尾田栄一郎

There's a Japanese game called Atchi Muite Hoi (Look That Way) where one player has to turn their head in one of the four directions while the other player points with a finger, hoping to guess the same direction. Well, I've invented a secret weapon called Atchi Muite Hoi 3-D that has ten directions instead. If a kid ever challenges you to Atchi Muite Hoi, use this method to childishly avoid losing!!

Here comes Volume 82!!!

-Eiichiro Oda, 2016

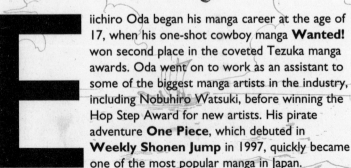

Eiichiro Oda began his manga career at the age of 17, when his one-shot cowboy manga **Wanted!** won second place in the coveted Tezuka manga awards. Oda went on to work as an assistant to some of the biggest manga artists in the industry, including Nobuhiro Watsuki, before winning the Hop Step Award for new artists. His pirate adventure **One Piece**, which debuted in **Weekly Shonen Jump** in 1997, quickly became one of the most popular manga in Japan.

ONE PIECE VOL. 82
NEW WORLD PART 22

SHONEN JUMP Manga Edition

STORY AND ART BY EIICHIRO ODA

Translation/Stephen Paul
Touch-up Art & Lettering/Vanessa Satone
Design/Yukiko Whitley
Editor/Alexis Kirsch

ONE PIECE © 1997 by Eiichiro Oda. All rights reserved.
First published in Japan in 1997 by SHUEISHA Inc., Tokyo.
English translation rights arranged by SHUEISHA Inc.

The stories, characters and incidents mentioned
in this publication are entirely fictional.

Printed in the U.S.A.

Published by VIZ Media, LLC
P.O. Box 77010
San Francisco, CA 94107

10 9 8 7 6 5 4 3 2 1
First printing, May 2017

SHONEN JUMP MANGA

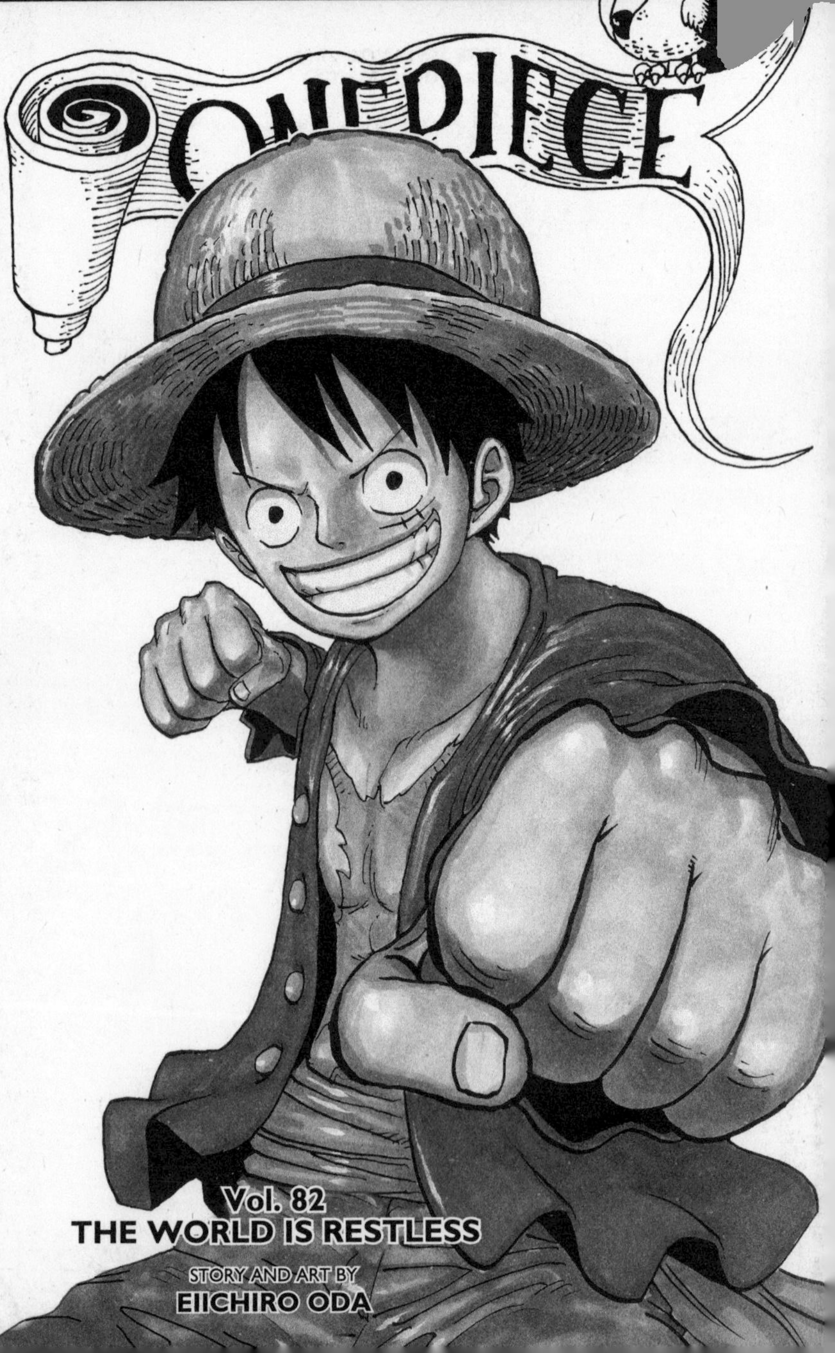
ONE PIECE

Vol. 82
THE WORLD IS RESTLESS

STORY AND ART BY
EIICHIRO ODA

The Straw Hat Crew

Tony Tony Chopper

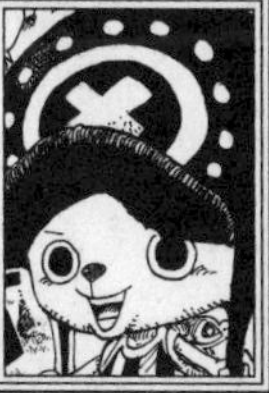

After researching powerful medicine in Birdie Kingdom, he reunited with the rest of the crew.

Ship's Doctor, Bounty: 100 berries

Monkey D. Luffy

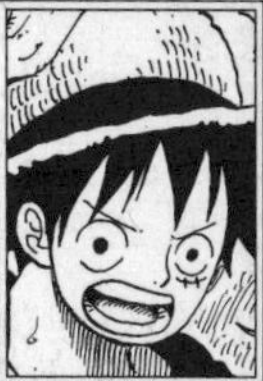

A young man who dreams of becoming the Pirate King. After training with Rayleigh, he and his crew head for the New World!

Captain, Bounty: 500 million berries

Nico Robin

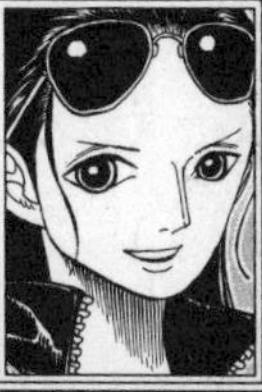

She spent her time in Baltigo with the leader of the Revolutionary Army: Luffy's father, Dragon.

Archeologist, Bounty: 130 million berries

Roronoa Zolo

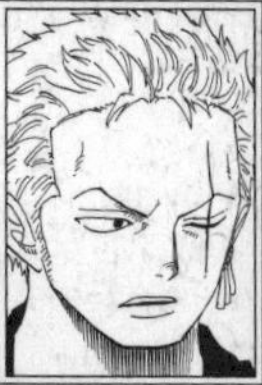

He swallowed his pride and asked to be trained by Mihawk on Gloom Island before reuniting with the rest of the crew.

Fighter, Bounty: 320 million berries

Franky

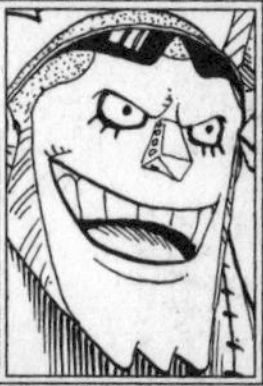

He modified himself in Future Land Baldimore and turned himself into Armored Franky before reuniting with the rest of the crew.

Shipwright, Bounty: 94 million berries

Nami

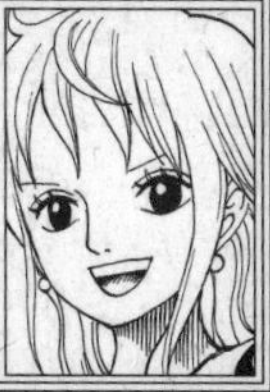

She studied the weather of the New World on the small Sky Island Weatheria, a place where weather is studied as a science.

Navigator, Bounty: 66 million berries

Brook

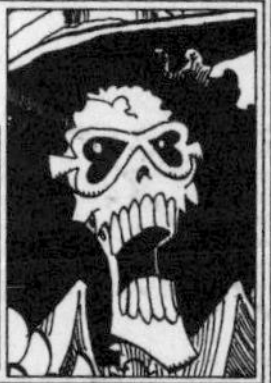

After being captured and used as a freak show by the Longarm Tribe, he became a famous rock star called "Soul King" Brook.

Musician, Bounty: 83 million berries

Usopp

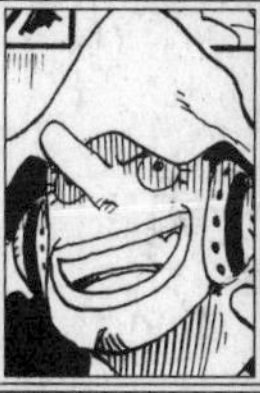

He trained under Heracles at the Bowin Islands to become the King of Snipers.

Sniper, Bounty: 200 million berries

Shanks

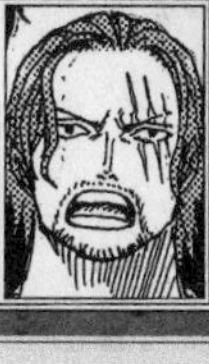

One of the Four Emperors. Waits for Luffy in the "New World," the second half of the Grand Line.

Captain of the Red-Haired Pirates

Sanji

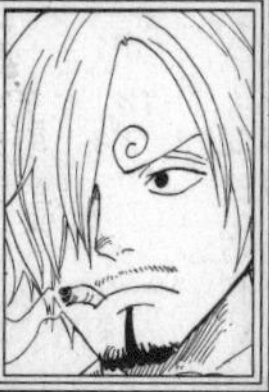

After fighting the New Kama Karate masters in the Kamabakka Kingdom, he returned to the crew.

Cook, Bounty: 177 million berries

kingdom from his control. After an exhausting battle, they remove Doflamingo from the land he torments! Luffy's team then sails ahead to catch up and regroup with Nami's team on the island of Zou. When they get there, it turns out that Kaido's crony Jack has already leveled the city. The minks were hiding the samurai Jack sought, but to them, the Kozuki Clan are like family that they would never sell out, even if their country fell to ruin. The crew is stunned by this heartfelt loyalty... Meanwhile, Sanji's family background is revealed, and events take a sudden, unexpected turn!

The story of ONE PIECE 1»82

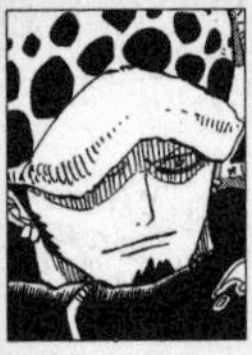
Trafalgar Law
Captain of the Heart Pirates

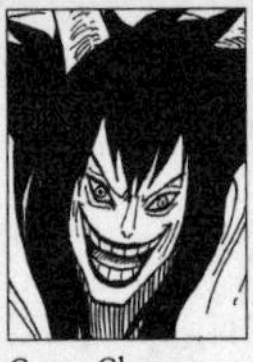
Caesar Clown
Former Govt Scientist

Wano Kingdom

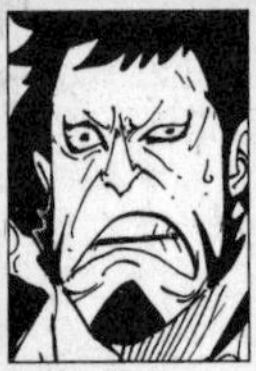
Foxfire Kin'emon
Samurai of Wano

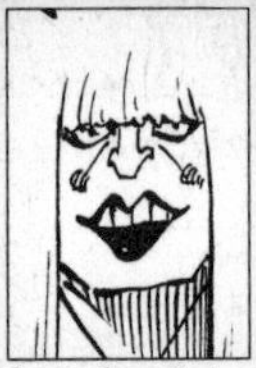
Evening Shower Kanjuro
Samurai of Wano

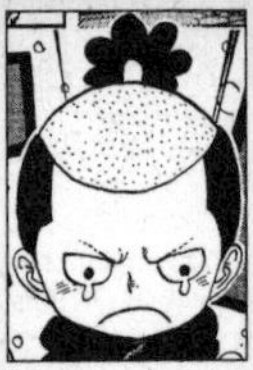
Momonosuke
Kin'emon's Son

Mokomo Dukedom

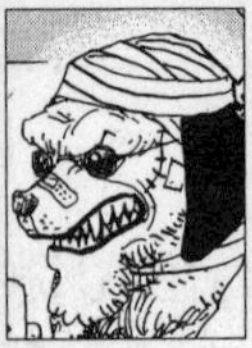
Duke Dogstorm
King of the Day

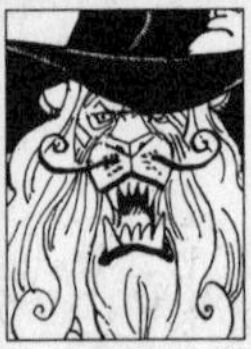
Full-Power Shishilian (Lion Mink)
Captain of the Dogstorm Musketeers

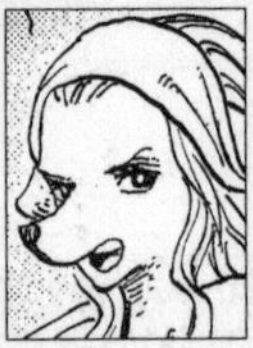
Wanda (Dog Mink)
Battlebeast Tribe

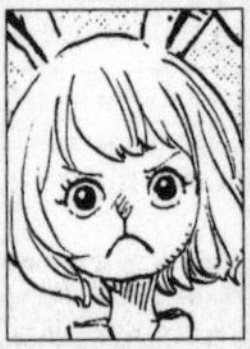
Carrot (Bunny Mink)
Battlebeast Tribe

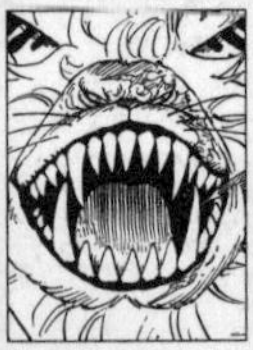
The Cat Viper
Spirit of the Whale Forest, King of the Night

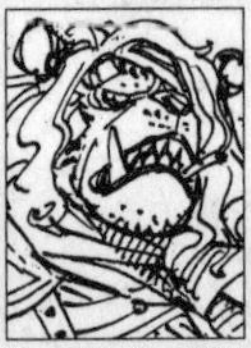
Treetop Pedro (Jaguar Mink)
Leader of the Guardians

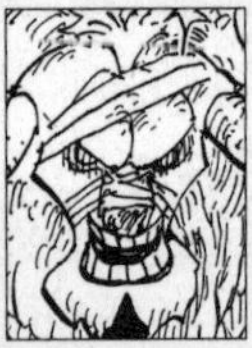
Roddy (Bull Mink)
Guardian of the Whale Forest

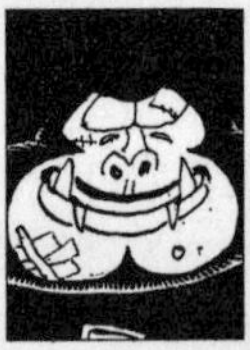
BB (Gorilla Mink)
Guardian of the Whale Forest

Animal Kingdom Pirates

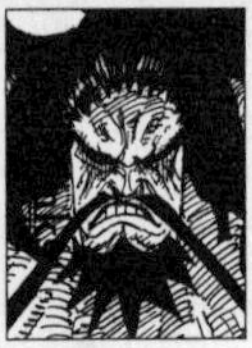
Kaido, King of the Beasts
Captain of the Animal Kingdom Pirates

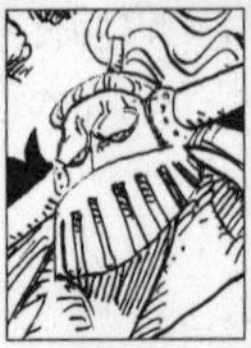
Jack the Drought
Lead Performer of the A.K. Pirates

Big Mom Pirates

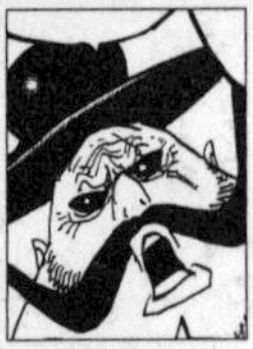
Baron Tamago
Fighter, Big Mom Pirates

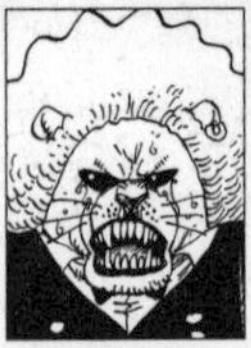
Pekoms
Fighter, Big Mom Pirates

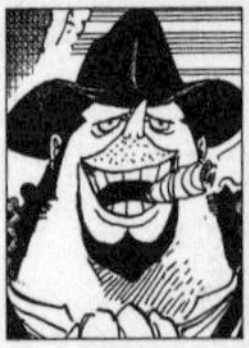
Capone "Gang" Bege
Captain of the Firetank Pirates

Story

After two years of hard training, the Straw Hat pirates are back together, first at the Sabaody Archipelago and then through Fish-Man Island to their next stage: the New World!!

The crew happens across Trafalgar Law on the island of Punk Hazard. At his suggestion, they form a new pirate alliance that seeks to take down one of the Four Emperors. The group infiltrates the kingdom of Dressrosa in an attempt to take down Doflamingo, Kaido's trading partner, and find themselves in a battle to liberate the

Vol. 82
THE WORLD IS RESTLESS

CONTENTS

Chapter 817: Raizo of the Mist   011

Chapter 818: Inside the Whale   029

Chapter 819: Momonosuke, Heir to the Kozuki Clan   047

Chapter 820: Cats and Dogs Have a History   065

Chapter 821: Understood   082

Chapter 822: Descending the Elephant   103

Chapter 823: The World Is Restless   121

Chapter 824: Playing Pirates   138

Chapter 825: Comic Strip   159

Chapter 826: 0 and 4   173

Chapter 827: Totto Land   191

ONE PIECE

Hereafter, the 82nd volume will start.

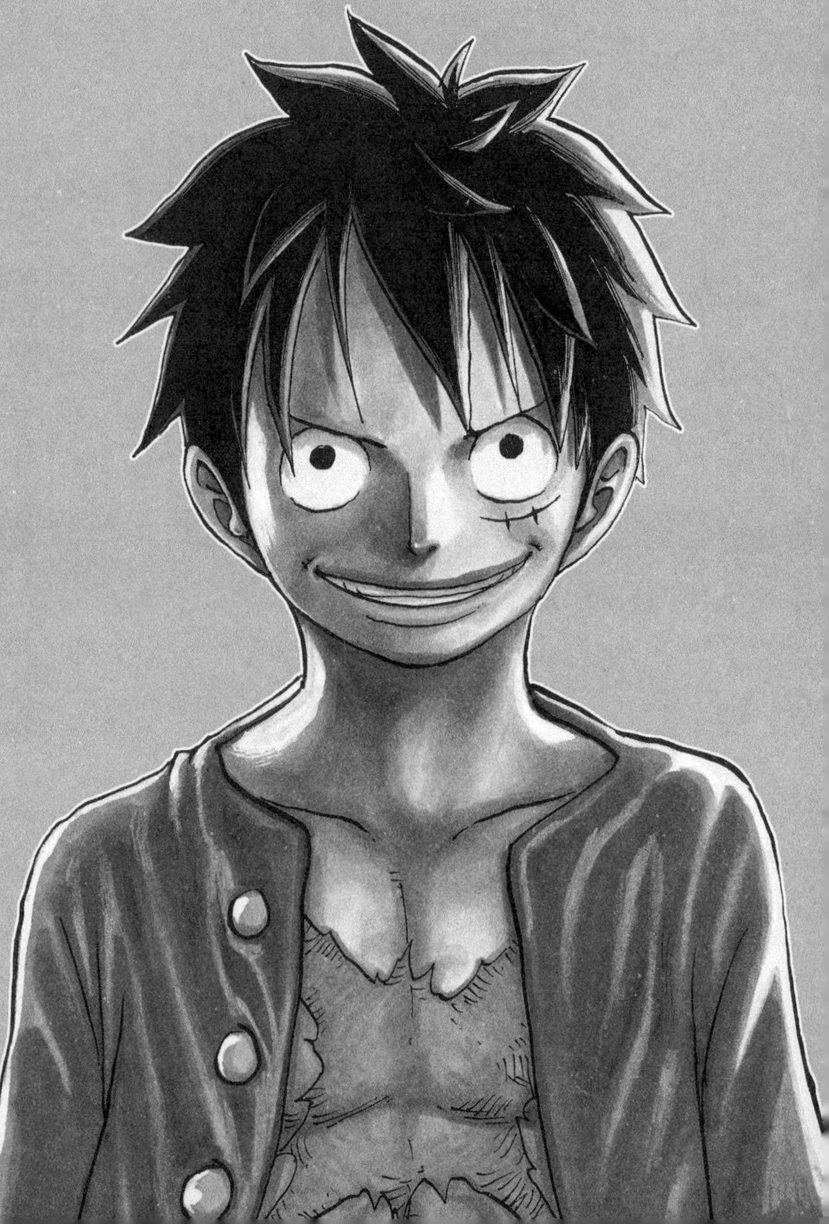

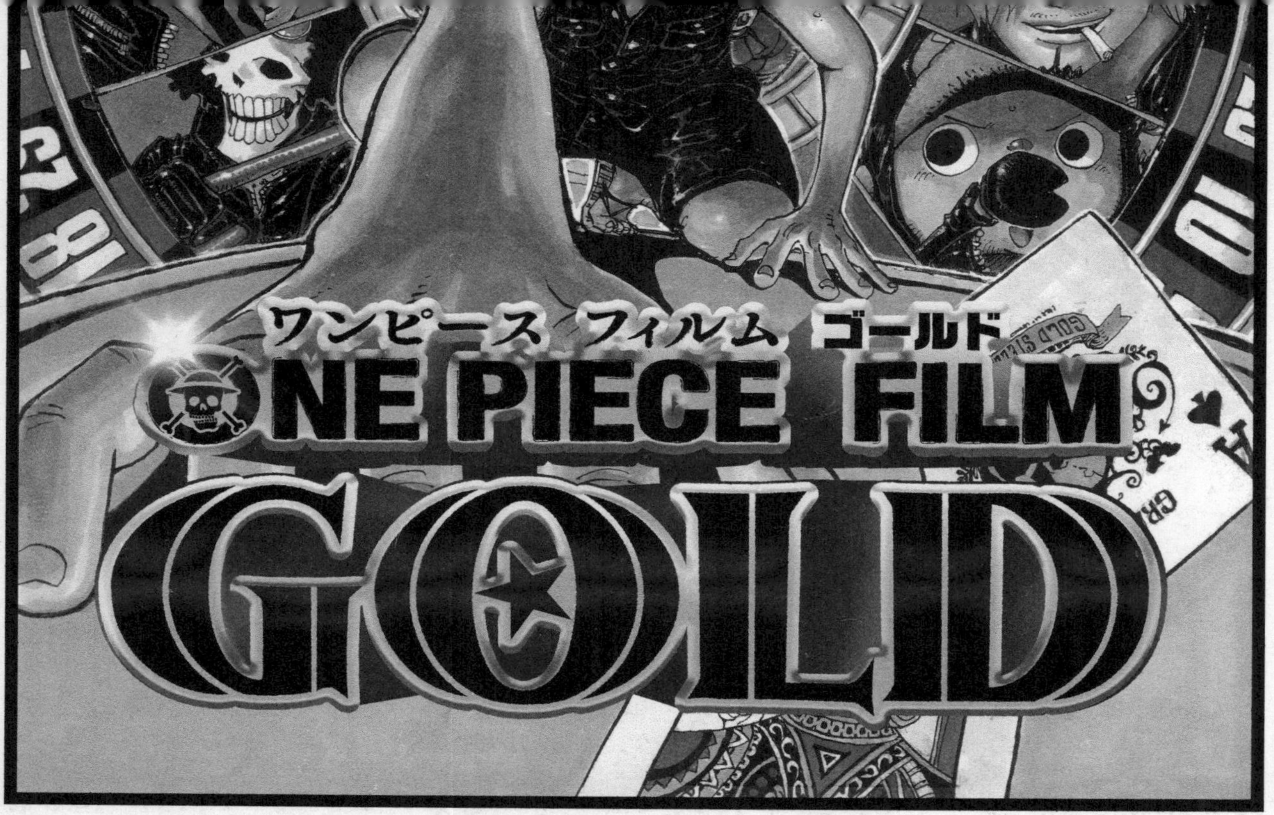
ワンピース フィルム ゴールド
ONE PIECE FILM
GOLD

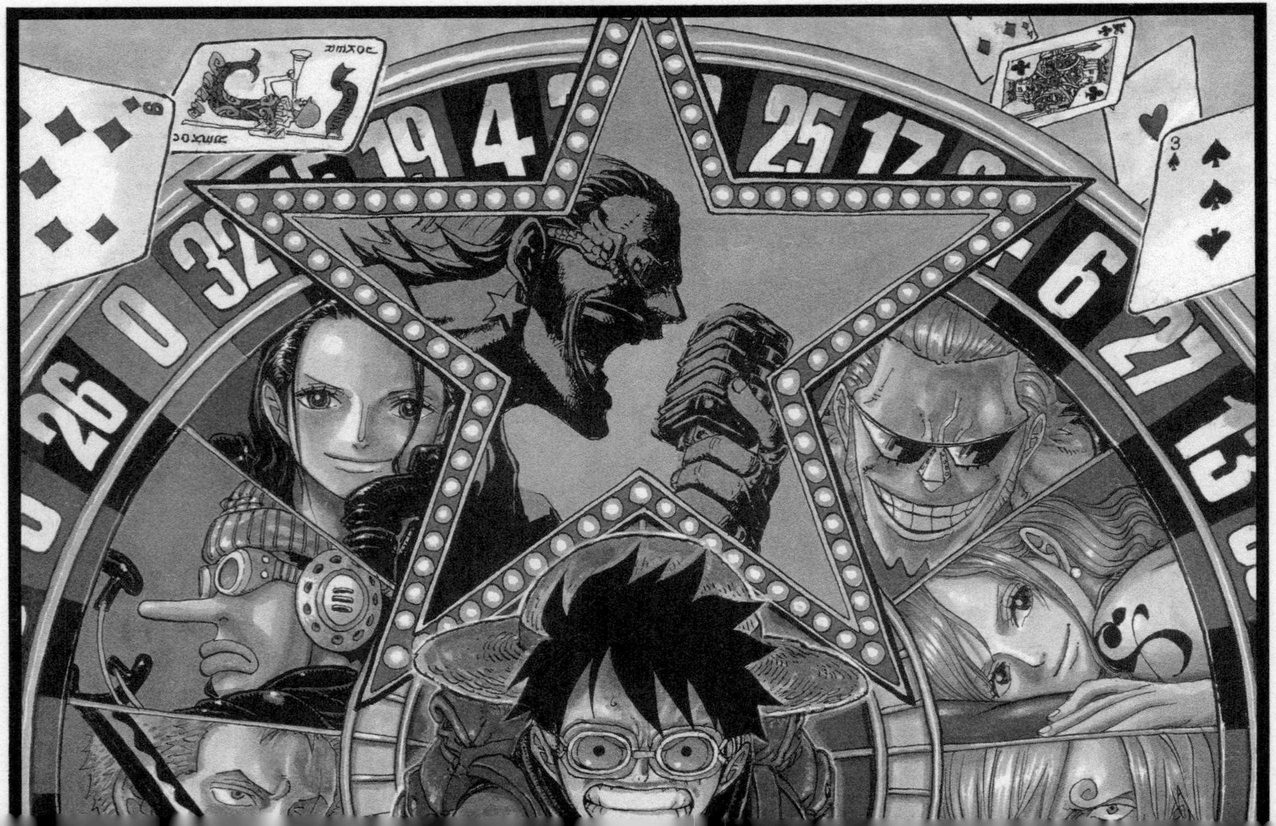

vol.82
ONE PIECE

DO I LOOK DEAD TO YOU?!

WHAT DO YOU THINK?!

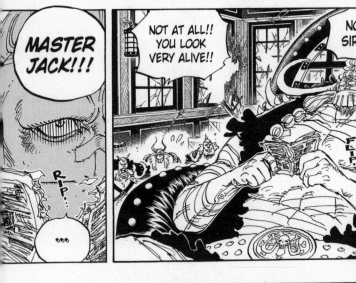

MASTER JACK!!!

R.I.P....

...

NOT AT ALL!! YOU LOOK VERY ALIVE!!

NO, SIR!!

AND NOW...

TUG

...TO YOU ALL!!!

DOON!!

KURAU CITY, ZOU

I AM GRATEFUL...

CHAPTER 817: RAIZO OF THE MIST

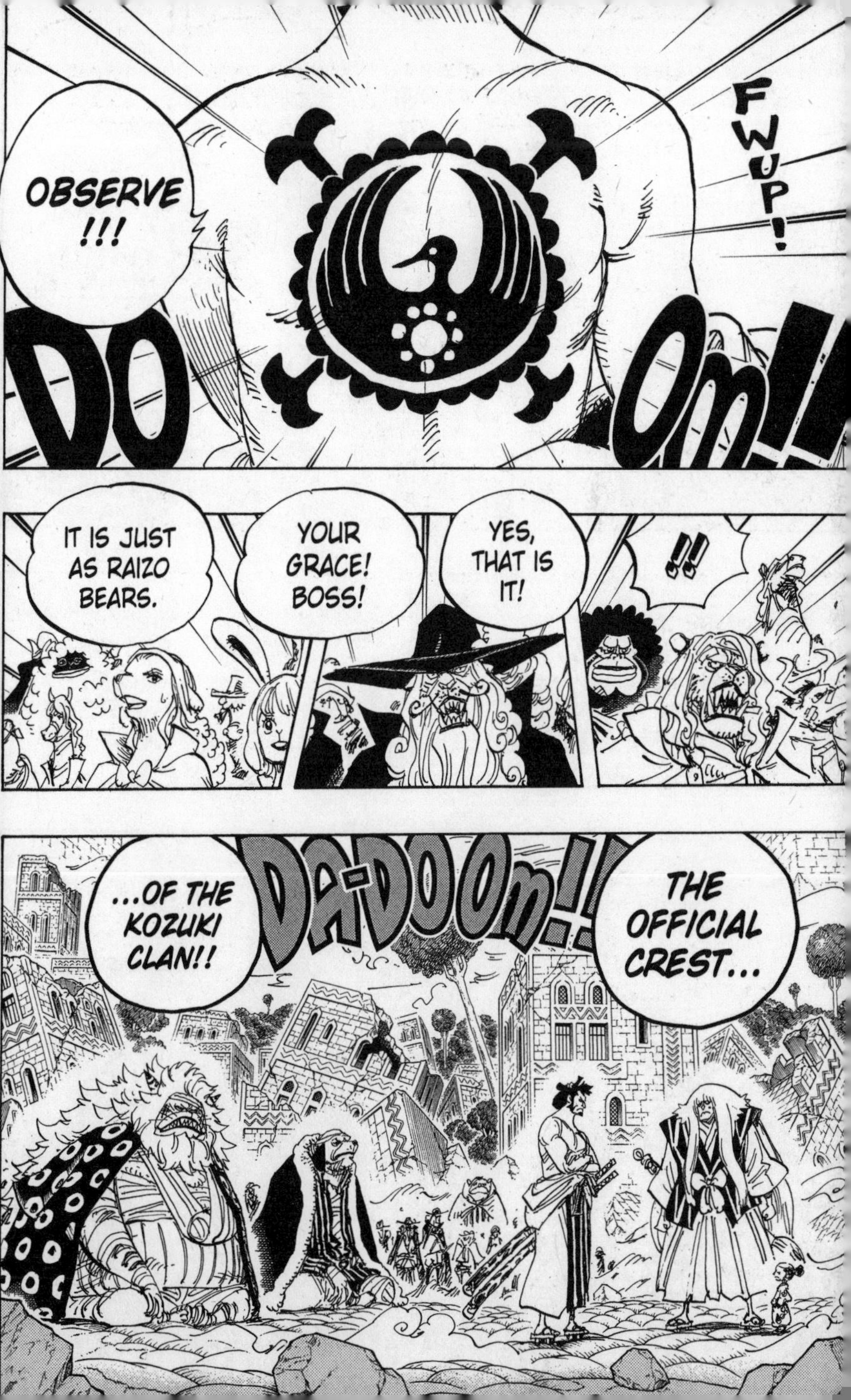
FWUP!
OBSERVE !!!
DOOM!!
!!
YES, THAT IS IT!
YOUR GRACE! BOSS!
IT IS JUST AS RAIZO BEARS.
THE OFFICIAL CREST...
DA-DOOM!!
...OF THE KOZUKI CLAN!!

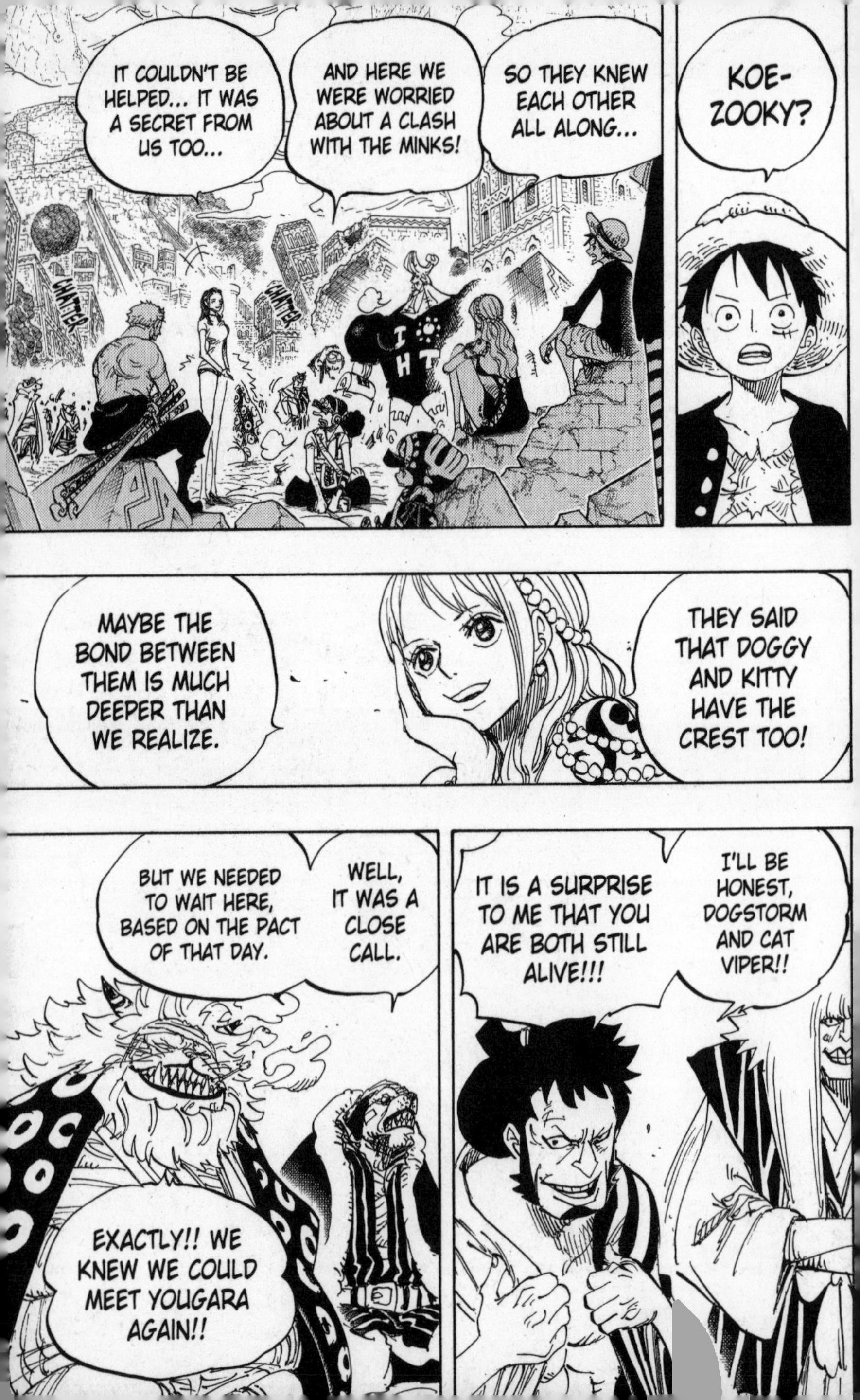
KOE-ZOOKY?
SO THEY KNEW EACH OTHER ALL ALONG...
AND HERE WE WERE WORRIED ABOUT A CLASH WITH THE MINKS!
IT COULDN'T BE HELPED... IT WAS A SECRET FROM US TOO...
CHATTER
CHATTER
THEY SAID THAT DOGGY AND KITTY HAVE THE CREST TOO!
MAYBE THE BOND BETWEEN THEM IS MUCH DEEPER THAN WE REALIZE.
I'LL BE HONEST, DOGSTORM AND CAT VIPER!!
IT IS A SURPRISE TO ME THAT YOU ARE BOTH STILL ALIVE!!!
WELL, IT WAS A CLOSE CALL.
BUT WE NEEDED TO WAIT HERE, BASED ON THE PACT OF THAT DAY.
EXACTLY!! WE KNEW WE COULD MEET YOUGARA AGAIN!!

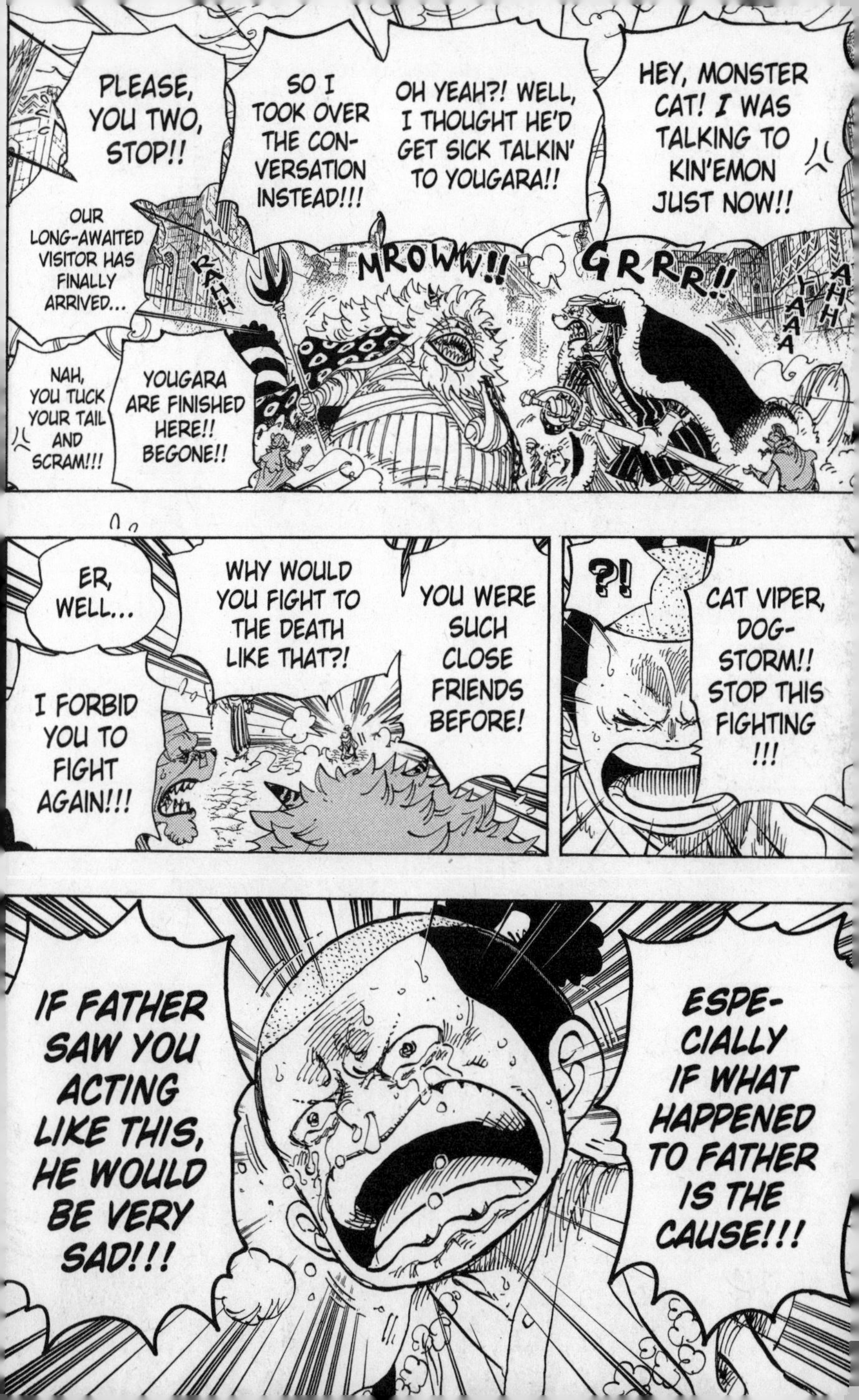
HEY, MONSTER CAT! I WAS TALKING TO KIN'EMON JUST NOW!!
OH YEAH?! WELL, I THOUGHT HE'D GET SICK TALKIN' TO YOUGARA!!
SO I TOOK OVER THE CON-VERSATION INSTEAD!!!
PLEASE, YOU TWO, STOP!!
GRRRR!!
AHH YAAAA
MROWW!!
RAHH
OUR LONG-AWAITED VISITOR HAS FINALLY ARRIVED...
YOUGARA ARE FINISHED HERE!! BEGONE!!
NAH, YOU TUCK YOUR TAIL AND SCRAM!!!
?!
CAT VIPER, DOG-STORM!! STOP THIS FIGHTING!!!
YOU WERE SUCH CLOSE FRIENDS BEFORE!
WHY WOULD YOU FIGHT TO THE DEATH LIKE THAT?!
ER, WELL...
I FORBID YOU TO FIGHT AGAIN!!!
ESPE-CIALLY IF WHAT HAPPENED TO FATHER IS THE CAUSE!!!
IF FATHER SAW YOU ACTING LIKE THIS, HE WOULD BE VERY SAD!!!

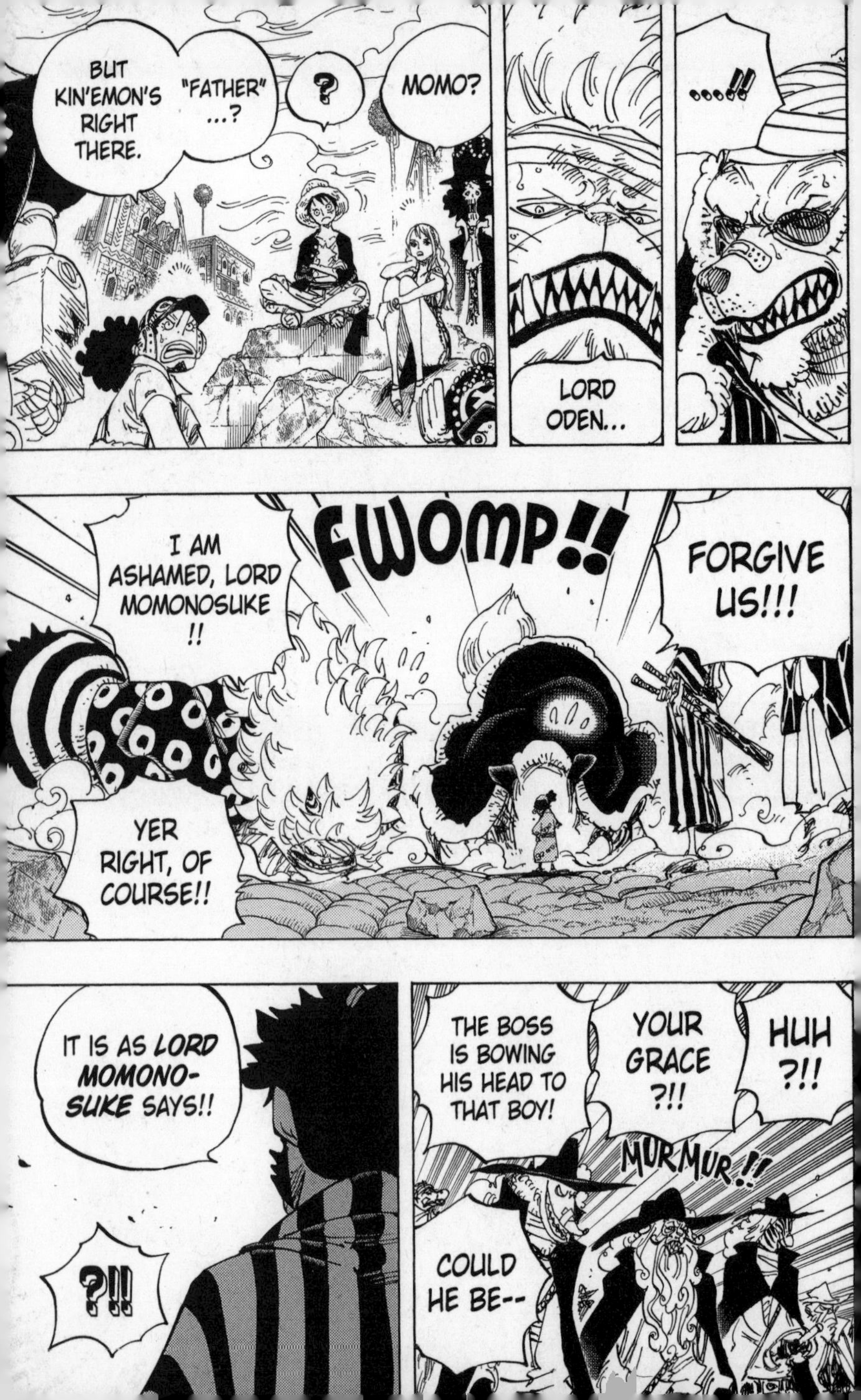
...!!
LORD ODEN...
MOMO?
?
"FATHER" ...?
BUT KIN'EMON'S RIGHT THERE.
FORGIVE US!!!
FWOMP!!
I AM ASHAMED, LORD MOMONOSUKE !!
YER RIGHT, OF COURSE!!
HUH ?!!
YOUR GRACE ?!!
THE BOSS IS BOWING HIS HEAD TO THAT BOY!
MURMUR!!
COULD HE BE--
IT IS AS LORD MOMONOSUKE SAYS!!
?!!

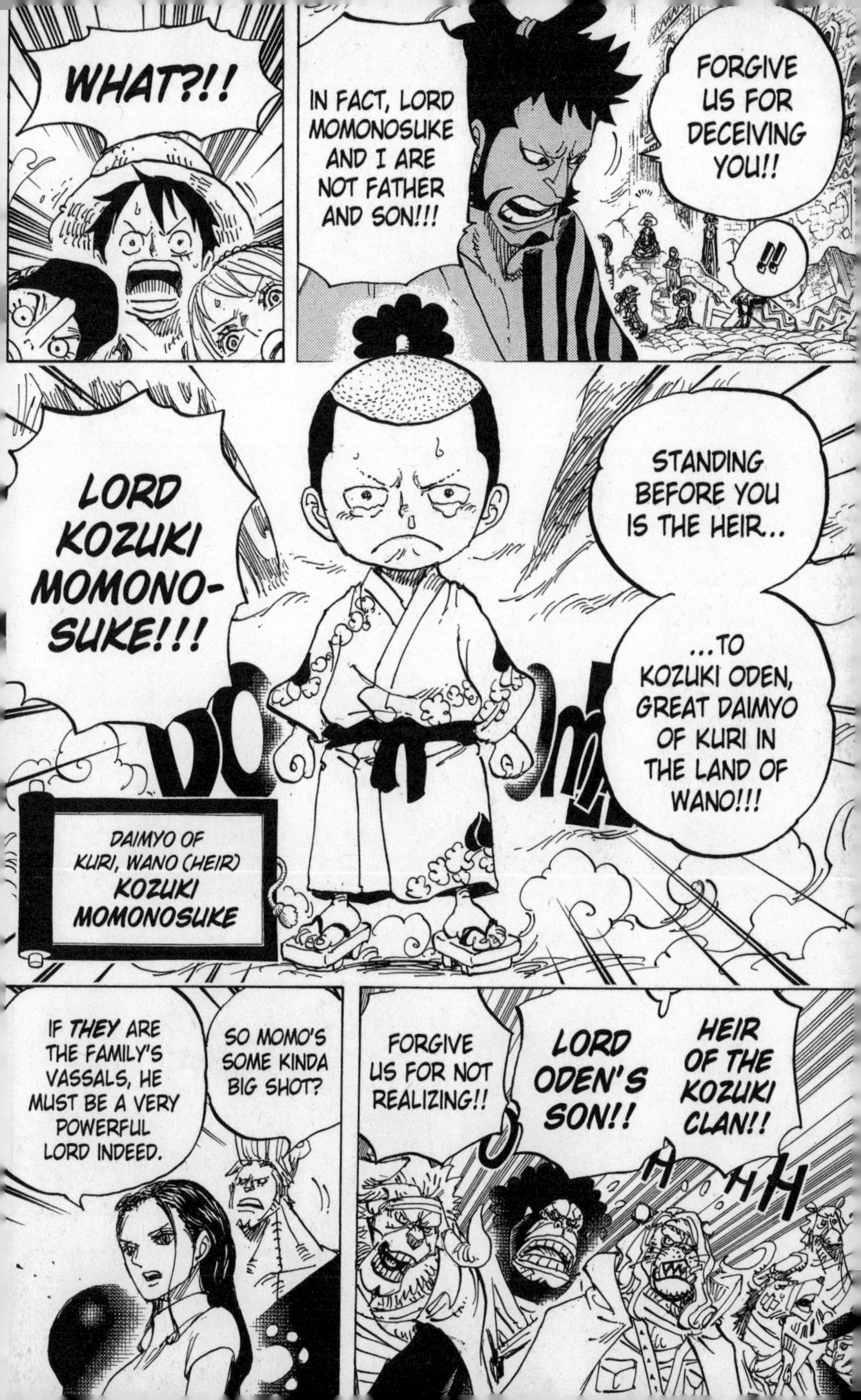
FORGIVE US FOR DECEIVING YOU!!
!!
IN FACT, LORD MOMONOSUKE AND I ARE NOT FATHER AND SON!!!
WHAT?!!
STANDING BEFORE YOU IS THE HEIR...
...TO KOZUKI ODEN, GREAT DAIMYO OF KURI IN THE LAND OF WANO!!!
LORD KOZUKI MOMONO-SUKE!!!
DAIMYO OF KURI, WANO (HEIR) KOZUKI MOMONOSUKE
HEIR OF THE KOZUKI CLAN!!
LORD ODEN'S SON!!
FORGIVE US FOR NOT REALIZING!!
SO MOMO'S SOME KINDA BIG SHOT?
IF THEY ARE THE FAMILY'S VASSALS, HE MUST BE A VERY POWERFUL LORD INDEED.

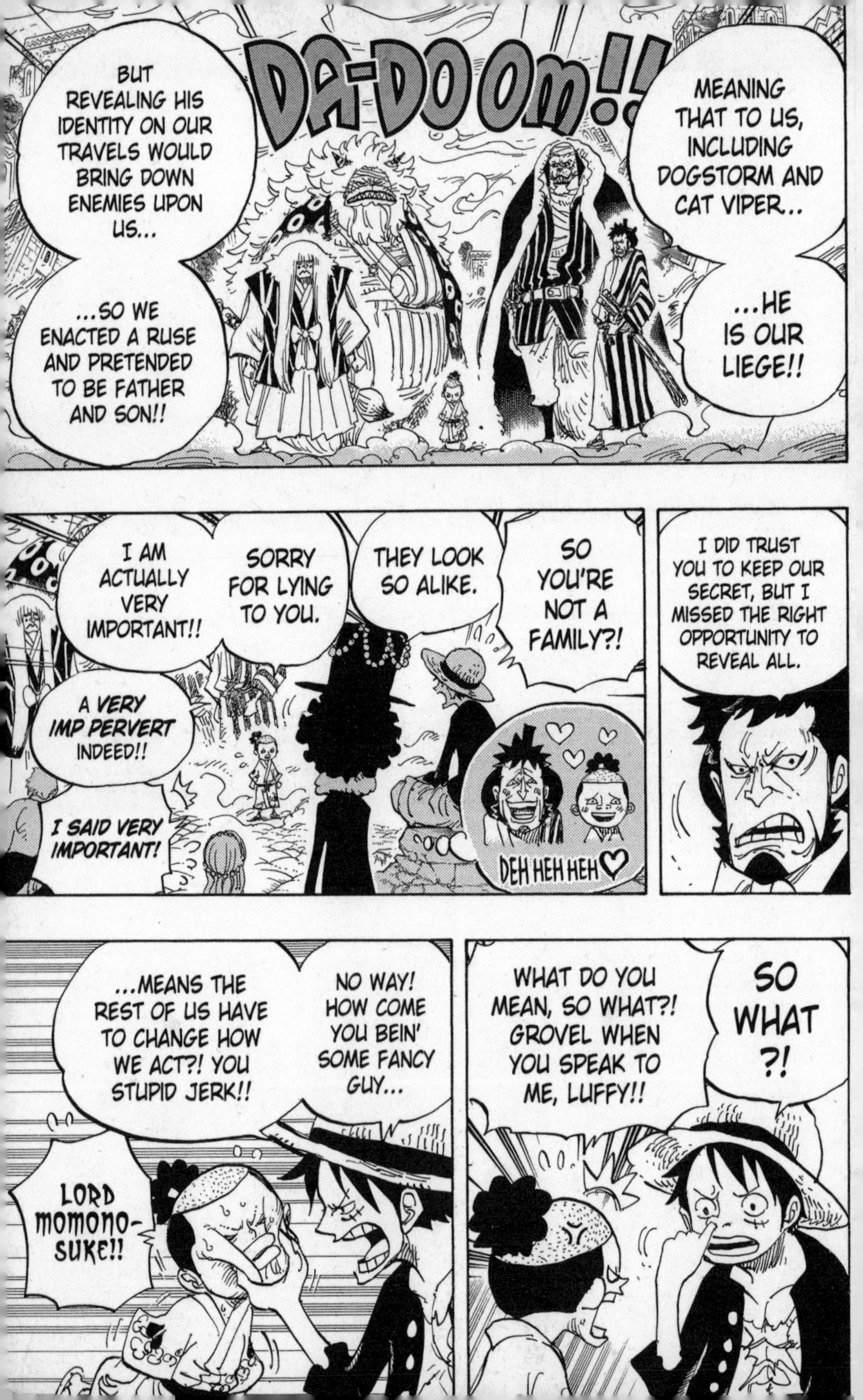
MEANING THAT TO US, INCLUDING DOGSTORM AND CAT VIPER...
...HE IS OUR LIEGE!!
DA-DOOM!!
BUT REVEALING HIS IDENTITY ON OUR TRAVELS WOULD BRING DOWN ENEMIES UPON US...
...SO WE ENACTED A RUSE AND PRETENDED TO BE FATHER AND SON!!
I DID TRUST YOU TO KEEP OUR SECRET, BUT I MISSED THE RIGHT OPPORTUNITY TO REVEAL ALL.
SO YOU'RE NOT A FAMILY?!
THEY LOOK SO ALIKE.
DEH HEH HEH
SORRY FOR LYING TO YOU.
I AM ACTUALLY VERY IMPORTANT!!
A VERY IMP PERVERT INDEED!!
I SAID VERY IMPORTANT!
SO WHAT?!
WHAT DO YOU MEAN, SO WHAT?! GROVEL WHEN YOU SPEAK TO ME, LUFFY!!
NO WAY! HOW COME YOU BEIN' SOME FANCY GUY...
...MEANS THE REST OF US HAVE TO CHANGE HOW WE ACT?! YOU STUPID JERK!!
LORD MOMONOSUKE!!

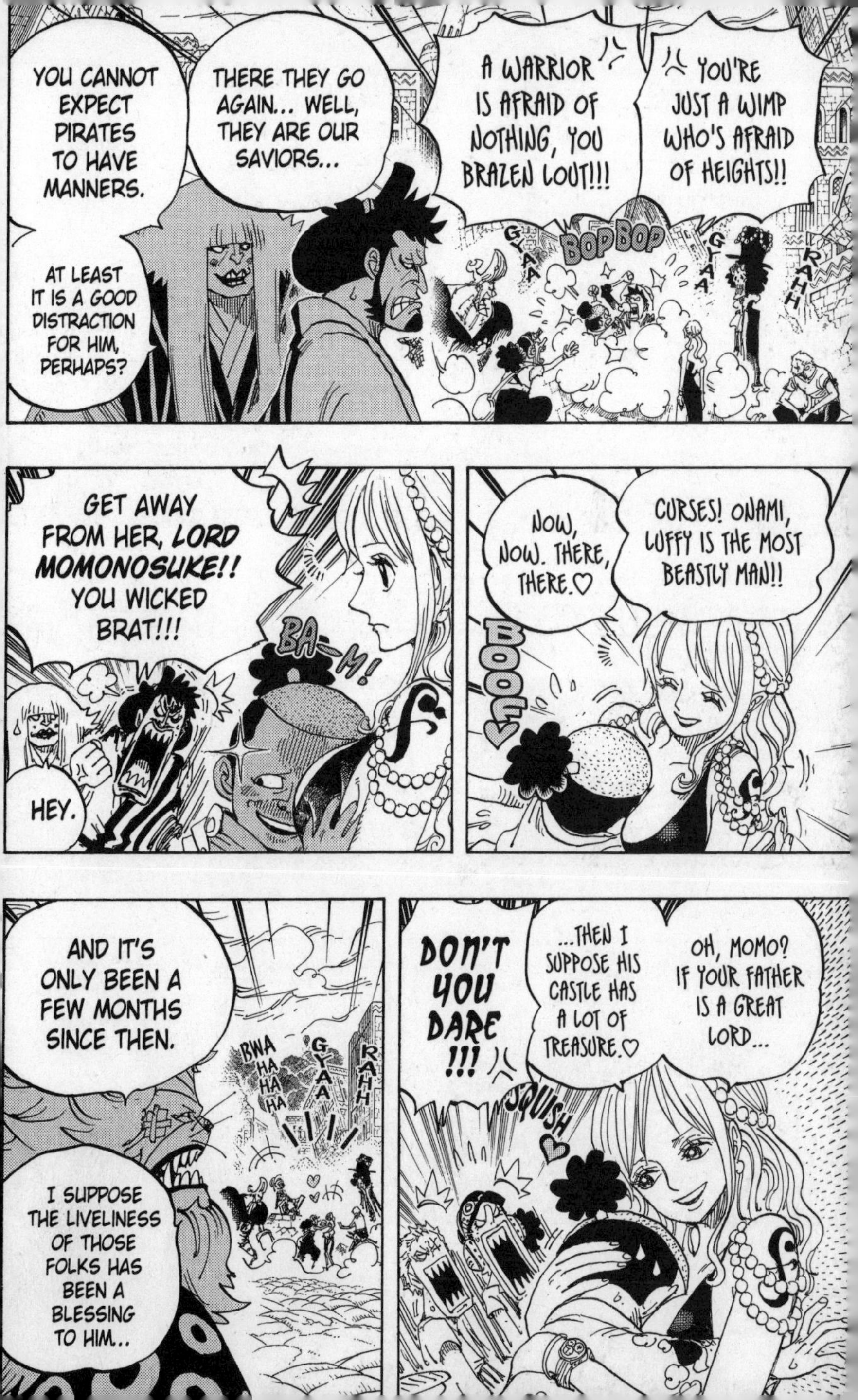

YOU'RE JUST A WIMP WHO'S AFRAID OF HEIGHTS!!
A WARRIOR IS AFRAID OF NOTHING, YOU BRAZEN LOUT!!!
RAHH
GYAA
BOP BOP
GYAA
THERE THEY GO AGAIN... WELL, THEY ARE OUR SAVIORS...
YOU CANNOT EXPECT PIRATES TO HAVE MANNERS.
AT LEAST IT IS A GOOD DISTRACTION FOR HIM, PERHAPS?
CURSES! ONAMI, LUFFY IS THE MOST BEASTLY MAN!!
NOW, NOW. THERE, THERE.♡
BOOF
GET AWAY FROM HER, LORD MOMONOSUKE!! YOU WICKED BRAT!!!
BA-M!
HEY.
OH, MOMO? IF YOUR FATHER IS A GREAT LORD...
...THEN I SUPPOSE HIS CASTLE HAS A LOT OF TREASURE.♡
DON'T YOU DARE!!!
SQUISH
AND IT'S ONLY BEEN A FEW MONTHS SINCE THEN.
RAHH
GYAA
BWA HA HA HA
I SUPPOSE THE LIVELINESS OF THOSE FOLKS HAS BEEN A BLESSING TO HIM...

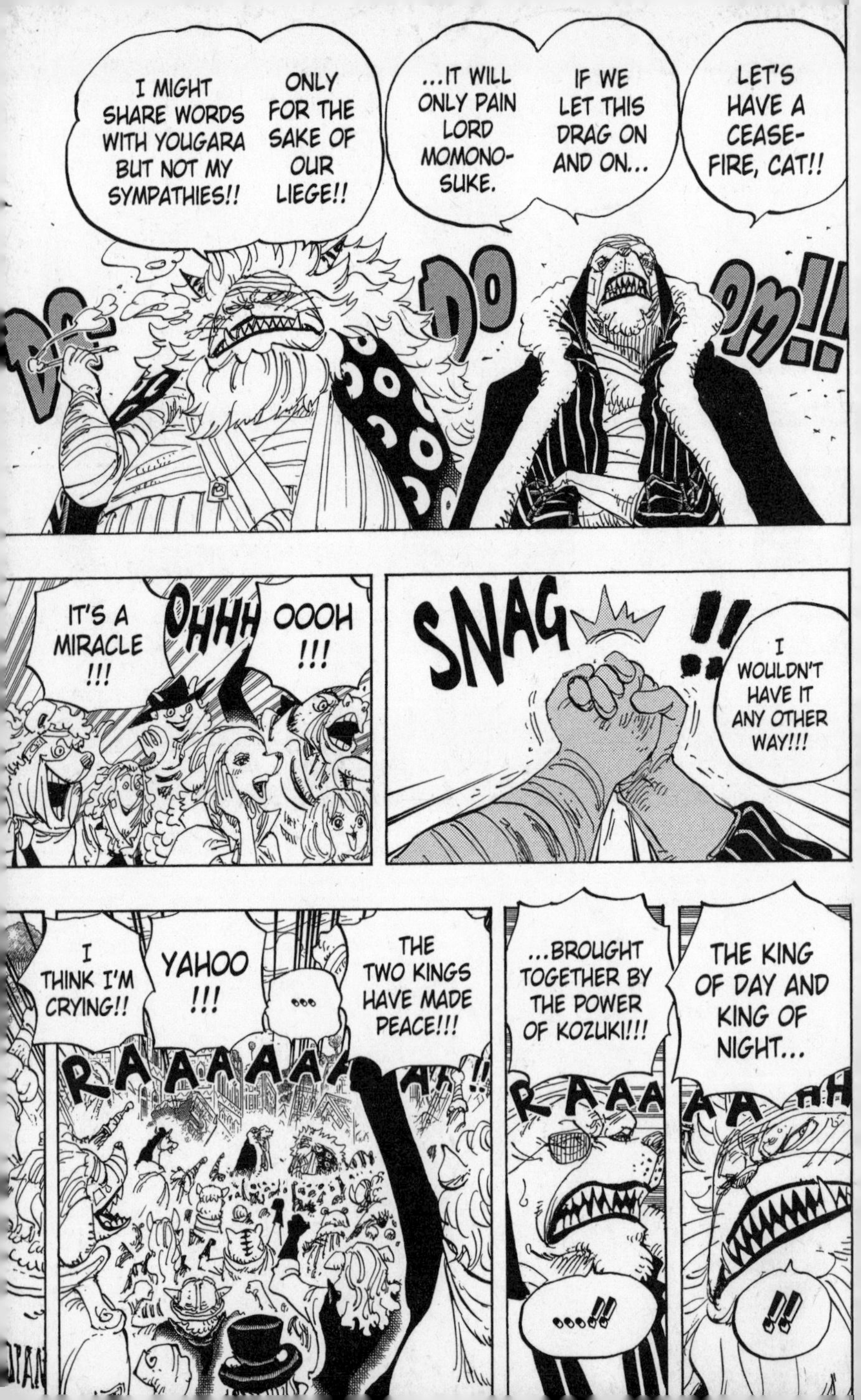
LET'S HAVE A CEASE-FIRE, CAT!!
IF WE LET THIS DRAG ON AND ON...
...IT WILL ONLY PAIN LORD MOMONOSUKE.
ONLY FOR THE SAKE OF OUR LIEGE!!
I MIGHT SHARE WORDS WITH YOUGARA BUT NOT MY SYMPATHIES!!
DOOM!!
SNAG!!
I WOULDN'T HAVE IT ANY OTHER WAY!!!
OOOH!!!
OHHH
IT'S A MIRACLE!!!
THE KING OF DAY AND KING OF NIGHT...
!!
...BROUGHT TOGETHER BY THE POWER OF KOZUKI!!!
RAAAAAHH
....!!
THE TWO KINGS HAVE MADE PEACE!!!
...
YAHOO!!!
I THINK I'M CRYING!!
RAAAAAAH!!

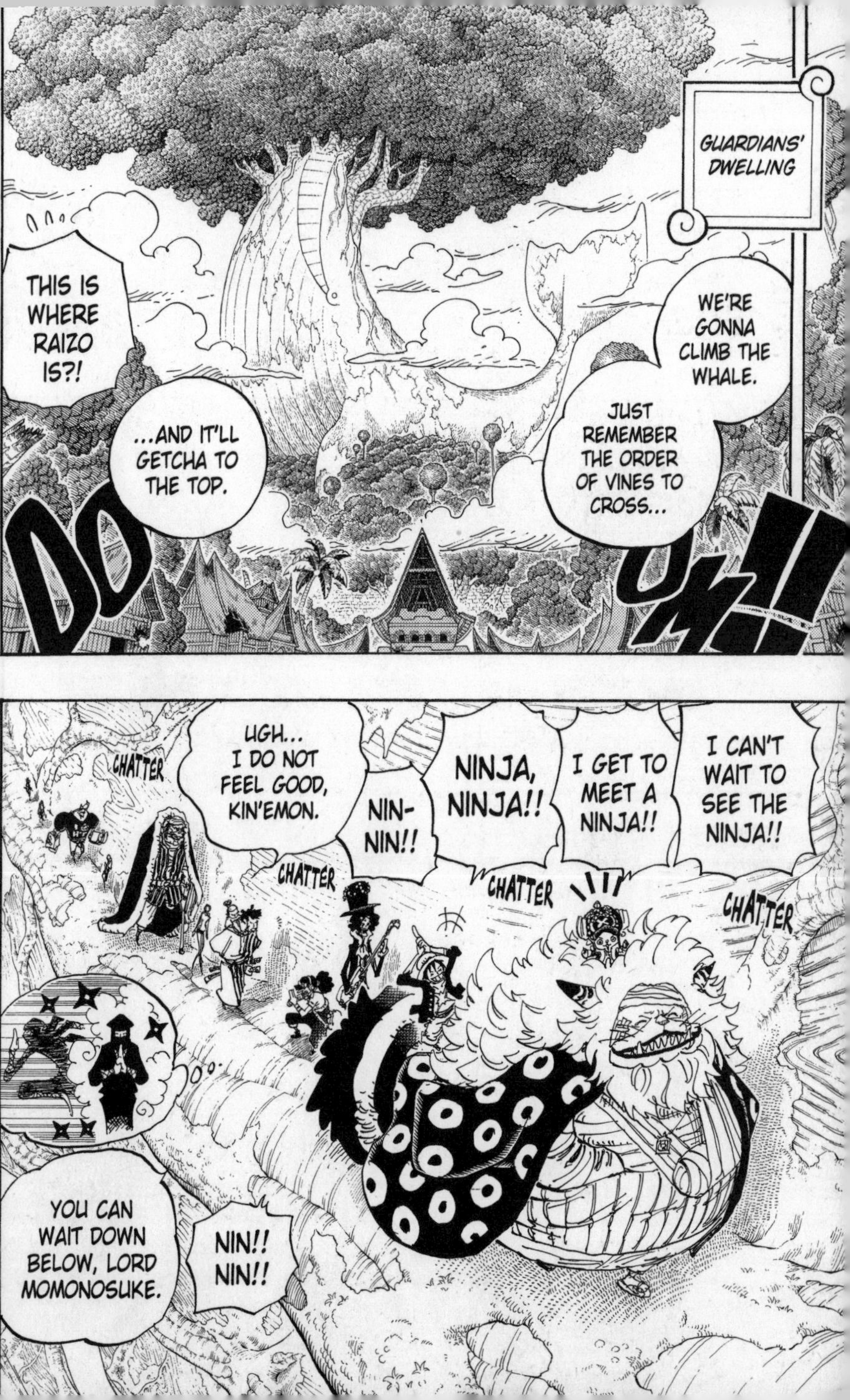
GUARDIANS' DWELLING
WE'RE GONNA CLIMB THE WHALE.
JUST REMEMBER THE ORDER OF VINES TO CROSS...
...AND IT'LL GETCHA TO THE TOP.
THIS IS WHERE RAIZO IS?!
DO
ON!!
I CAN'T WAIT TO SEE THE NINJA!!
I GET TO MEET A NINJA!!
NINJA, NINJA!!
NIN-NIN!!
UGH... I DO NOT FEEL GOOD, KIN'EMON.
CHATTER
CHATTER
CHATTER
CHATTER
NIN!! NIN!!
YOU CAN WAIT DOWN BELOW, LORD MOMONOSUKE.

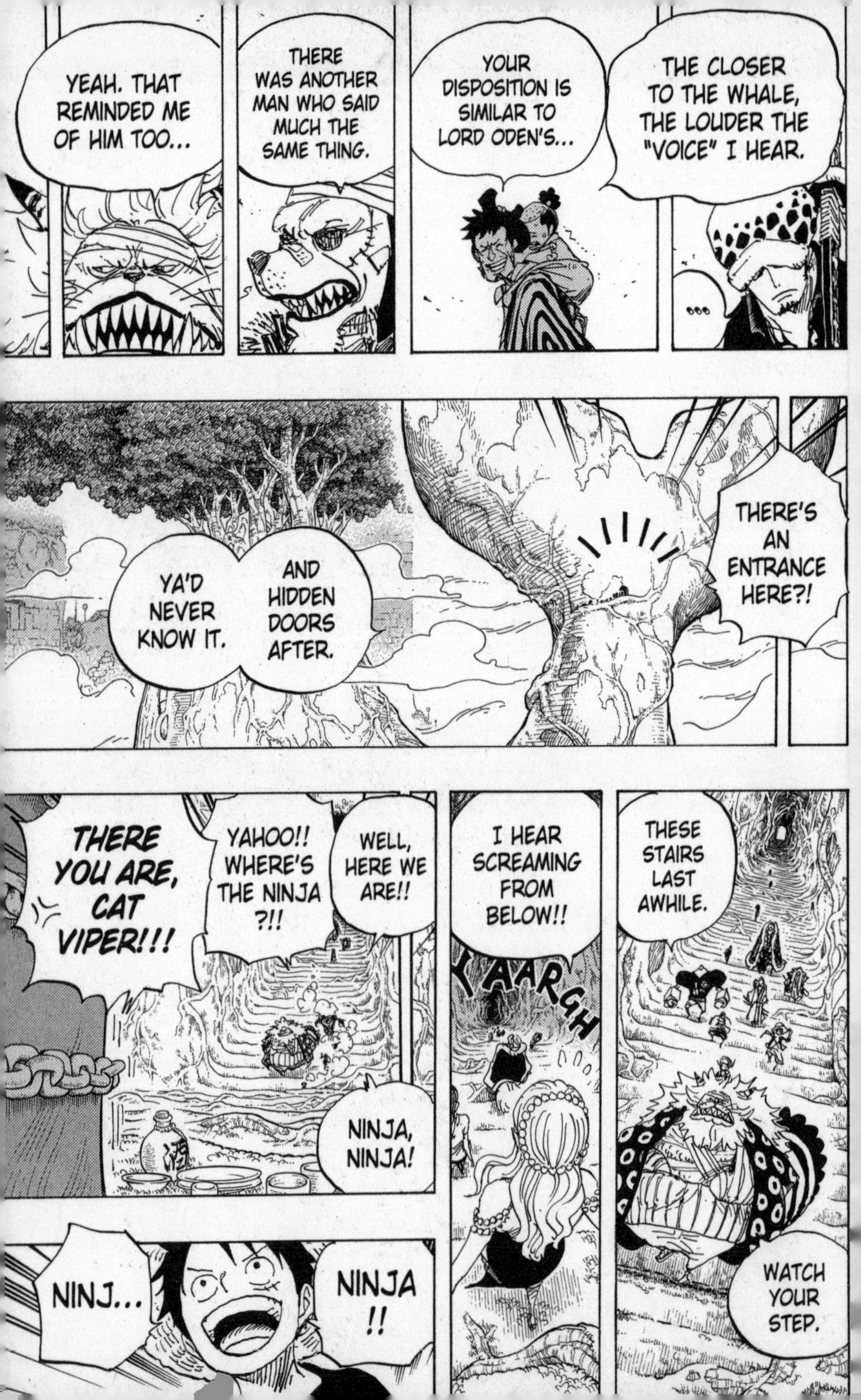
THE CLOSER TO THE WHALE, THE LOUDER THE "VOICE" I HEAR.
...
YOUR DISPOSITION IS SIMILAR TO LORD ODEN'S...
THERE WAS ANOTHER MAN WHO SAID MUCH THE SAME THING.
YEAH. THAT REMINDED ME OF HIM TOO...
THERE'S AN ENTRANCE HERE?!
AND HIDDEN DOORS AFTER.
YA'D NEVER KNOW IT.
THESE STAIRS LAST AWHILE.
WATCH YOUR STEP.
I HEAR SCREAMING FROM BELOW!!
YAARGH
WELL, HERE WE ARE!!
YAHOO!! WHERE'S THE NINJA ?!!
THERE YOU ARE, CAT VIPER!!!
NINJA, NINJA!
NINJA !!
NINJ...

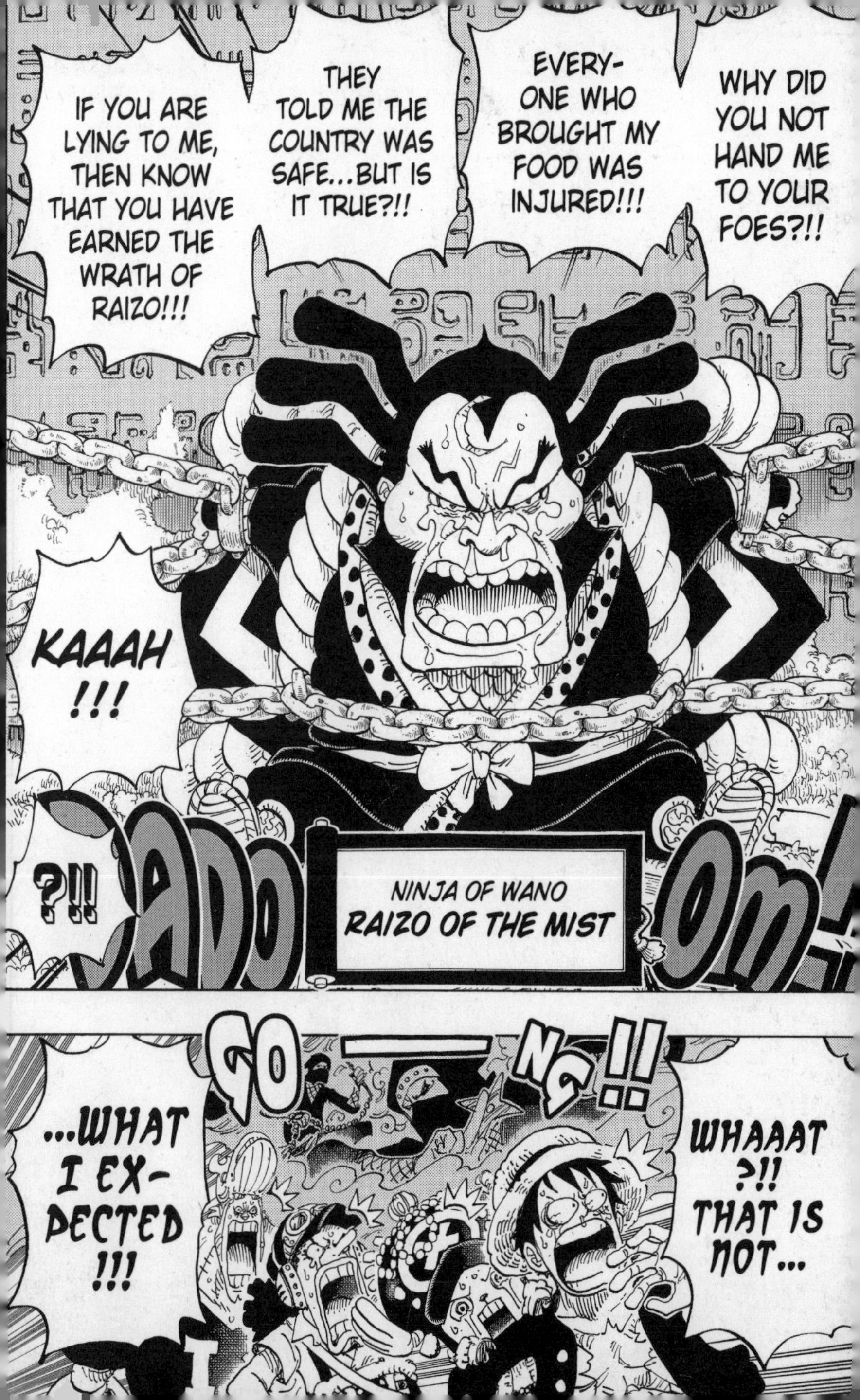
WHY DID YOU NOT HAND ME TO YOUR FOES?!!
EVERYONE WHO BROUGHT MY FOOD WAS INJURED!!!
THEY TOLD ME THE COUNTRY WAS SAFE...BUT IS IT TRUE?!!
IF YOU ARE LYING TO ME, THEN KNOW THAT YOU HAVE EARNED THE WRATH OF RAIZO!!!
KAAAH!!!
DO OM!
?!!
NINJA OF WANO
RAIZO OF THE MIST
GO—NG!!
WHAAAT?!! THAT IS NOT...
...WHAT I EXPECTED!!!

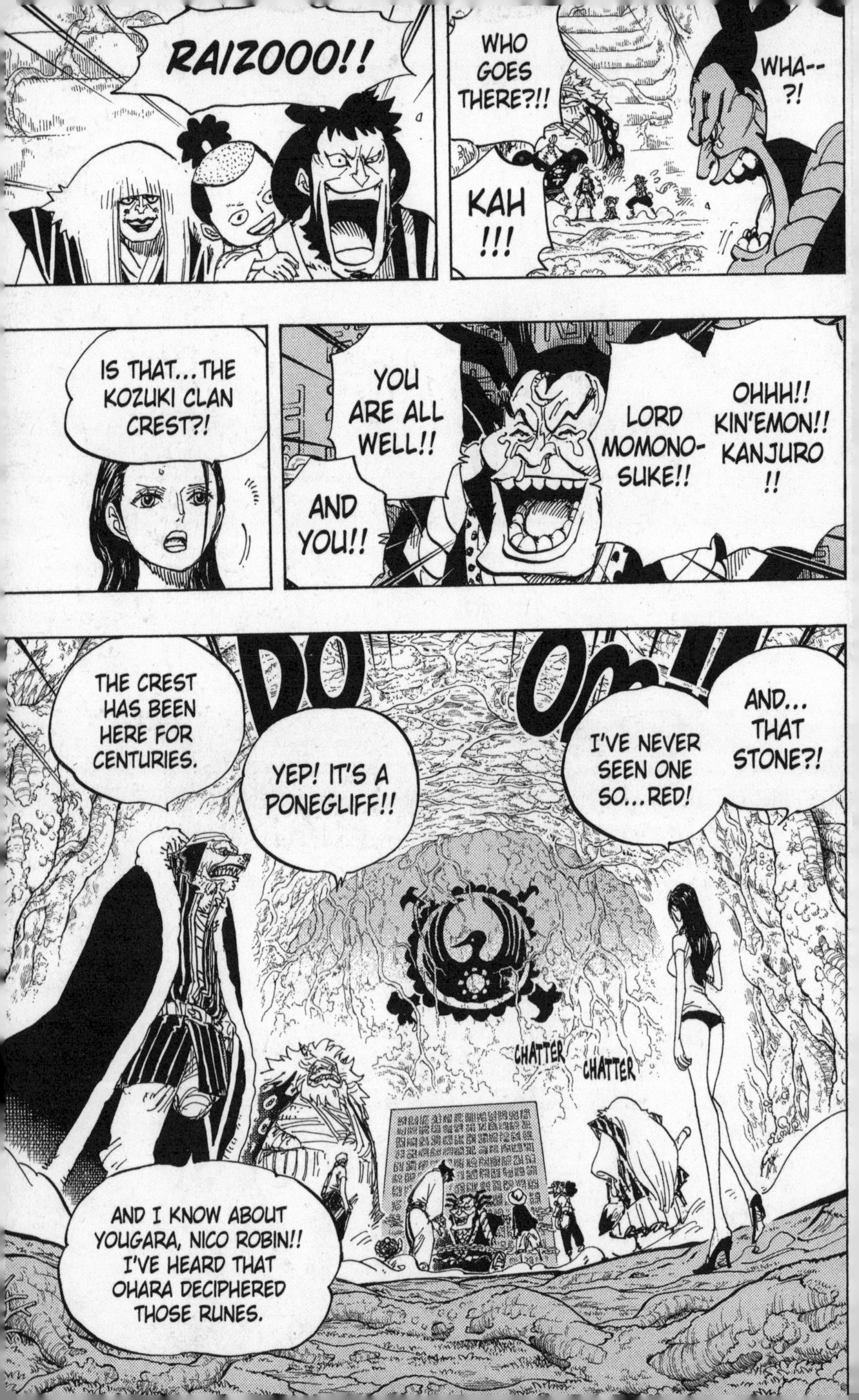
WHA-- ?!
WHO GOES THERE?!!
KAH !!!
RAIZOOO!!
OHHH!! KIN'EMON!! KANJURO !!
LORD MOMONO-SUKE!!
YOU ARE ALL WELL!!
AND YOU!!
IS THAT...THE KOZUKI CLAN CREST?!
AND... THAT STONE?!
I'VE NEVER SEEN ONE SO...RED!
YEP! IT'S A PONEGLIFF!!
THE CREST HAS BEEN HERE FOR CENTURIES.
CHATTER
CHATTER
AND I KNOW ABOUT YOUGARA, NICO ROBIN!! I'VE HEARD THAT OHARA DECIPHERED THOSE RUNES.

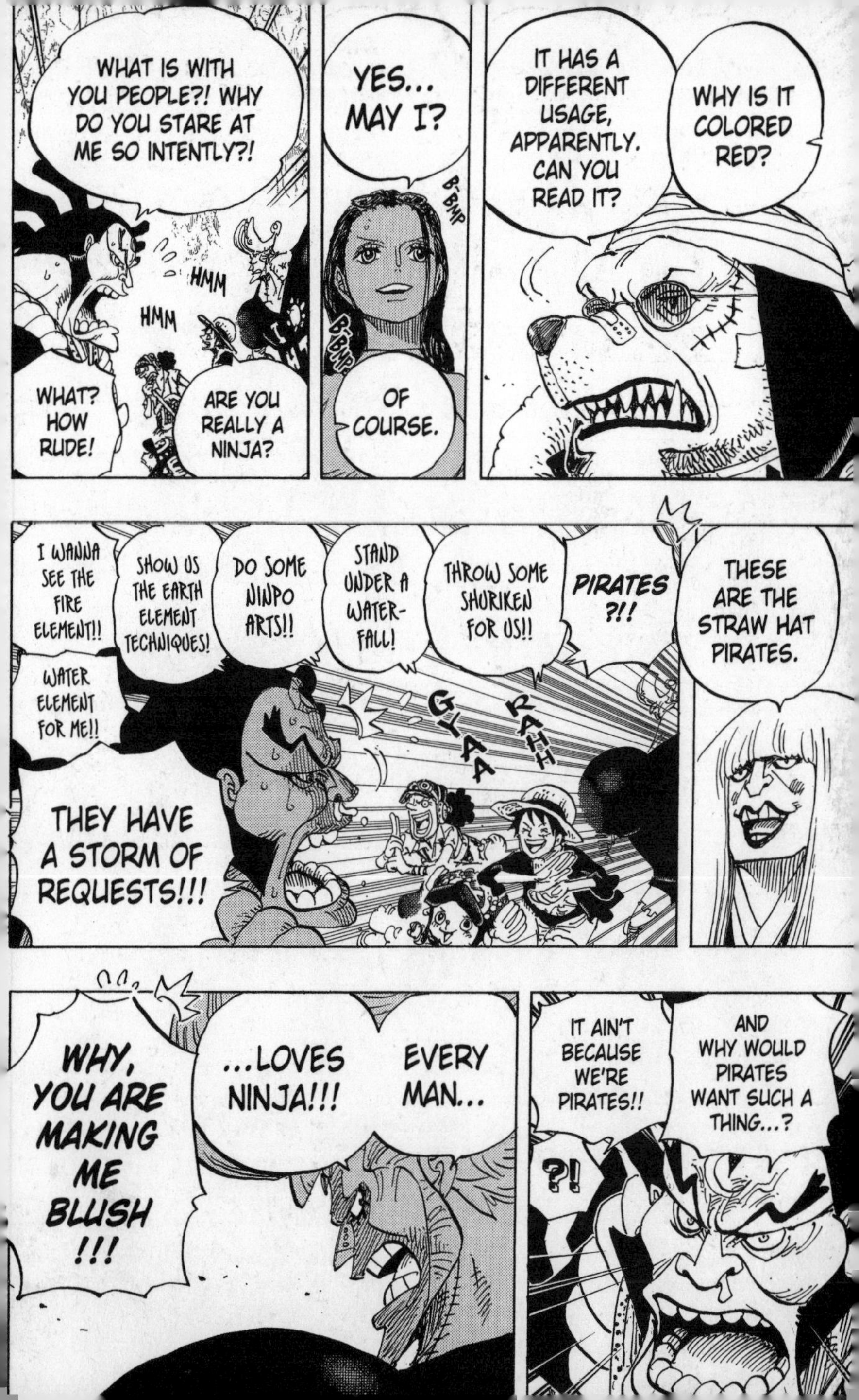

WHY IS IT COLORED RED?
IT HAS A DIFFERENT USAGE, APPARENTLY. CAN YOU READ IT?
YES... MAY I?
B'BMP
B'BMP
OF COURSE.
WHAT IS WITH YOU PEOPLE?! WHY DO YOU STARE AT ME SO INTENTLY?!
HMM
HMM
ARE YOU REALLY A NINJA?
WHAT? HOW RUDE!
THESE ARE THE STRAW HAT PIRATES.
PIRATES?!!
THROW SOME SHURIKEN FOR US!!
STAND UNDER A WATER-FALL!
DO SOME NINPO ARTS!!
SHOW US THE EARTH ELEMENT TECHNIQUES!
I WANNA SEE THE FIRE ELEMENT!!
WATER ELEMENT FOR ME!!
RAHH
GYAA
THEY HAVE A STORM OF REQUESTS!!!
AND WHY WOULD PIRATES WANT SUCH A THING...?
IT AIN'T BECAUSE WE'RE PIRATES!!
?!
EVERY MAN...
...LOVES NINJA!!!
WHY, YOU ARE MAKING ME BLUSH!!!

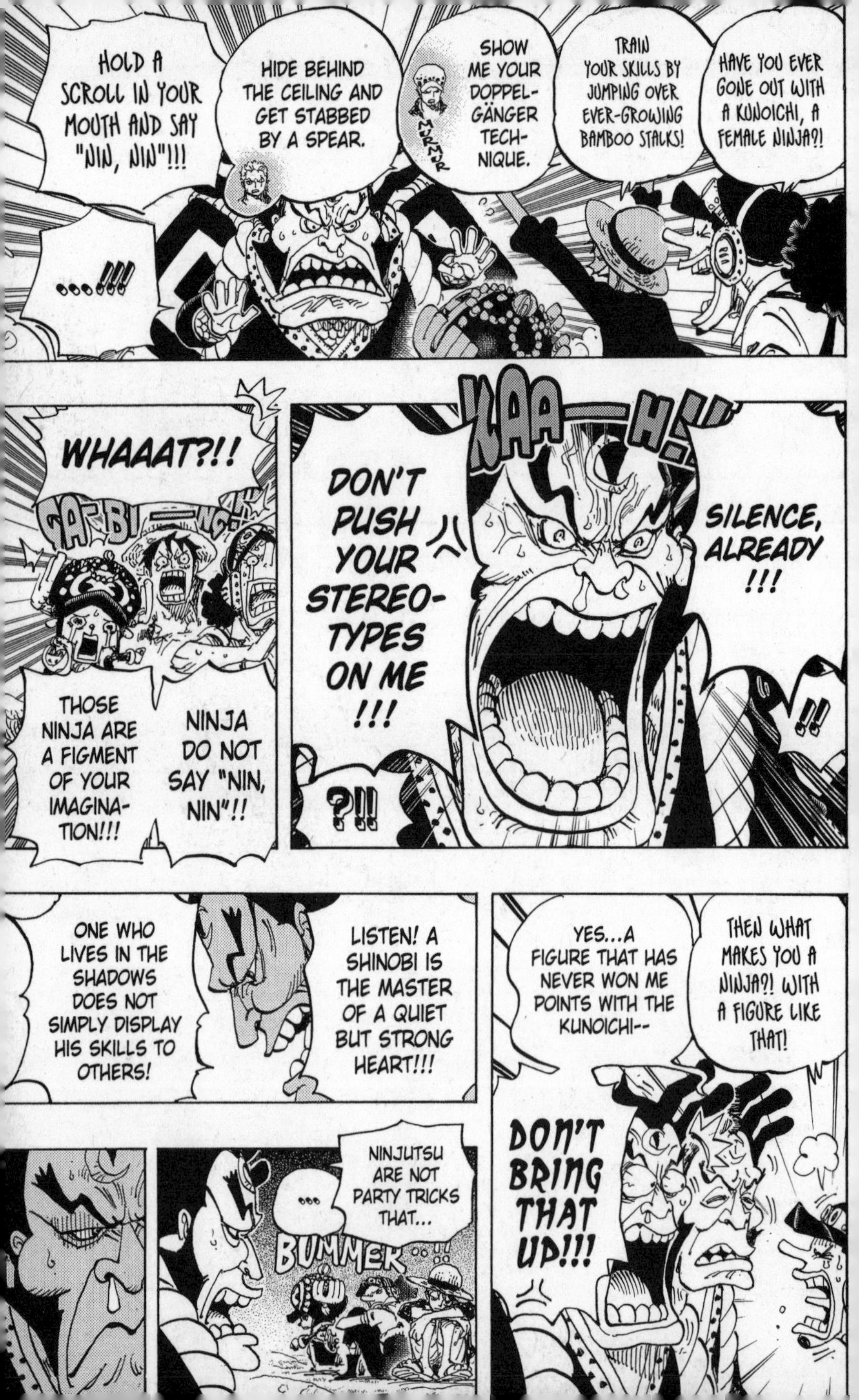
HAVE YOU EVER GONE OUT WITH A KUNOICHI, A FEMALE NINJA?!
TRAIN YOUR SKILLS BY JUMPING OVER EVER-GROWING BAMBOO STALKS!
SHOW ME YOUR DOPPEL-GÄNGER TECH-NIQUE.
MURMUR
HIDE BEHIND THE CEILING AND GET STABBED BY A SPEAR.
HOLD A SCROLL IN YOUR MOUTH AND SAY "NIN, NIN"!!!
...!!!
KLAA—H!!
SILENCE, ALREADY!!!
DON'T PUSH YOUR STEREO-TYPES ON ME!!!
!!
?!!
WHAAAT?!!
GA-BI—NG!
NINJA DO NOT SAY "NIN, NIN"!!
THOSE NINJA ARE A FIGMENT OF YOUR IMAGINA-TION!!!
THEN WHAT MAKES YOU A NINJA?! WITH A FIGURE LIKE THAT!
YES...A FIGURE THAT HAS NEVER WON ME POINTS WITH THE KUNOICHI--
DON'T BRING THAT UP!!!
LISTEN! A SHINOBI IS THE MASTER OF A QUIET BUT STRONG HEART!!!
ONE WHO LIVES IN THE SHADOWS DOES NOT SIMPLY DISPLAY HIS SKILLS TO OTHERS!
NINJUTSU ARE NOT PARTY TRICKS THAT...
...
BUMMER..!!

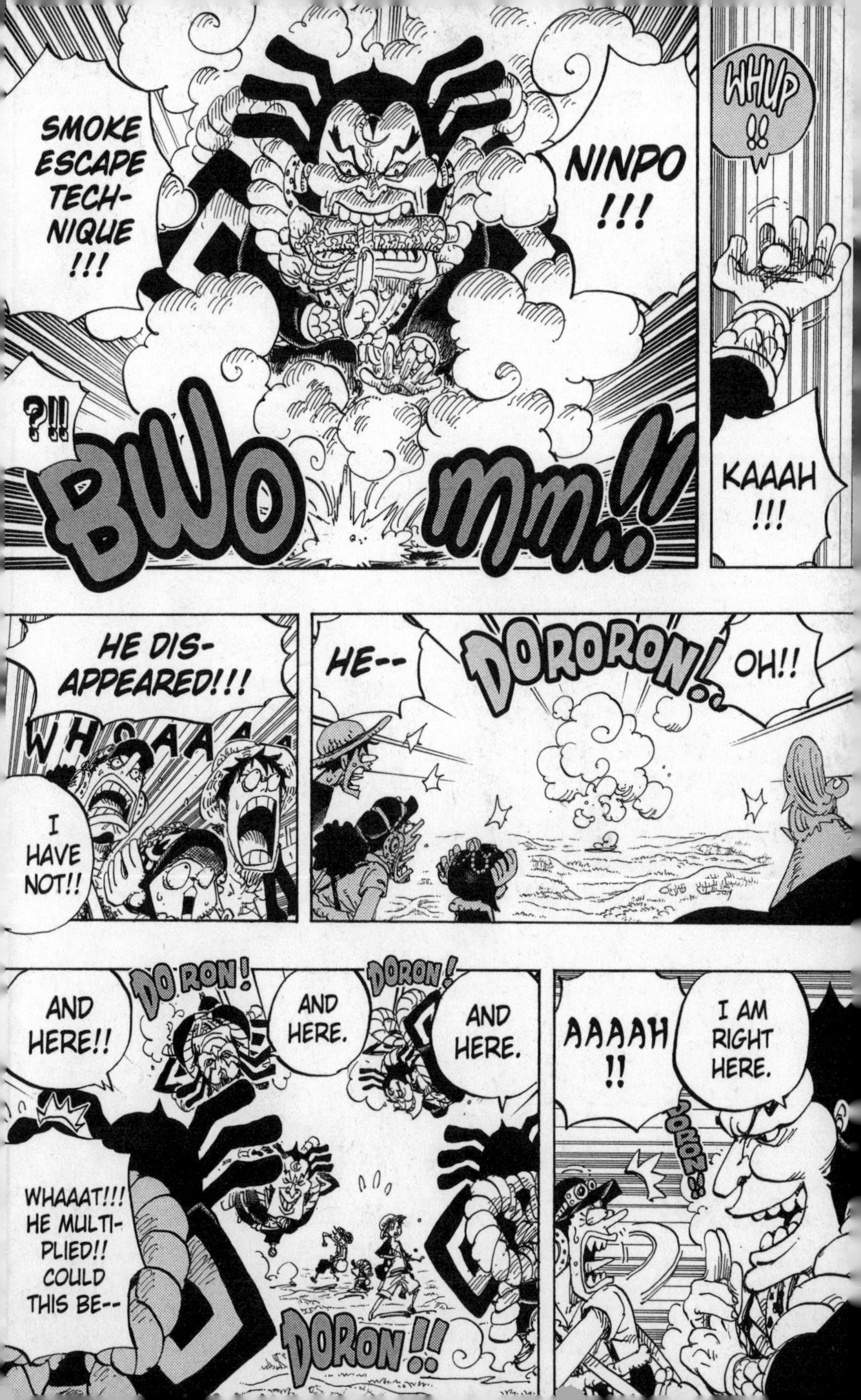
WHUP!!
KAAAH!!!
NINPO!!!
SMOKE ESCAPE TECH-NIQUE!!!
?!!
BWOMM..!!
OH!!
DORORON..!
HE--
HE DIS-APPEARED!!!
WHOAAA
I HAVE NOT!!
I AM RIGHT HERE.
AAAAH!!
DORON!!
AND HERE.
DORON!
AND HERE.
DO RON!
AND HERE!!
WHAAAT!!! HE MULTI-PLIED!! COULD THIS BE--
DORON!!

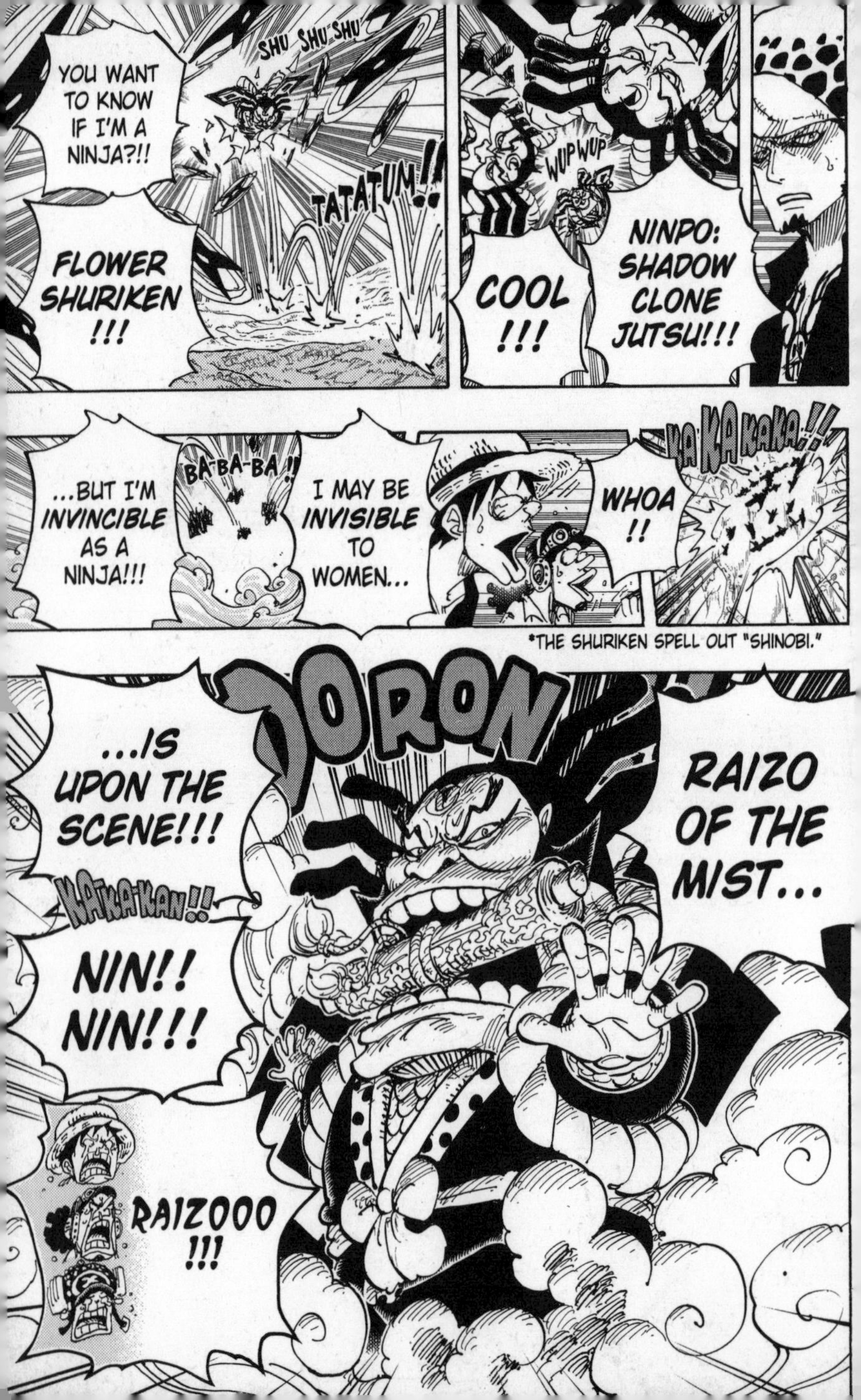
NINPO: SHADOW CLONE JUTSU!!!
WUP WUP
COOL !!!
YOU WANT TO KNOW IF I'M A NINJA?!!
SHU SHU SHU
TATATUM!!
FLOWER SHURIKEN !!!
KA KA KAKA!!!
WHOA !!
I MAY BE INVISIBLE TO WOMEN...
BA-BA-BA!!
...BUT I'M INVINCIBLE AS A NINJA!!!
RAIZO OF THE MIST...
DORON
...IS UPON THE SCENE!!!
KA-KA-KAN!!
NIN!! NIN!!!
RAIZOOO !!!
*THE SHURIKEN SPELL OUT "SHINOBI."

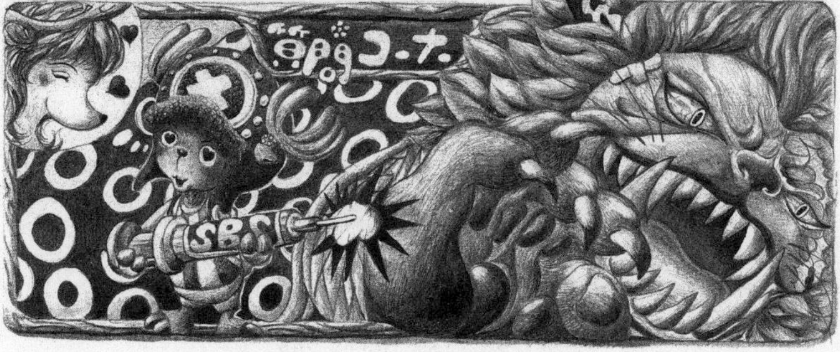
SBS

(Takahisa Fujimoto, Nara)

A: Hello there. I suppose we'll get started with our question and ans—

Q: I recognize that face… You're Eiichiro Oda, aren't ya? I hear you're having trouble with your SBS segment getting hijacked... So you tried to line up at the SBS arena first thing in the morning. Nice try, pal!!! I lined up three days ago. So **I'm** gonna say the words…

"Let's start the SBS!!"

--Komashu

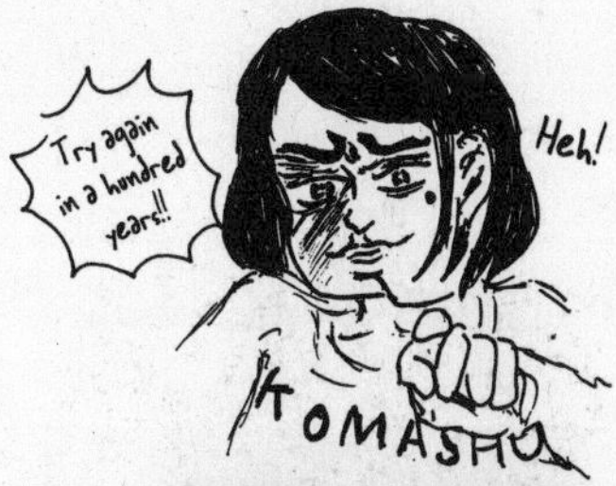
Try again in a hundred years!!
Heh!
KOMASHU

A: Whoaaaa!!
I have to wait a hundred years to try again?!

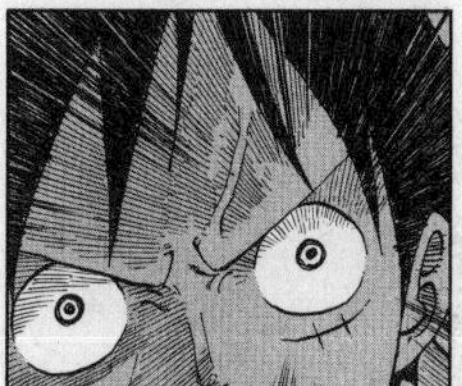

Q: Oda Sensei, I've got big trouble. Akainu is standing right behind me. What should I do?

--Junpei T.

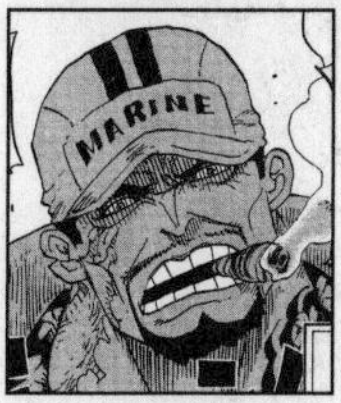
MARINE

A: First, stay calm. I'm going to show you the pose that will allow you to get past Akainu. Shape your mouth into a "3" sign, look up and to the left, and start whistling. This will help you slip past most major threats: bears, ghosts, you name it.

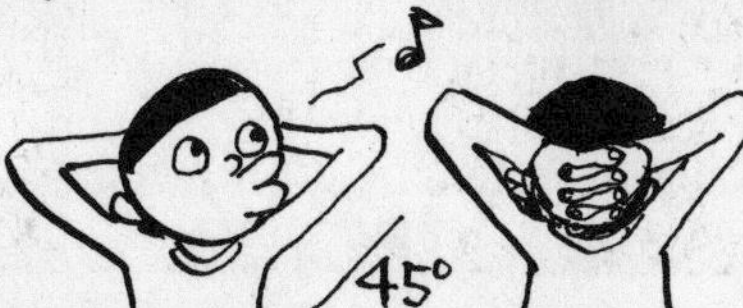
45°

Chapter 818:
INSIDE THE WHALE

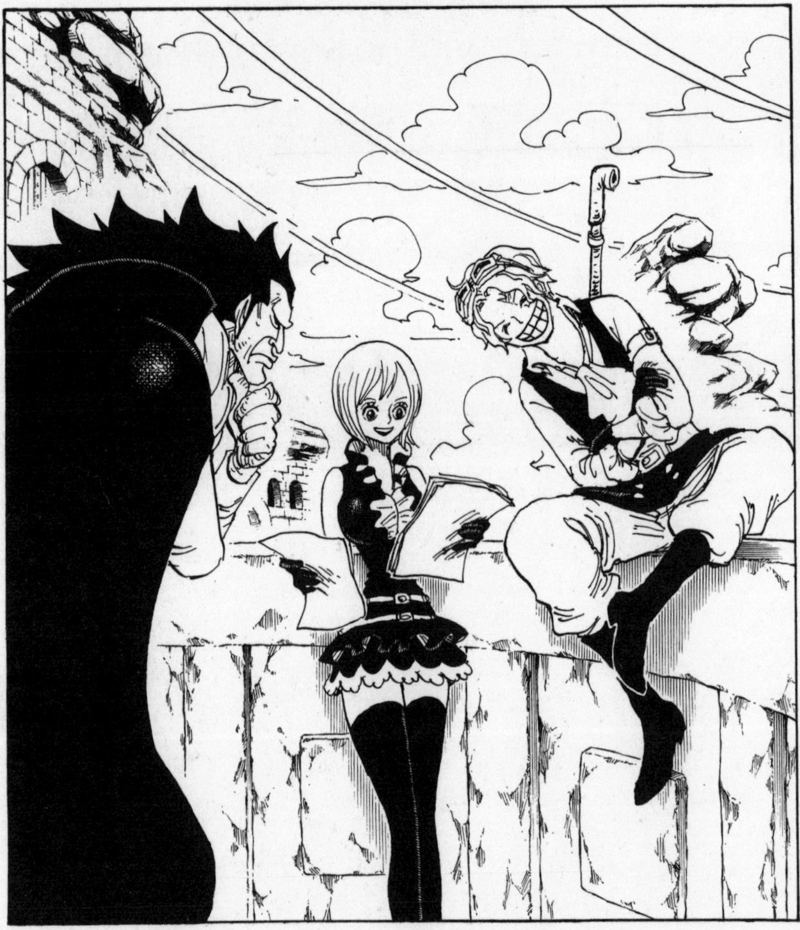

DECKS OF THE WORLD, 500-MILLION-MAN ARC,
VOL. 11: "BALTIGO"

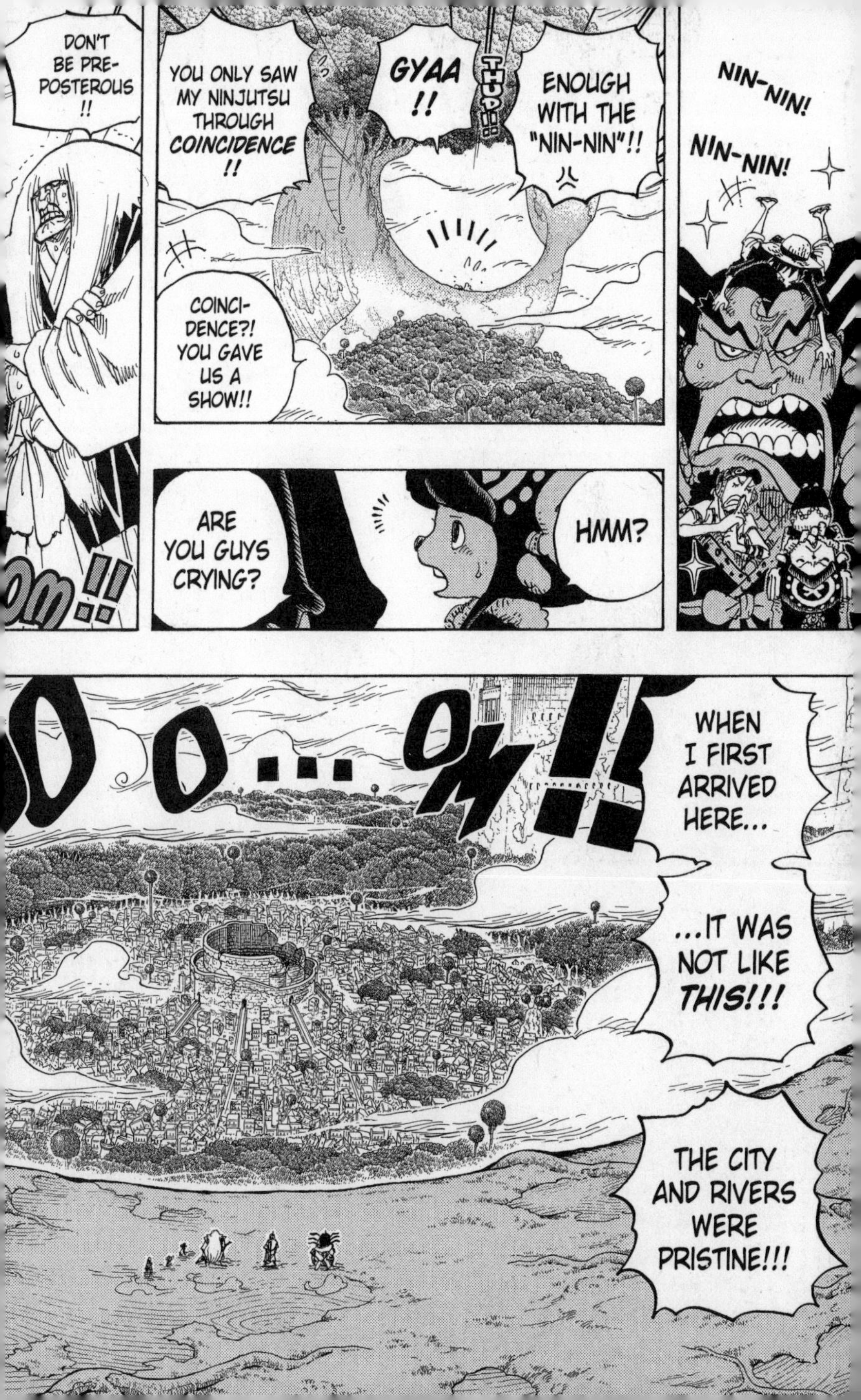
NIN-NIN!
NIN-NIN!
ENOUGH WITH THE "NIN-NIN"!!
THUD!!
GYAA!!
YOU ONLY SAW MY NINJUTSU THROUGH COINCIDENCE!!
COINCIDENCE?! YOU GAVE US A SHOW!!
HMM?
ARE YOU GUYS CRYING?
DON'T BE PREPOSTEROUS!!
WHEN I FIRST ARRIVED HERE...
...IT WAS NOT LIKE THIS!!!
THE CITY AND RIVERS WERE PRISTINE!!!

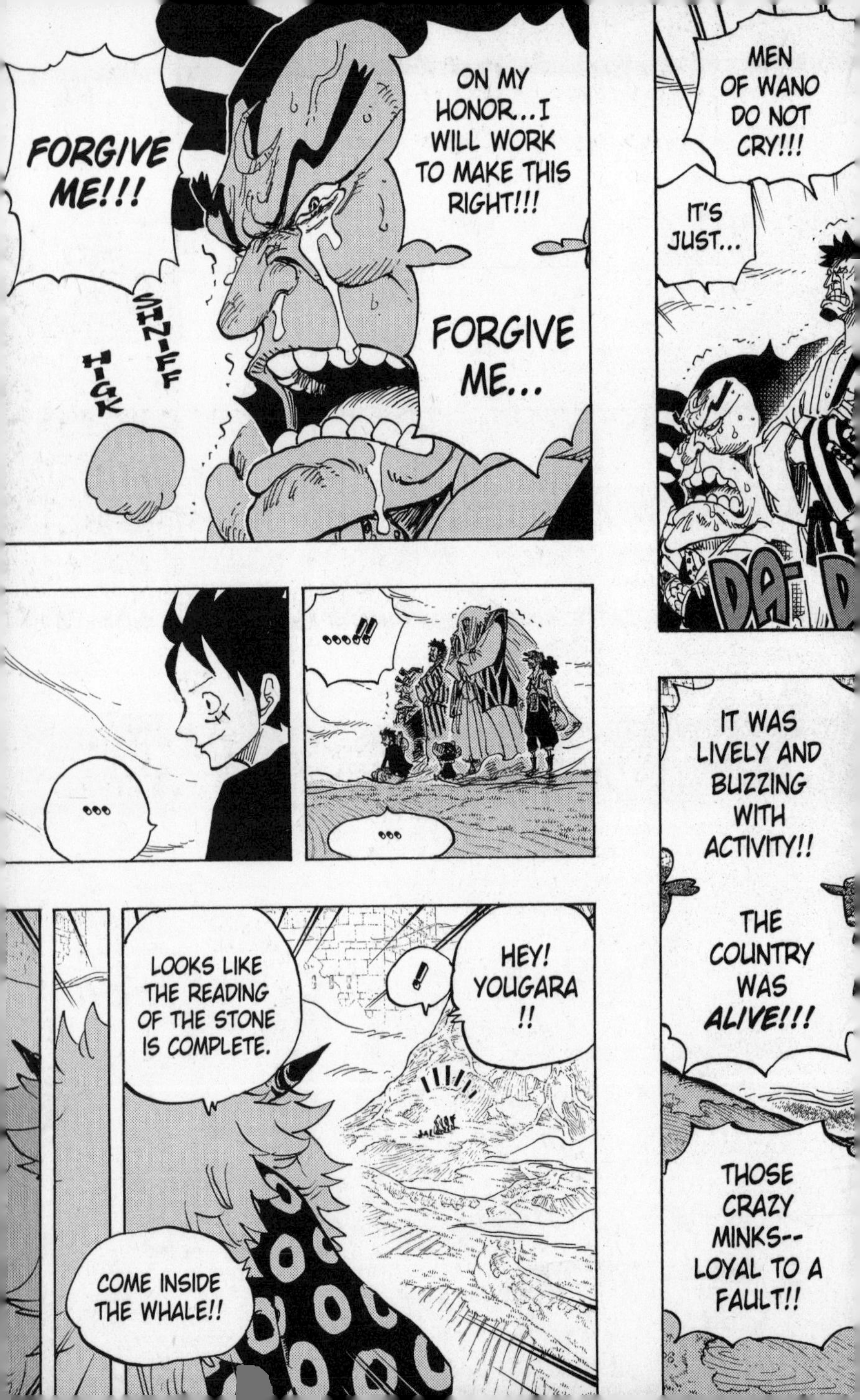
MEN OF WANO DO NOT CRY!!!
IT'S JUST...
DA-D
IT WAS LIVELY AND BUZZING WITH ACTIVITY!!
THE COUNTRY WAS ALIVE!!!
THOSE CRAZY MINKS-- LOYAL TO A FAULT!!
ON MY HONOR...I WILL WORK TO MAKE THIS RIGHT!!!
FORGIVE ME!!!
FORGIVE ME...
SHNIFF
HICK
.....!!
...
...
HEY! YOUGARA!!
!
LOOKS LIKE THE READING OF THE STONE IS COMPLETE.
COME INSIDE THE WHALE!!

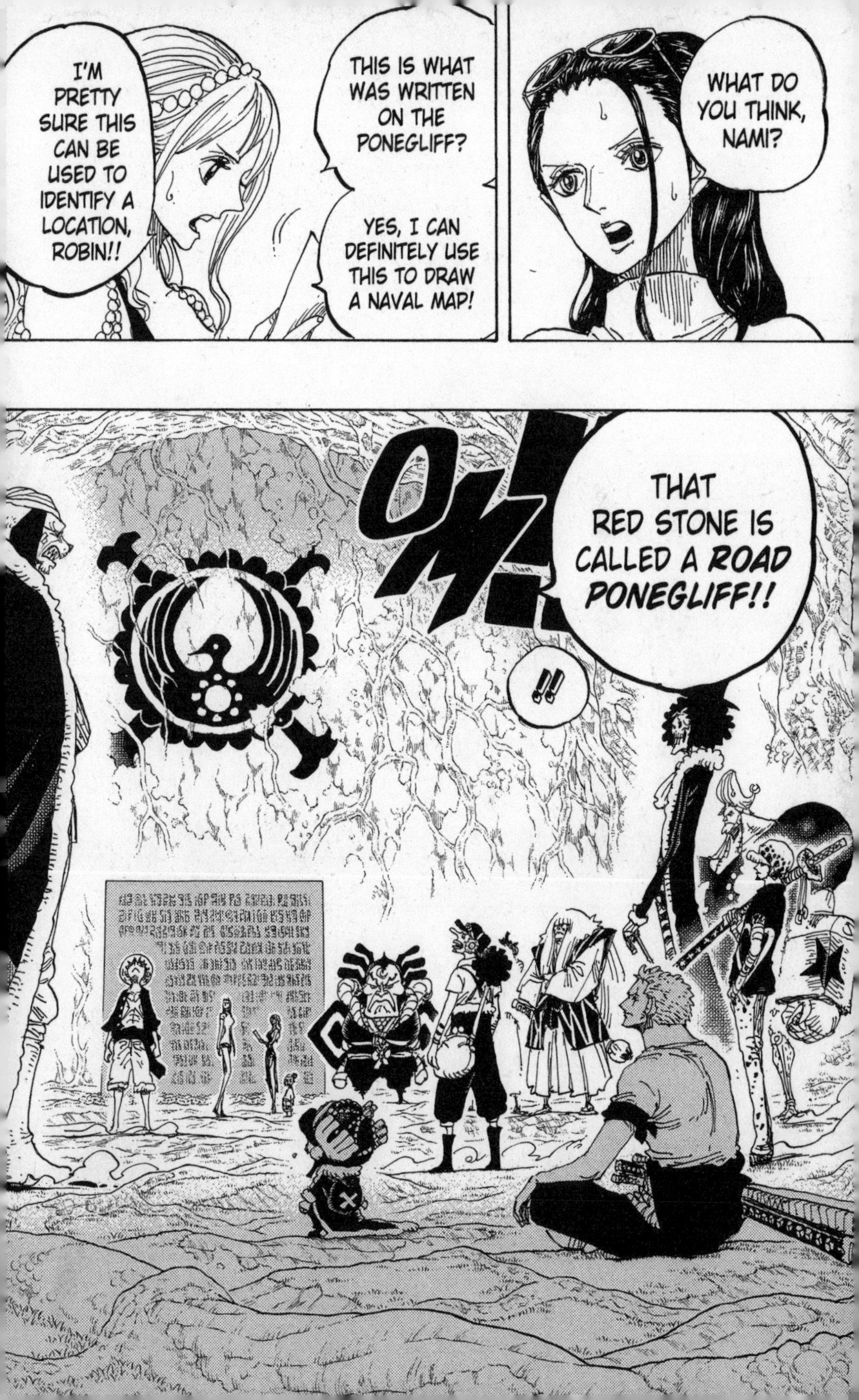

WHAT DO YOU THINK, NAMI?
THIS IS WHAT WAS WRITTEN ON THE PONEGLIFF?
YES, I CAN DEFINITELY USE THIS TO DRAW A NAVAL MAP!
I'M PRETTY SURE THIS CAN BE USED TO IDENTIFY A LOCATION, ROBIN!!
THAT RED STONE IS CALLED A *ROAD PONEGLIFF!!*
OH!!
!!

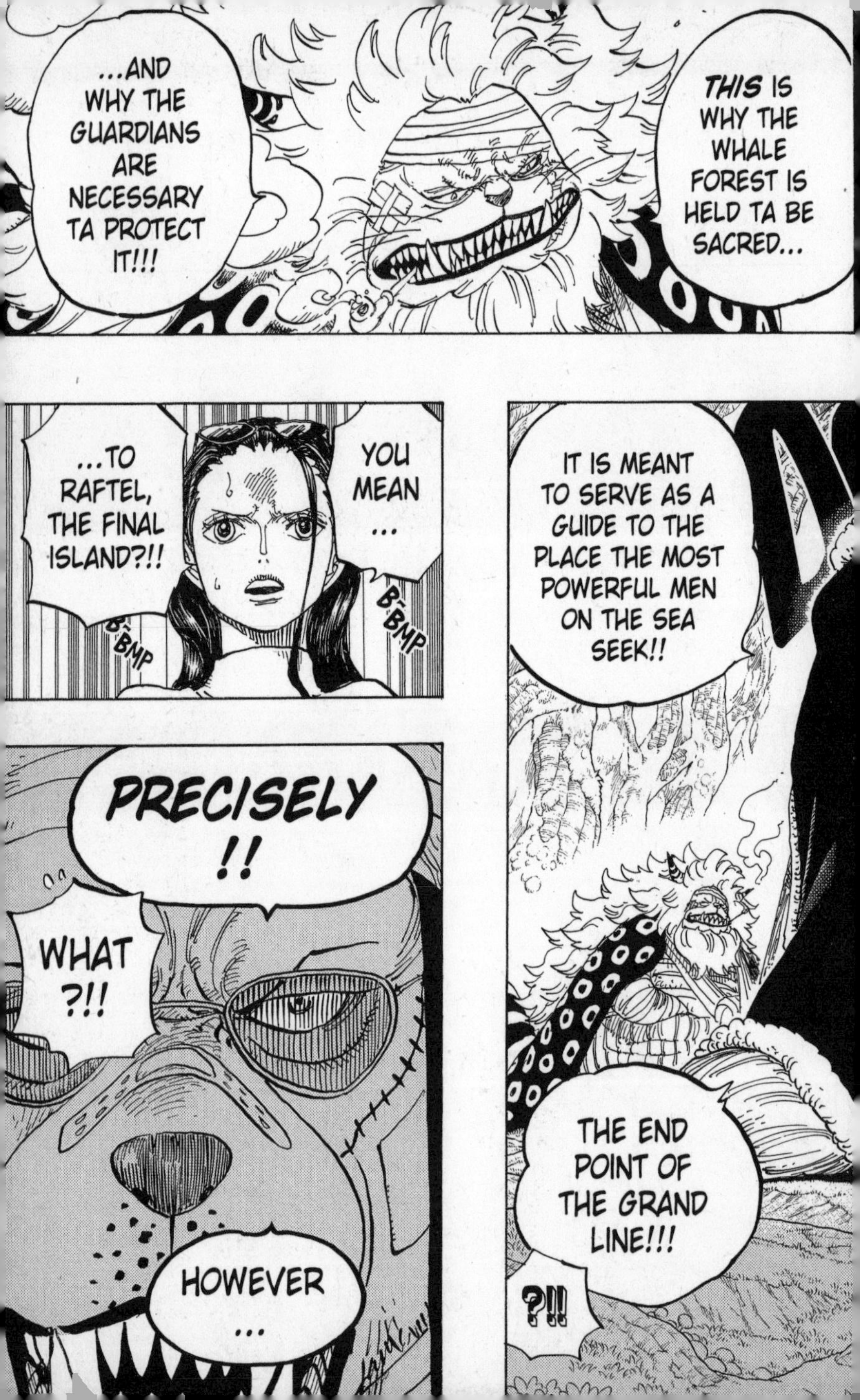
THIS IS WHY THE WHALE FOREST IS HELD TA BE SACRED...
...AND WHY THE GUARDIANS ARE NECESSARY TA PROTECT IT!!!
IT IS MEANT TO SERVE AS A GUIDE TO THE PLACE THE MOST POWERFUL MEN ON THE SEA SEEK!!
THE END POINT OF THE GRAND LINE!!!
?!!
YOU MEAN...
...TO RAFTEL, THE FINAL ISLAND?!!
B-BMP
B-BMP
PRECISELY!!
WHAT?!!
HOWEVER...

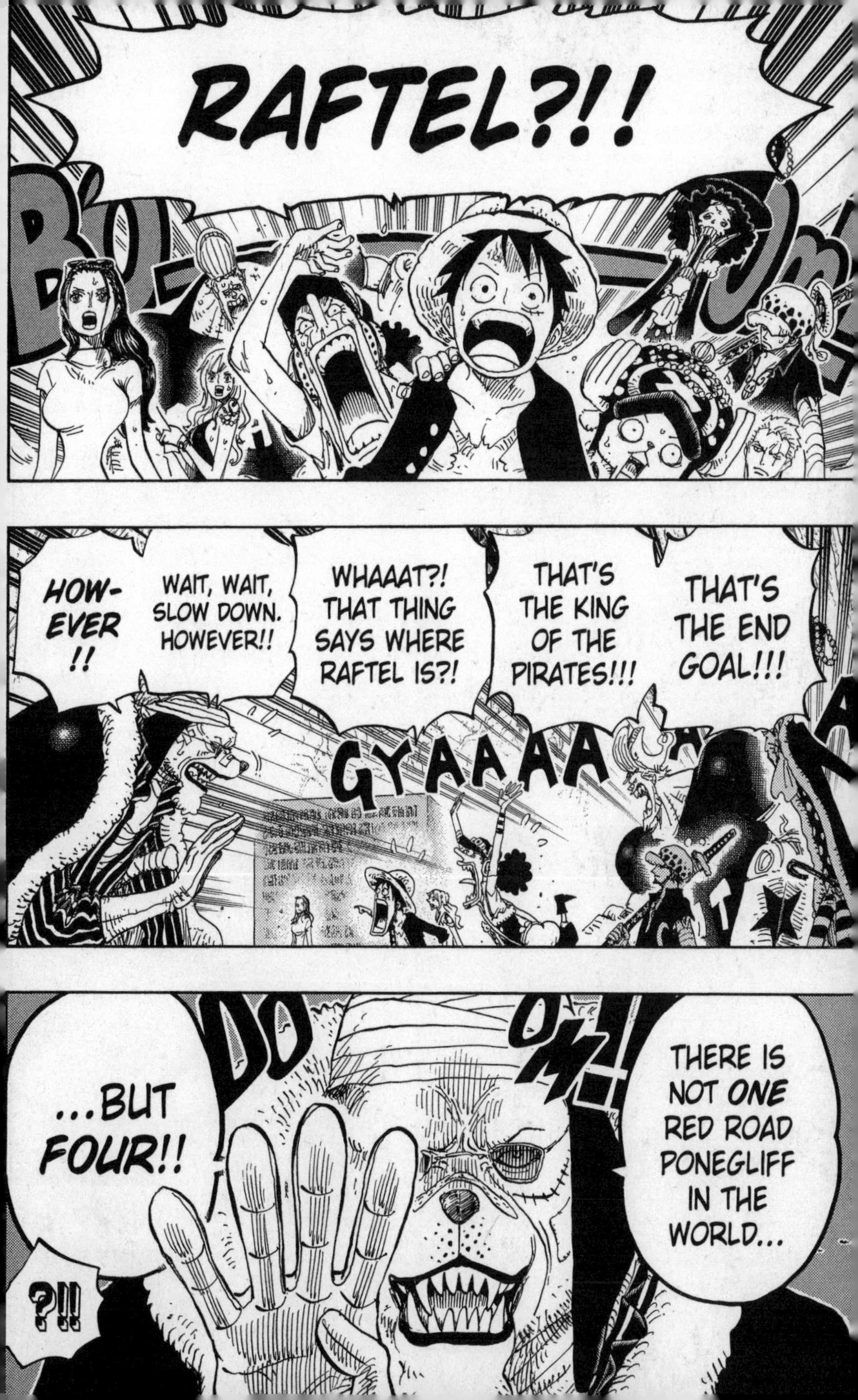
RAFTEL?!!
THAT'S THE END GOAL!!!
THAT'S THE KING OF THE PIRATES!!!
WHAAAT?! THAT THING SAYS WHERE RAFTEL IS?!
WAIT, WAIT, SLOW DOWN. HOWEVER!!
HOW-EVER !!
GYAAAAA
THERE IS NOT *ONE* RED ROAD PONEGLIFF IN THE WORLD...
...BUT FOUR!!
?!!

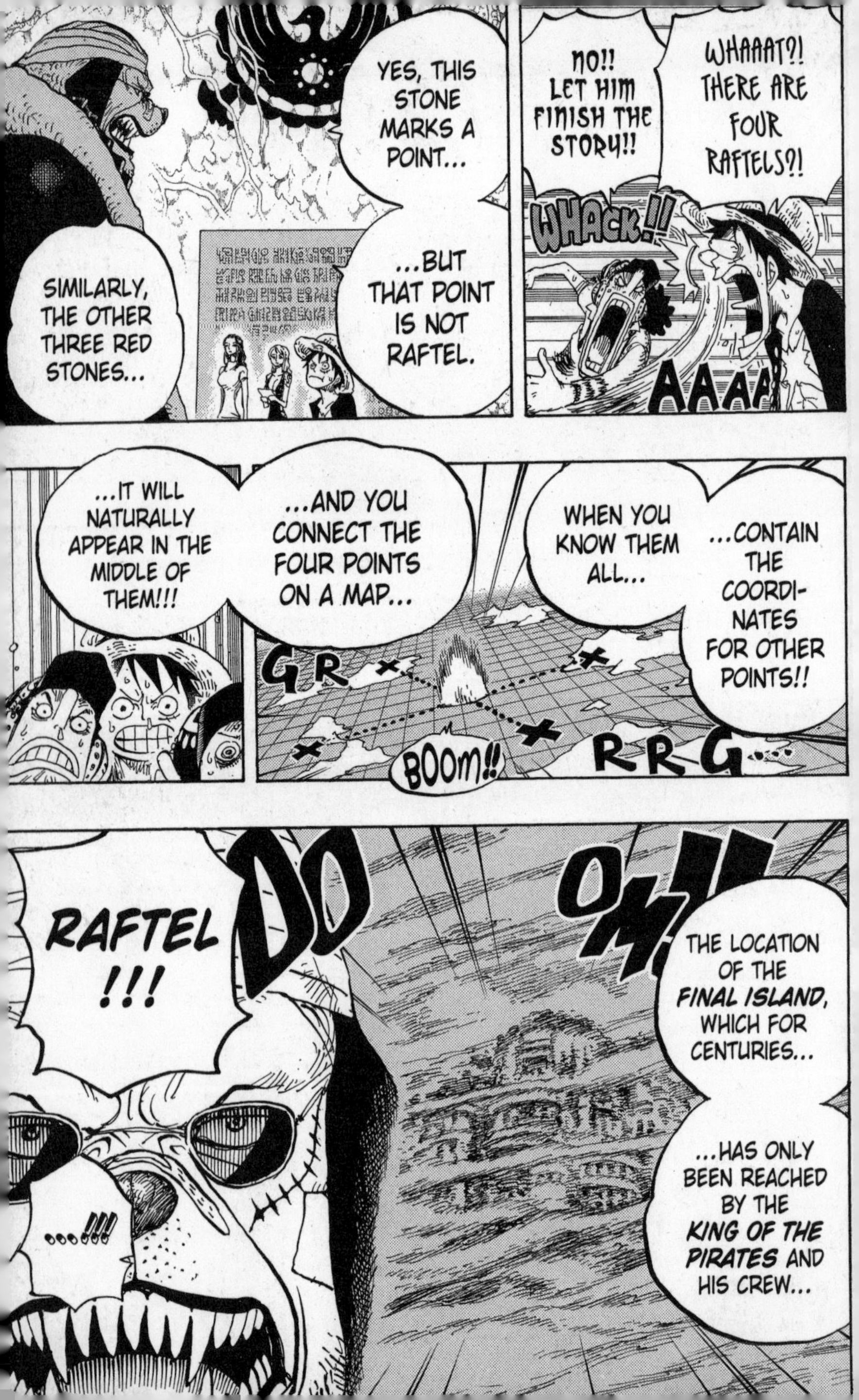
WHAAAT?! THERE ARE FOUR RAFTELS?!
NO!! LET HIM FINISH THE STORY!!
WHACK!!
AAAA
YES, THIS STONE MARKS A POINT...
...BUT THAT POINT IS NOT RAFTEL.
SIMILARLY, THE OTHER THREE RED STONES...
...CONTAIN THE COORDINATES FOR OTHER POINTS!!
WHEN YOU KNOW THEM ALL...
...AND YOU CONNECT THE FOUR POINTS ON A MAP...
RRG
BOOM!!
GR
...IT WILL NATURALLY APPEAR IN THE MIDDLE OF THEM!!!
THE LOCATION OF THE FINAL ISLAND, WHICH FOR CENTURIES...
...HAS ONLY BEEN REACHED BY THE KING OF THE PIRATES AND HIS CREW...
DOOM!!
RAFTEL!!!
...!!!

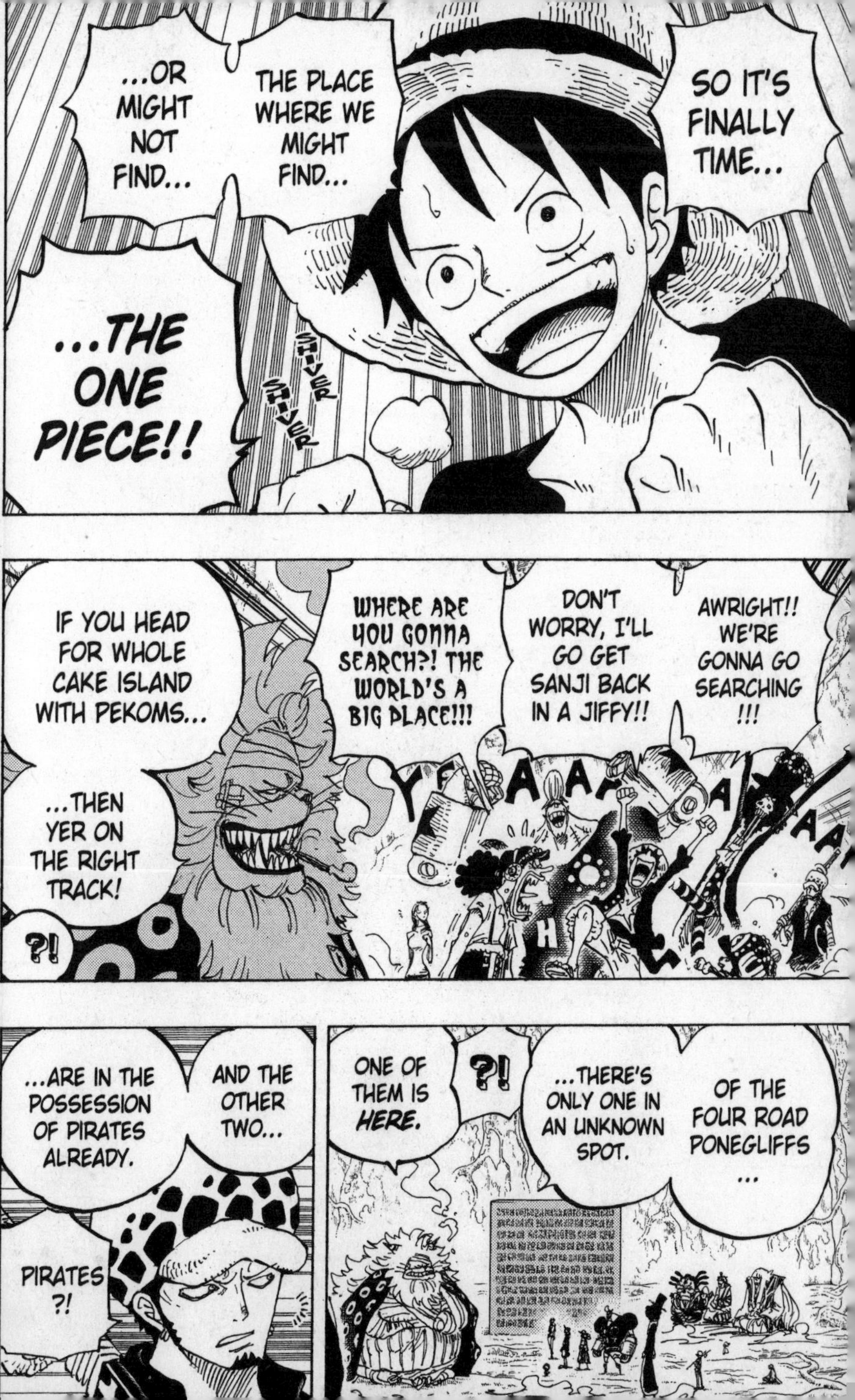
SO IT'S FINALLY TIME...
THE PLACE WHERE WE MIGHT FIND...
...OR MIGHT NOT FIND...
...THE ONE PIECE!!
SHIVER SHIVER
AWRIGHT!! WE'RE GONNA GO SEARCHING !!!
DON'T WORRY, I'LL GO GET SANJI BACK IN A JIFFY!!
WHERE ARE YOU GONNA SEARCH?! THE WORLD'S A BIG PLACE!!!
IF YOU HEAD FOR WHOLE CAKE ISLAND WITH PEKOMS...
...THEN YER ON THE RIGHT TRACK!
?!
OF THE FOUR ROAD PONEGLIFFS ...
...THERE'S ONLY ONE IN AN UNKNOWN SPOT.
?!
ONE OF THEM IS *HERE.*
AND THE OTHER TWO...
...ARE IN THE POSSESSION OF PIRATES ALREADY.
PIRATES ?!

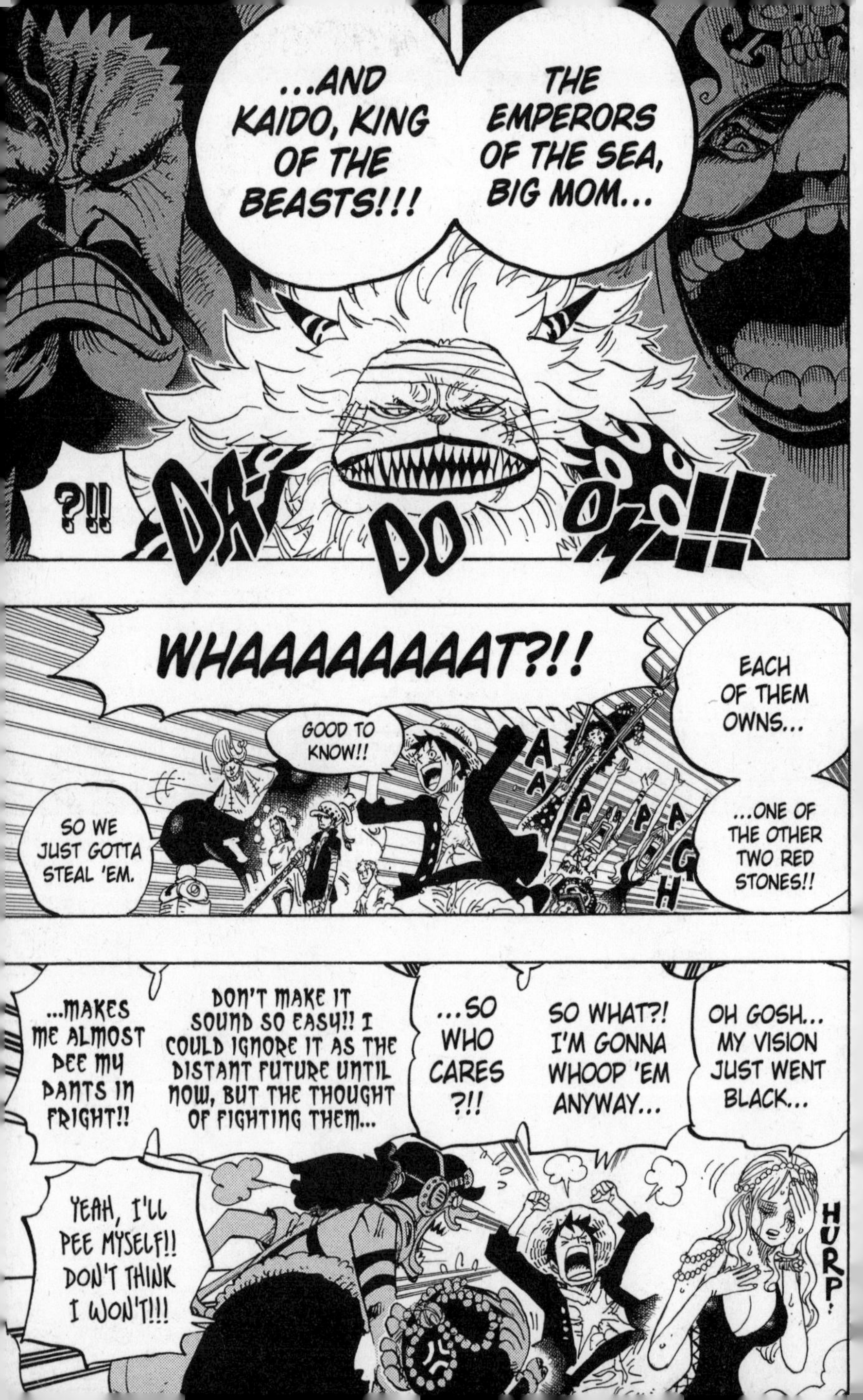
THE EMPERORS OF THE SEA, BIG MOM...
...AND KAIDO, KING OF THE BEASTS!!!
DA DO OOOM!!
?!!
EACH OF THEM OWNS...
...ONE OF THE OTHER TWO RED STONES!!
WHAAAAAAAAT?!!
AAAPPAGH
GOOD TO KNOW!!
SO WE JUST GOTTA STEAL 'EM.
OH GOSH... MY VISION JUST WENT BLACK...
HURP!
SO WHAT?! I'M GONNA WHOOP 'EM ANYWAY...
...SO WHO CARES?!!
DON'T MAKE IT SOUND SO EASY!! I COULD IGNORE IT AS THE DISTANT FUTURE UNTIL NOW, BUT THE THOUGHT OF FIGHTING THEM...
...MAKES ME ALMOST PEE MY PANTS IN FRIGHT!!
YEAH, I'LL PEE MYSELF!! DON'T THINK I WON'T!!!

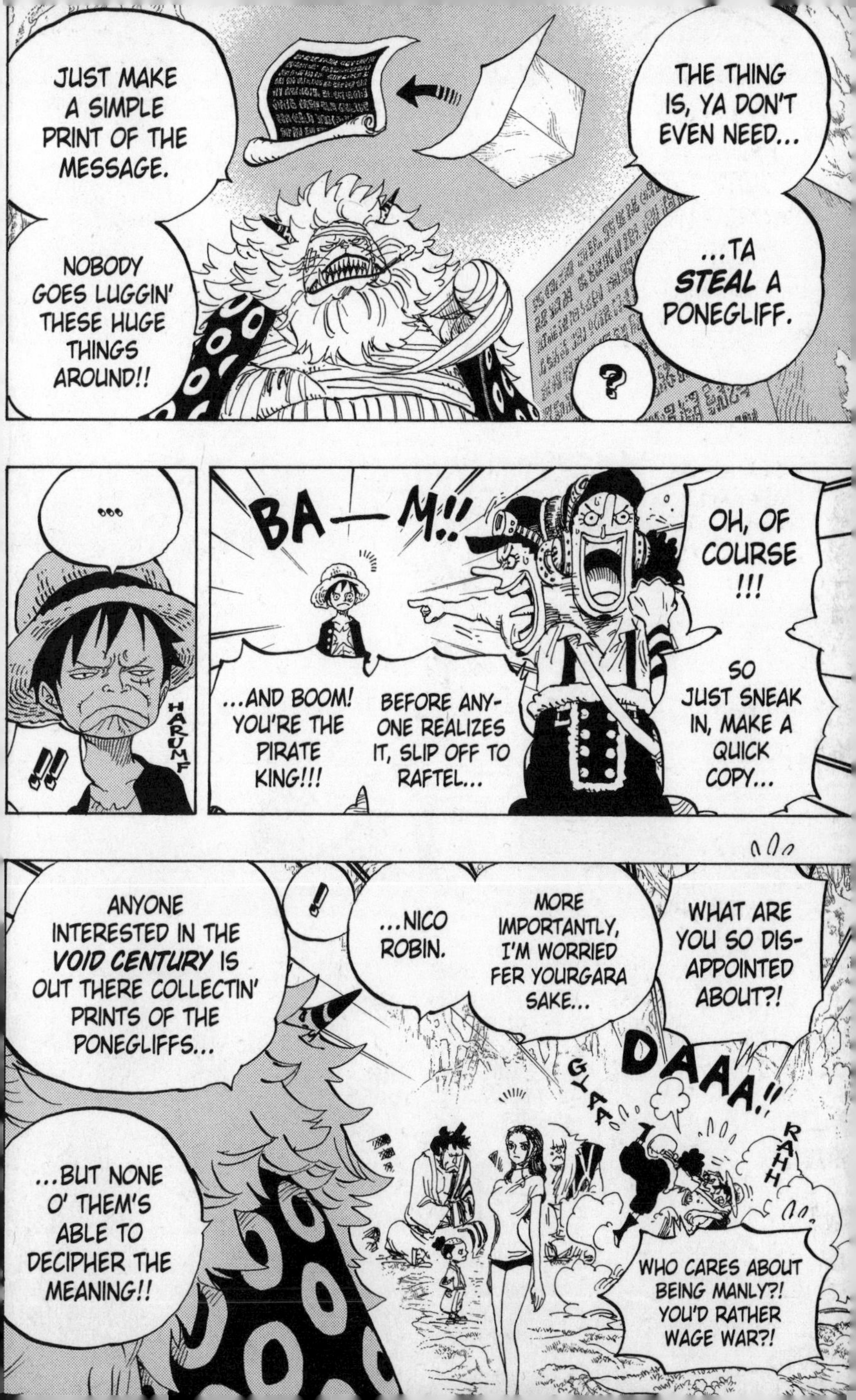
THE THING IS, YA DON'T EVEN NEED...
...TA *STEAL* A PONEGLIFF.
?
JUST MAKE A SIMPLE PRINT OF THE MESSAGE.
NOBODY GOES LUGGIN' THESE HUGE THINGS AROUND!!
BA—M!!
OH, OF COURSE!!!
SO JUST SNEAK IN, MAKE A QUICK COPY...
BEFORE ANY-ONE REALIZES IT, SLIP OFF TO RAFTEL...
...AND BOOM! YOU'RE THE PIRATE KING!!!
...
HARUMF
!!
WHAT ARE YOU SO DIS-APPOINTED ABOUT?!
MORE IMPORTANTLY, I'M WORRIED FER YOURGARA SAKE...
...NICO ROBIN.
!
ANYONE INTERESTED IN THE *VOID CENTURY* IS OUT THERE COLLECTIN' PRINTS OF THE PONEGLIFFS...
DAAAA!!
GYAA
RAHH
WHO CARES ABOUT BEING MANLY?! YOU'D RATHER WAGE WAR?!
...BUT NONE O' THEM'S ABLE TO DECIPHER THE MEANING!!

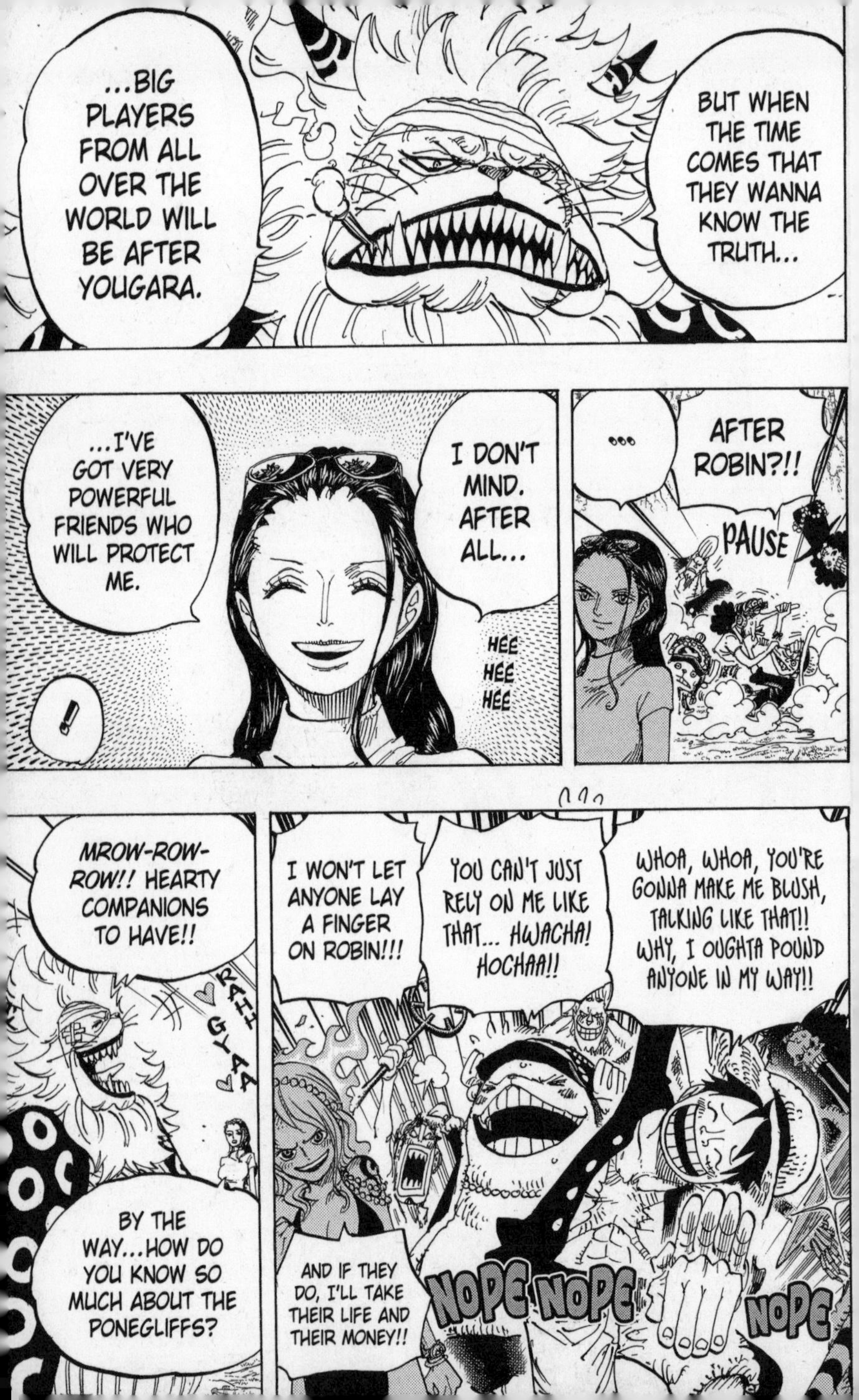
BUT WHEN THE TIME COMES THAT THEY WANNA KNOW THE TRUTH...
...BIG PLAYERS FROM ALL OVER THE WORLD WILL BE AFTER YOUGARA.
AFTER ROBIN?!!
...
PAUSE
I DON'T MIND. AFTER ALL...
...I'VE GOT VERY POWERFUL FRIENDS WHO WILL PROTECT ME.
HEE HEE HEE
!
WHOA, WHOA, YOU'RE GONNA MAKE ME BLUSH, TALKING LIKE THAT!! WHY, I OUGHTA POUND ANYONE IN MY WAY!!
YOU CAN'T JUST RELY ON ME LIKE THAT... HWACHA! HOCHAA!!
I WON'T LET ANYONE LAY A FINGER ON ROBIN!!!
AND IF THEY DO, I'LL TAKE THEIR LIFE AND THEIR MONEY!!
NOPE NOPE NOPE
MROW-ROW-ROW!! HEARTY COMPANIONS TO HAVE!!
RAHH
GYAA
BY THE WAY...HOW DO YOU KNOW SO MUCH ABOUT THE PONEGLIFFS?

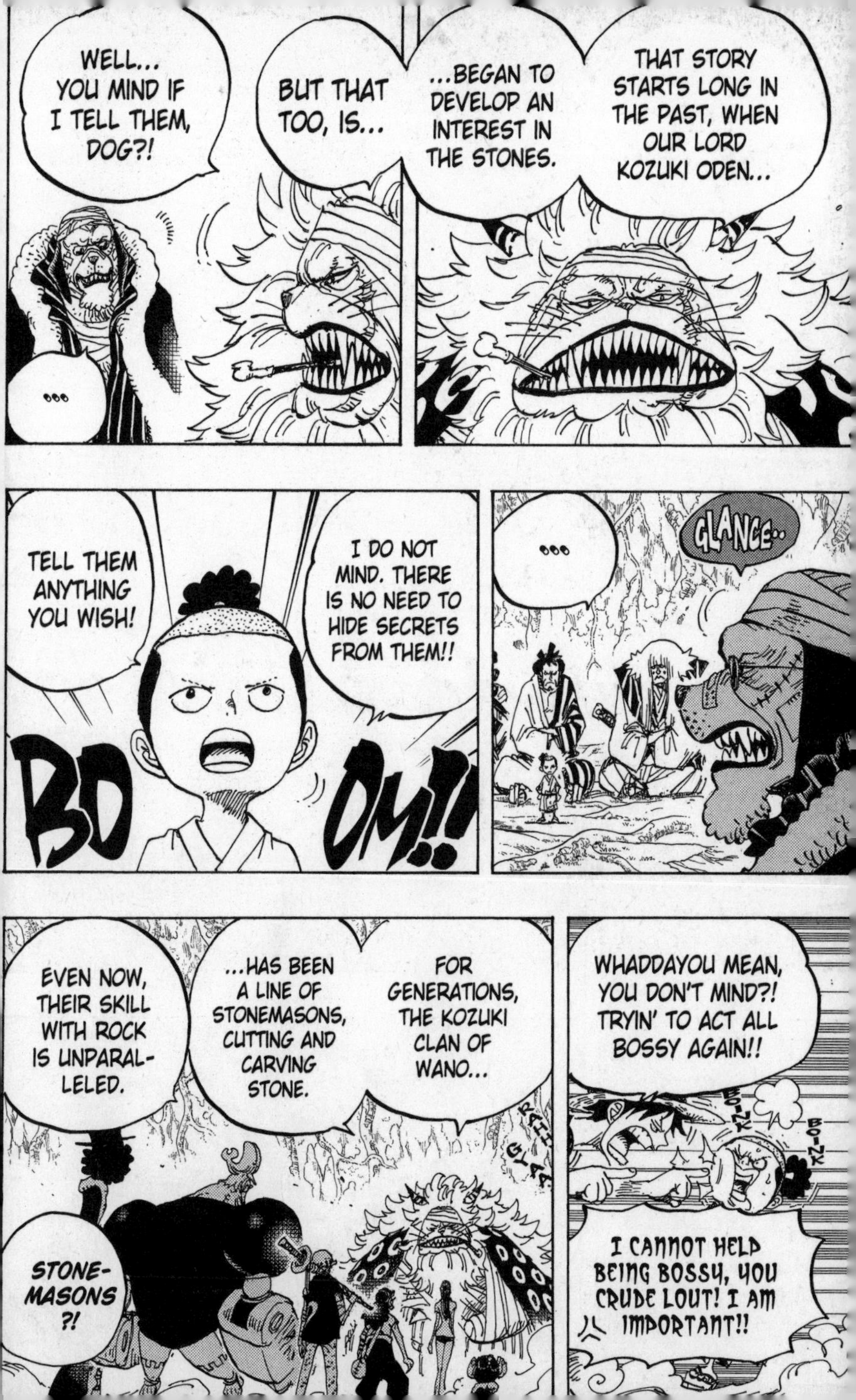
THAT STORY STARTS LONG IN THE PAST, WHEN OUR LORD KOZUKI ODEN...
...BEGAN TO DEVELOP AN INTEREST IN THE STONES.
BUT THAT TOO, IS...
WELL... YOU MIND IF I TELL THEM, DOG?!
...
GLANCE..
...
I DO NOT MIND. THERE IS NO NEED TO HIDE SECRETS FROM THEM!!
TELL THEM ANYTHING YOU WISH!
BOOM!!
WHADDAYOU MEAN, YOU DON'T MIND?! TRYIN' TO ACT ALL BOSSY AGAIN!!
BOINK
BOINK
I CANNOT HELP BEING BOSSY, YOU CRUDE LOUT! I AM IMPORTANT!!
FOR GENERATIONS, THE KOZUKI CLAN OF WANO...
...HAS BEEN A LINE OF STONEMASONS, CUTTING AND CARVING STONE.
EVEN NOW, THEIR SKILL WITH ROCK IS UNPARAL-LELED.
STONE-MASONS ?!

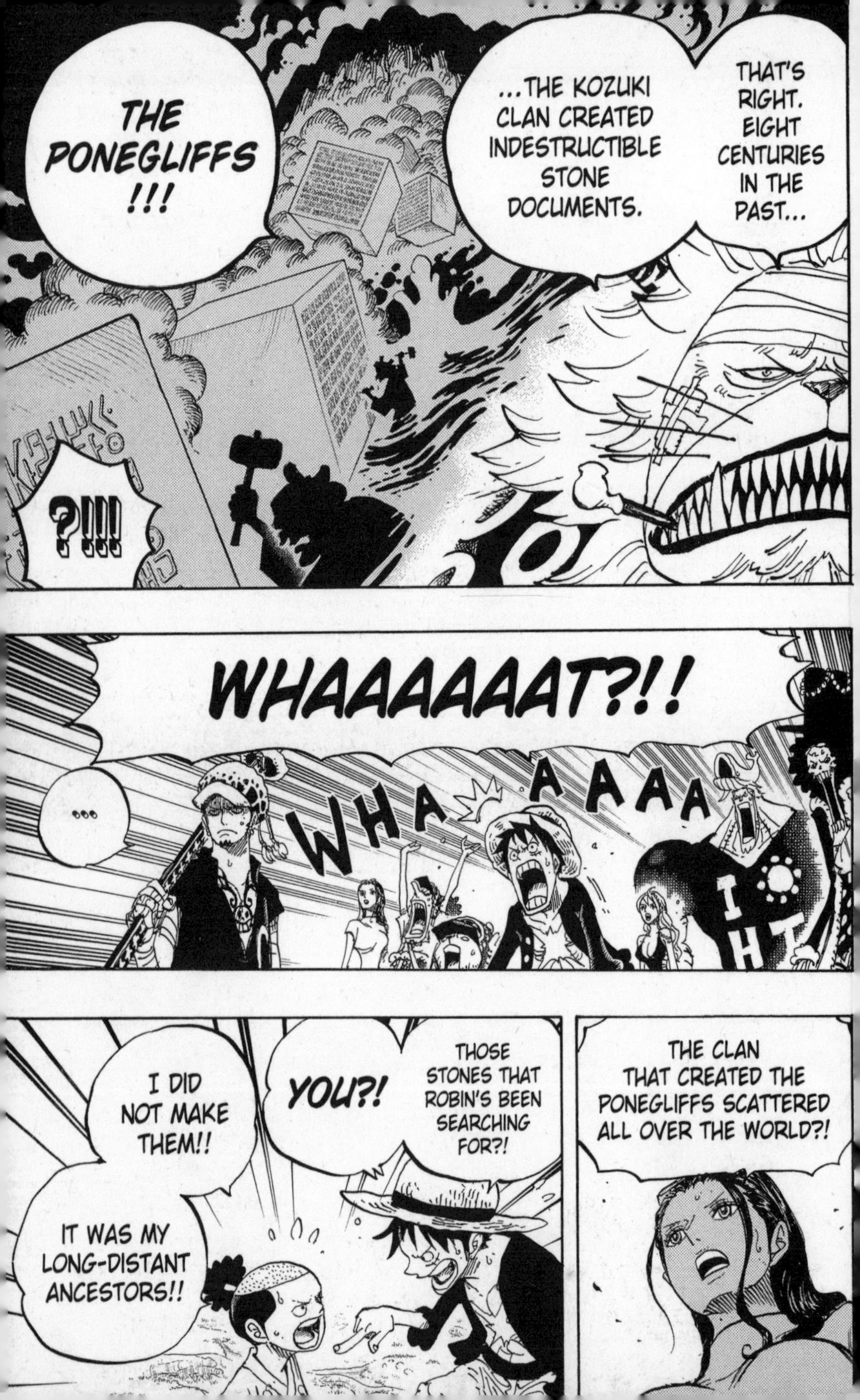
THAT'S RIGHT. EIGHT CENTURIES IN THE PAST...
...THE KOZUKI CLAN CREATED INDESTRUCTIBLE STONE DOCUMENTS.
THE PONEGLIFFS!!!
?!!!
WHAAAAAAT?!!
WHAAAAA
...
THE CLAN THAT CREATED THE PONEGLIFFS SCATTERED ALL OVER THE WORLD?!
THOSE STONES THAT ROBIN'S BEEN SEARCHING FOR?!
YOU?!
I DID NOT MAKE THEM!!
IT WAS MY LONG-DISTANT ANCESTORS!!

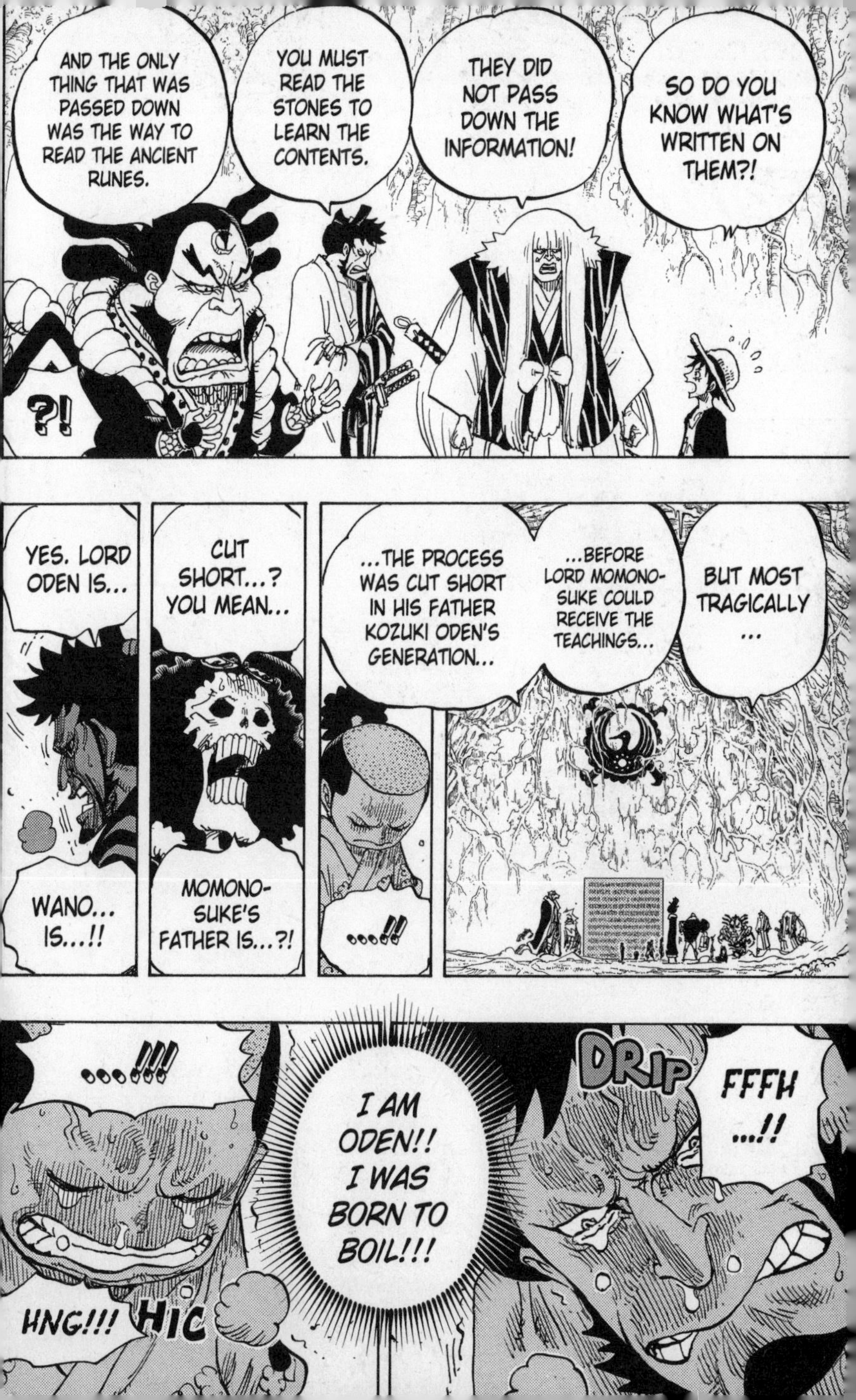

SO DO YOU KNOW WHAT'S WRITTEN ON THEM?!
THEY DID NOT PASS DOWN THE INFORMATION!
YOU MUST READ THE STONES TO LEARN THE CONTENTS.
AND THE ONLY THING THAT WAS PASSED DOWN WAS THE WAY TO READ THE ANCIENT RUNES.
?!
BUT MOST TRAGICALLY ...
...BEFORE LORD MOMONO-SUKE COULD RECEIVE THE TEACHINGS...
...THE PROCESS WAS CUT SHORT IN HIS FATHER KOZUKI ODEN'S GENERATION...
...!!
CUT SHORT...? YOU MEAN...
MOMONO-SUKE'S FATHER IS...?!
YES. LORD ODEN IS...
WANO... IS...!!
DRIP
FFFH ...!!
I AM ODEN!! I WAS BORN TO BOIL!!!
...!!!
HNG!!!
HIC

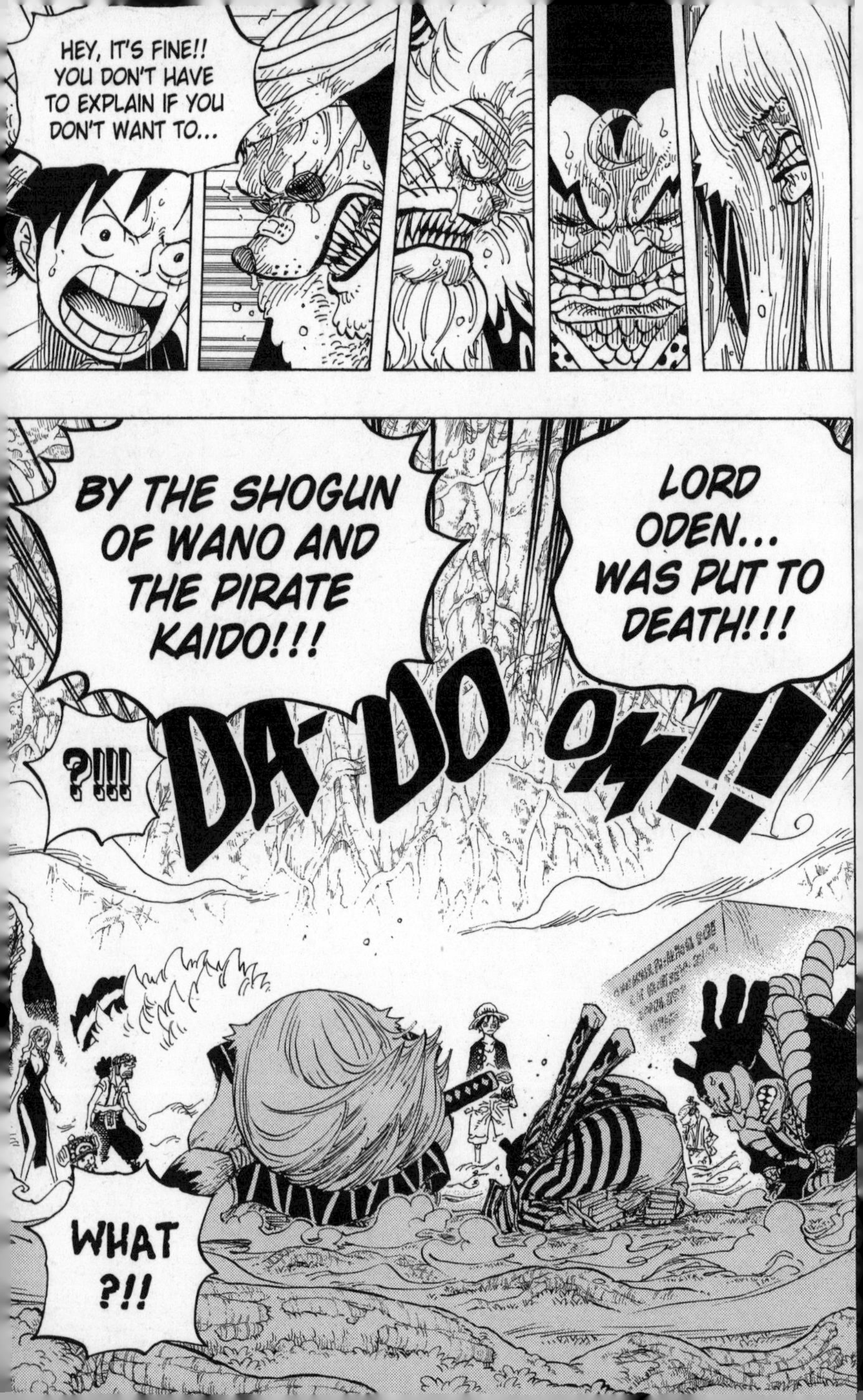
HEY, IT'S FINE!! YOU DON'T HAVE TO EXPLAIN IF YOU DON'T WANT TO...
LORD ODEN... WAS PUT TO DEATH!!!
BY THE SHOGUN OF WANO AND THE PIRATE KAIDO!!!
DA-DOOM!!
?!!!
WHAT ?!!

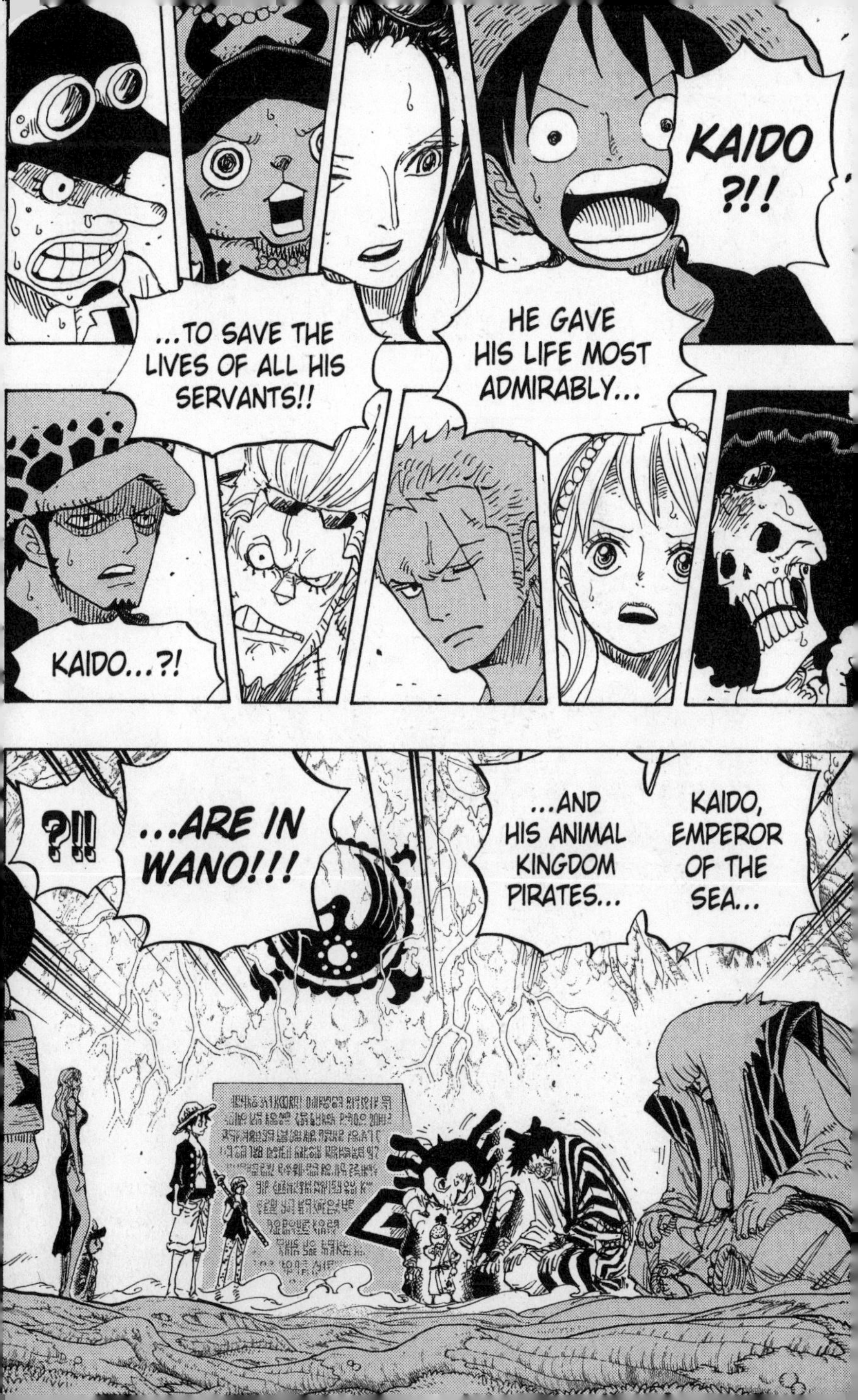
KAIDO ?!!
HE GAVE HIS LIFE MOST ADMIRABLY...
...TO SAVE THE LIVES OF ALL HIS SERVANTS!!
KAIDO...?!
KAIDO, EMPEROR OF THE SEA...
...AND HIS ANIMAL KINGDOM PIRATES...
...ARE IN WANO!!!
?!!

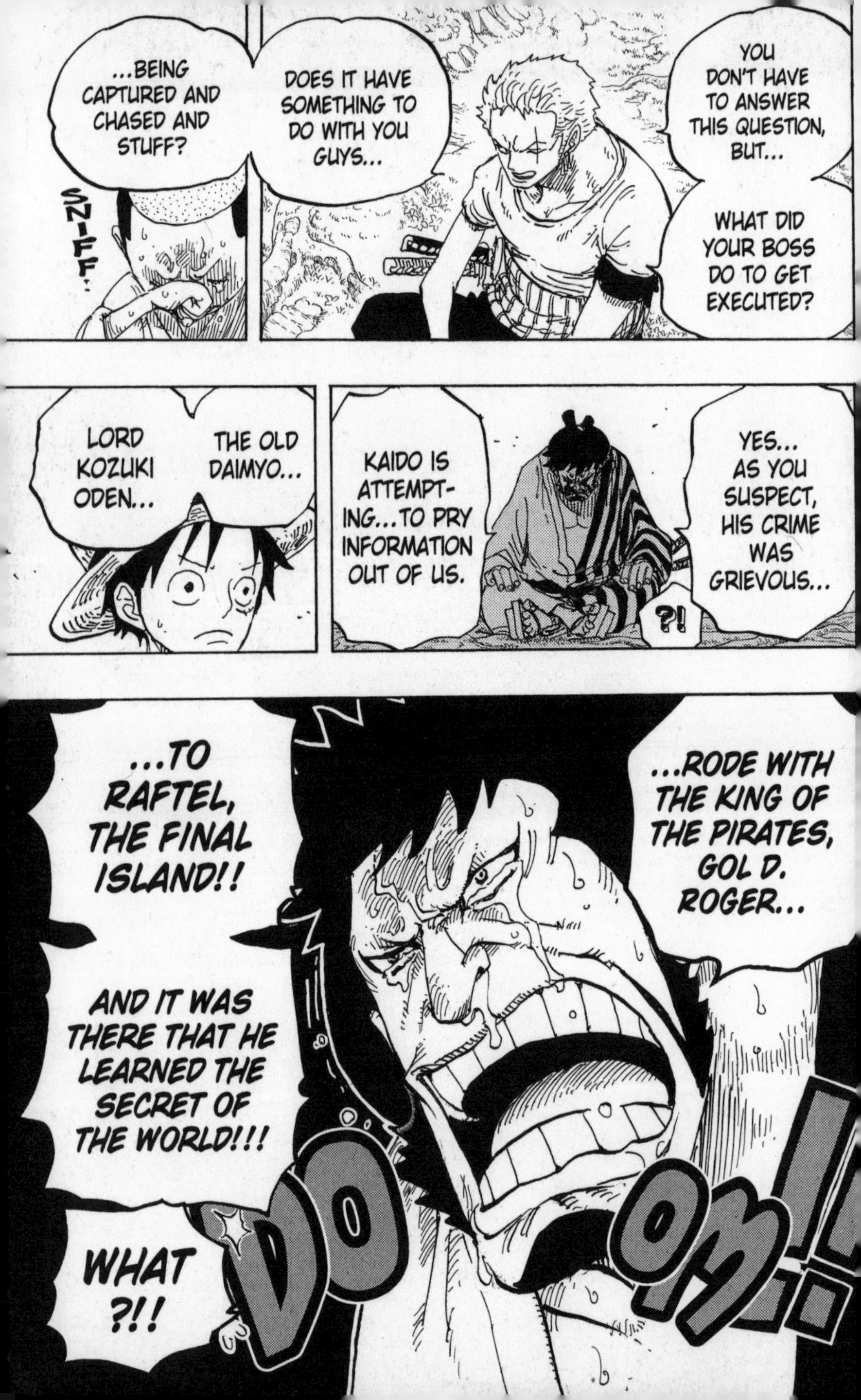
YOU DON'T HAVE TO ANSWER THIS QUESTION, BUT...
WHAT DID YOUR BOSS DO TO GET EXECUTED?
DOES IT HAVE SOMETHING TO DO WITH YOU GUYS...
...BEING CAPTURED AND CHASED AND STUFF?
SNIFF
YES... AS YOU SUSPECT, HIS CRIME WAS GRIEVOUS...
KAIDO IS ATTEMPT-ING...TO PRY INFORMATION OUT OF US.
?!
THE OLD DAIMYO...
LORD KOZUKI ODEN...
...RODE WITH THE KING OF THE PIRATES, GOL D. ROGER...
...TO RAFTEL, THE FINAL ISLAND!!
AND IT WAS THERE THAT HE LEARNED THE SECRET OF THE WORLD!!!
DOOOM!!
WHAT?!!

SBS Question Corner

質問コーナー

(Hayato Asami, Kanagawa)

Q: Oda Sensei! Please tell us the hobbies of the Worst Generation!

--K.S.9

A:

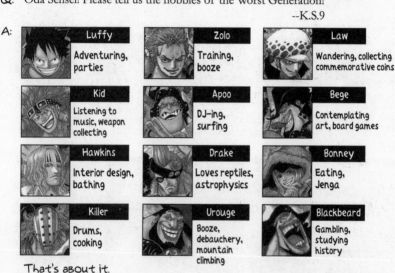

Luffy — Adventuring, parties	**Zolo** — Training, booze	**Law** — Wandering, collecting commemorative coins
Kid — Listening to music, weapon collecting	**Apoo** — DJ-ing, surfing	**Bege** — Contemplating art, board games
Hawkins — Interior design, bathing	**Drake** — Loves reptiles, astrophysics	**Bonney** — Eating, Jenga
Killer — Drums, cooking	**Urouge** — Booze, debauchery, mountain climbing	**Blackbeard** — Gambling, studying history

That's about it.

Q: In the Grand Ship Collection line of figurines, there's one simply titled "Trafalgar Law's Submarine." Doesn't it have a catchy name like the *Thousand Sunny?*

--Aspiring Heart Pirates Member

©Eiichiro Oda/Shueisha - Fuji TV - Toei Animation

A: Oh, they put one of those out, did they? It's called the *Polar Tang.* It's hard to work the names into the story, so these things slip through.

Q: Gorilla is yummy.
I like Lassen's dolphin paintings. --Taro Sasaki

A: Thank you for your letter.

Chapter 819: MOMONOSUKE, HEIR TO THE KOZUKI CLAN

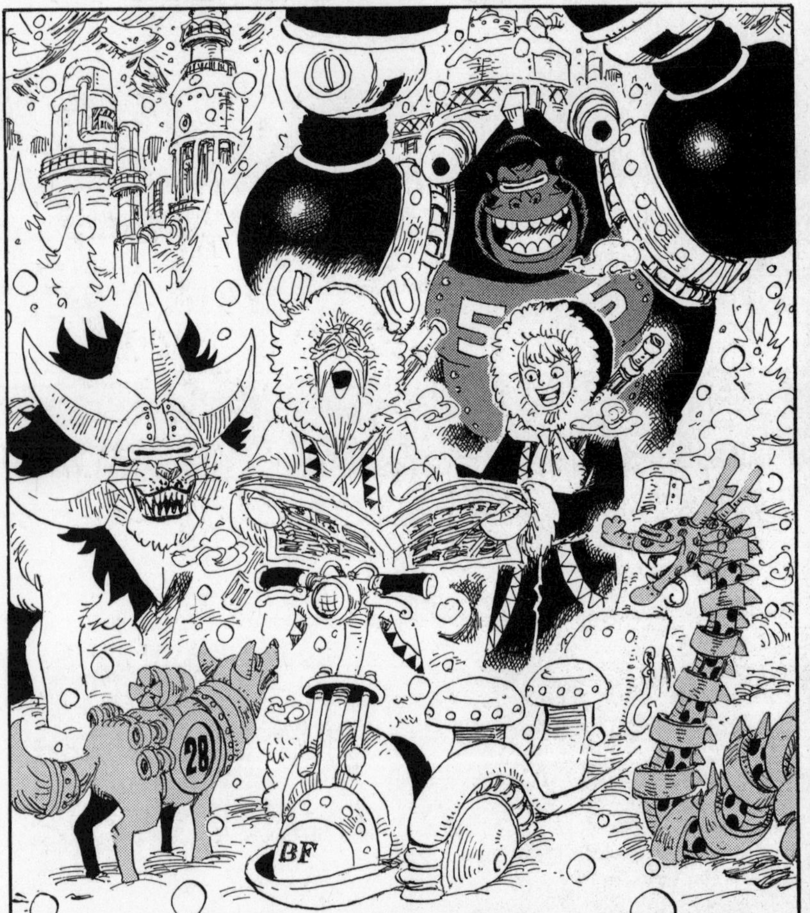
5
28
BF

DECKS OF THE WORLD, 500-MILLION-MAN ARC, VOL. 12: "FUTURE LAND BALDIMORE"

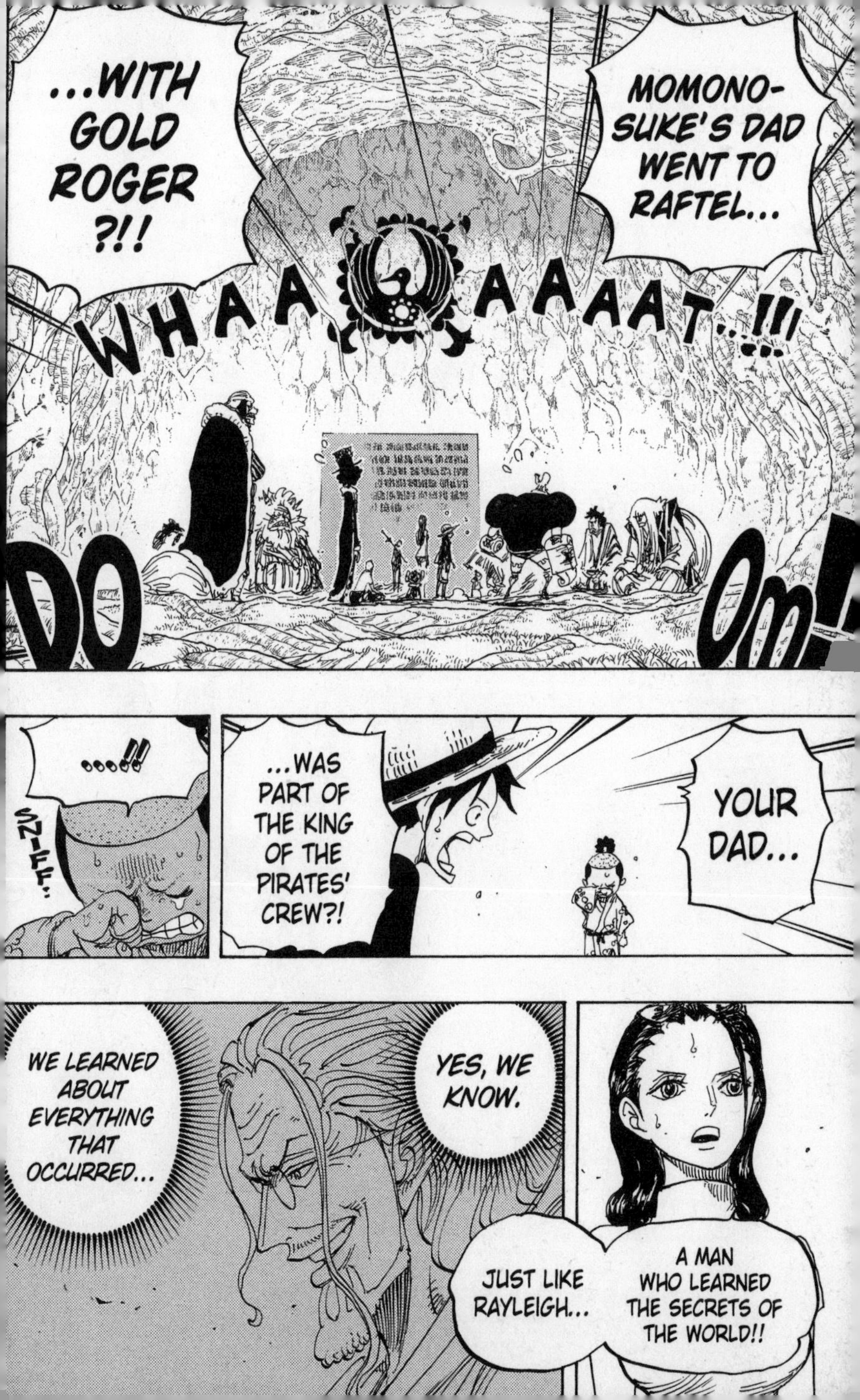
MOMONOSUKE'S DAD WENT TO RAFTEL...
...WITH GOLD ROGER?!!
WHAAAAAAT...!!!
DOOM!!
YOUR DAD...
...WAS PART OF THE KING OF THE PIRATES' CREW?!
.....!!
SNIFF...
A MAN WHO LEARNED THE SECRETS OF THE WORLD!!
JUST LIKE RAYLEIGH...
YES, WE KNOW.
WE LEARNED ABOUT EVERYTHING THAT OCCURRED...

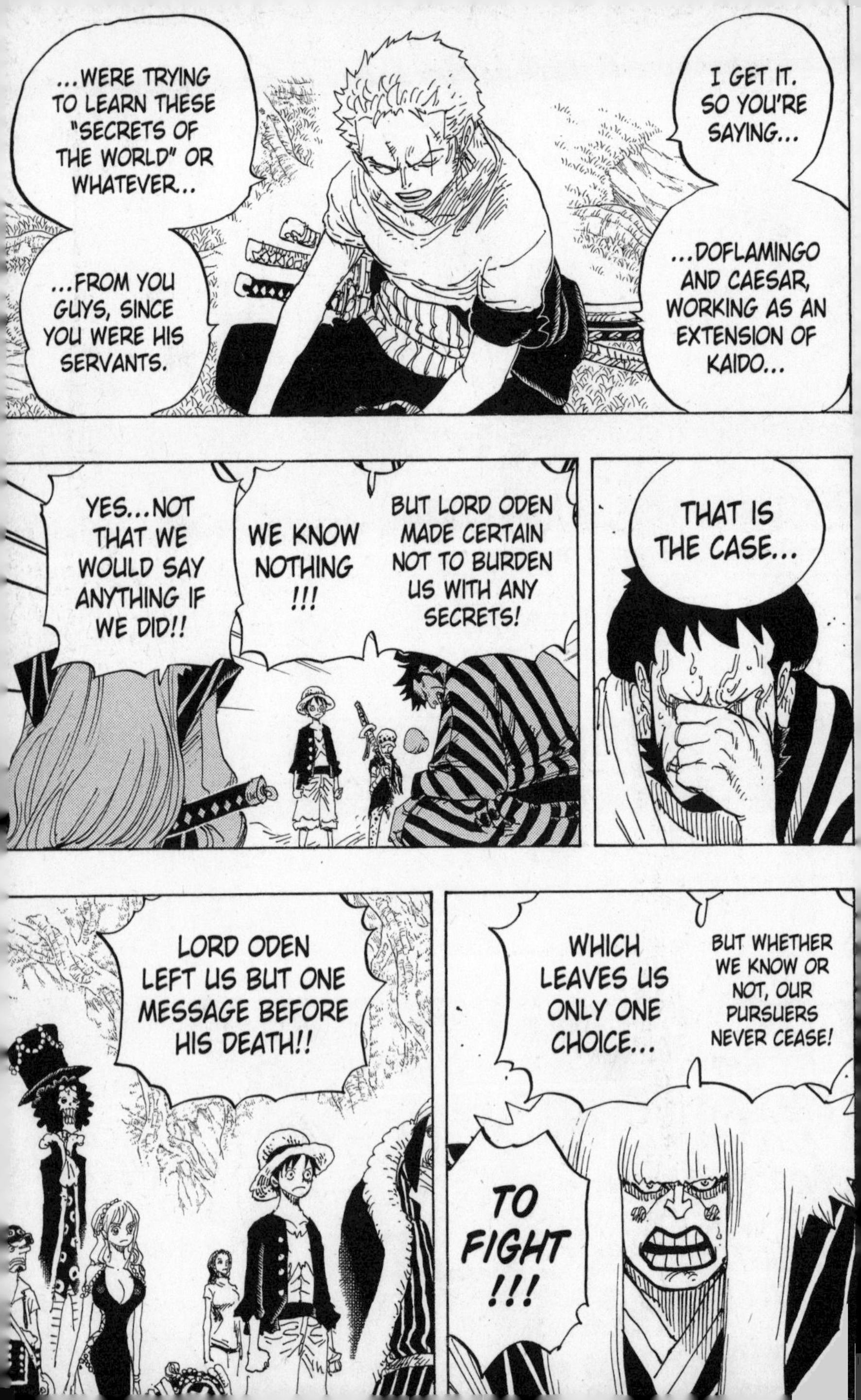

I GET IT. SO YOU'RE SAYING...
...DOFLAMINGO AND CAESAR, WORKING AS AN EXTENSION OF KAIDO...
...WERE TRYING TO LEARN THESE "SECRETS OF THE WORLD" OR WHATEVER...
...FROM YOU GUYS, SINCE YOU WERE HIS SERVANTS.
THAT IS THE CASE...
BUT LORD ODEN MADE CERTAIN NOT TO BURDEN US WITH ANY SECRETS!
WE KNOW NOTHING !!!
YES...NOT THAT WE WOULD SAY ANYTHING IF WE DID!!
BUT WHETHER WE KNOW OR NOT, OUR PURSUERS NEVER CEASE!
WHICH LEAVES US ONLY ONE CHOICE...
TO FIGHT !!!
LORD ODEN LEFT US BUT ONE MESSAGE BEFORE HIS DEATH!!

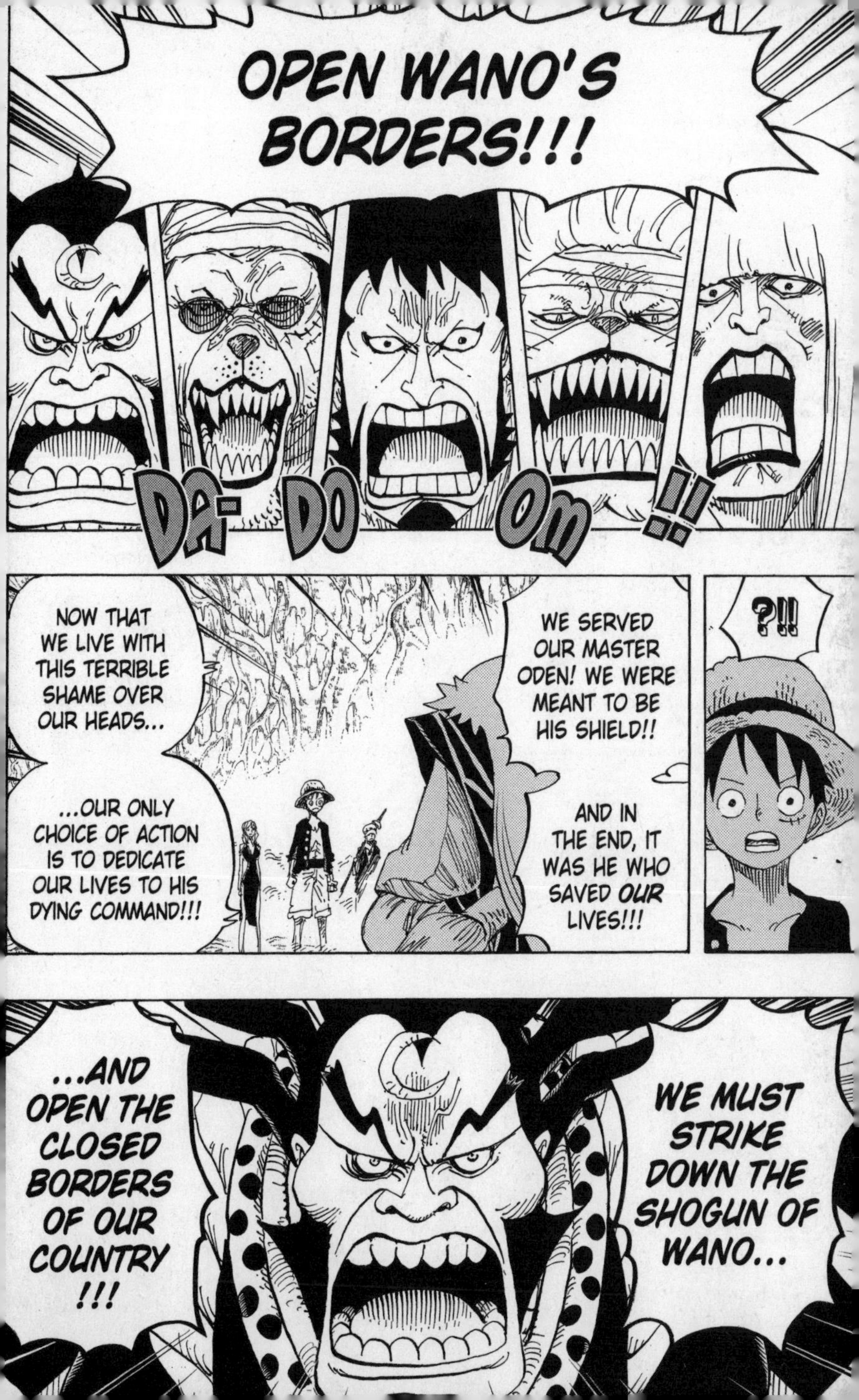
OPEN WANO'S BORDERS!!!
DA-DOOM!!
?!!
WE SERVED OUR MASTER ODEN! WE WERE MEANT TO BE HIS SHIELD!!
AND IN THE END, IT WAS HE WHO SAVED OUR LIVES!!!
NOW THAT WE LIVE WITH THIS TERRIBLE SHAME OVER OUR HEADS...
...OUR ONLY CHOICE OF ACTION IS TO DEDICATE OUR LIVES TO HIS DYING COMMAND!!!
WE MUST STRIKE DOWN THE SHOGUN OF WANO...
...AND OPEN THE CLOSED BORDERS OF OUR COUNTRY!!!

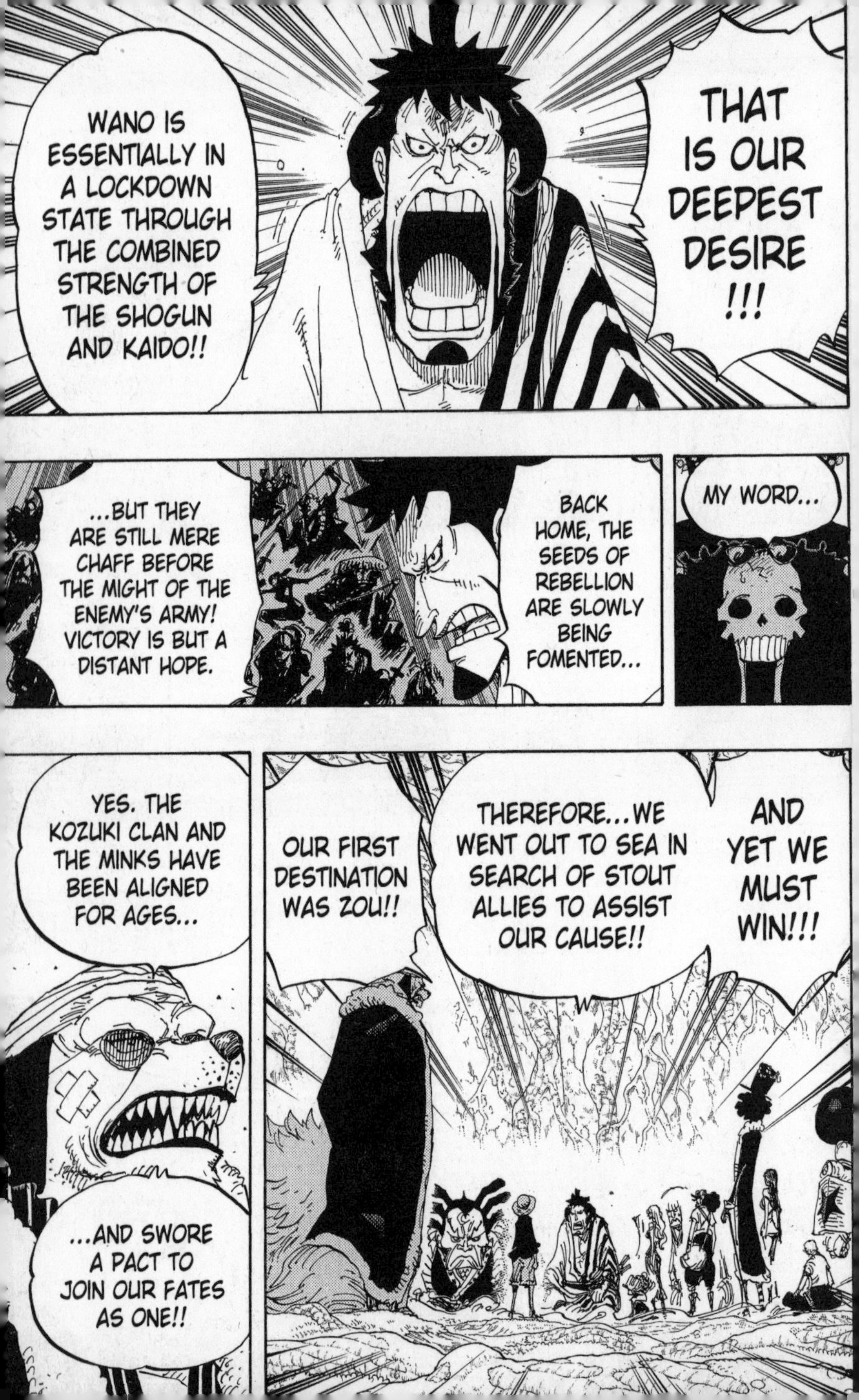
THAT IS OUR DEEPEST DESIRE!!!
WANO IS ESSENTIALLY IN A LOCKDOWN STATE THROUGH THE COMBINED STRENGTH OF THE SHOGUN AND KAIDO!!
MY WORD...
BACK HOME, THE SEEDS OF REBELLION ARE SLOWLY BEING FOMENTED...
...BUT THEY ARE STILL MERE CHAFF BEFORE THE MIGHT OF THE ENEMY'S ARMY! VICTORY IS BUT A DISTANT HOPE.
AND YET WE MUST WIN!!!
THEREFORE...WE WENT OUT TO SEA IN SEARCH OF STOUT ALLIES TO ASSIST OUR CAUSE!!
OUR FIRST DESTINATION WAS ZOU!!
YES. THE KOZUKI CLAN AND THE MINKS HAVE BEEN ALIGNED FOR AGES...
...AND SWORE A PACT TO JOIN OUR FATES AS ONE!!

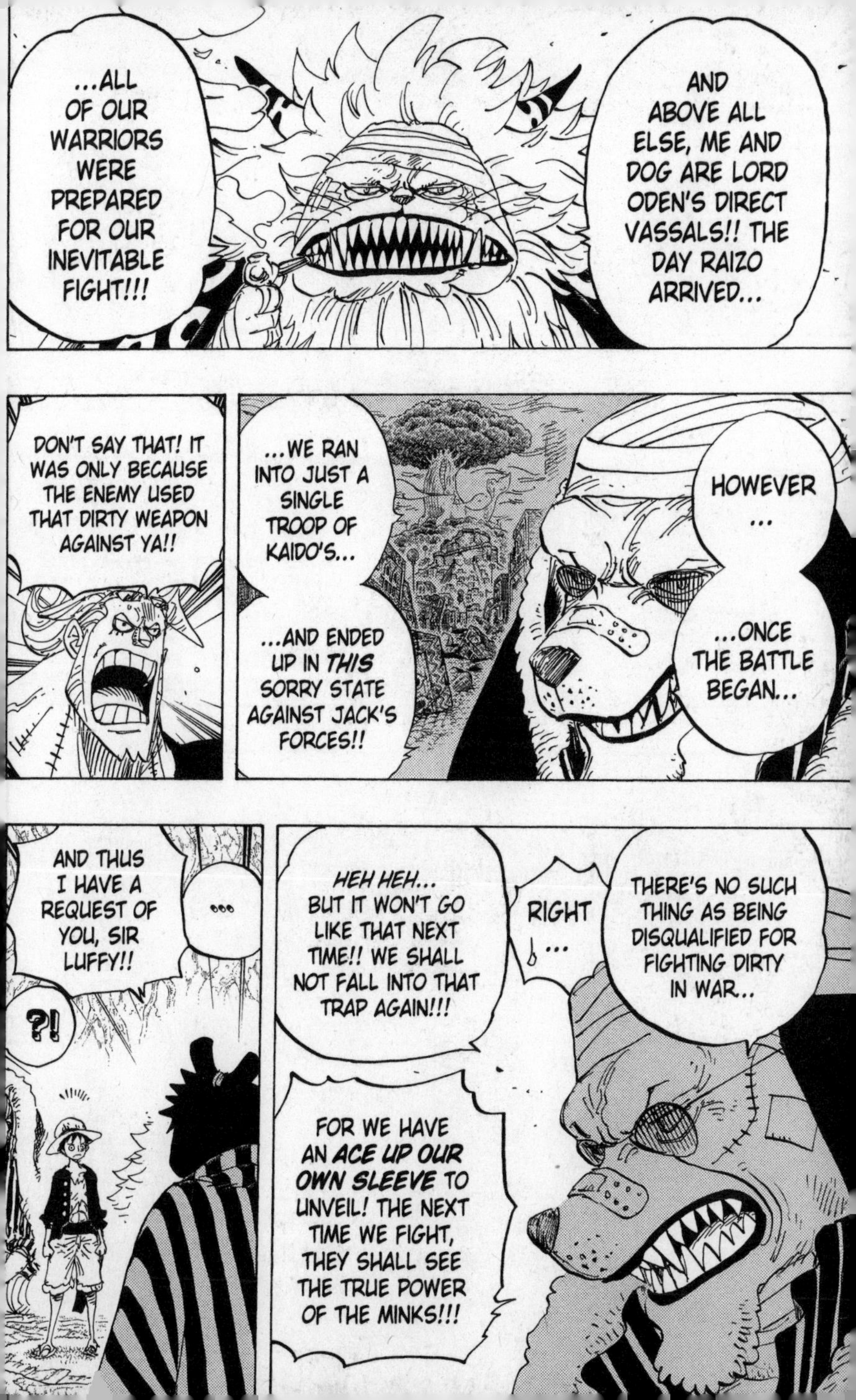
AND ABOVE ALL ELSE, ME AND DOG ARE LORD ODEN'S DIRECT VASSALS!! THE DAY RAIZO ARRIVED...
...ALL OF OUR WARRIORS WERE PREPARED FOR OUR INEVITABLE FIGHT!!!
HOWEVER...
...ONCE THE BATTLE BEGAN...
...WE RAN INTO JUST A SINGLE TROOP OF KAIDO'S...
...AND ENDED UP IN *THIS* SORRY STATE AGAINST JACK'S FORCES!!
DON'T SAY THAT! IT WAS ONLY BECAUSE THE ENEMY USED THAT DIRTY WEAPON AGAINST YA!!
THERE'S NO SUCH THING AS BEING DISQUALIFIED FOR FIGHTING DIRTY IN WAR...
RIGHT...
HEH HEH... BUT IT WON'T GO LIKE THAT NEXT TIME!! WE SHALL NOT FALL INTO THAT TRAP AGAIN!!!
FOR WE HAVE AN ***ACE UP OUR OWN SLEEVE*** TO UNVEIL! THE NEXT TIME WE FIGHT, THEY SHALL SEE THE TRUE POWER OF THE MINKS!!!
...
AND THUS I HAVE A REQUEST OF YOU, SIR LUFFY!!
?!

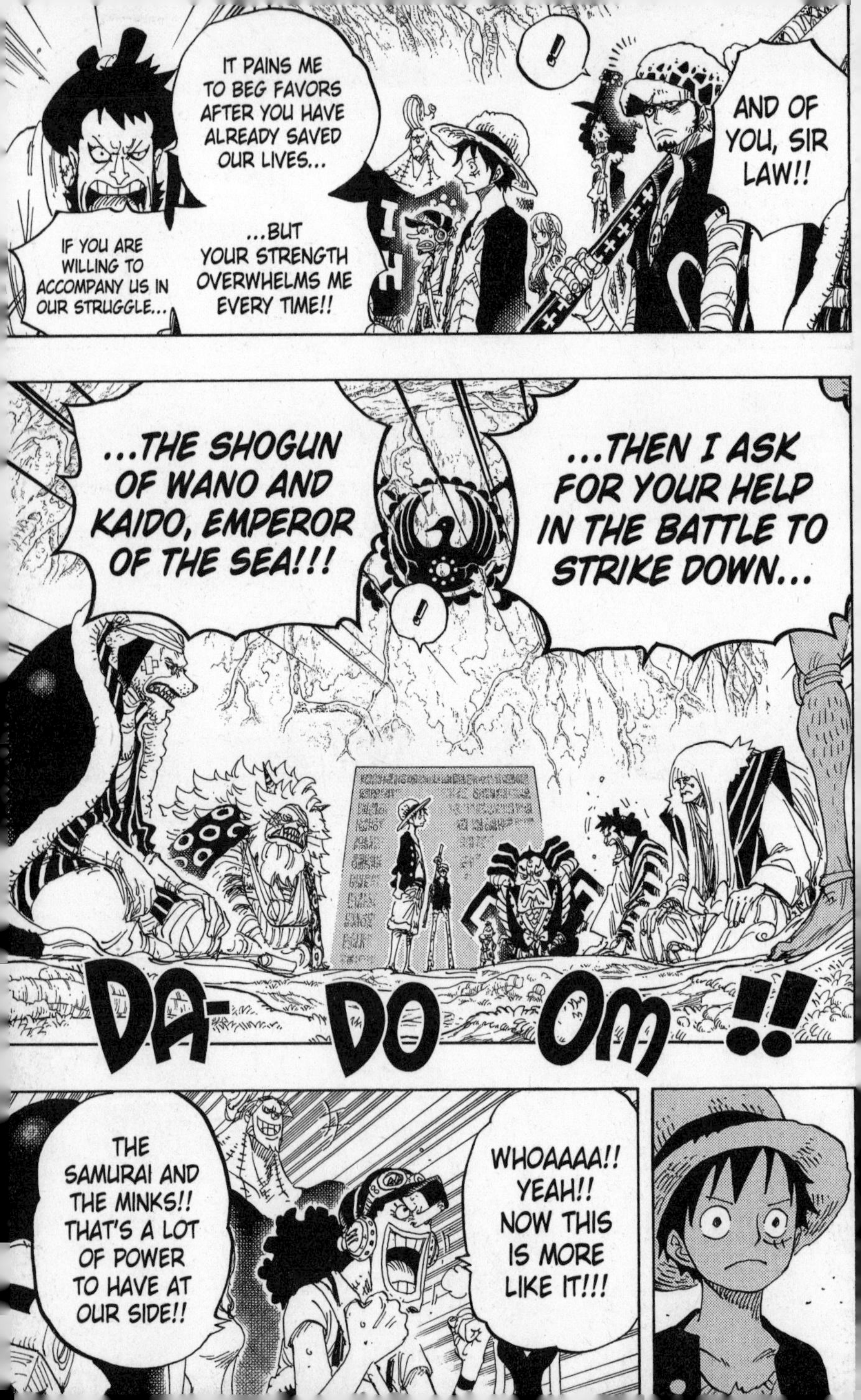
IT PAINS ME TO BEG FAVORS AFTER YOU HAVE ALREADY SAVED OUR LIVES...
...BUT YOUR STRENGTH OVERWHELMS ME EVERY TIME!!
!
AND OF YOU, SIR LAW!!
IF YOU ARE WILLING TO ACCOMPANY US IN OUR STRUGGLE...
...THEN I ASK FOR YOUR HELP IN THE BATTLE TO STRIKE DOWN...
...THE SHOGUN OF WANO AND KAIDO, EMPEROR OF THE SEA!!!
!
DA-DO-OM!!
WHOAAAA!! YEAH!! NOW THIS IS MORE LIKE IT!!!
THE SAMURAI AND THE MINKS!! THAT'S A LOT OF POWER TO HAVE AT OUR SIDE!!

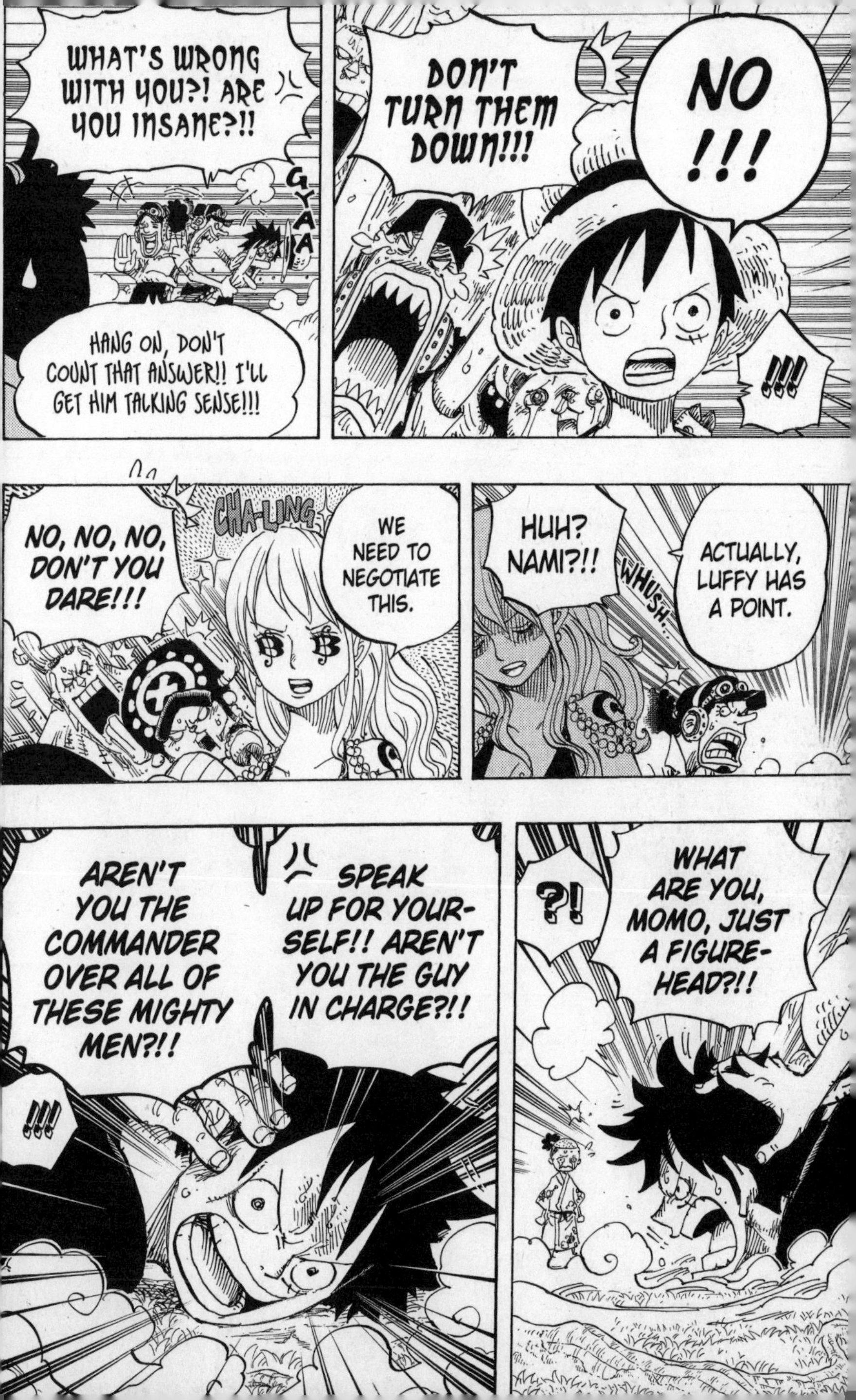
NO !!!
DON'T TURN THEM DOWN!!!
!!!
WHAT'S WRONG WITH YOU?! ARE YOU INSANE?!!
GYAA
HANG ON, DON'T COUNT THAT ANSWER!! I'LL GET HIM TALKING SENSE!!!
ACTUALLY, LUFFY HAS A POINT.
HUH? NAMI?!!
WHUSH
WE NEED TO NEGOTIATE THIS.
CHA-LING
NO, NO, NO, DON'T YOU DARE!!!
WHAT ARE YOU, MOMO, JUST A FIGURE-HEAD?!!
?!
SPEAK UP FOR YOUR-SELF!! AREN'T YOU THE GUY IN CHARGE?!!
AREN'T YOU THE COMMANDER OVER ALL OF THESE MIGHTY MEN?!!
!!!

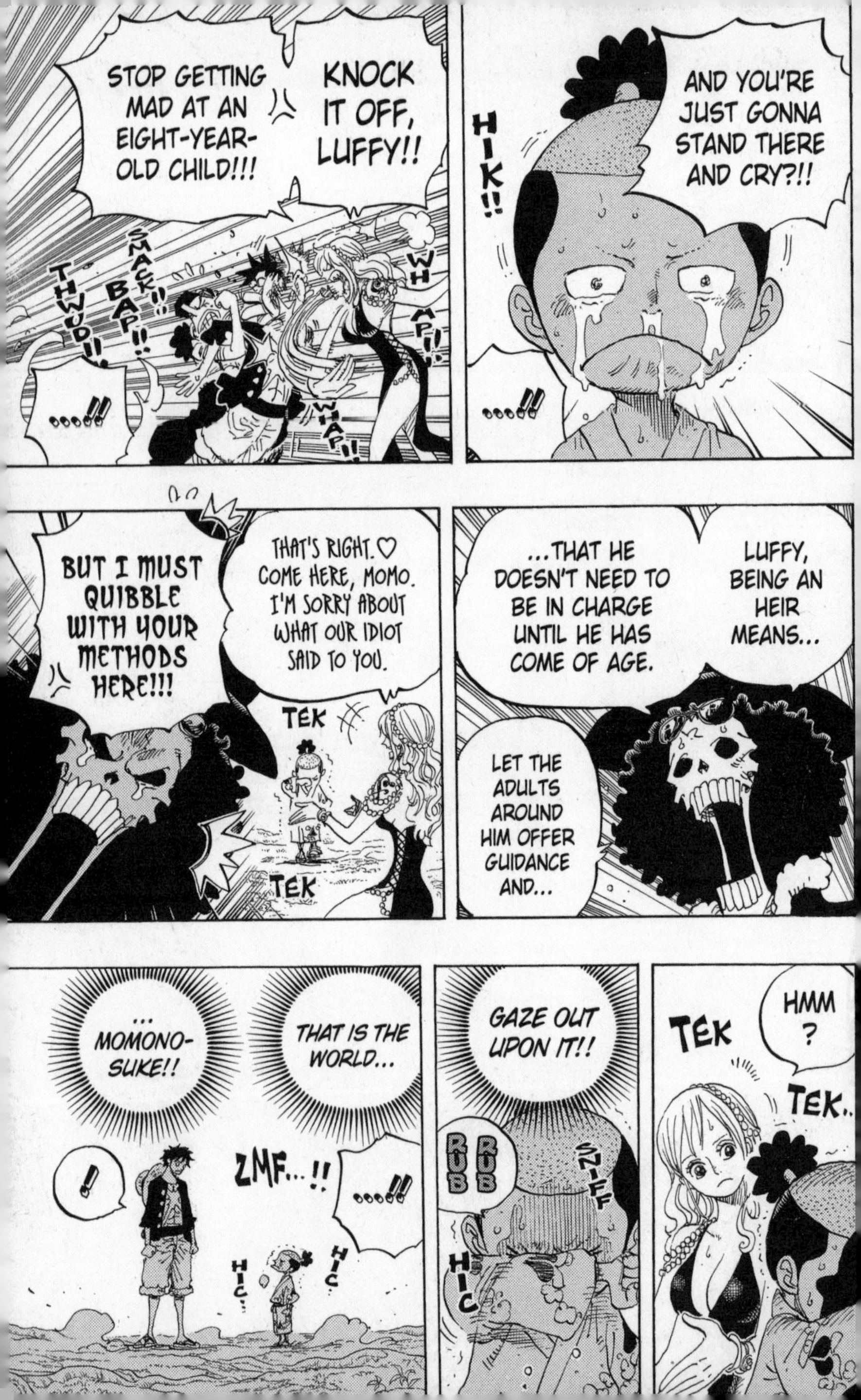
AND YOU'RE JUST GONNA STAND THERE AND CRY?!!
HIK!!
...!!
KNOCK IT OFF, LUFFY!!
STOP GETTING MAD AT AN EIGHT-YEAR-OLD CHILD!!!
WHAMP!!
SMACK!!
BAP!!
THWUD!!
WHAP!!
...!!
LUFFY, BEING AN HEIR MEANS...
...THAT HE DOESN'T NEED TO BE IN CHARGE UNTIL HE HAS COME OF AGE.
LET THE ADULTS AROUND HIM OFFER GUIDANCE AND...
THAT'S RIGHT.♡ COME HERE, MOMO. I'M SORRY ABOUT WHAT OUR IDIOT SAID TO YOU.
BUT I MUST QUIBBLE WITH YOUR METHODS HERE!!!
TEK
TEK
HMM ?
TEK
TEK..
GAZE OUT UPON IT!!
SNIFF
RUB RUB
HIC
THAT IS THE WORLD...
... MOMONOSUKE!!
...!!
ZMF...!!
!
HIC
HIC

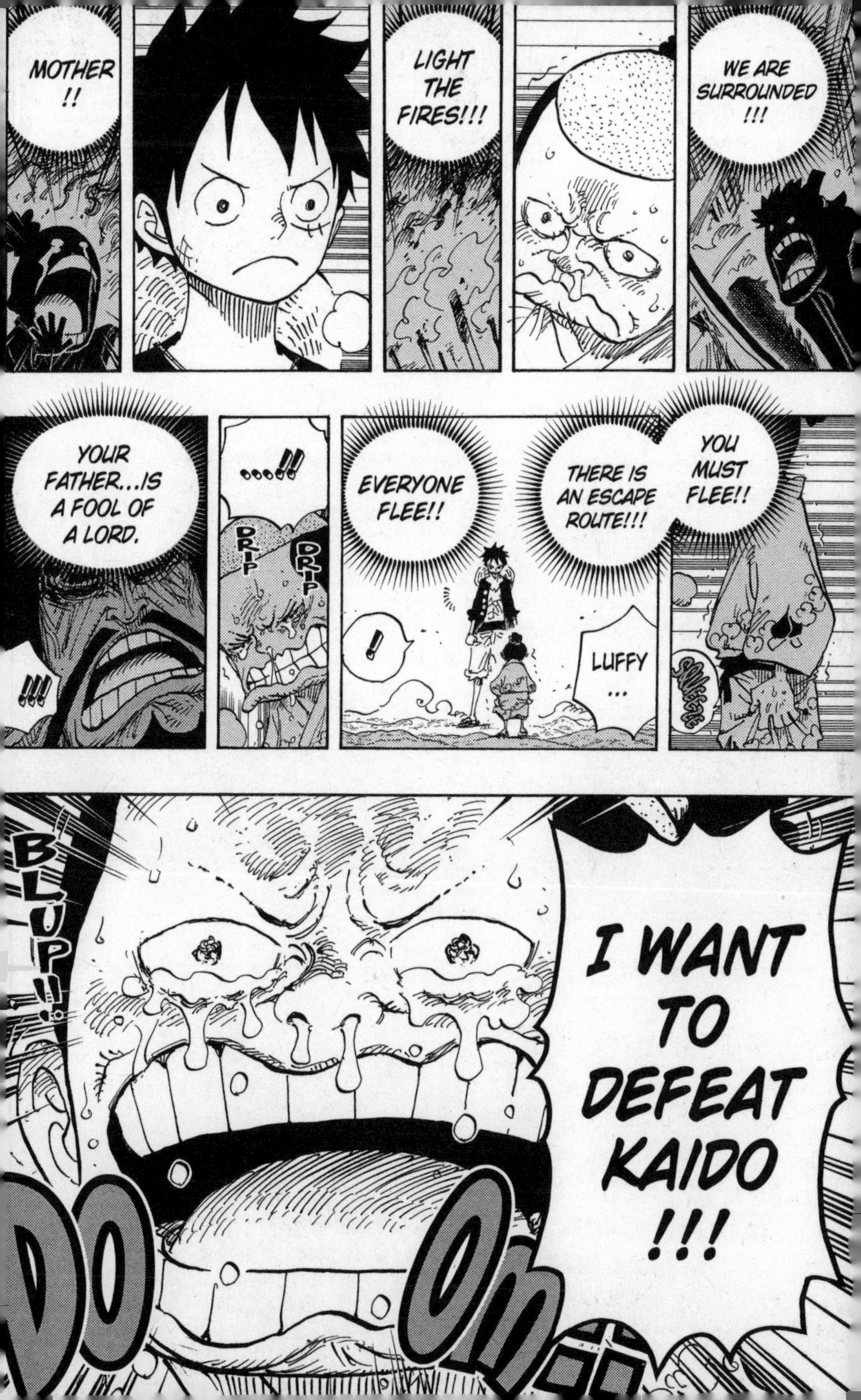
WE ARE SURROUNDED !!!
LIGHT THE FIRES!!!
MOTHER !!
YOU MUST FLEE!!
THERE IS AN ESCAPE ROUTE!!!
EVERYONE FLEE!!
LUFFY ...
!
......!!
DRIP
DRIP
YOUR FATHER...IS A FOOL OF A LORD.
!!!
I WANT TO DEFEAT KAIDO !!!
BLUP!!

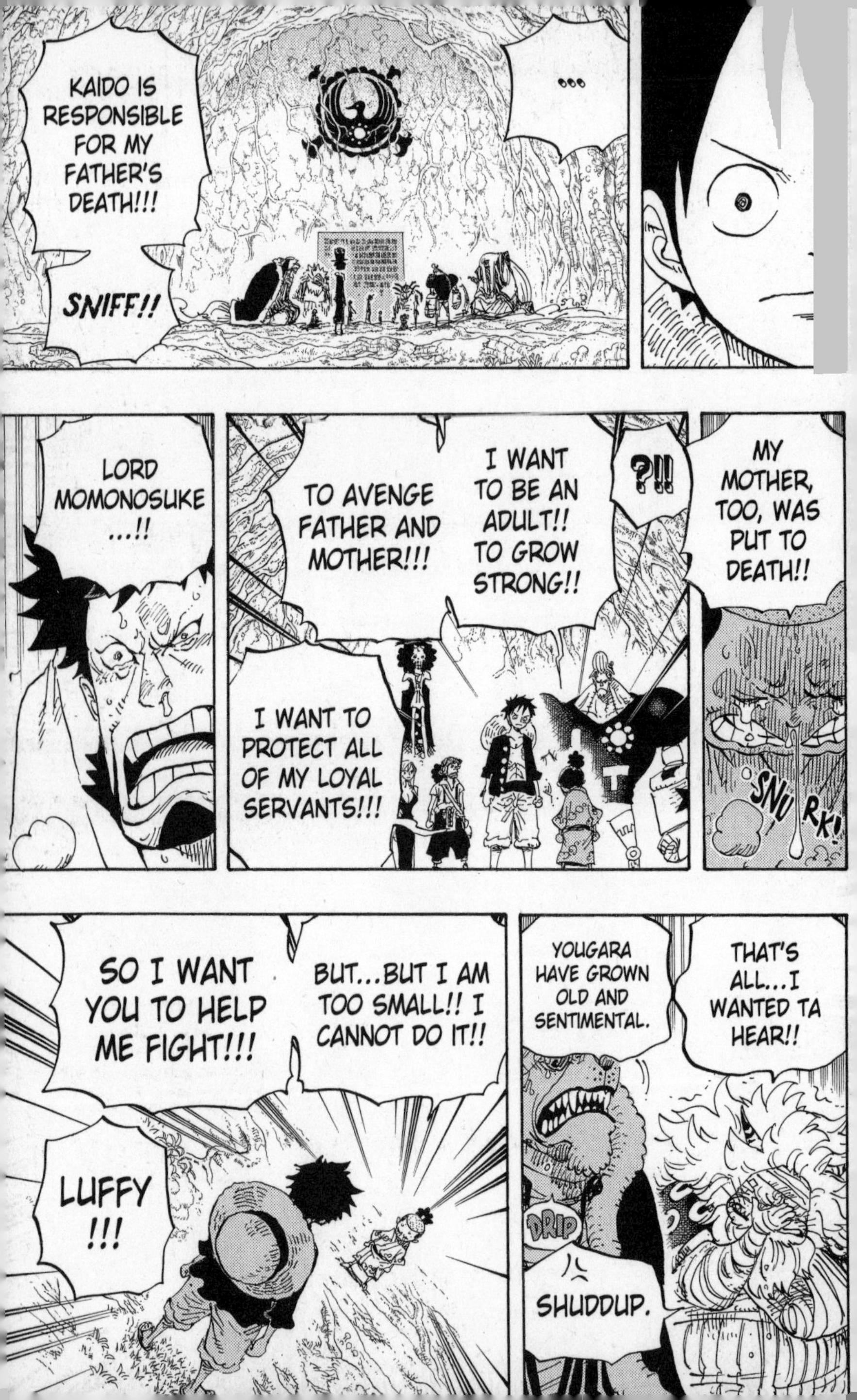
...
KAIDO IS RESPONSIBLE FOR MY FATHER'S DEATH!!!
SNIFF!!
MY MOTHER, TOO, WAS PUT TO DEATH!!
SNURK!
?!!
I WANT TO BE AN ADULT!! TO GROW STRONG!!
TO AVENGE FATHER AND MOTHER!!!
I WANT TO PROTECT ALL OF MY LOYAL SERVANTS!!!
LORD MOMONOSUKE ...!!
THAT'S ALL...I WANTED TA HEAR!!
YOUGARA HAVE GROWN OLD AND SENTIMENTAL.
DRIP
SHUDDUP.
BUT...BUT I AM TOO SMALL!! I CANNOT DO IT!!
SO I WANT YOU TO HELP ME FIGHT!!!
LUFFY!!!

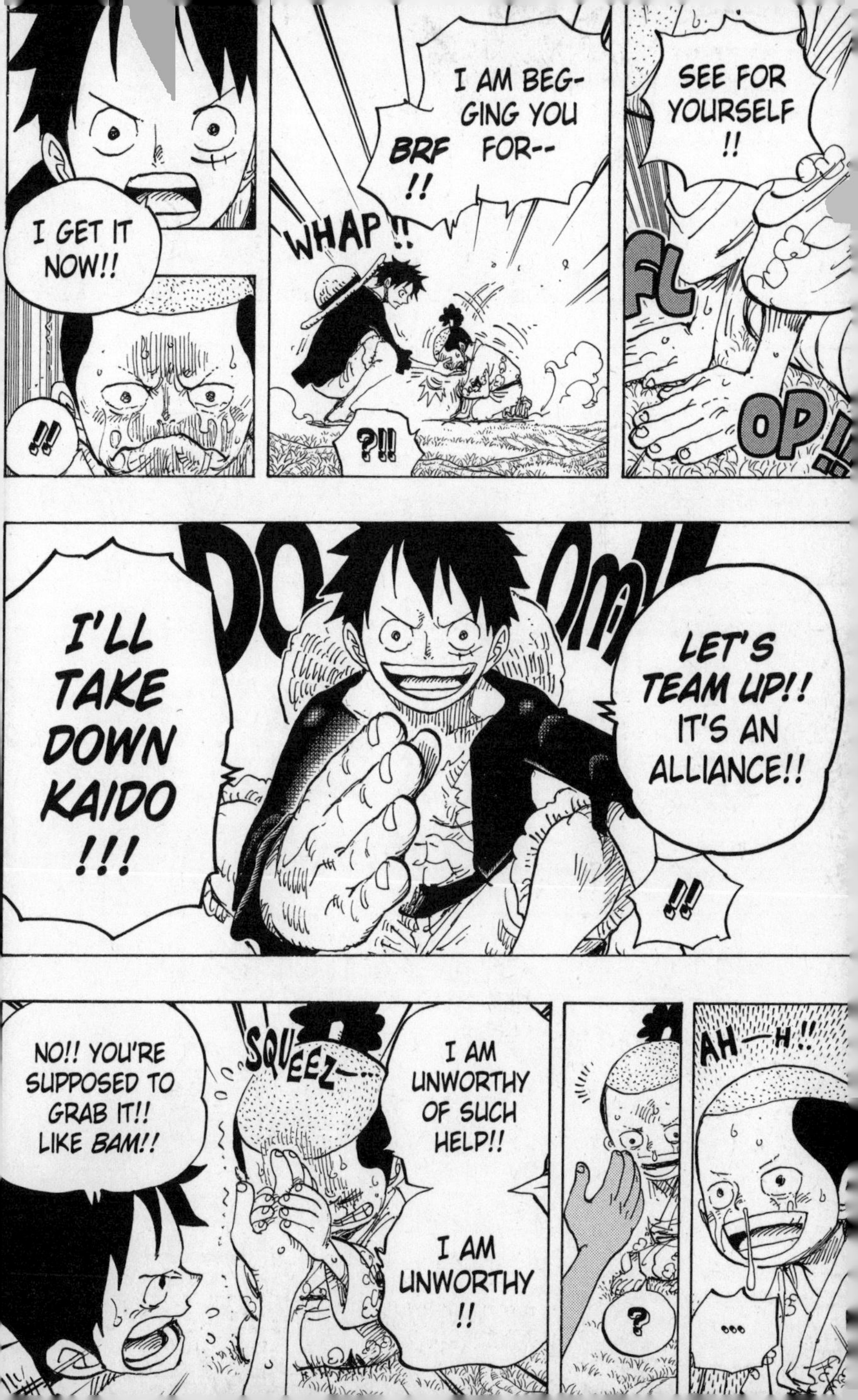

SEE FOR YOURSELF!!
FL
OP!!
I AM BEG-GING YOU FOR--
BRF!!
WHAP!!
?!!
I GET IT NOW!!
!!
LET'S TEAM UP!! IT'S AN ALLIANCE!!
DO
OM!!
I'LL TAKE DOWN KAIDO!!!
!!
AH—H!!
...
?
I AM UNWORTHY OF SUCH HELP!!
SQUEEZ—..
I AM UNWORTHY!!
NO!! YOU'RE SUPPOSED TO GRAB IT!! LIKE BAM!!

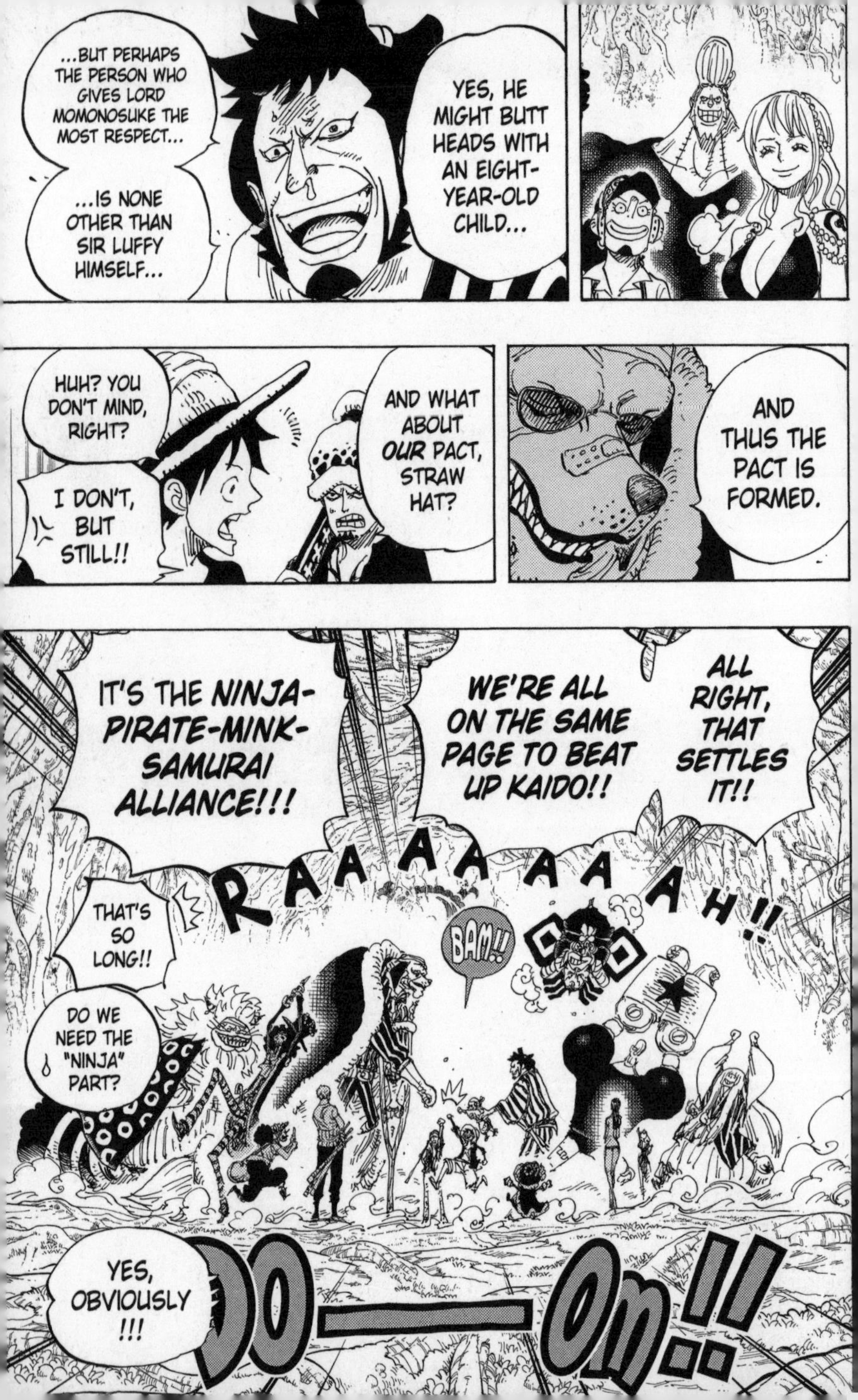
YES, HE MIGHT BUTT HEADS WITH AN EIGHT-YEAR-OLD CHILD...
...BUT PERHAPS THE PERSON WHO GIVES LORD MOMONOSUKE THE MOST RESPECT...
...IS NONE OTHER THAN SIR LUFFY HIMSELF...
AND THUS THE PACT IS FORMED.
AND WHAT ABOUT *OUR* PACT, STRAW HAT?
HUH? YOU DON'T MIND, RIGHT?
I DON'T, BUT STILL!!
ALL RIGHT, THAT SETTLES IT!!
WE'RE ALL ON THE SAME PAGE TO BEAT UP KAIDO!!
IT'S THE *NINJA-PIRATE-MINK-SAMURAI ALLIANCE!!!*
RAAAAAAAH!!
BAM!!
THAT'S SO LONG!!
DO WE NEED THE "NINJA" PART?
YES, OBVIOUSLY!!!
DOO—OM!!

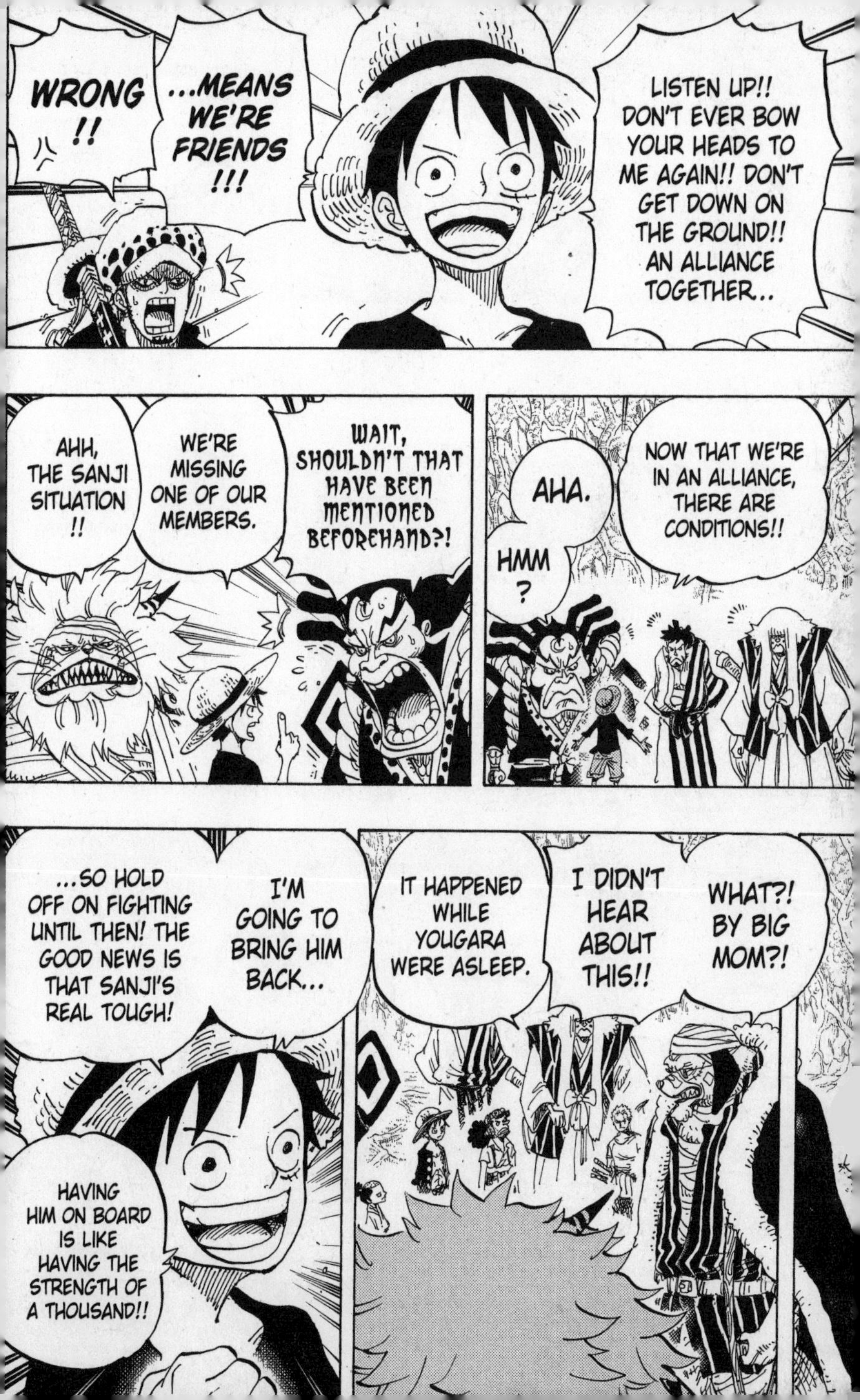
LISTEN UP!! DON'T EVER BOW YOUR HEADS TO ME AGAIN!! DON'T GET DOWN ON THE GROUND!! AN ALLIANCE TOGETHER..
...MEANS WE'RE FRIENDS!!!
WRONG!!
NOW THAT WE'RE IN AN ALLIANCE, THERE ARE CONDITIONS!!
AHA.
HMM?
WAIT, SHOULDN'T THAT HAVE BEEN MENTIONED BEFOREHAND?!
WE'RE MISSING ONE OF OUR MEMBERS.
AHH, THE SANJI SITUATION!!
WHAT?! BY BIG MOM?!
I DIDN'T HEAR ABOUT THIS!!
IT HAPPENED WHILE YOUGARA WERE ASLEEP.
I'M GOING TO BRING HIM BACK...
...SO HOLD OFF ON FIGHTING UNTIL THEN! THE GOOD NEWS IS THAT SANJI'S REAL TOUGH!
HAVING HIM ON BOARD IS LIKE HAVING THE STRENGTH OF A THOUSAND!!

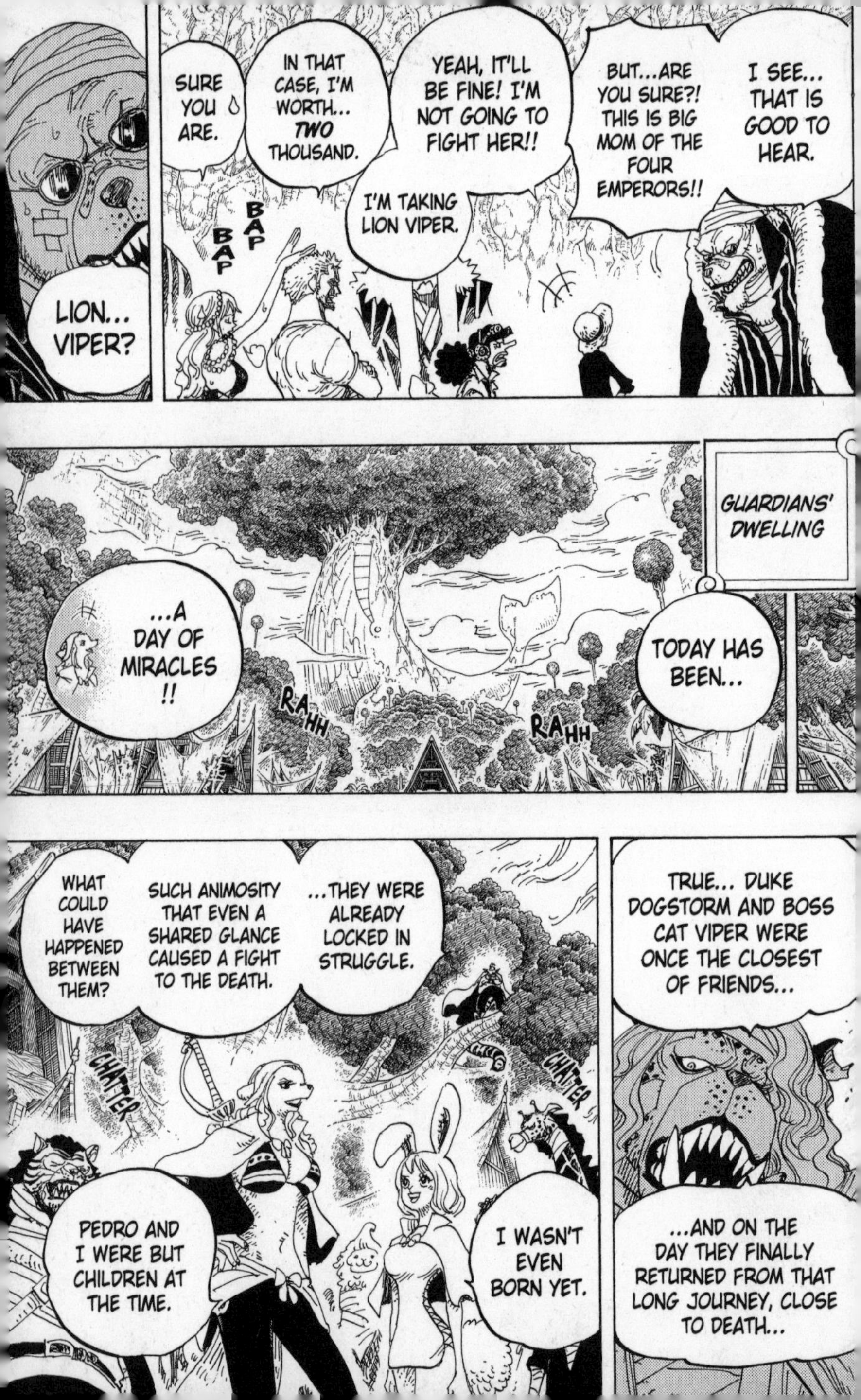
I SEE... THAT IS GOOD TO HEAR.
BUT...ARE YOU SURE?! THIS IS BIG MOM OF THE FOUR EMPERORS!!
YEAH, IT'LL BE FINE! I'M NOT GOING TO FIGHT HER!!
I'M TAKING LION VIPER.
IN THAT CASE, I'M WORTH... TWO THOUSAND.
SURE YOU ARE.
BAP BAP
LION... VIPER?
GUARDIANS' DWELLING
TODAY HAS BEEN...
...A DAY OF MIRACLES!!
RAHH
RAHH
TRUE... DUKE DOGSTORM AND BOSS CAT VIPER WERE ONCE THE CLOSEST OF FRIENDS...
...AND ON THE DAY THEY FINALLY RETURNED FROM THAT LONG JOURNEY, CLOSE TO DEATH...
...THEY WERE ALREADY LOCKED IN STRUGGLE.
SUCH ANIMOSITY THAT EVEN A SHARED GLANCE CAUSED A FIGHT TO THE DEATH.
WHAT COULD HAVE HAPPENED BETWEEN THEM?
CHATTER
CHATTER
I WASN'T EVEN BORN YET.
PEDRO AND I WERE BUT CHILDREN AT THE TIME.

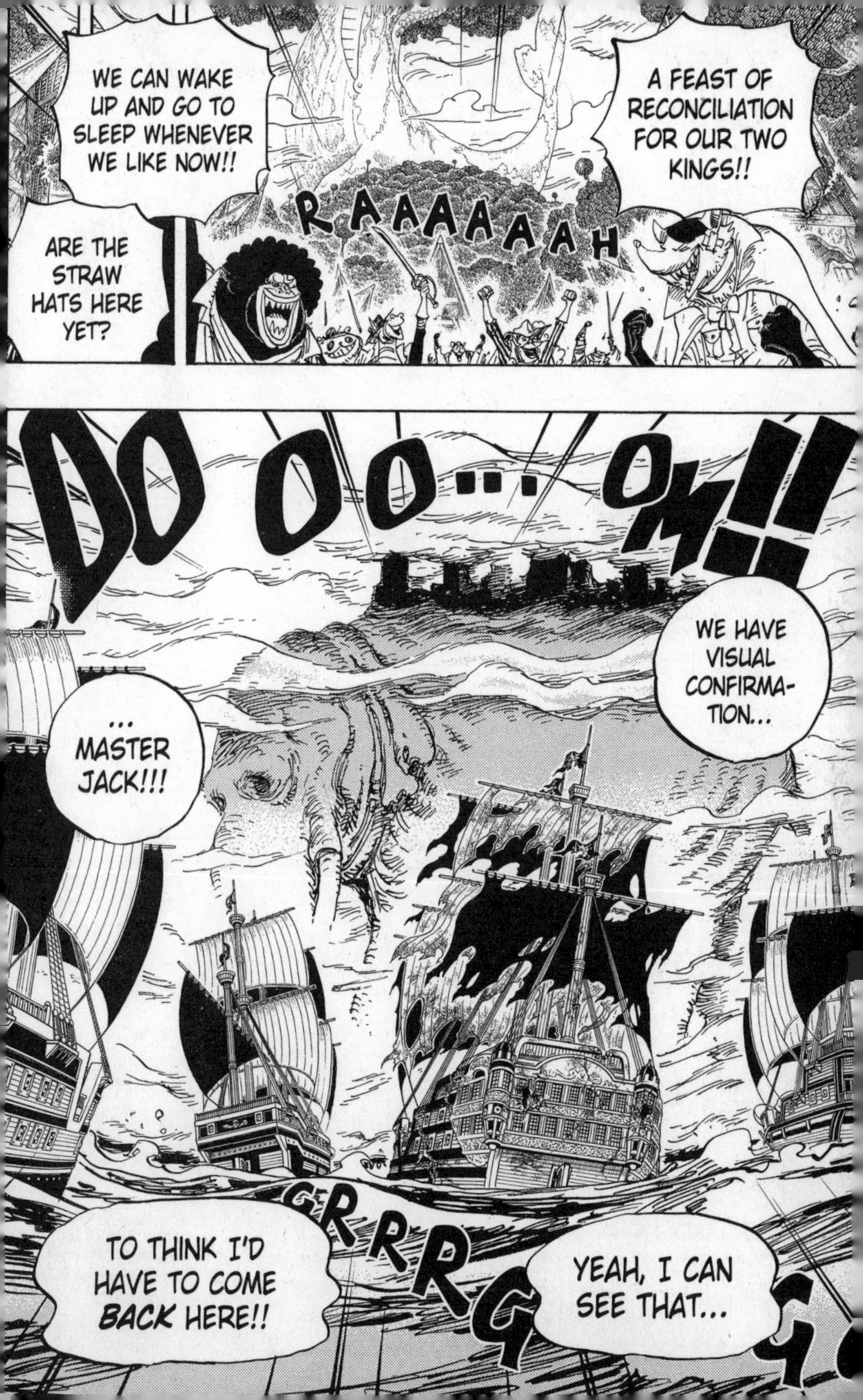
A FEAST OF RECONCILIATION FOR OUR TWO KINGS!!
WE CAN WAKE UP AND GO TO SLEEP WHENEVER WE LIKE NOW!!
RAAAAAAAH
ARE THE STRAW HATS HERE YET?
DO OO... OM!!
WE HAVE VISUAL CONFIRMATION...
... MASTER JACK!!!
YEAH, I CAN SEE THAT...
TO THINK I'D HAVE TO COME BACK HERE!!
GRRRG

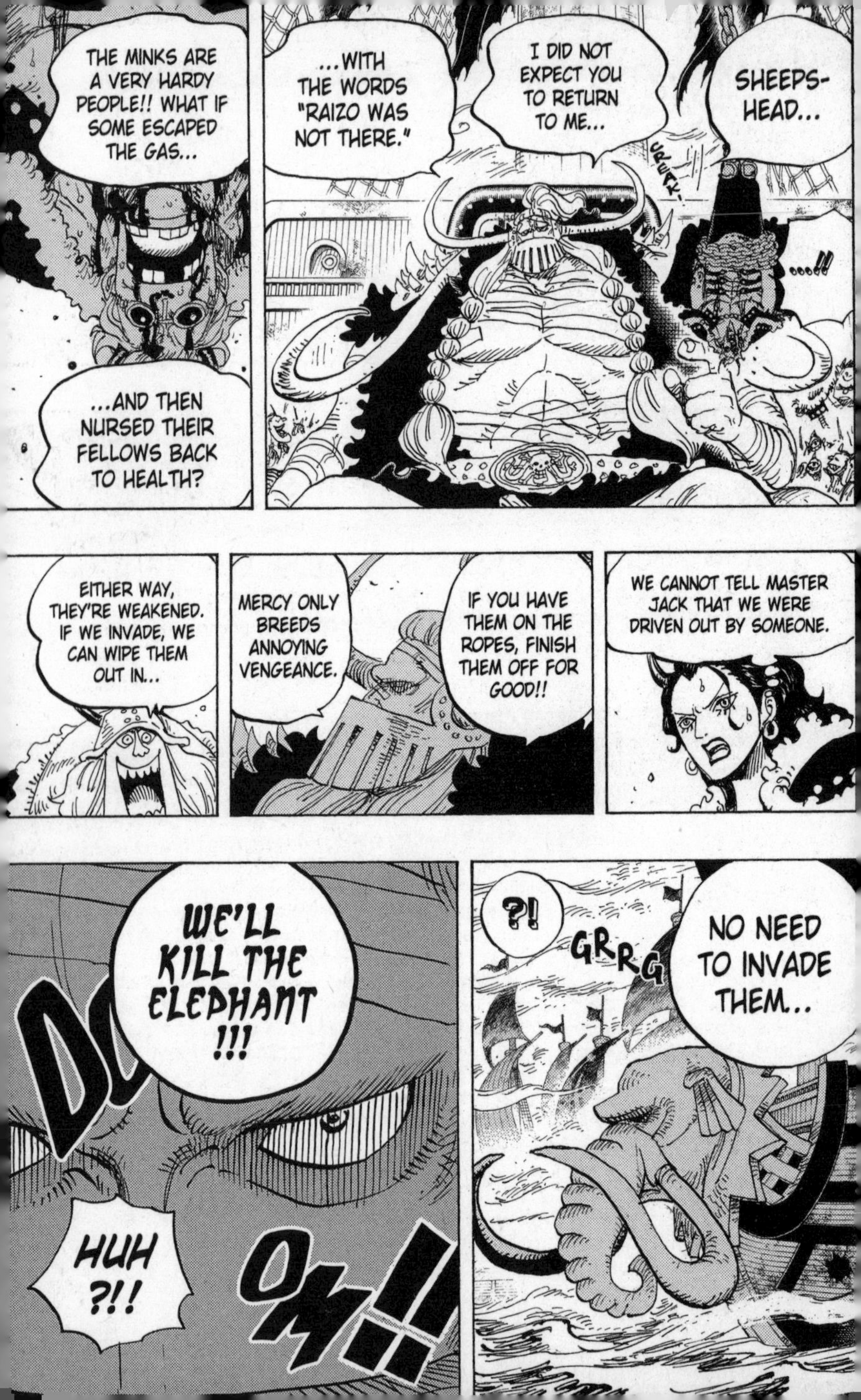
SHEEPS-HEAD...
I DID NOT EXPECT YOU TO RETURN TO ME...
...WITH THE WORDS "RAIZO WAS NOT THERE."
CREAK
...!!
THE MINKS ARE A VERY HARDY PEOPLE!! WHAT IF SOME ESCAPED THE GAS...
...AND THEN NURSED THEIR FELLOWS BACK TO HEALTH?
WE CANNOT TELL MASTER JACK THAT WE WERE DRIVEN OUT BY SOMEONE.
IF YOU HAVE THEM ON THE ROPES, FINISH THEM OFF FOR GOOD!!
MERCY ONLY BREEDS ANNOYING VENGEANCE.
EITHER WAY, THEY'RE WEAKENED. IF WE INVADE, WE CAN WIPE THEM OUT IN...
?!
GRRG
NO NEED TO INVADE THEM...
WE'LL KILL THE ELEPHANT!!!
DO
HUH ?!!
OM!!

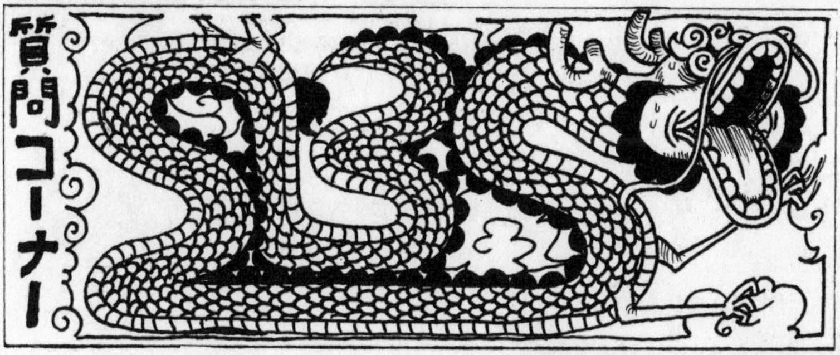
質問コーナー

(Can☆, Aomori)

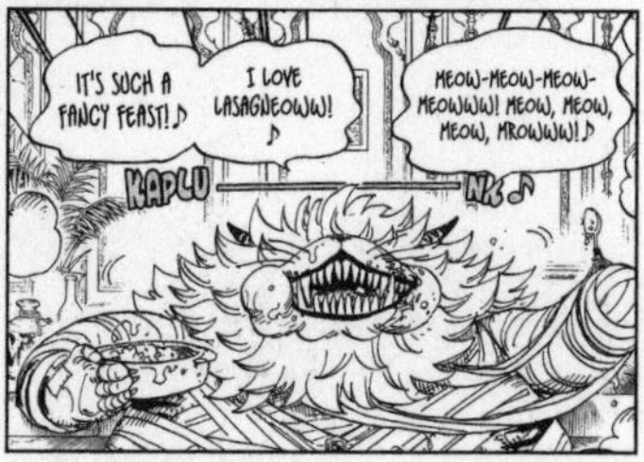
MEOW-MEOW-MEOW-MEOWWW! MEOW, MEOW, MEOW, MROWWW!♪
I LOVE LASAGNEOWW! ♪
IT'S SUCH A FANCY FEAST!♪
KAPLU—NK♪

Q: Hey, I just noticed something!! Is it possible that in the scene where the Cat Viper is singing in the bath, he's actually singing Beethoven's Ninth? Meow-meow-meow meowww, meow-meow-meow meowww!♪

--Samurai Ryota

A: Ooh, good call! It fits perfectly. I never realized that Beethoven's Ninth had lyrics! Try singing them in music class at school.

Q: There certainly are a lot of old men in *One Piece*. Is it a consequence of the story setting that there are so many old characters? Or do you just have a bad case of "Gotta-Draw-Old-Men-or-I'll-Die-itis"?

--Bootylicia

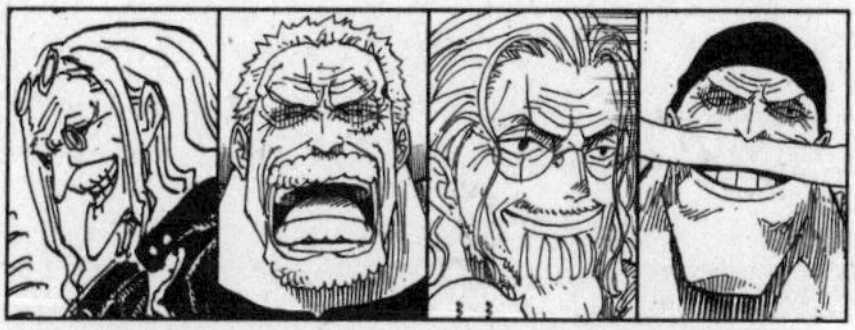

A: I love old dudes! I think that both men and women grow deeper and more interesting as they age. They're very often fascinating figures! However, reality means that you also grow physically weaker as you age. I've always had a deep disgust for young people who insult and disrespect their elders for this inevitable fact of life. So one of the fantasies that I depict in One Piece is a world in which old dudes, old ladies, gram-grams and pop-pops are still kickin' butt and takin' names. You'll be old like them one day too. Wouldn't it be cool to be this tough?

Q: Since you're the author of *One Piece,* have you ever worn a one piece dress? Also, how old is Silvers Rayleigh?

--Jabras Rayleigh

A: I always wear a one piece while at work. Rayleigh is 78 years old. On that note, Roger would be 77, Garp is 78, Sengoku is 79, and Otsuru is 76.

Chapter 820:

CATS AND DOGS HAVE A HISTORY

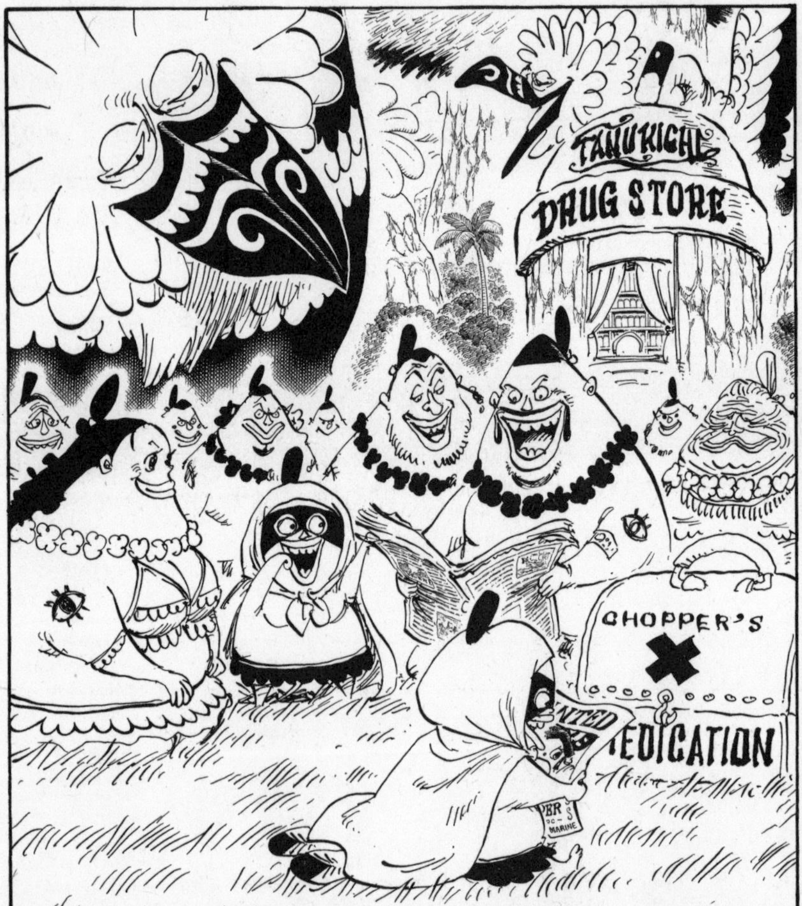
TANUKICHI
DRUG STORE
CHOPPER'S
EDICATION

DECKS OF THE WORLD, 500-MILLION-MAN ARC, VOL. 13: "BIRDIE KINGDOM"

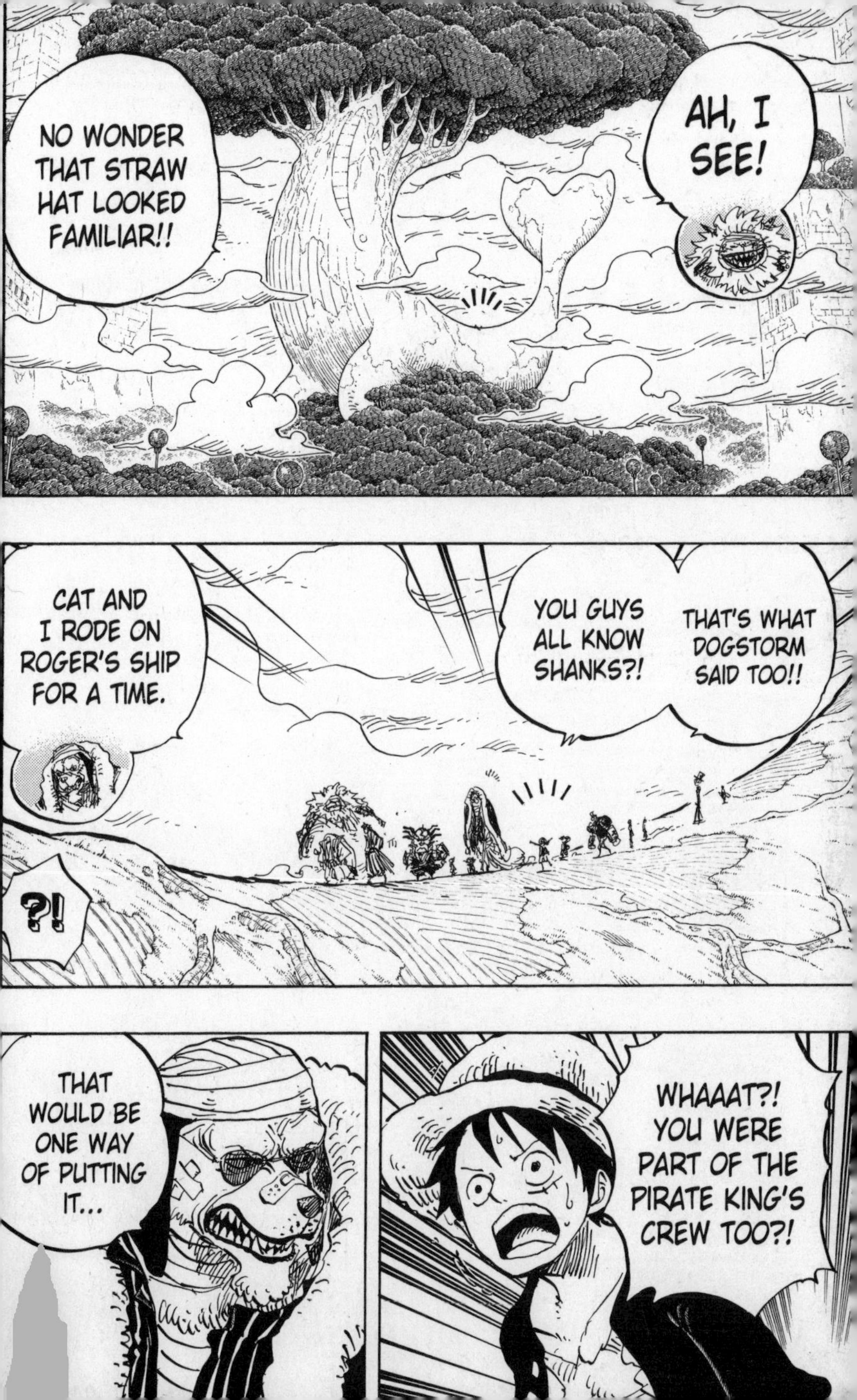
AH, I SEE!
NO WONDER THAT STRAW HAT LOOKED FAMILIAR!!
THAT'S WHAT DOGSTORM SAID TOO!!
YOU GUYS ALL KNOW SHANKS?!
CAT AND I RODE ON ROGER'S SHIP FOR A TIME.
?!
WHAAAT?! YOU WERE PART OF THE PIRATE KING'S CREW TOO?!
THAT WOULD BE ONE WAY OF PUTTING IT...

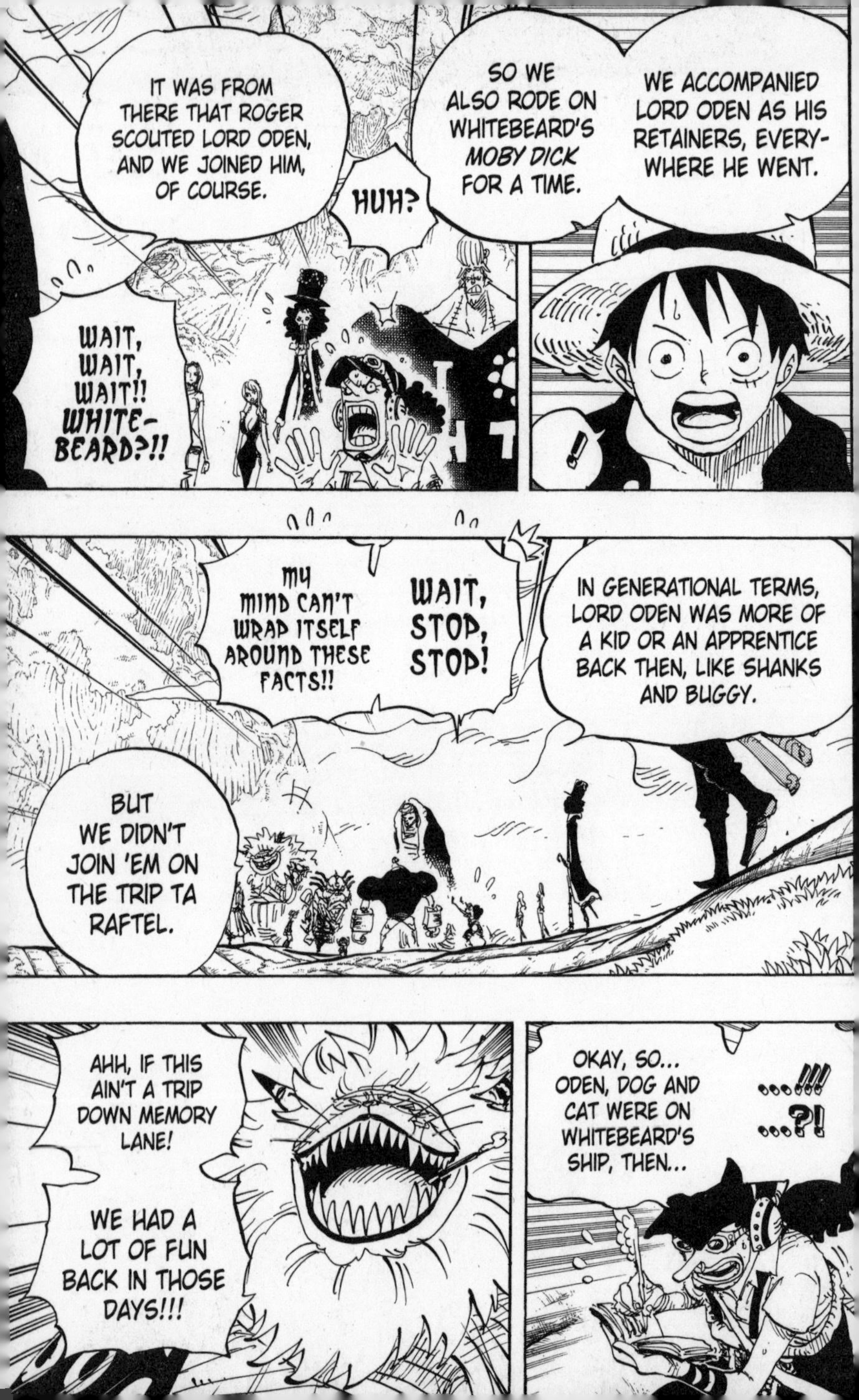

WE ACCOMPANIED LORD ODEN AS HIS RETAINERS, EVERY-WHERE HE WENT.
SO WE ALSO RODE ON WHITEBEARD'S *MOBY DICK* FOR A TIME.
!
IT WAS FROM THERE THAT ROGER SCOUTED LORD ODEN, AND WE JOINED HIM, OF COURSE.
HUH?
WAIT, WAIT, WAIT!! WHITE-BEARD?!!
IN GENERATIONAL TERMS, LORD ODEN WAS MORE OF A KID OR AN APPRENTICE BACK THEN, LIKE SHANKS AND BUGGY.
WAIT, STOP, STOP!
MY MIND CAN'T WRAP ITSELF AROUND THESE FACTS!!
BUT WE DIDN'T JOIN 'EM ON THE TRIP TA RAFTEL.
OKAY, SO... ODEN, DOG AND CAT WERE ON WHITEBEARD'S SHIP, THEN...
...!!!
...?!
AHH, IF THIS AIN'T A TRIP DOWN MEMORY LANE!
WE HAD A LOT OF FUN BACK IN THOSE DAYS!!!

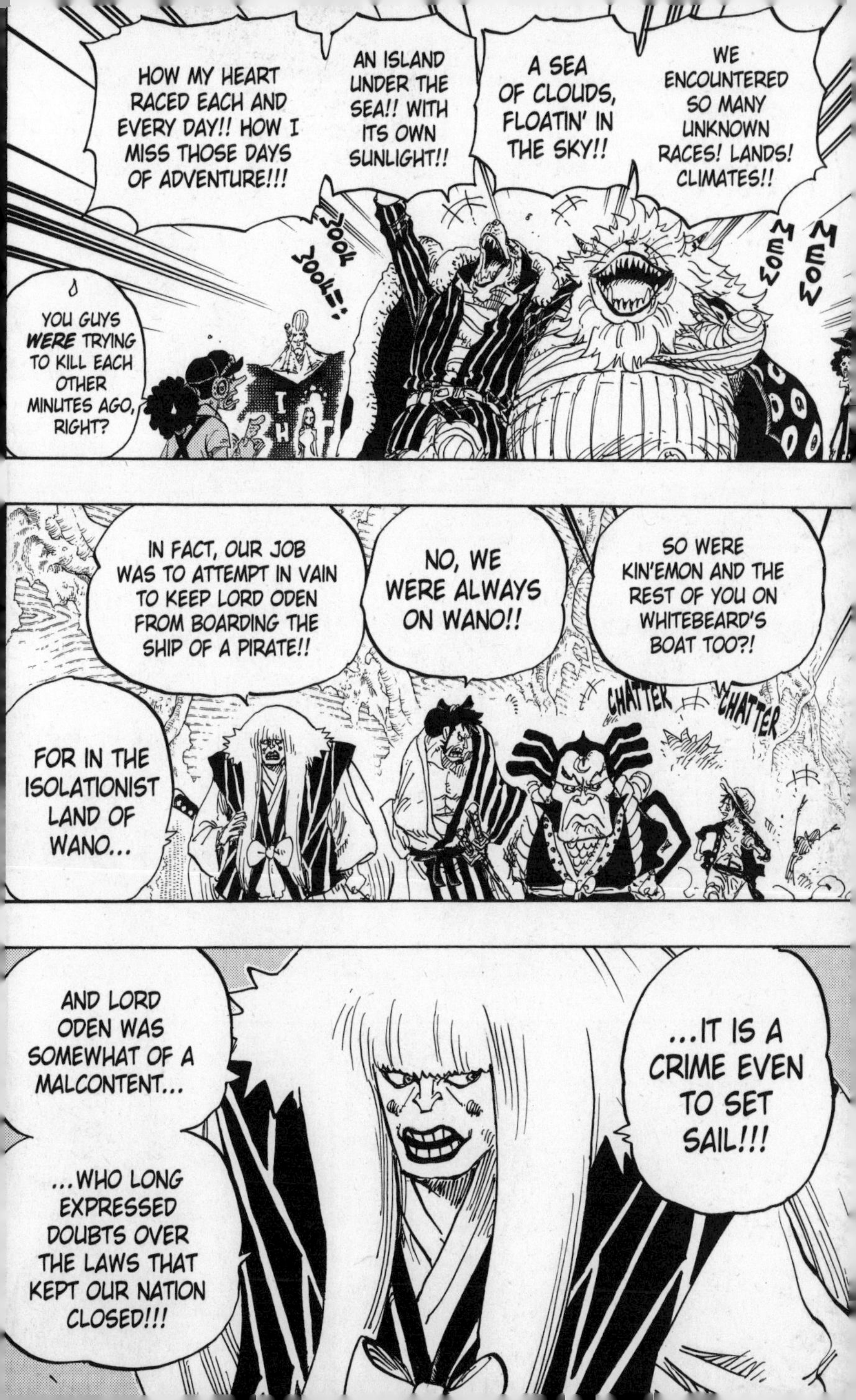
WE ENCOUNTERED SO MANY UNKNOWN RACES! LANDS! CLIMATES!!
A SEA OF CLOUDS, FLOATIN' IN THE SKY!!
AN ISLAND UNDER THE SEA!! WITH ITS OWN SUNLIGHT!!
HOW MY HEART RACED EACH AND EVERY DAY!! HOW I MISS THOSE DAYS OF ADVENTURE!!!
MEOW
MEOW
WOOF WOOF!!
YOU GUYS *WERE* TRYING TO KILL EACH OTHER MINUTES AGO, RIGHT?
SO WERE KIN'EMON AND THE REST OF YOU ON WHITEBEARD'S BOAT TOO?!
NO, WE WERE ALWAYS ON WANO!!
IN FACT, OUR JOB WAS TO ATTEMPT IN VAIN TO KEEP LORD ODEN FROM BOARDING THE SHIP OF A PIRATE!!
CHATTER
CHATTER
FOR IN THE ISOLATIONIST LAND OF WANO...
...IT IS A CRIME EVEN TO SET SAIL!!!
AND LORD ODEN WAS SOMEWHAT OF A MALCONTENT...
...WHO LONG EXPRESSED DOUBTS OVER THE LAWS THAT KEPT OUR NATION CLOSED!!!

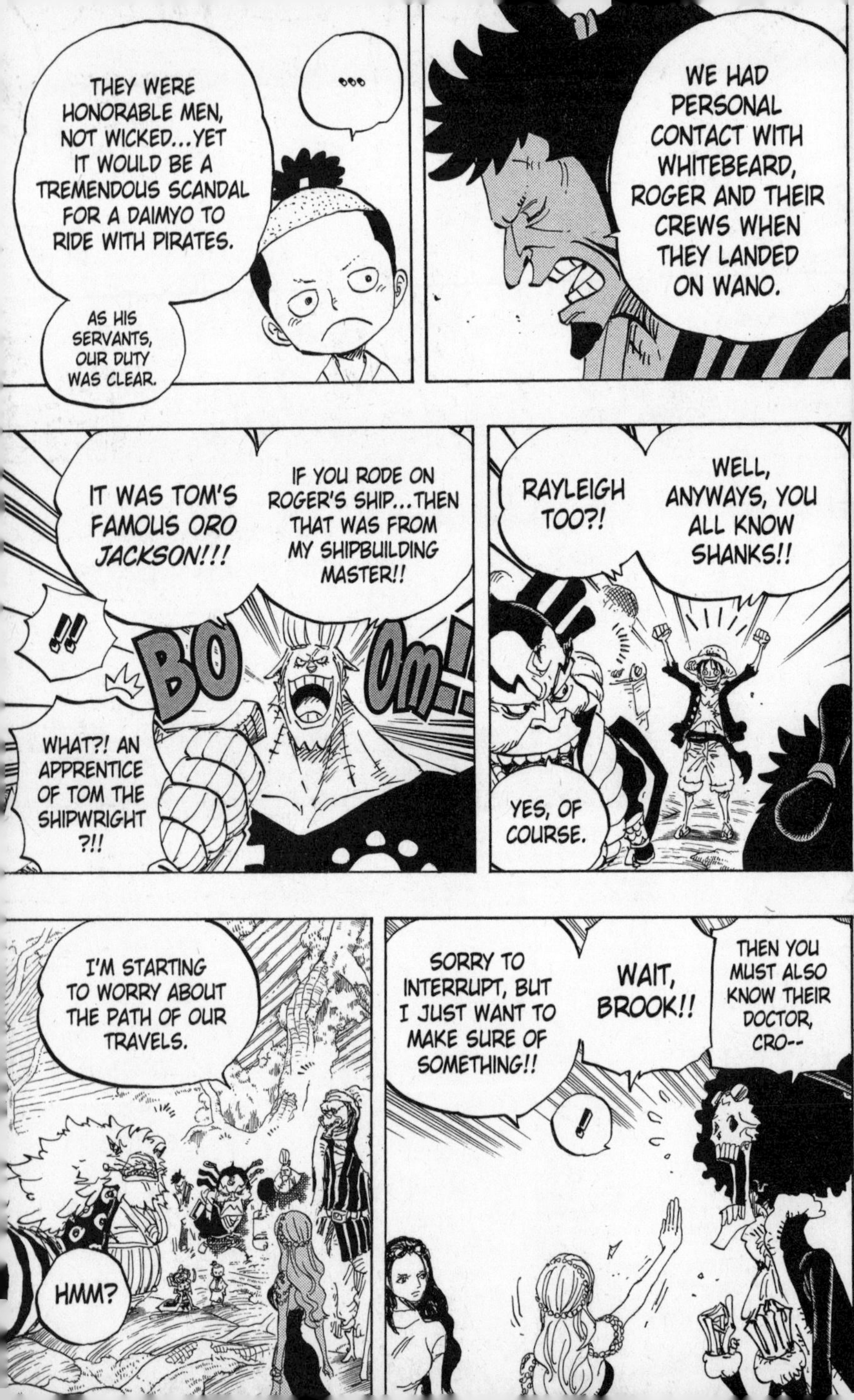
WE HAD PERSONAL CONTACT WITH WHITEBEARD, ROGER AND THEIR CREWS WHEN THEY LANDED ON WANO.
...
THEY WERE HONORABLE MEN, NOT WICKED...YET IT WOULD BE A TREMENDOUS SCANDAL FOR A DAIMYO TO RIDE WITH PIRATES.
AS HIS SERVANTS, OUR DUTY WAS CLEAR.
WELL, ANYWAYS, YOU ALL KNOW SHANKS!!
RAYLEIGH TOO?!
YES, OF COURSE.
IF YOU RODE ON ROGER'S SHIP...THEN THAT WAS FROM MY SHIPBUILDING MASTER!!
IT WAS TOM'S FAMOUS ORO JACKSON!!!
!!
BOOM!!
WHAT?! AN APPRENTICE OF TOM THE SHIPWRIGHT?!!
THEN YOU MUST ALSO KNOW THEIR DOCTOR, CRO--
WAIT, BROOK!!
SORRY TO INTERRUPT, BUT I JUST WANT TO MAKE SURE OF SOMETHING!!
!
I'M STARTING TO WORRY ABOUT THE PATH OF OUR TRAVELS.
HMM?

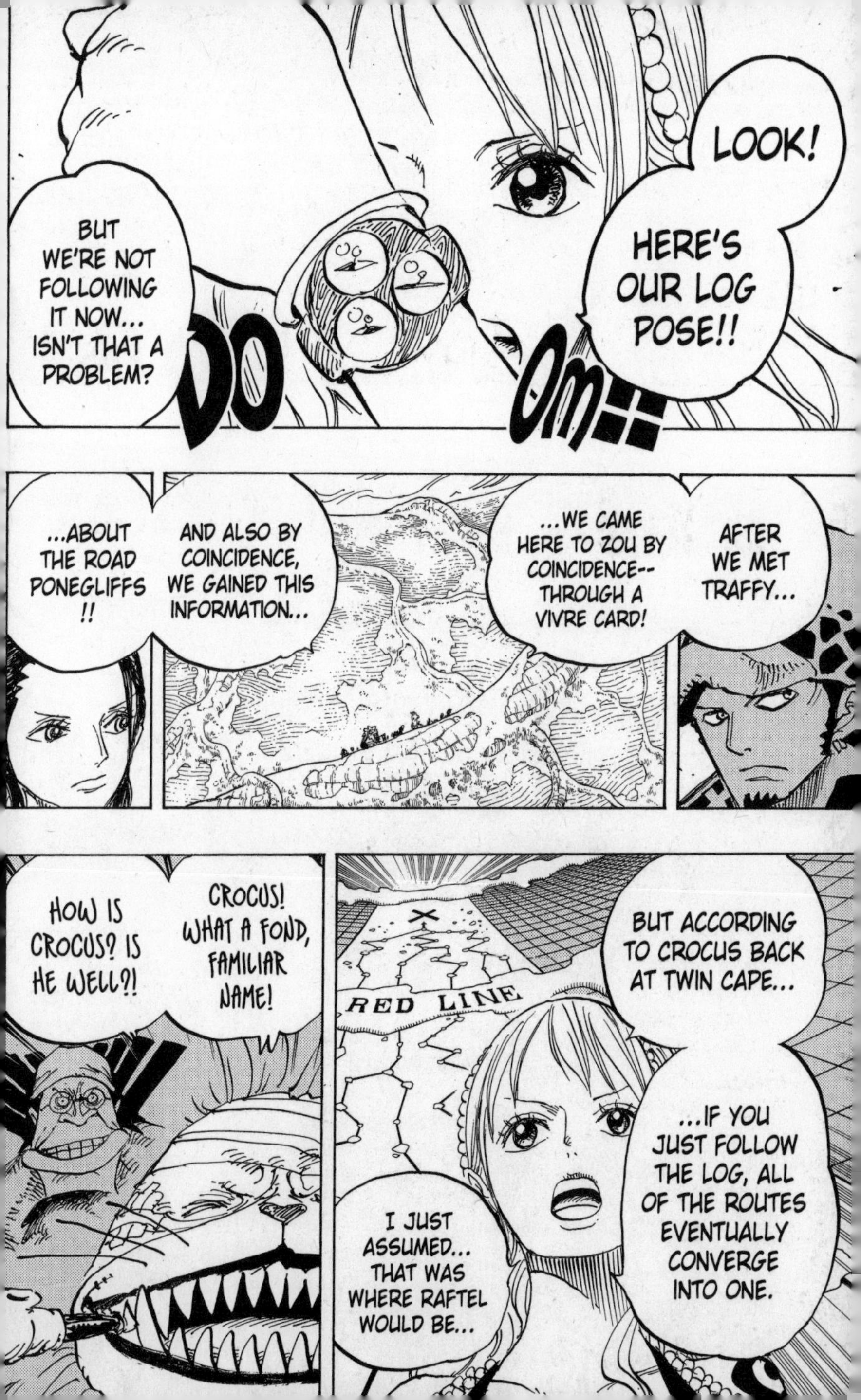
LOOK!
HERE'S OUR LOG POSE!!
DOOM
BUT WE'RE NOT FOLLOWING IT NOW... ISN'T THAT A PROBLEM?
AFTER WE MET TRAFFY...
...WE CAME HERE TO ZOU BY COINCIDENCE-- THROUGH A VIVRE CARD!
AND ALSO BY COINCIDENCE, WE GAINED THIS INFORMATION...
...ABOUT THE ROAD PONEGLIFFS !!
RED LINE
BUT ACCORDING TO CROCUS BACK AT TWIN CAPE...
...IF YOU JUST FOLLOW THE LOG, ALL OF THE ROUTES EVENTUALLY CONVERGE INTO ONE.
I JUST ASSUMED... THAT WAS WHERE RAFTEL WOULD BE...
CROCUS! WHAT A FOND, FAMILIAR NAME!
HOW IS CROCUS? IS HE WELL?!

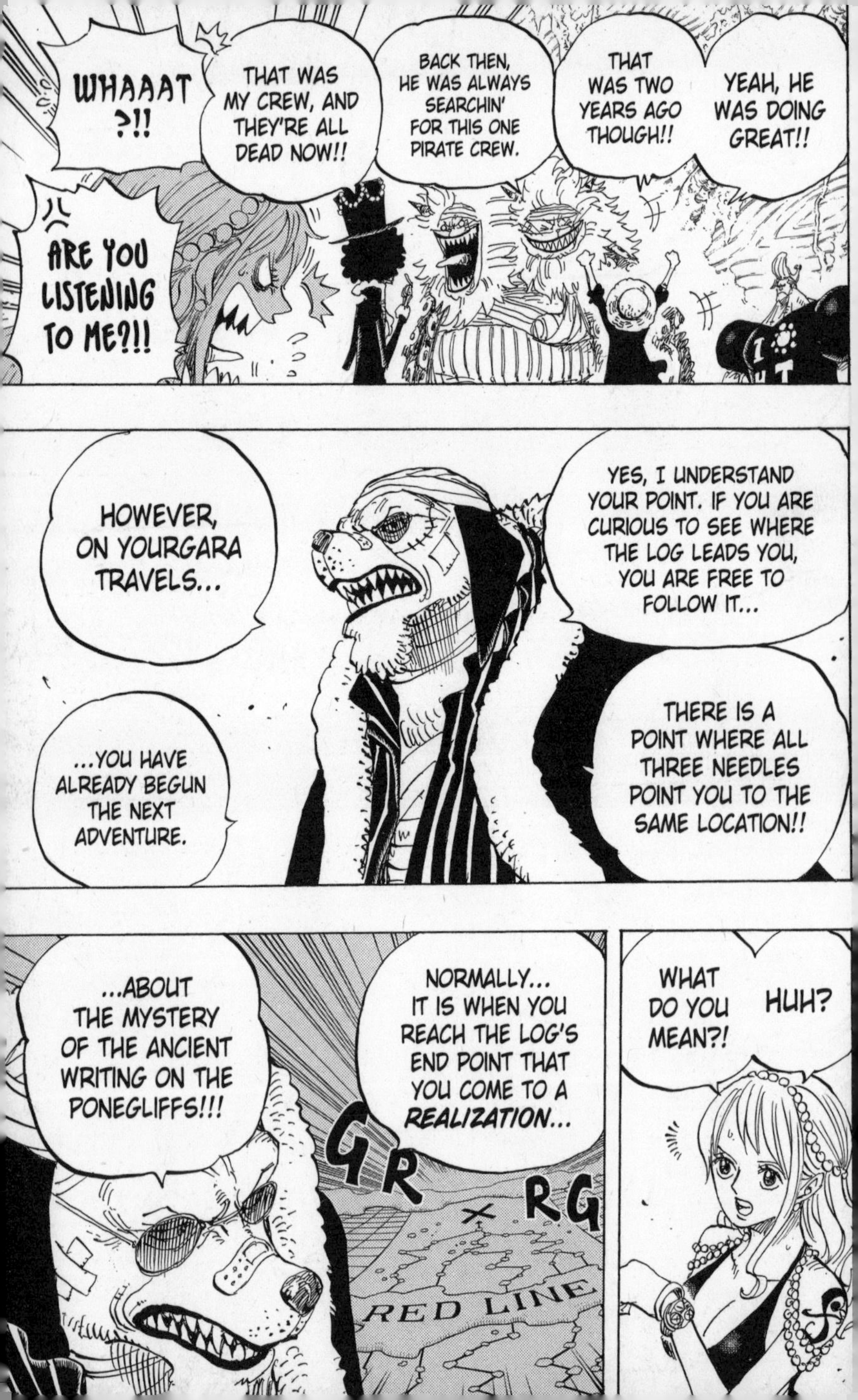
YEAH, HE WAS DOING GREAT!!
THAT WAS TWO YEARS AGO THOUGH!!
BACK THEN, HE WAS ALWAYS SEARCHIN' FOR THIS ONE PIRATE CREW.
THAT WAS MY CREW, AND THEY'RE ALL DEAD NOW!!
WHAAAT ?!!
ARE YOU LISTENING TO ME?!!
YES, I UNDERSTAND YOUR POINT. IF YOU ARE CURIOUS TO SEE WHERE THE LOG LEADS YOU, YOU ARE FREE TO FOLLOW IT...
HOWEVER, ON YOURGARA TRAVELS...
THERE IS A POINT WHERE ALL THREE NEEDLES POINT YOU TO THE SAME LOCATION!!
...YOU HAVE ALREADY BEGUN THE NEXT ADVENTURE.
HUH?
WHAT DO YOU MEAN?!
NORMALLY... IT IS WHEN YOU REACH THE LOG'S END POINT THAT YOU COME TO A *REALIZATION*...
GR RG
...ABOUT THE MYSTERY OF THE ANCIENT WRITING ON THE PONEGLIFFS!!!
RED LINE

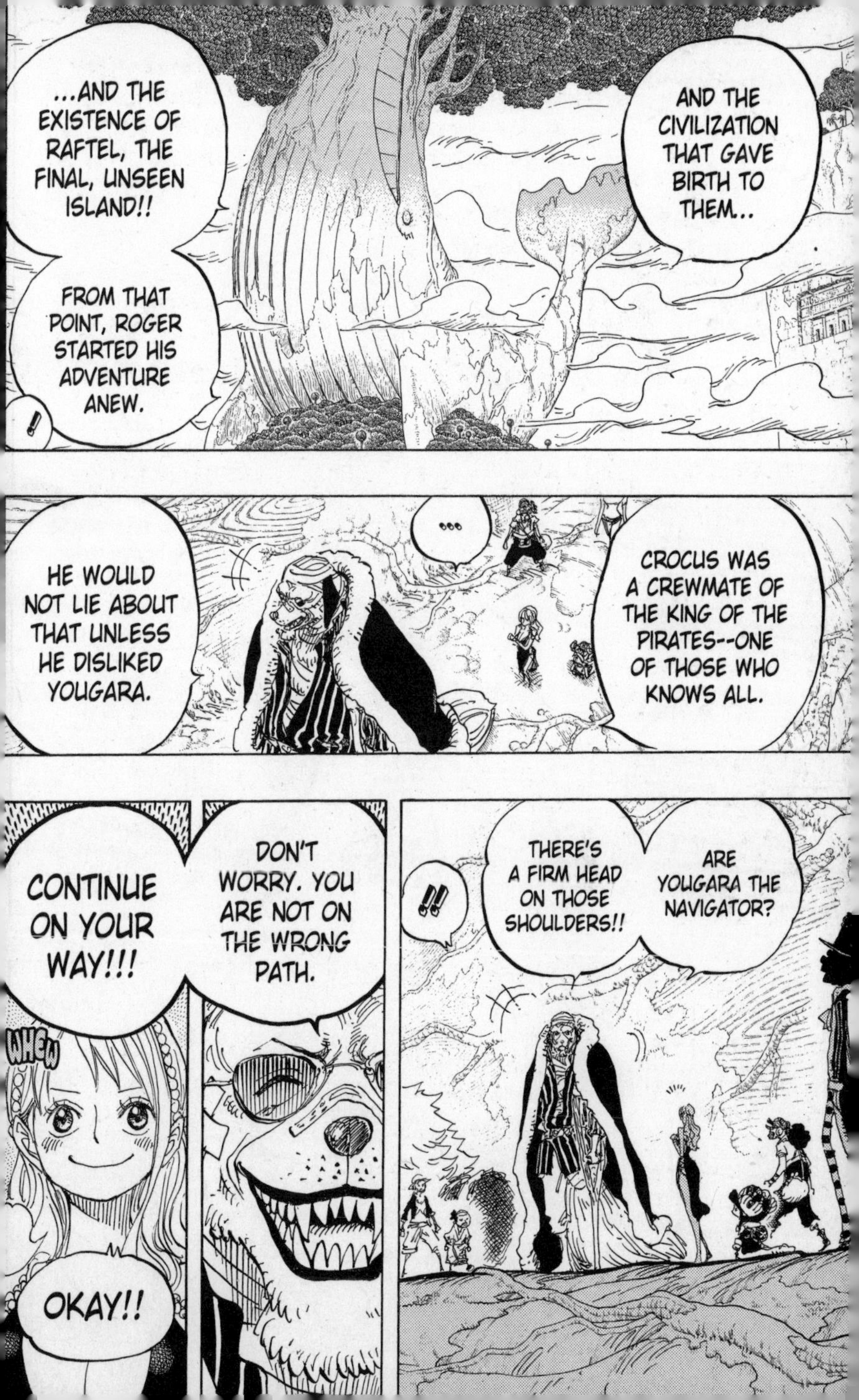

AND THE CIVILIZATION THAT GAVE BIRTH TO THEM...
...AND THE EXISTENCE OF RAFTEL, THE FINAL, UNSEEN ISLAND!!
FROM THAT POINT, ROGER STARTED HIS ADVENTURE ANEW.
!
CROCUS WAS A CREWMATE OF THE KING OF THE PIRATES--ONE OF THOSE WHO KNOWS ALL.
...
HE WOULD NOT LIE ABOUT THAT UNLESS HE DISLIKED YOUGARA.
ARE YOUGARA THE NAVIGATOR?
THERE'S A FIRM HEAD ON THOSE SHOULDERS!!
!!
DON'T WORRY. YOU ARE NOT ON THE WRONG PATH.
CONTINUE ON YOUR WAY!!!
WHEW
OKAY!!

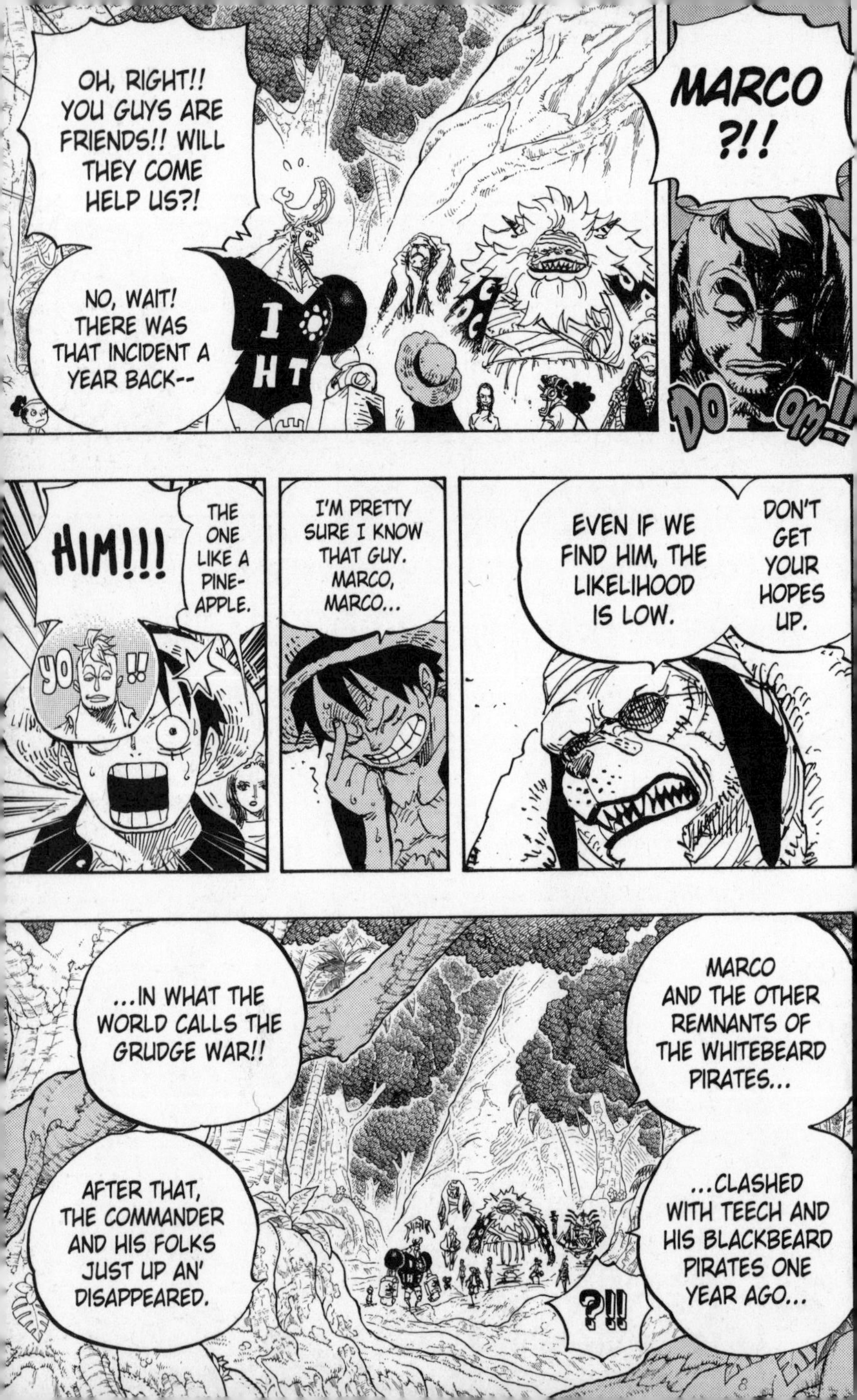
MARCO ?!!
DOOM!!
OH, RIGHT!! YOU GUYS ARE FRIENDS!! WILL THEY COME HELP US?!
NO, WAIT! THERE WAS THAT INCIDENT A YEAR BACK--
DON'T GET YOUR HOPES UP.
EVEN IF WE FIND HIM, THE LIKELIHOOD IS LOW.
I'M PRETTY SURE I KNOW THAT GUY. MARCO, MARCO...
THE ONE LIKE A PINE-APPLE.
HIM!!!
YO!!
MARCO AND THE OTHER REMNANTS OF THE WHITEBEARD PIRATES...
...CLASHED WITH TEECH AND HIS BLACKBEARD PIRATES ONE YEAR AGO...
...IN WHAT THE WORLD CALLS THE GRUDGE WAR!!
?!!
AFTER THAT, THE COMMANDER AND HIS FOLKS JUST UP AN' DISAPPEARED.

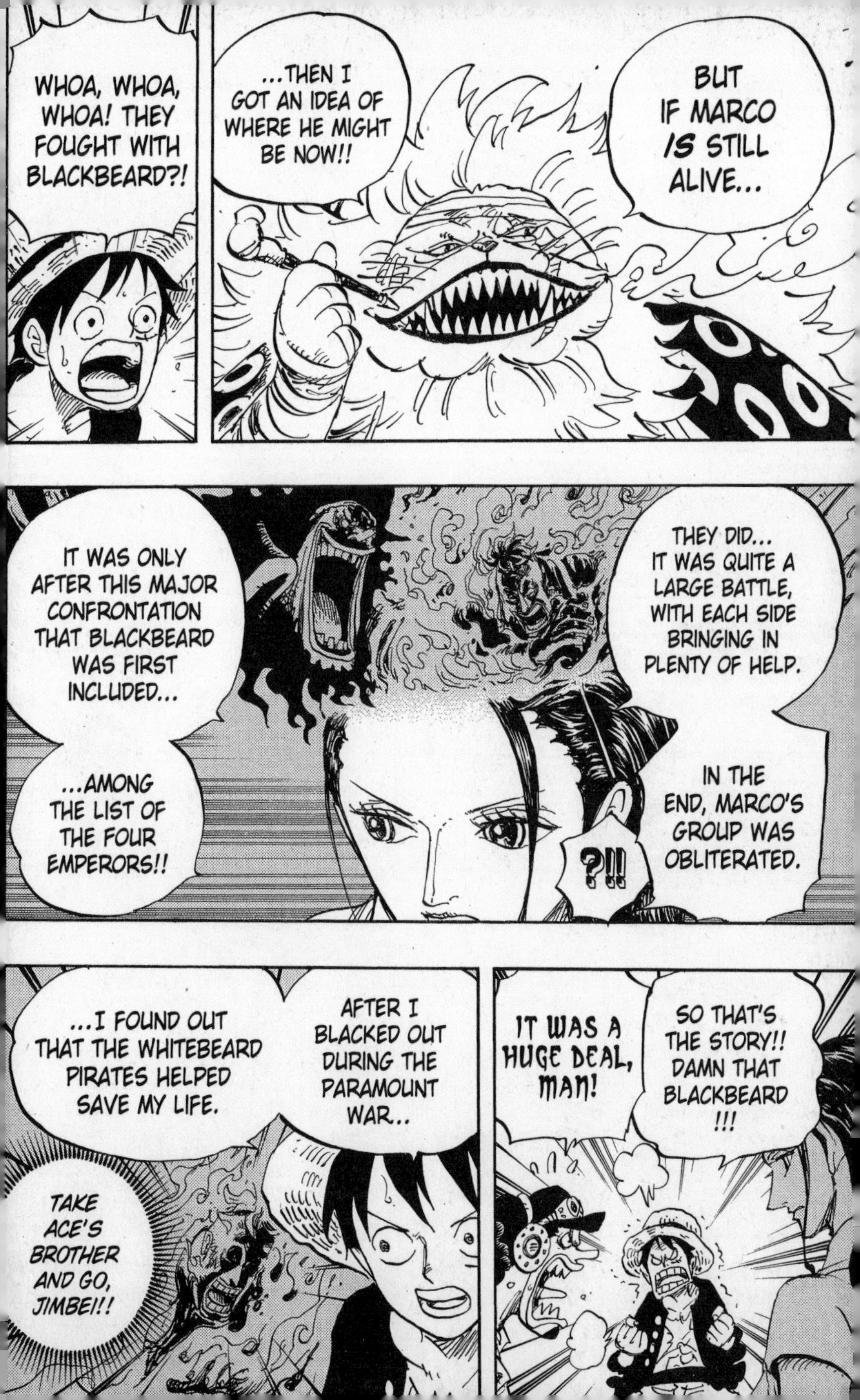
BUT IF MARCO *IS* STILL ALIVE...
...THEN I GOT AN IDEA OF WHERE HE MIGHT BE NOW!!
WHOA, WHOA, WHOA! THEY FOUGHT WITH BLACKBEARD?!
THEY DID... IT WAS QUITE A LARGE BATTLE, WITH EACH SIDE BRINGING IN PLENTY OF HELP.
IN THE END, MARCO'S GROUP WAS OBLITERATED.
?!!
IT WAS ONLY AFTER THIS MAJOR CONFRONTATION THAT BLACKBEARD WAS FIRST INCLUDED...
...AMONG THE LIST OF THE FOUR EMPERORS!!
SO THAT'S THE STORY!! DAMN THAT BLACKBEARD !!!
IT WAS A HUGE DEAL, MAN!
AFTER I BLACKED OUT DURING THE PARAMOUNT WAR...
...I FOUND OUT THAT THE WHITEBEARD PIRATES HELPED SAVE MY LIFE.
TAKE ACE'S BROTHER AND GO, JIMBEI!!

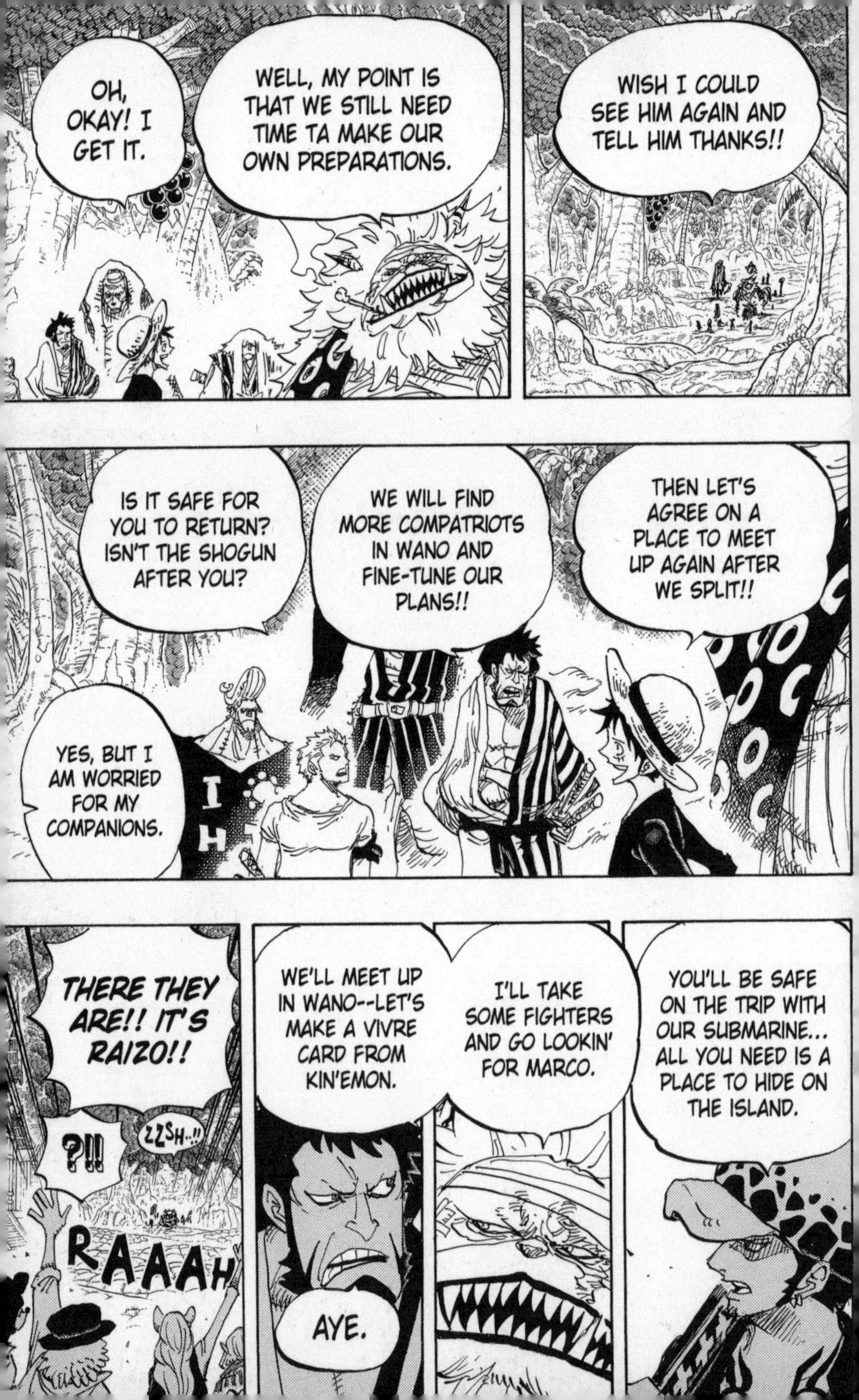
WISH I COULD SEE HIM AGAIN AND TELL HIM THANKS!!
WELL, MY POINT IS THAT WE STILL NEED TIME TA MAKE OUR OWN PREPARATIONS.
OH, OKAY! I GET IT.
THEN LET'S AGREE ON A PLACE TO MEET UP AGAIN AFTER WE SPLIT!!
WE WILL FIND MORE COMPATRIOTS IN WANO AND FINE-TUNE OUR PLANS!!
IS IT SAFE FOR YOU TO RETURN? ISN'T THE SHOGUN AFTER YOU?
YES, BUT I AM WORRIED FOR MY COMPANIONS.
YOU'LL BE SAFE ON THE TRIP WITH OUR SUBMARINE... ALL YOU NEED IS A PLACE TO HIDE ON THE ISLAND.
I'LL TAKE SOME FIGHTERS AND GO LOOKIN' FOR MARCO.
WE'LL MEET UP IN WANO--LET'S MAKE A VIVRE CARD FROM KIN'EMON.
AYE.
THERE THEY ARE!! IT'S RAIZO!!
ZZSH..!!
?!!
RAAAH

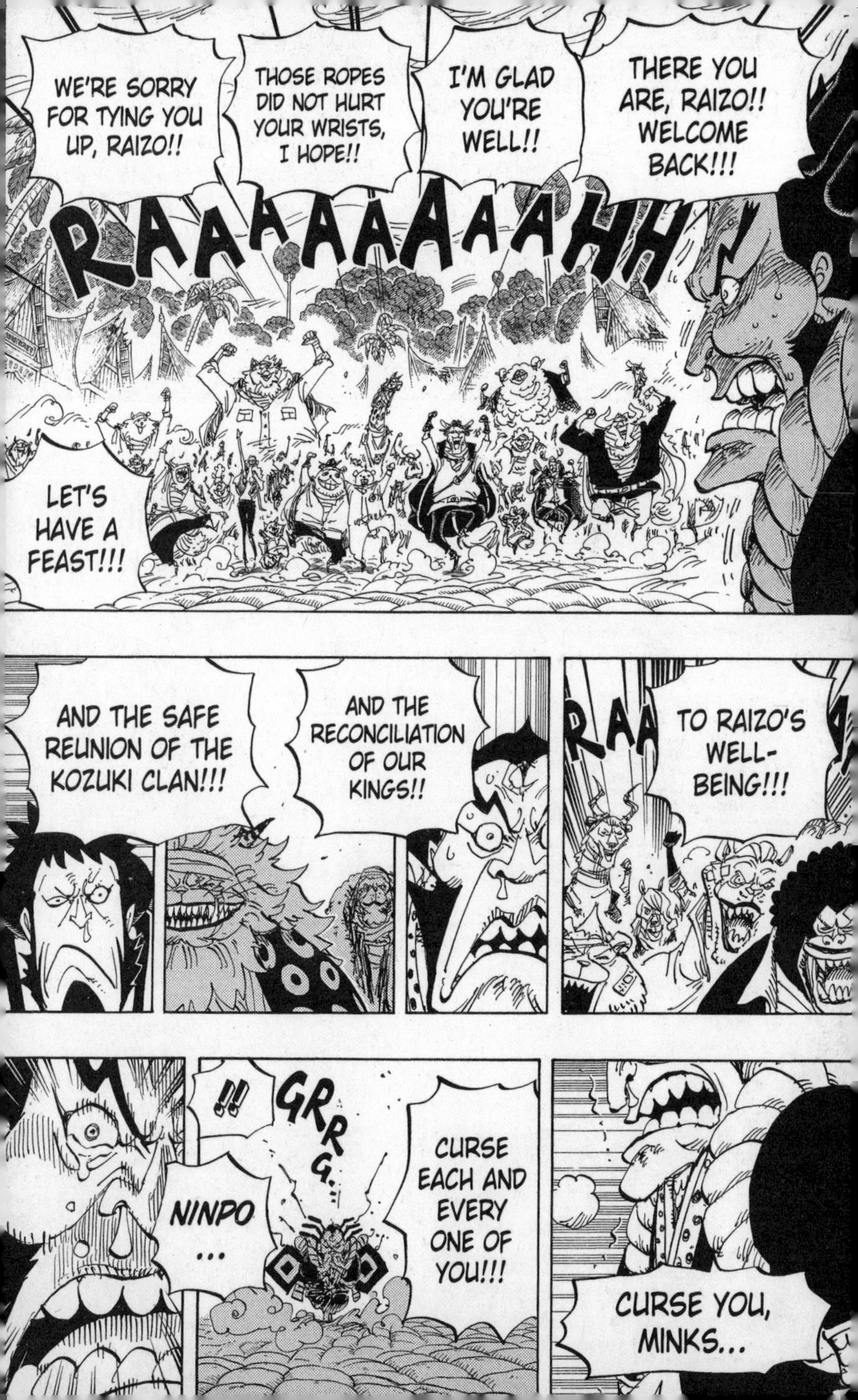
THERE YOU ARE, RAIZO!! WELCOME BACK!!!
I'M GLAD YOU'RE WELL!!
THOSE ROPES DID NOT HURT YOUR WRISTS, I HOPE!!
WE'RE SORRY FOR TYING YOU UP, RAIZO!!
RAAAAAAAAHH
LET'S HAVE A FEAST!!!
RAA
TO RAIZO'S WELL-BEING!!!
AND THE RECONCILIATION OF OUR KINGS!!
AND THE SAFE REUNION OF THE KOZUKI CLAN!!!
CURSE YOU, MINKS...
GRRRG.
!!
CURSE EACH AND EVERY ONE OF YOU!!!
NINPO ...

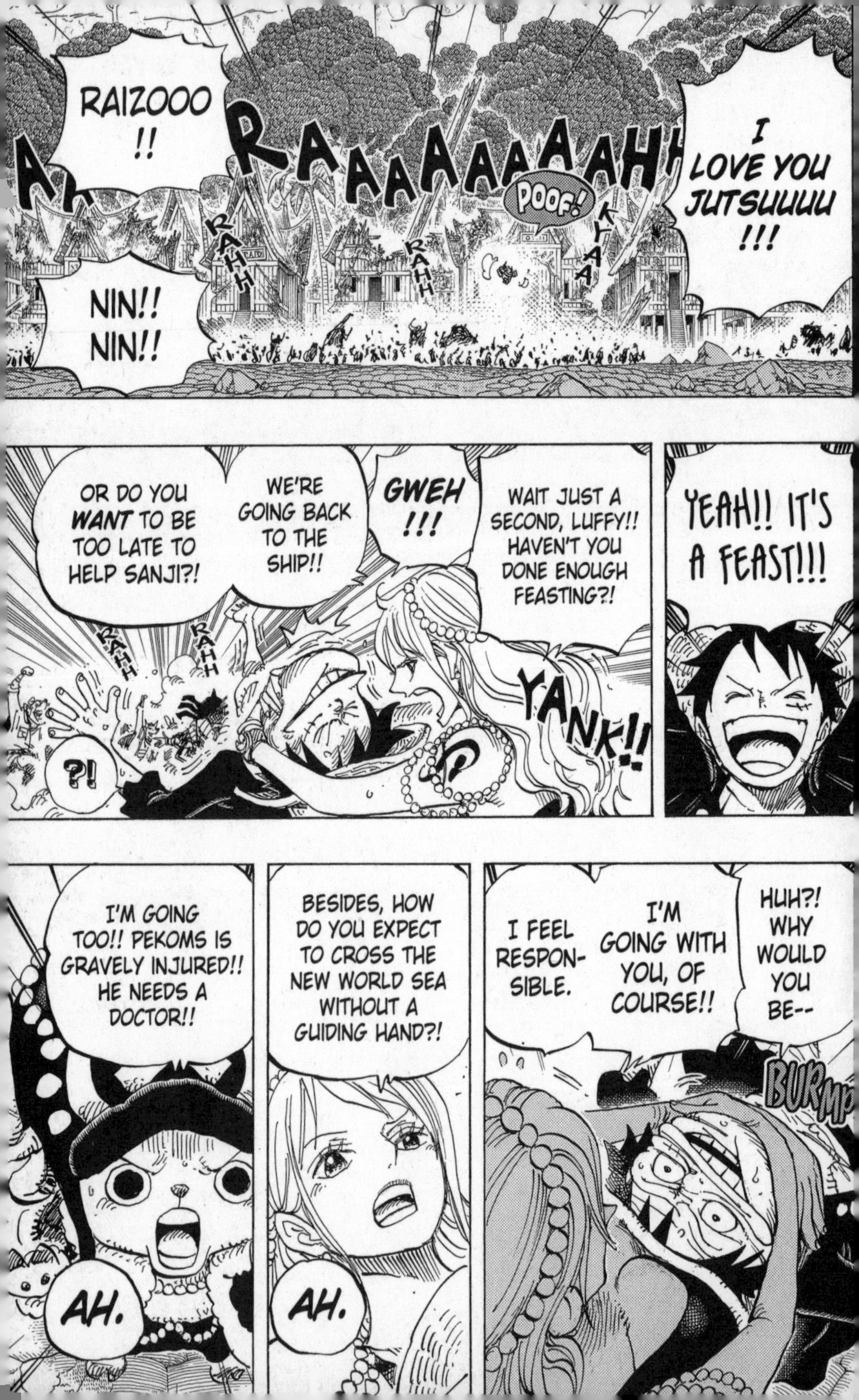

I LOVE YOU JUTSUUUU!!!
POOF!
KYAA
RAHH
RAHH
RAIZOOO!!
NIN!! NIN!!
YEAH!! IT'S A FEAST!!!
WAIT JUST A SECOND, LUFFY!! HAVEN'T YOU DONE ENOUGH FEASTING?!
GWEH!!!
WE'RE GOING BACK TO THE SHIP!!
OR DO YOU WANT TO BE TOO LATE TO HELP SANJI?!
YANK!!
RAHH
RAHH
?!
HUH?! WHY WOULD YOU BE--
I'M GOING WITH YOU, OF COURSE!!
I FEEL RESPON-SIBLE.
BURMP
BESIDES, HOW DO YOU EXPECT TO CROSS THE NEW WORLD SEA WITHOUT A GUIDING HAND?!
AH.
I'M GOING TOO!! PEKOMS IS GRAVELY INJURED!! HE NEEDS A DOCTOR!!
AH.

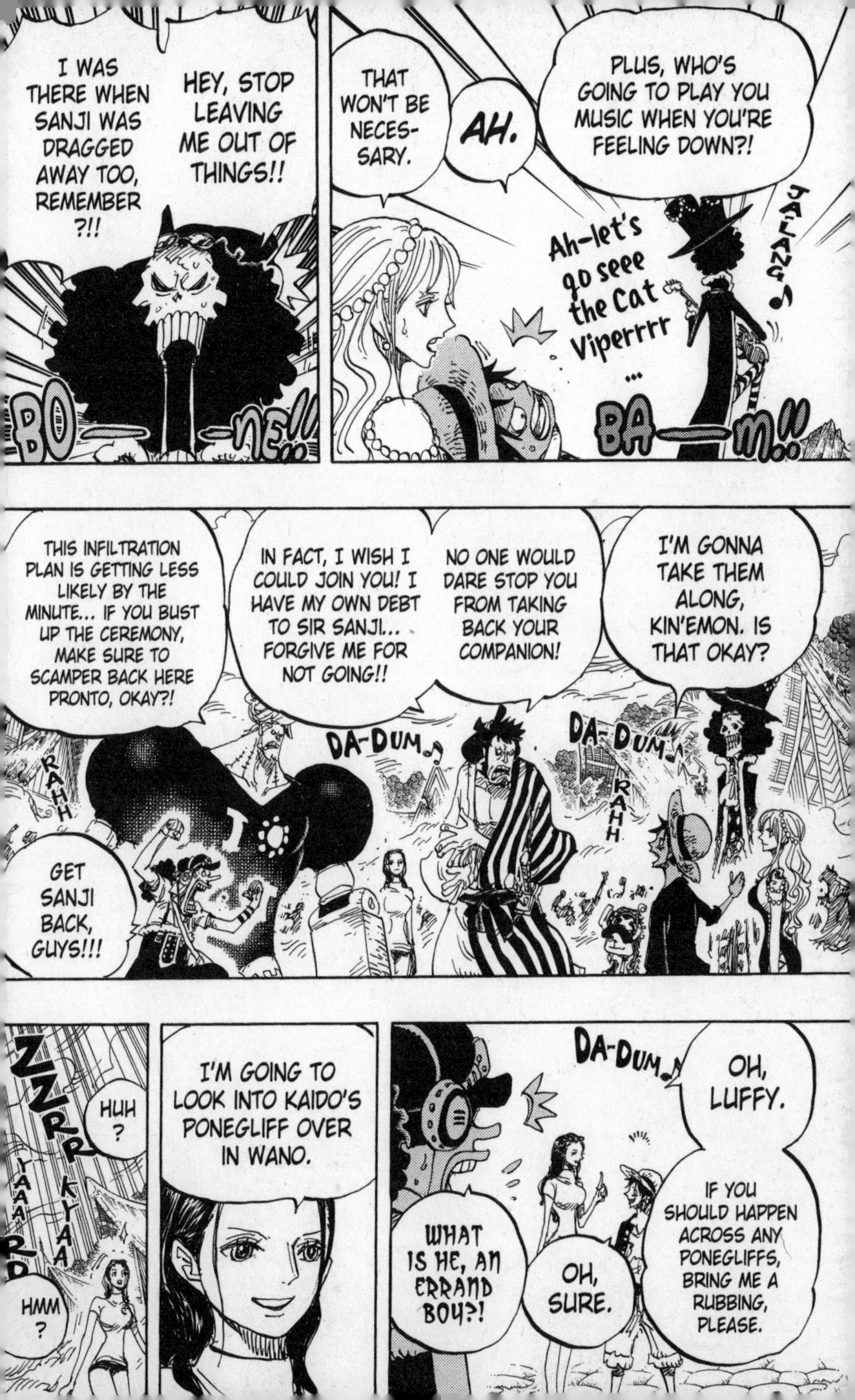
PLUS, WHO'S GOING TO PLAY YOU MUSIC WHEN YOU'RE FEELING DOWN?!
JA-LANG
AH.
THAT WON'T BE NECES-SARY.
Ah-let's go seee the Cat Viperrrr ...
BA—M!!
HEY, STOP LEAVING ME OUT OF THINGS!!
I WAS THERE WHEN SANJI WAS DRAGGED AWAY TOO, REMEMBER?!!
BO—NE!!
I'M GONNA TAKE THEM ALONG, KIN'EMON. IS THAT OKAY?
NO ONE WOULD DARE STOP YOU FROM TAKING BACK YOUR COMPANION!
IN FACT, I WISH I COULD JOIN YOU! I HAVE MY OWN DEBT TO SIR SANJI... FORGIVE ME FOR NOT GOING!!
DA-DUM
RAHH
DA-DUM
THIS INFILTRATION PLAN IS GETTING LESS LIKELY BY THE MINUTE... IF YOU BUST UP THE CEREMONY, MAKE SURE TO SCAMPER BACK HERE PRONTO, OKAY?!
RAHH
GET SANJI BACK, GUYS!!!
DA-DUM
OH, LUFFY.
IF YOU SHOULD HAPPEN ACROSS ANY PONEGLIFFS, BRING ME A RUBBING, PLEASE.
OH, SURE.
WHAT IS HE, AN ERRAND BOY?!
I'M GOING TO LOOK INTO KAIDO'S PONEGLIFF OVER IN WANO.
HUH?
KYAAA
HMM?

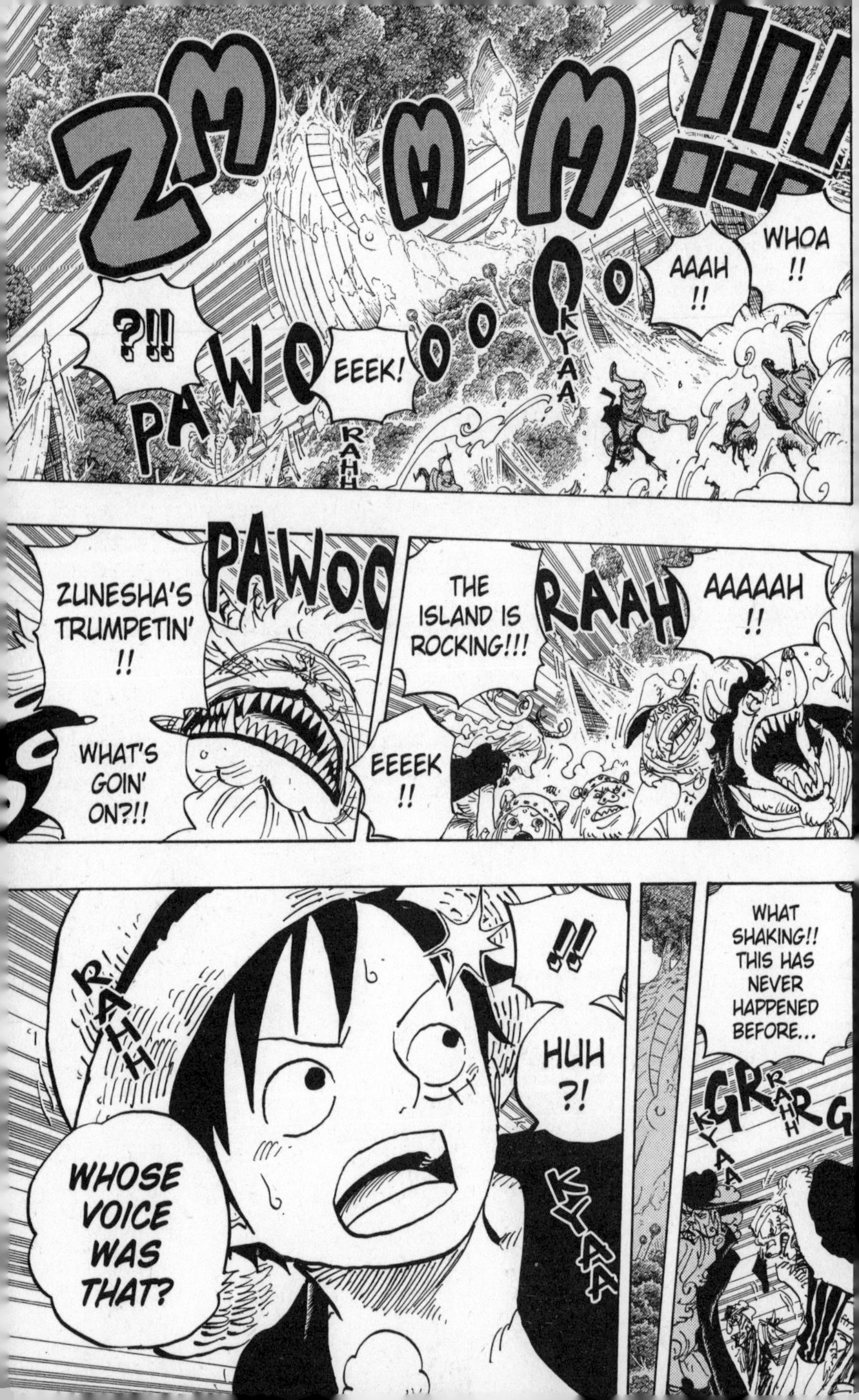
WHOA !!
AAAH !!
ZMMMM!!!!
?!!
PAWOOOOO
EEEK!
KYAA
RAHH
AAAAAH !!
RAAH
THE ISLAND IS ROCKING!!!
EEEEK !!
PAWOO
ZUNESHA'S TRUMPETIN' !!
WHAT'S GOIN' ON?!!
WHAT SHAKING!! THIS HAS NEVER HAPPENED BEFORE...
GRRAHHRG
KYAA
!!
HUH ?!
RAHH
KYAA
WHOSE VOICE WAS THAT?

Chapter 821: UNDERSTOOD

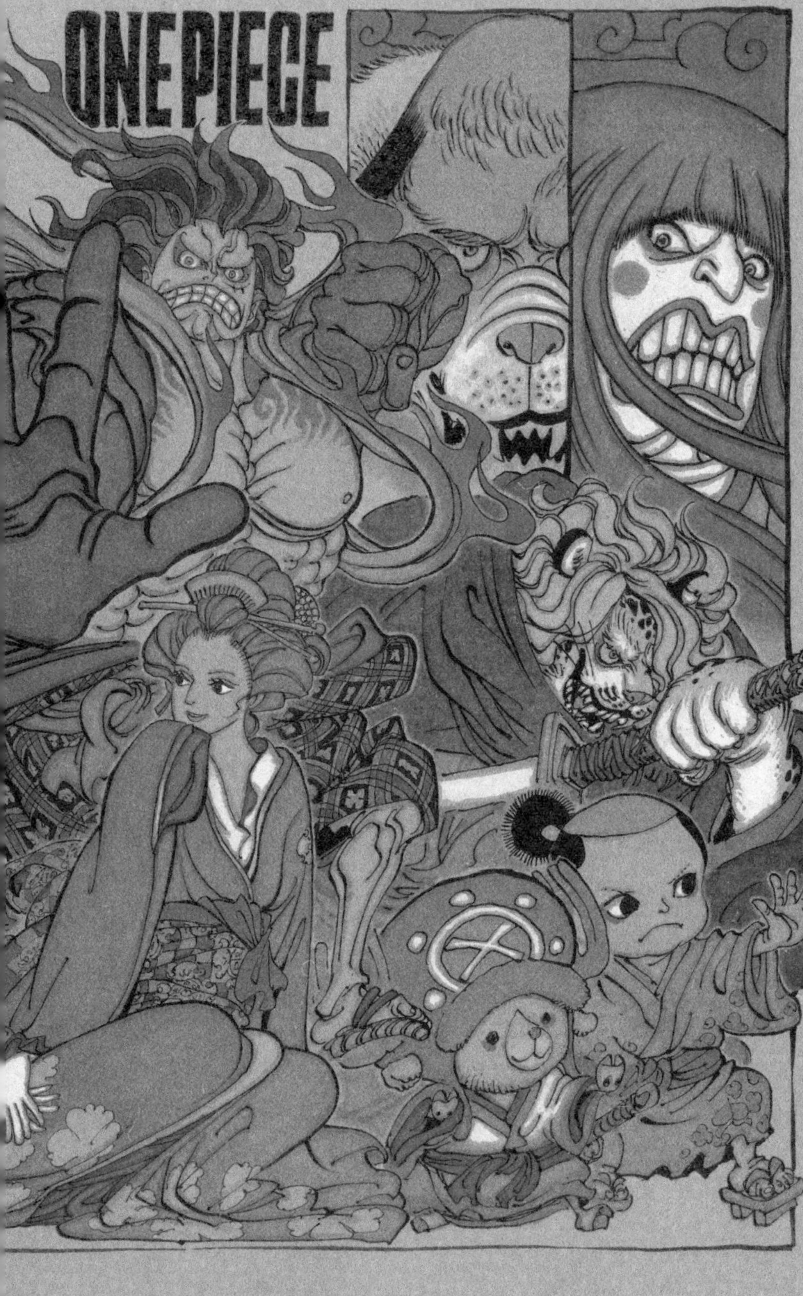
ONE PIECE

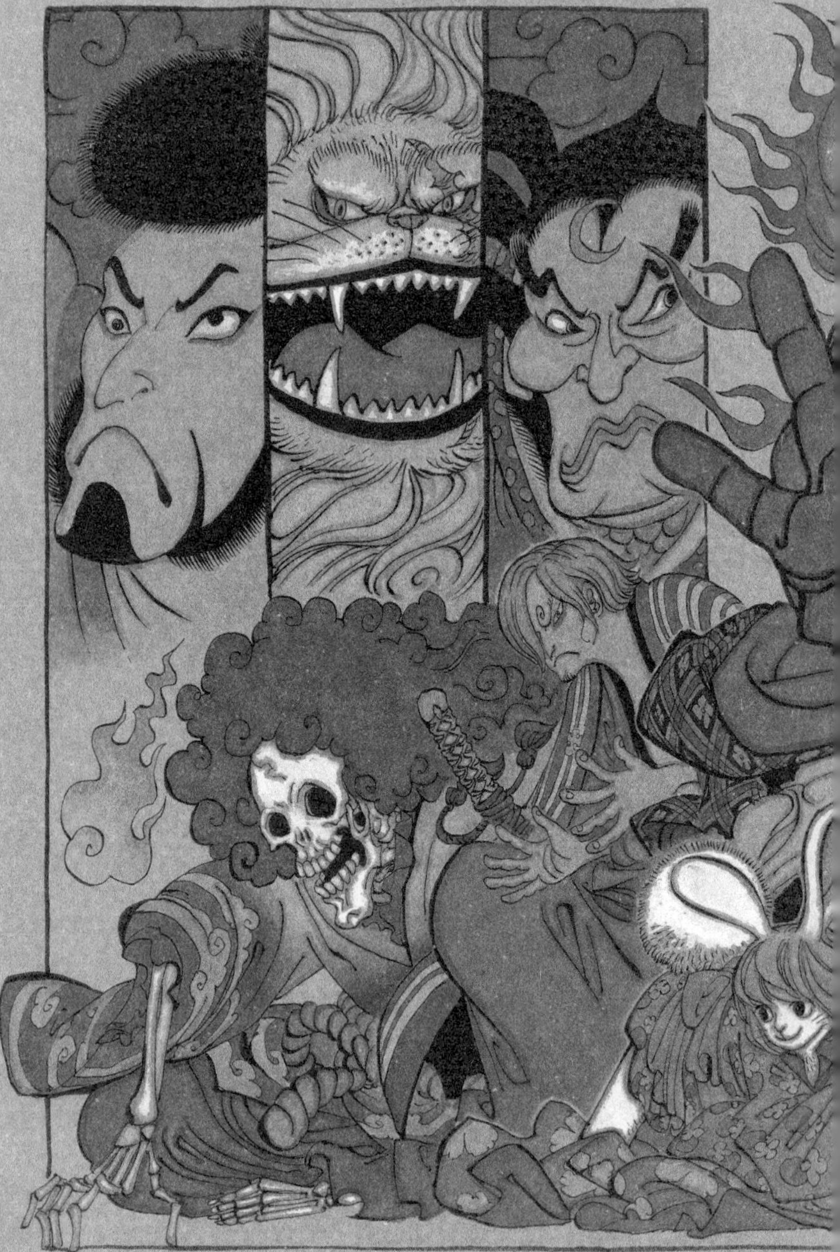

vol.82
ONE PIECE

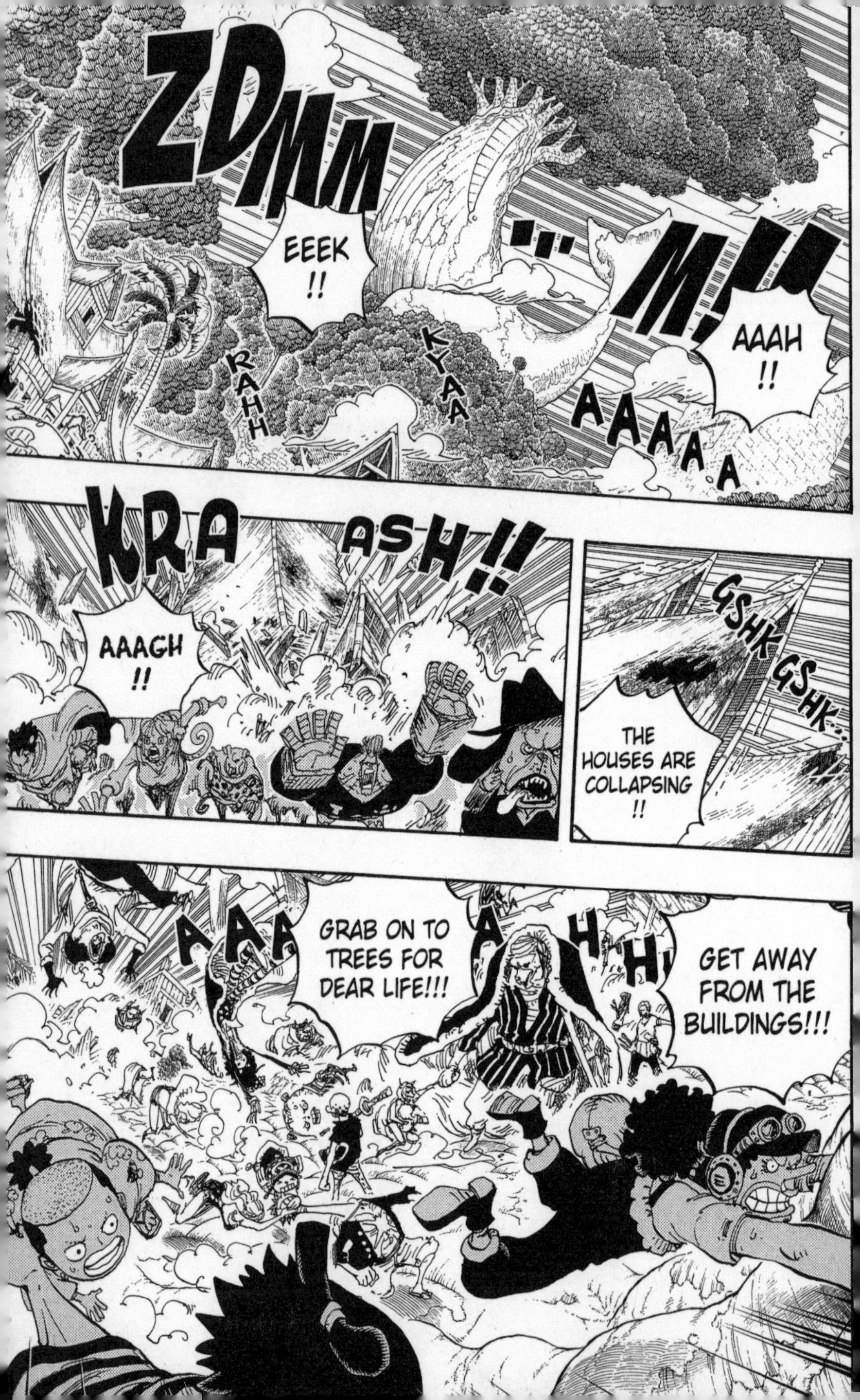
ZDMM...M!!
AAAH !!
AAAAAA
KYAA
EEEK !!
RAHH
GSHK GSHK...
THE HOUSES ARE COLLAPSING !!
KRAASH!!
AAAGH !!
GET AWAY FROM THE BUILDINGS!!!
AAAAHH
GRAB ON TO TREES FOR DEAR LIFE!!!

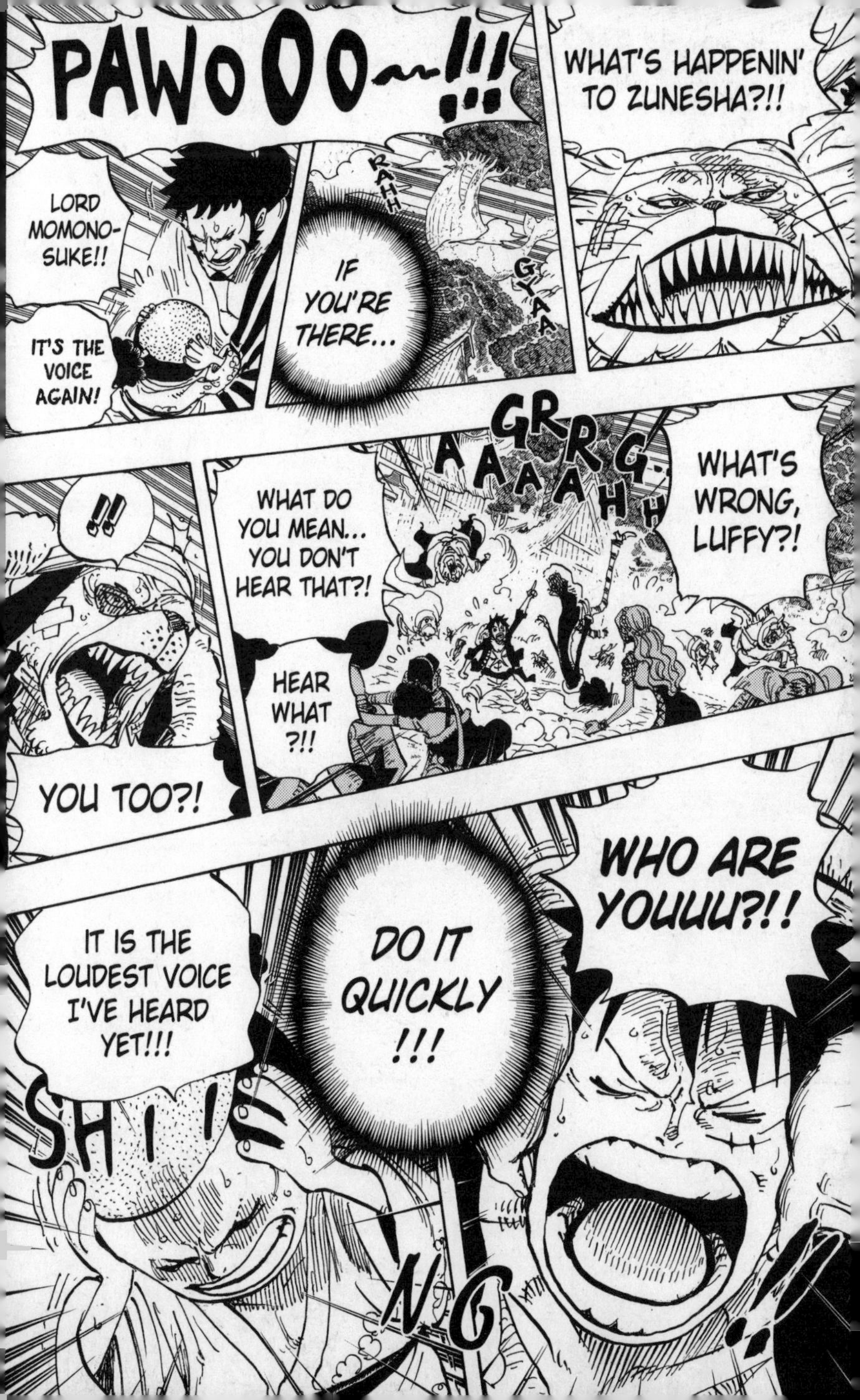
WHAT'S HAPPENIN' TO ZUNESHA?!!
PAWOOOO~~!!!!!
RAHH
GYAA
IF YOU'RE THERE...
LORD MOMONOSUKE!!
IT'S THE VOICE AGAIN!
GRRRG- AAAAAHHH
WHAT'S WRONG, LUFFY?!
WHAT DO YOU MEAN... YOU DON'T HEAR THAT?!
HEAR WHAT?!!
!!
YOU TOO?!
WHO ARE YOUUU?!!
DO IT QUICKLY!!!
IT IS THE LOUDEST VOICE I'VE HEARD YET!!!
SHING

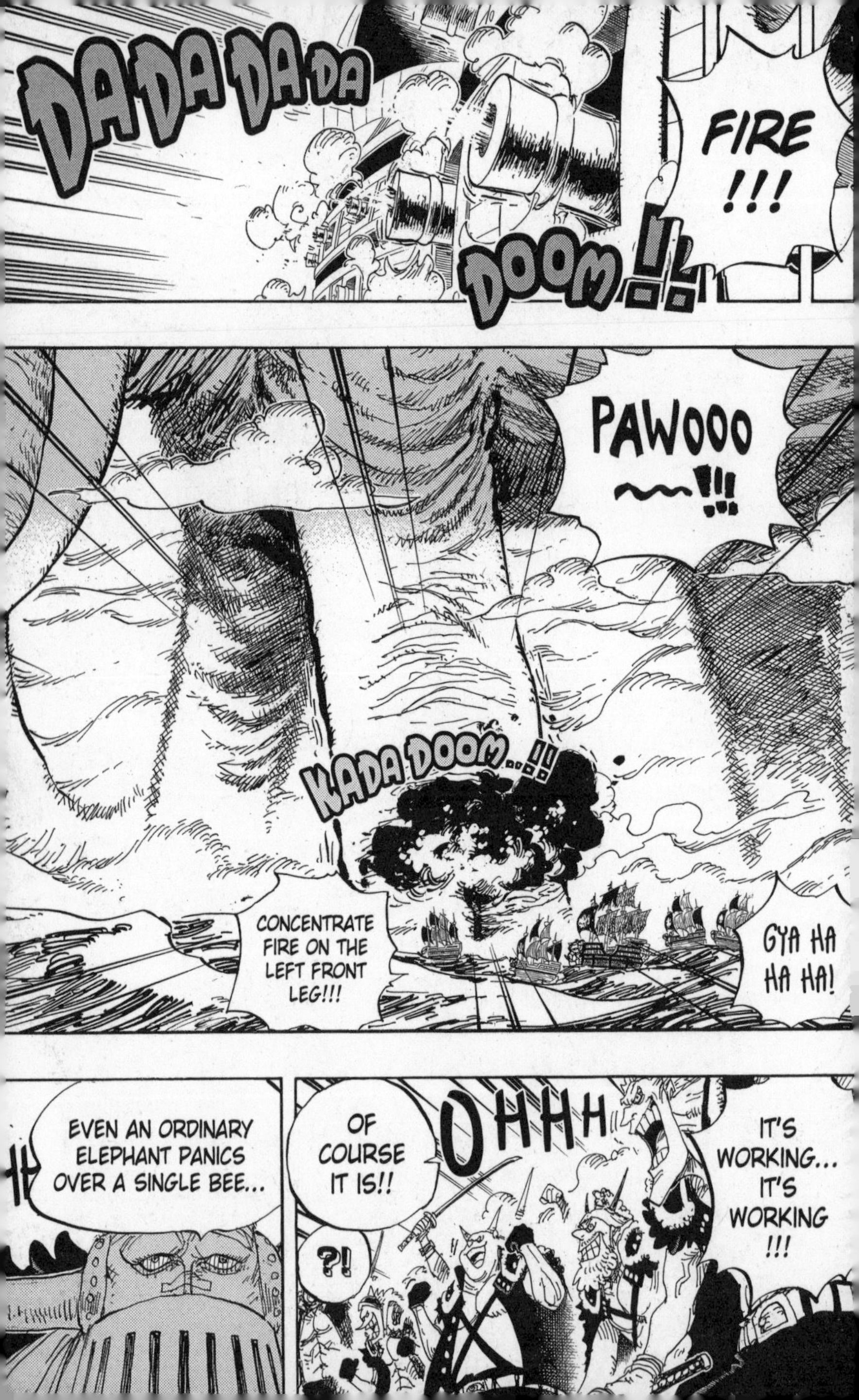
FIRE!!!
DOOM!!!
DA DA DA DA
PAWOOO~!!!
KADA DOOM...!!
GYA HA HA HA!
CONCENTRATE FIRE ON THE LEFT FRONT LEG!!!
IT'S WORKING... IT'S WORKING!!!
OHHH
OF COURSE IT IS!!
?!
EVEN AN ORDINARY ELEPHANT PANICS OVER A SINGLE BEE...

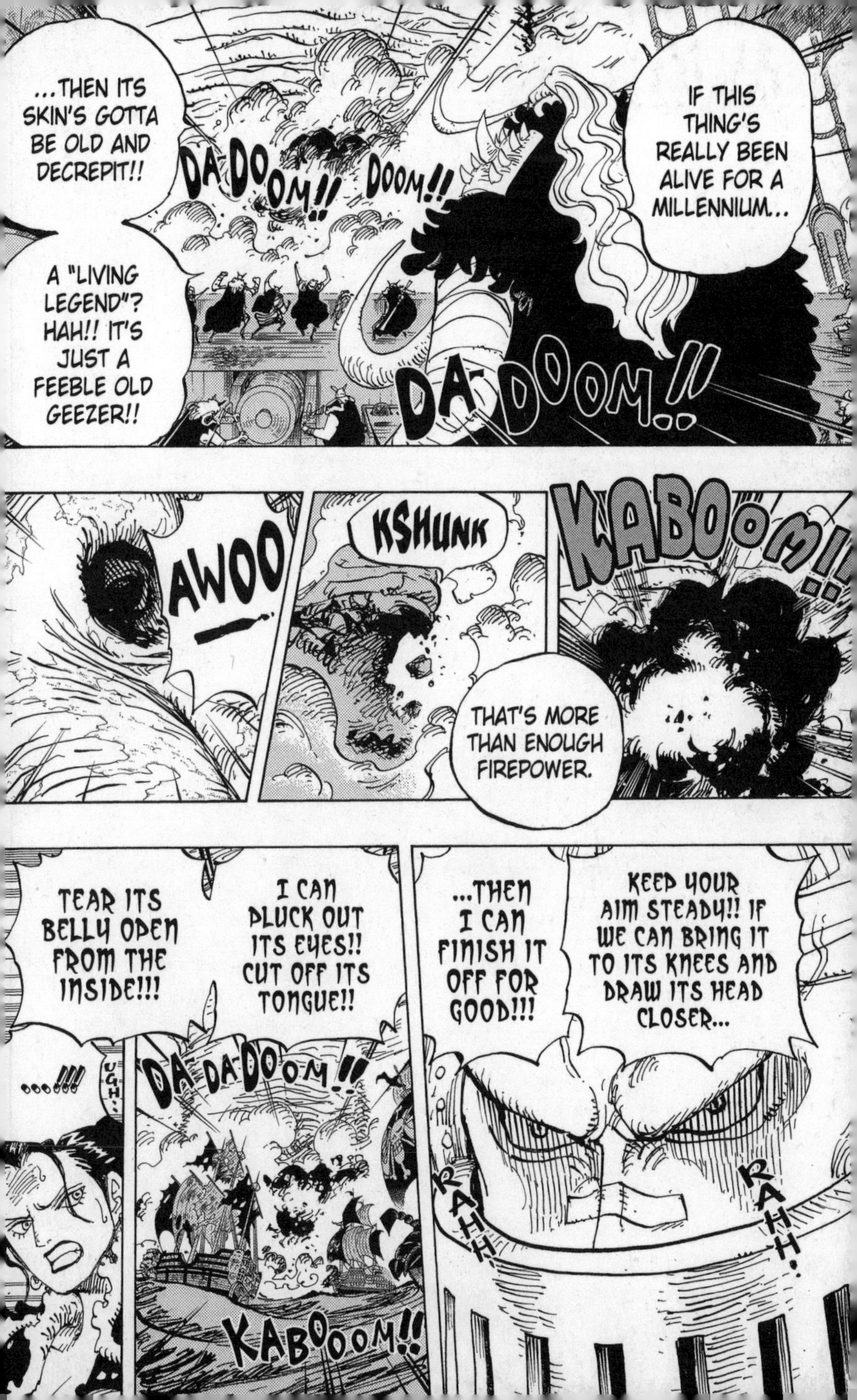
IF THIS THING'S REALLY BEEN ALIVE FOR A MILLENNIUM...
...THEN ITS SKIN'S GOTTA BE OLD AND DECREPIT!!
A "LIVING LEGEND"? HAH!! IT'S JUST A FEEBLE OLD GEEZER!!
DA-DOOM!!
DOOM!!
DA-DOOM!!
KABOOM!!
THAT'S MORE THAN ENOUGH FIREPOWER.
KSHUNK
AWOO—
KEEP YOUR AIM STEADY!! IF WE CAN BRING IT TO ITS KNEES AND DRAW ITS HEAD CLOSER...
...THEN I CAN FINISH IT OFF FOR GOOD!!!
RAHH
RAHH
I CAN PLUCK OUT ITS EYES!! CUT OFF ITS TONGUE!!
TEAR ITS BELLY OPEN FROM THE INSIDE!!!
DA-DA-DOOM!!
KABOOM!!
...!!!
UGH..

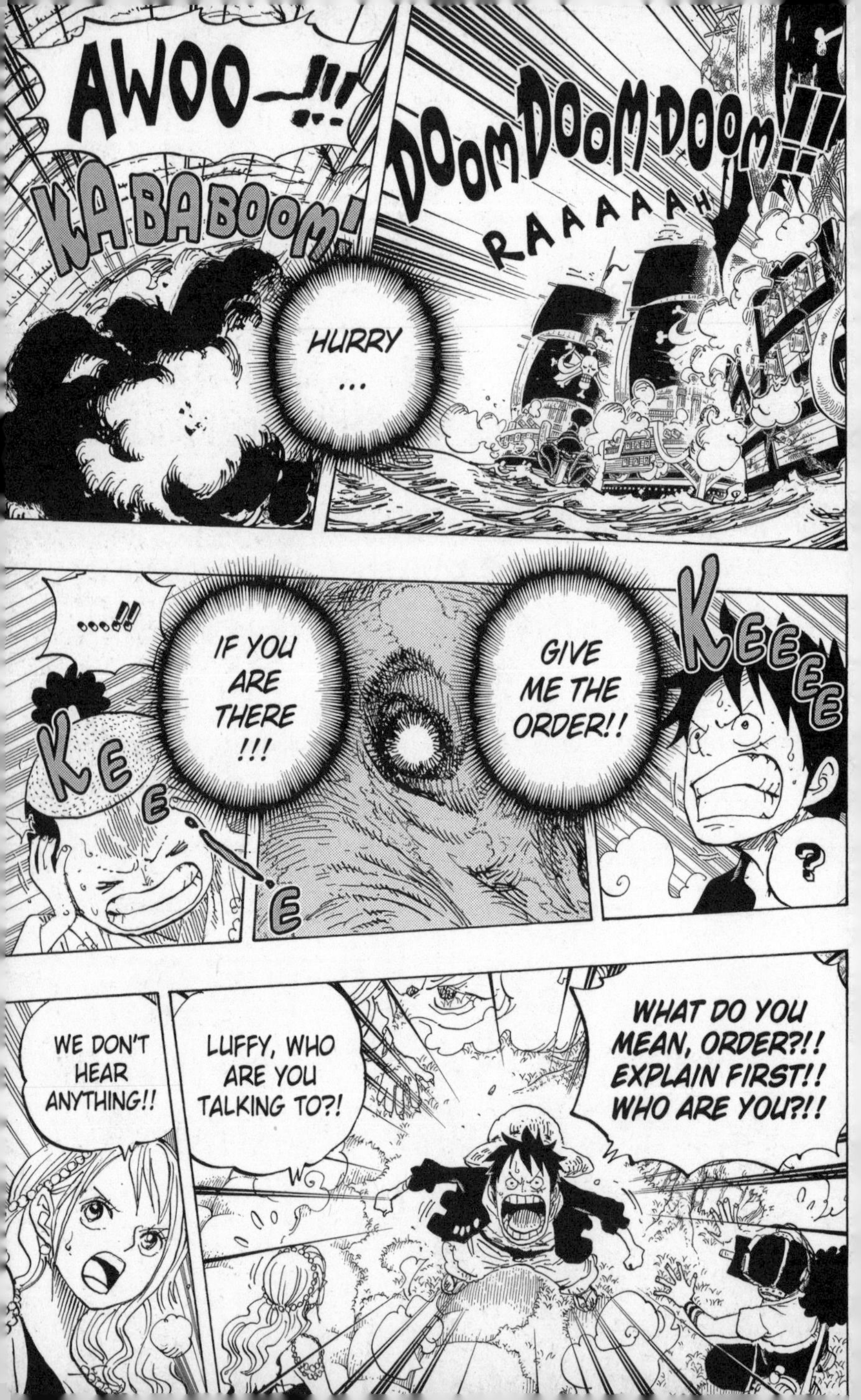
DOOM DOOM DOOM!!
RAAAAAH
HURRY...
AWOO—!!!
KABABOOM!
KEEEEE
GIVE ME THE ORDER!!
?
IF YOU ARE THERE!!!
...!!
KEEEE
WHAT DO YOU MEAN, ORDER?!! EXPLAIN FIRST!! WHO ARE YOU?!!
LUFFY, WHO ARE YOU TALKING TO?!
WE DON'T HEAR ANYTHING!!

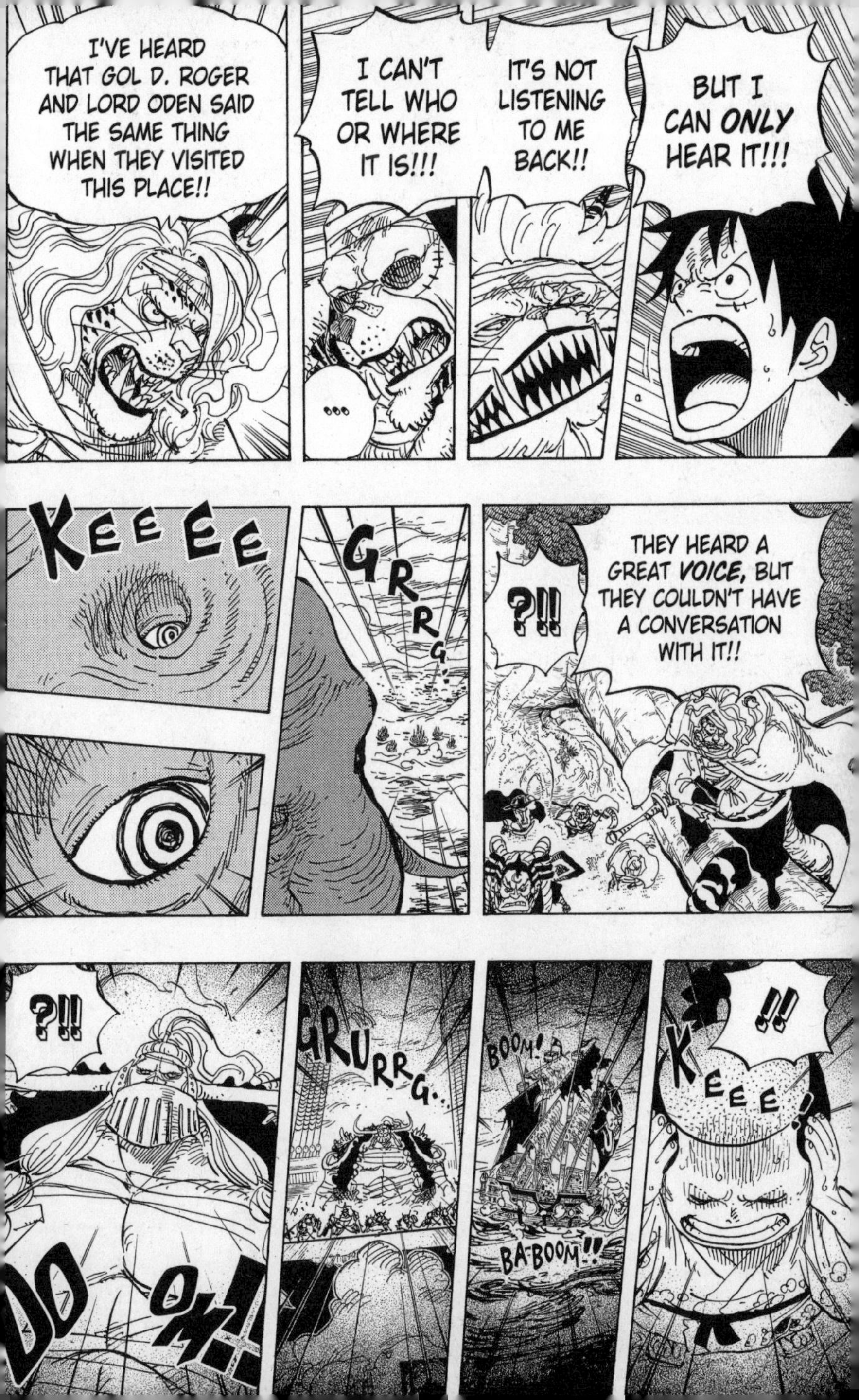

BUT I CAN ONLY HEAR IT!!!
IT'S NOT LISTENING TO ME BACK!!
I CAN'T TELL WHO OR WHERE IT IS!!!
...
I'VE HEARD THAT GOL D. ROGER AND LORD ODEN SAID THE SAME THING WHEN THEY VISITED THIS PLACE!!
THEY HEARD A GREAT VOICE, BUT THEY COULDN'T HAVE A CONVERSATION WITH IT!!
?!!
GRRRG..
KEEEE
!!
KEEE
BOOM!
BA-BOOM!!
GRURRRG..
?!!
DOOM!!

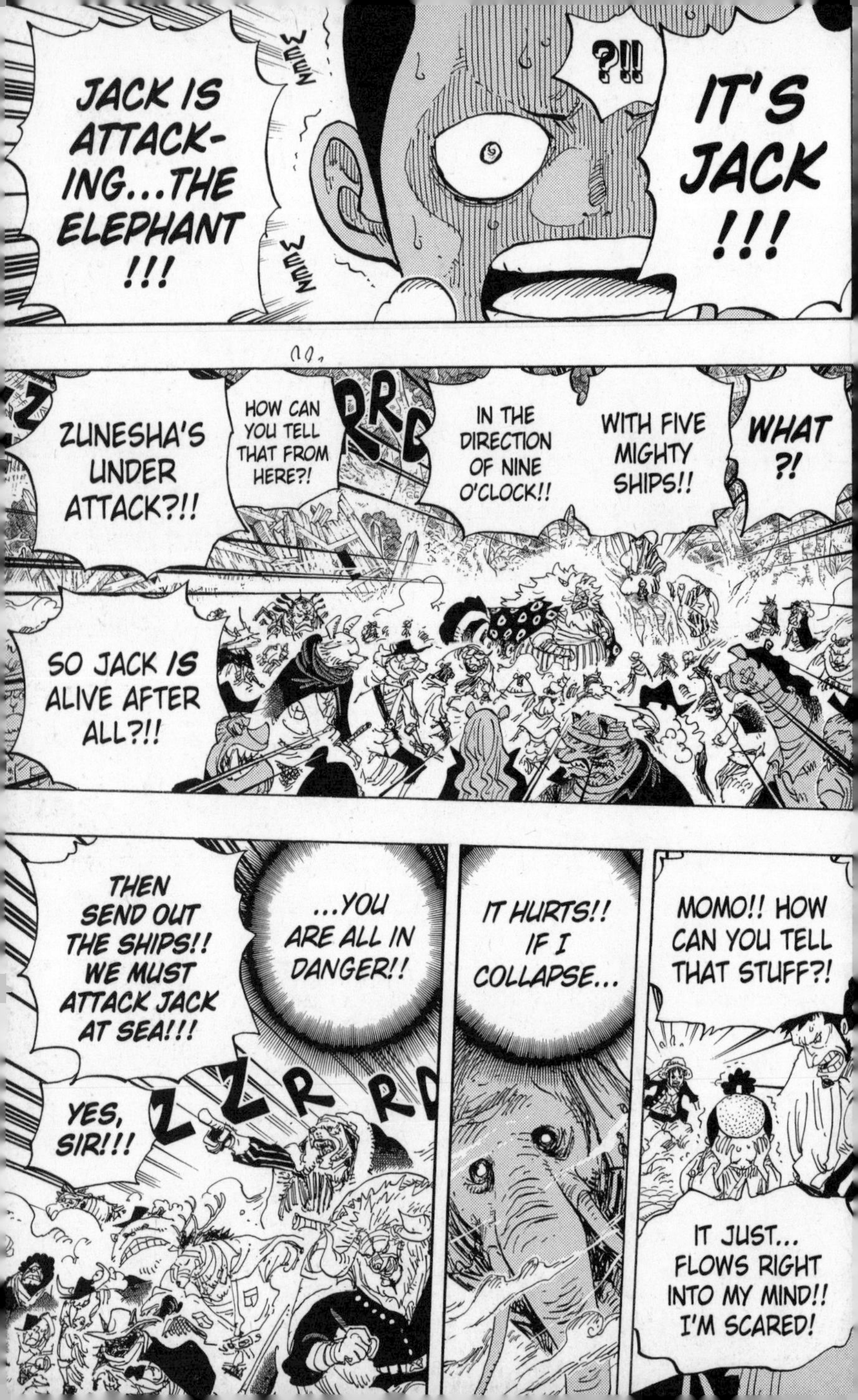
IT'S JACK!!!
?!!
JACK IS ATTACKING...THE ELEPHANT!!!
WEEN
WEEN
WHAT?!
WITH FIVE MIGHTY SHIPS!!
IN THE DIRECTION OF NINE O'CLOCK!!
HOW CAN YOU TELL THAT FROM HERE?!
ZUNESHA'S UNDER ATTACK?!!
SO JACK IS ALIVE AFTER ALL?!!
MOMO!! HOW CAN YOU TELL THAT STUFF?!
IT JUST... FLOWS RIGHT INTO MY MIND!! I'M SCARED!
IT HURTS!! IF I COLLAPSE...
...YOU ARE ALL IN DANGER!!
THEN SEND OUT THE SHIPS!! WE MUST ATTACK JACK AT SEA!!!
YES, SIR!!!

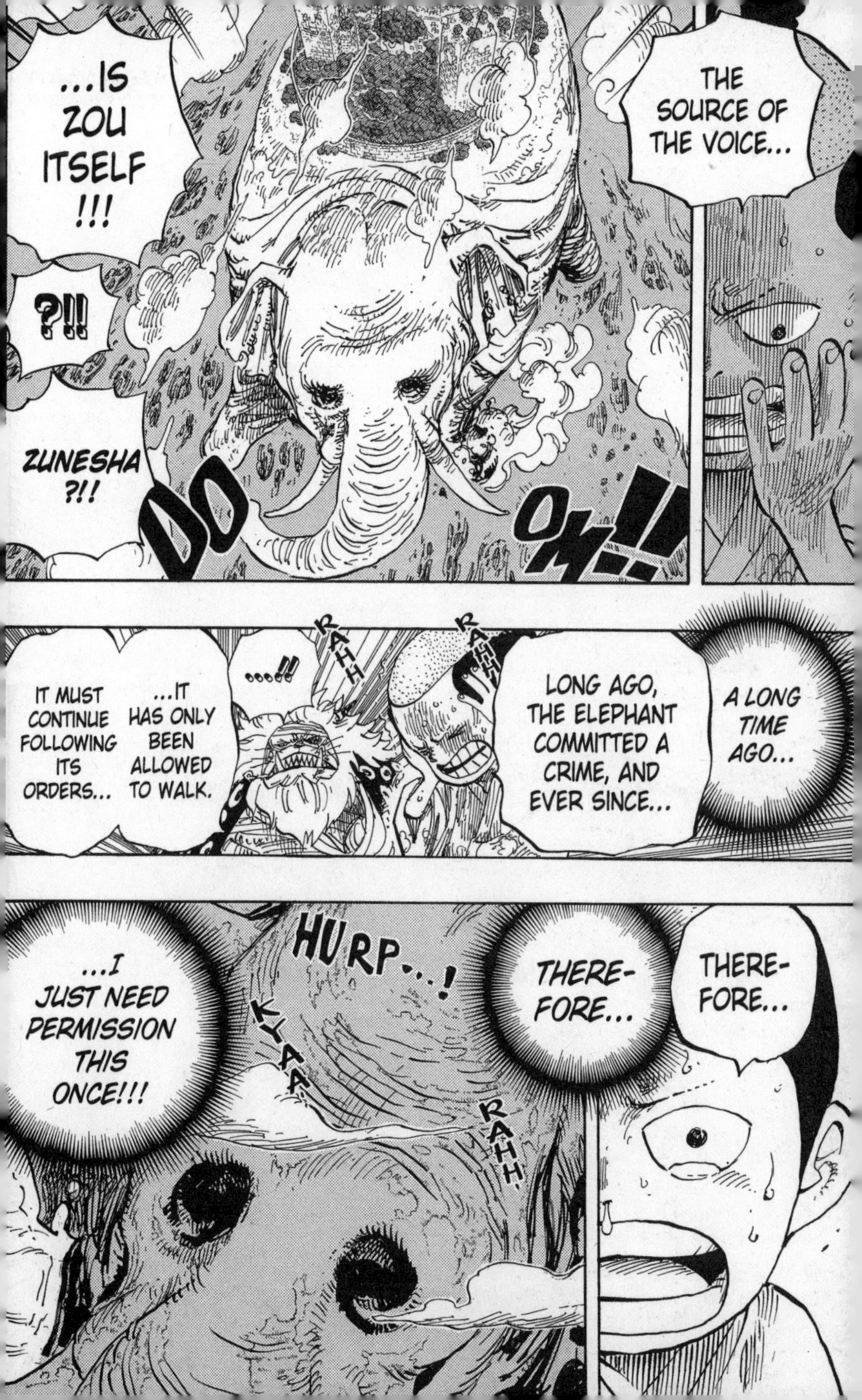
THE SOURCE OF THE VOICE...
...IS ZOU ITSELF!!!
?!!
ZUNESHA?!!
DO
OM!!
A LONG TIME AGO...
LONG AGO, THE ELEPHANT COMMITTED A CRIME, AND EVER SINCE...
RAHH
RAHH
...!!
...IT HAS ONLY BEEN ALLOWED TO WALK.
IT MUST CONTINUE FOLLOWING ITS ORDERS...
THERE-FORE...
THERE-FORE...
HURP...!
KYAA
RAHH
...I JUST NEED PERMISSION THIS ONCE!!!

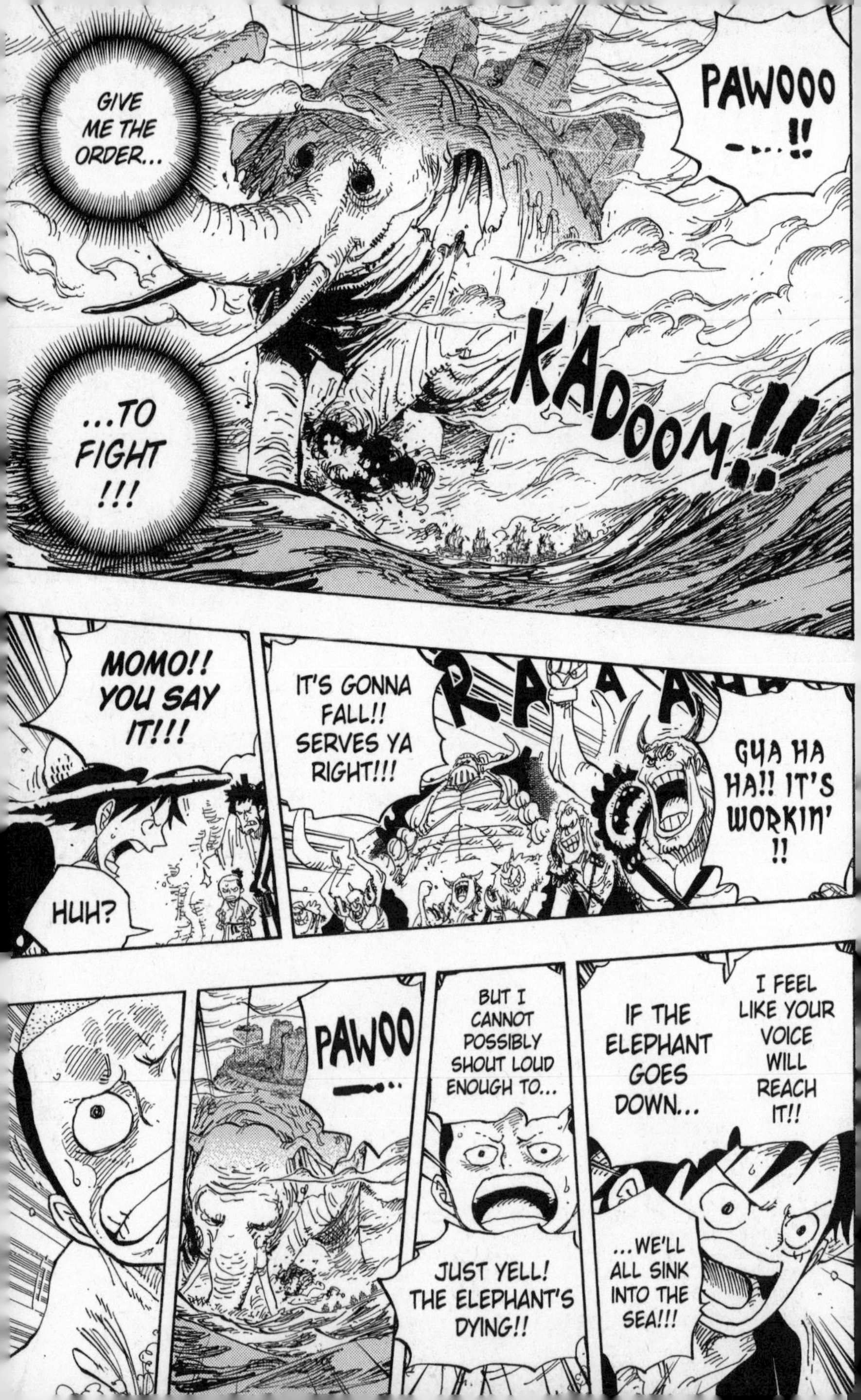
PAWOOO—!!
GIVE ME THE ORDER...
KADOOM!!
...TO FIGHT!!!
RAAA
GUA HA HA!! IT'S WORKIN' !!
IT'S GONNA FALL!! SERVES YA RIGHT!!!
MOMO!! YOU SAY IT!!!
HUH?
I FEEL LIKE YOUR VOICE WILL REACH IT!!
IF THE ELEPHANT GOES DOWN...
...WE'LL ALL SINK INTO THE SEA!!!
BUT I CANNOT POSSIBLY SHOUT LOUD ENOUGH TO...
JUST YELL! THE ELEPHANT'S DYING!!
PAWOO—...

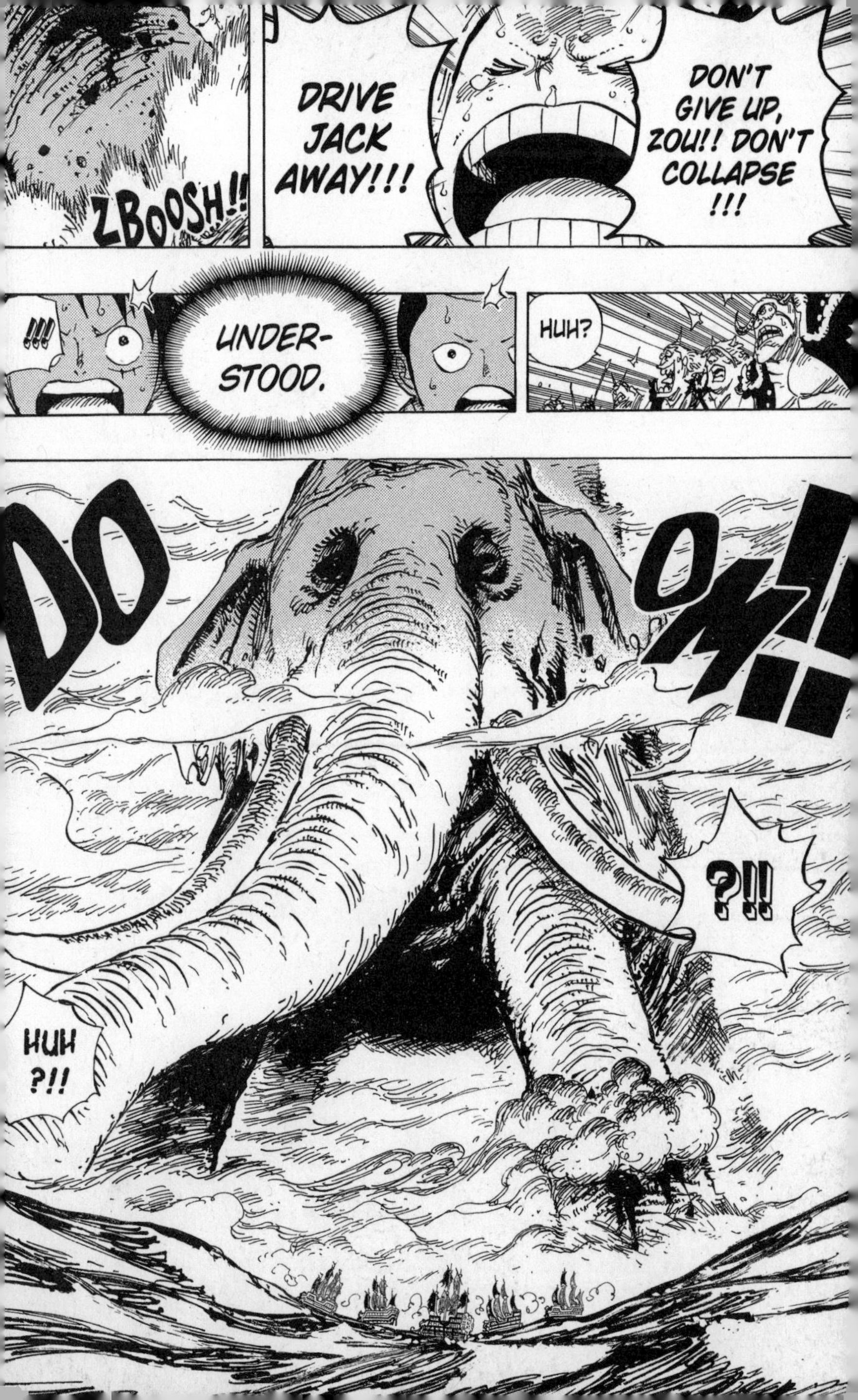
DON'T GIVE UP, ZOU!! DON'T COLLAPSE !!!
DRIVE JACK AWAY!!!
ZBOOSH!!
HUH?
UNDER-STOOD.
!!!
DOOM!!
?!!
HUH ?!!

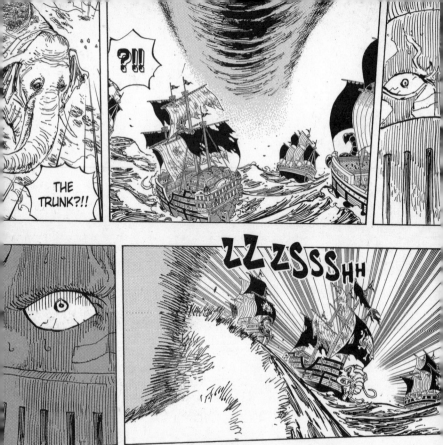

?!!

THE
TRUNK?!!

ZZ ZSSSHH

AAAAAH
!!!

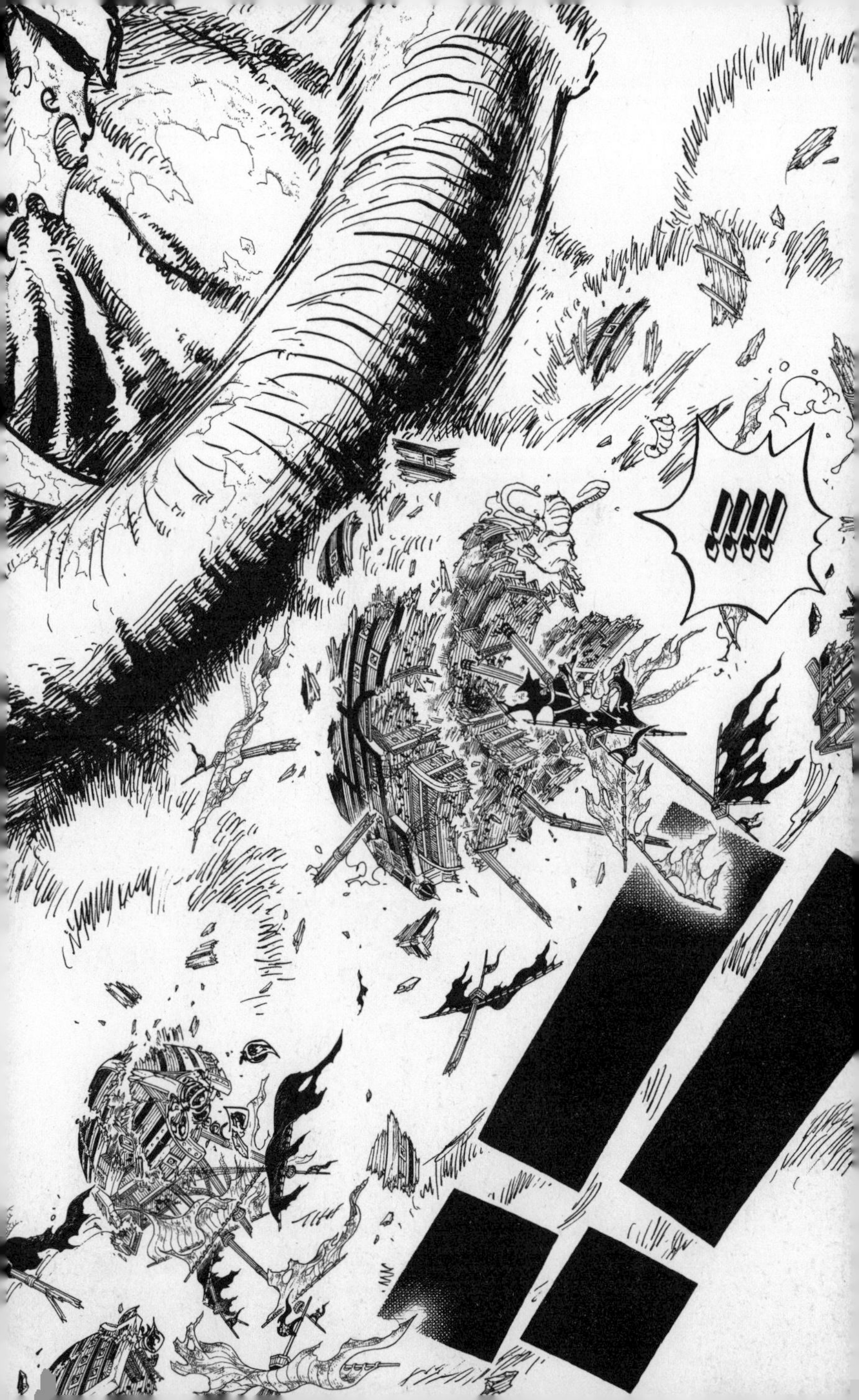
!!!!

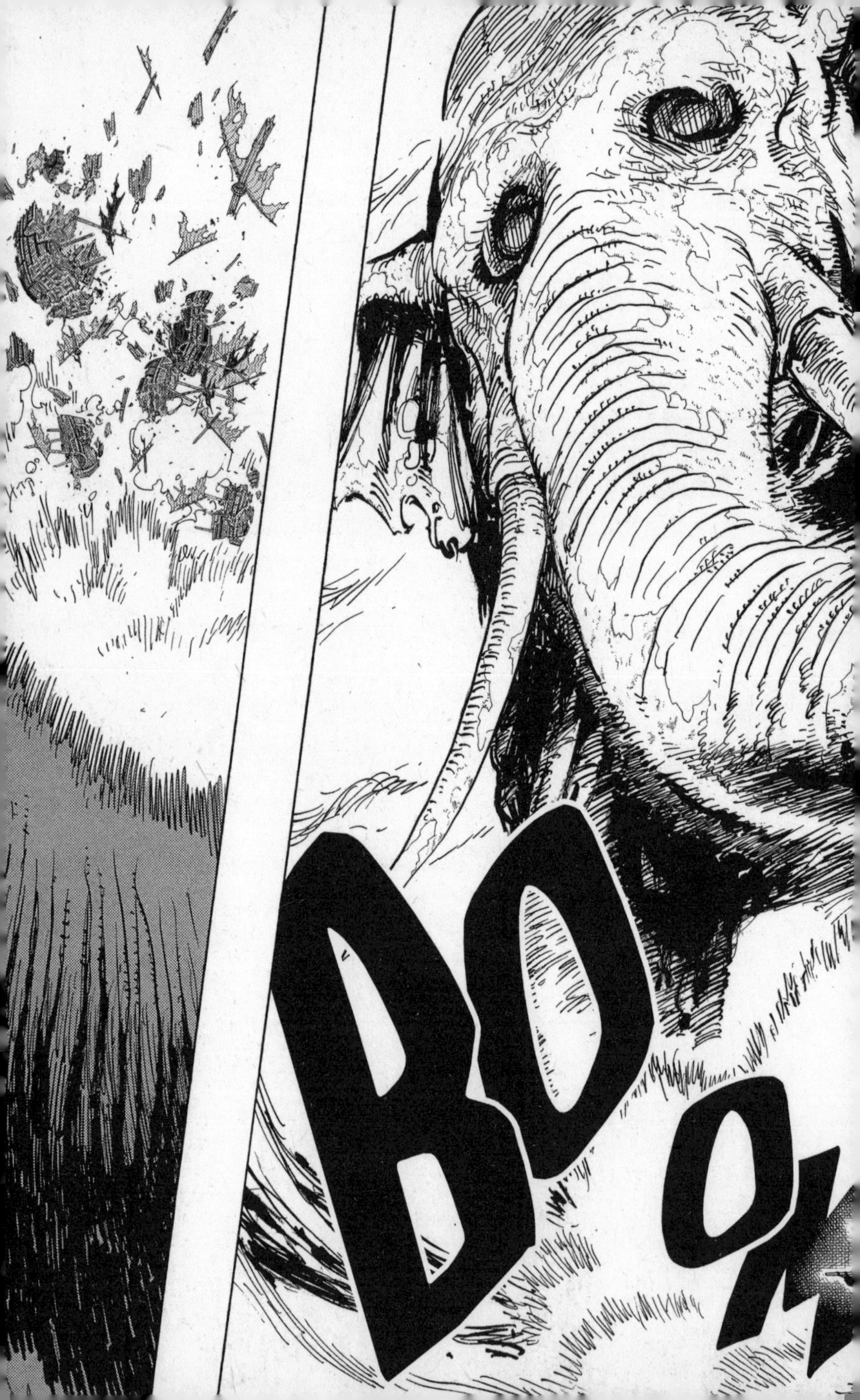
BOOM

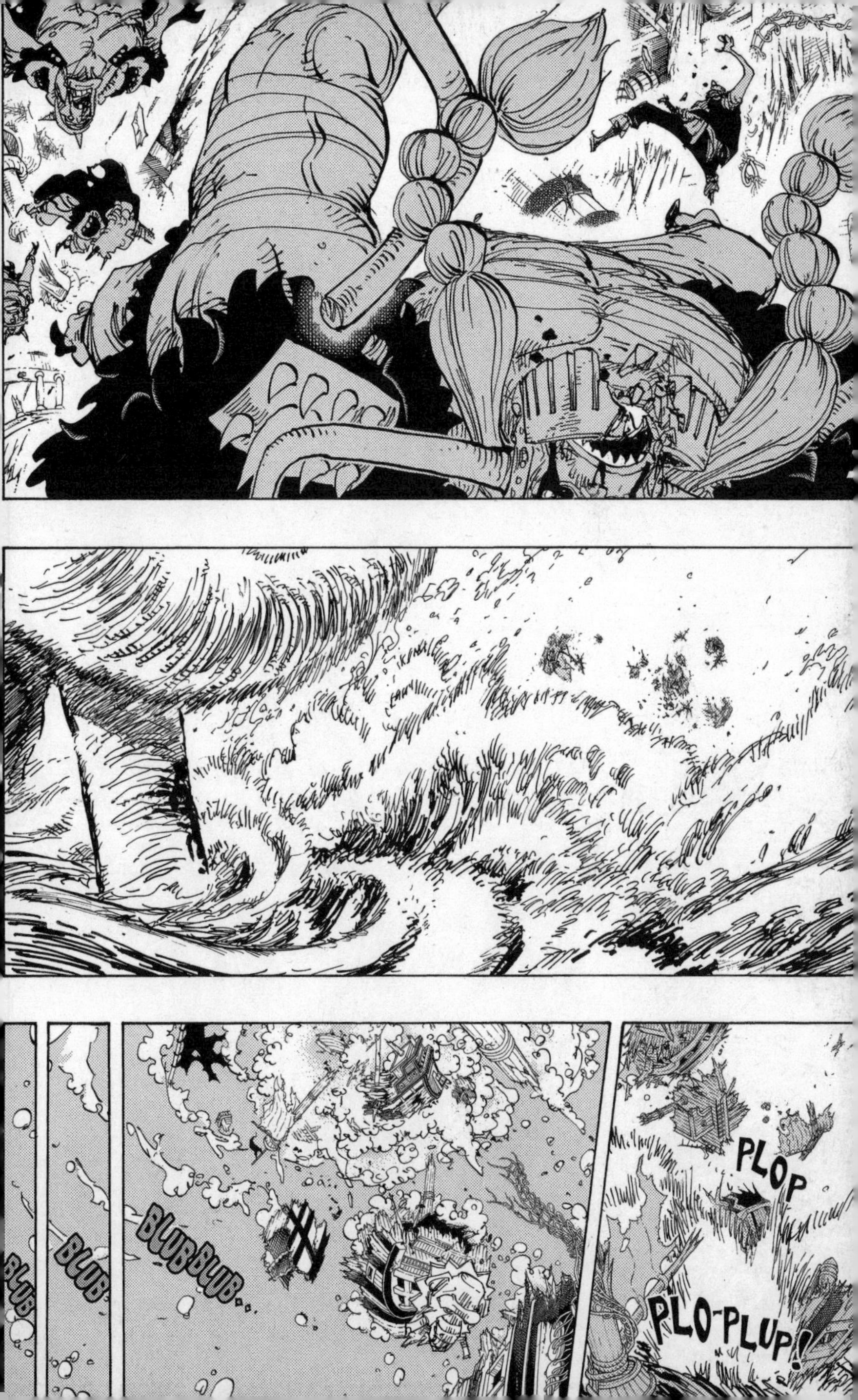
PLOP
PLO-PLUP!
BLUB BLUB...
BLUB
BLUB

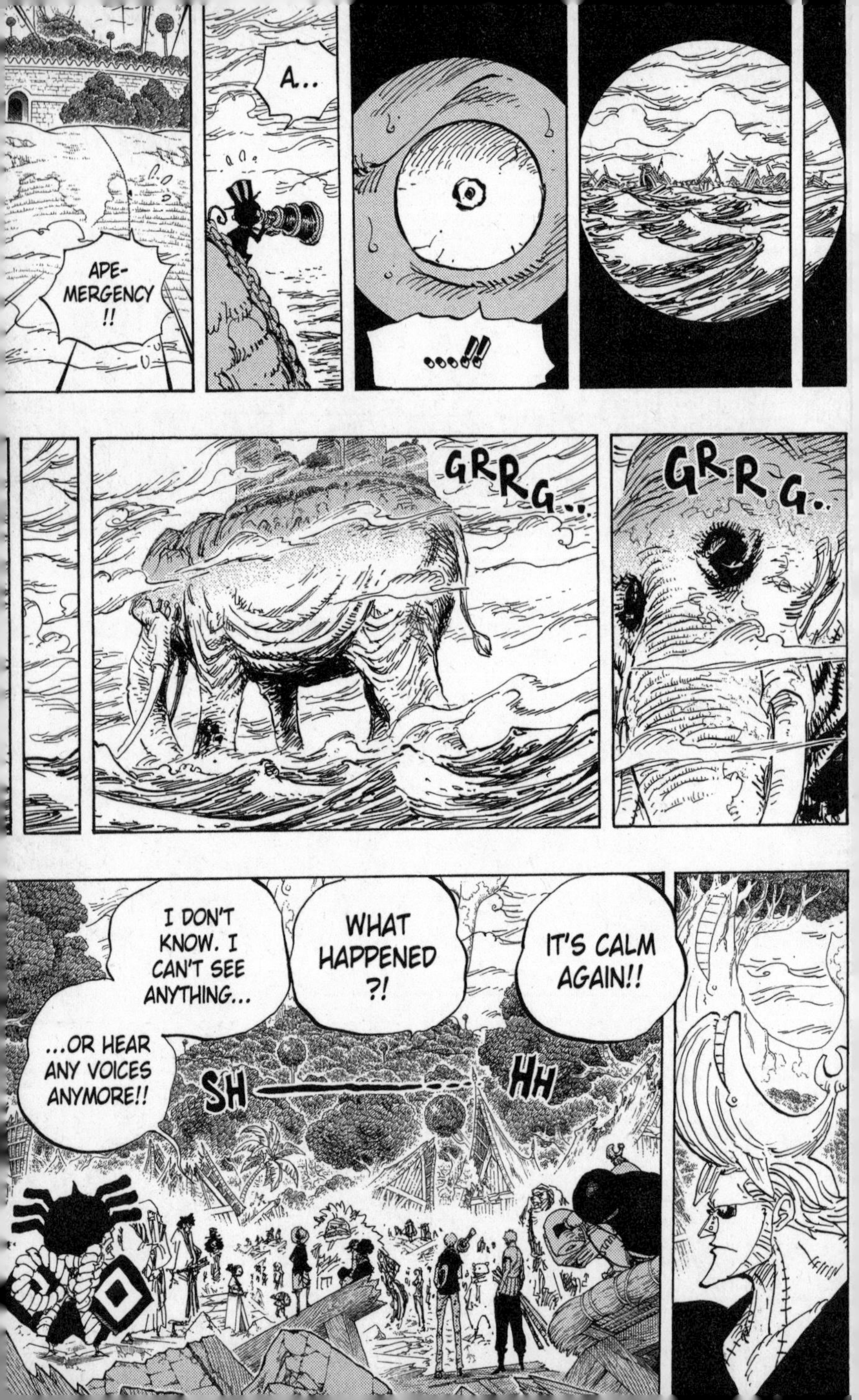
....!!
A...
APE-MERGENCY !!
GRRG..
GRRG..
IT'S CALM AGAIN!!
WHAT HAPPENED ?!
I DON'T KNOW. I CAN'T SEE ANYTHING...
...OR HEAR ANY VOICES ANYMORE!!
SH—HH

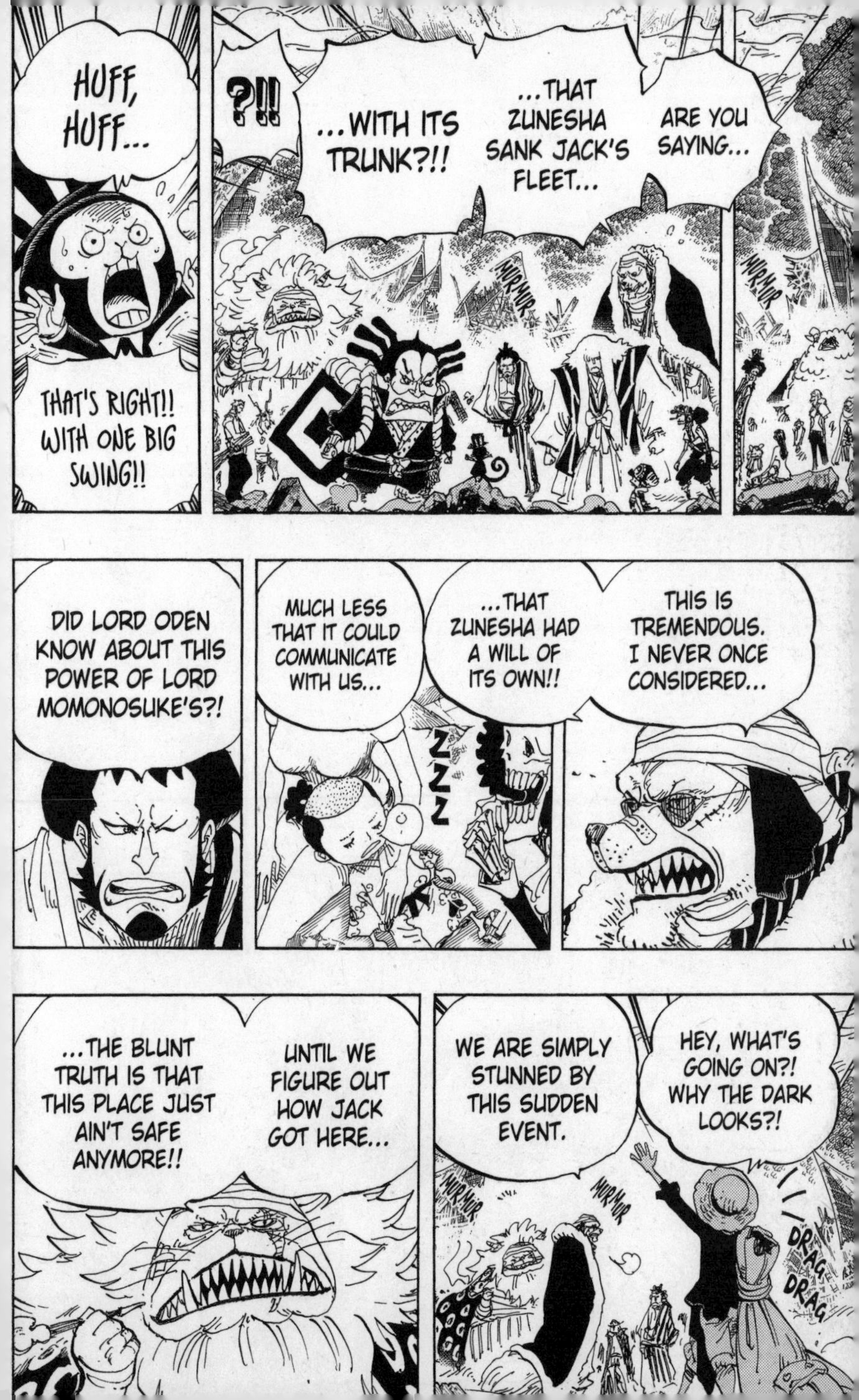
ARE YOU SAYING...
...THAT ZUNESHA SANK JACK'S FLEET...
...WITH ITS TRUNK?!!
?!!
MURMUR
MURMUR
HUFF, HUFF...
THAT'S RIGHT!! WITH ONE BIG SWING!!
THIS IS TREMENDOUS. I NEVER ONCE CONSIDERED...
...THAT ZUNESHA HAD A WILL OF ITS OWN!!
MUCH LESS THAT IT COULD COMMUNICATE WITH US...
ZZZ
DID LORD ODEN KNOW ABOUT THIS POWER OF LORD MOMONOSUKE'S?!
HEY, WHAT'S GOING ON?! WHY THE DARK LOOKS?!
WE ARE SIMPLY STUNNED BY THIS SUDDEN EVENT.
MURMUR
MURMUR
DRAG DRAG
UNTIL WE FIGURE OUT HOW JACK GOT HERE...
...THE BLUNT TRUTH IS THAT THIS PLACE JUST AIN'T SAFE ANYMORE!!

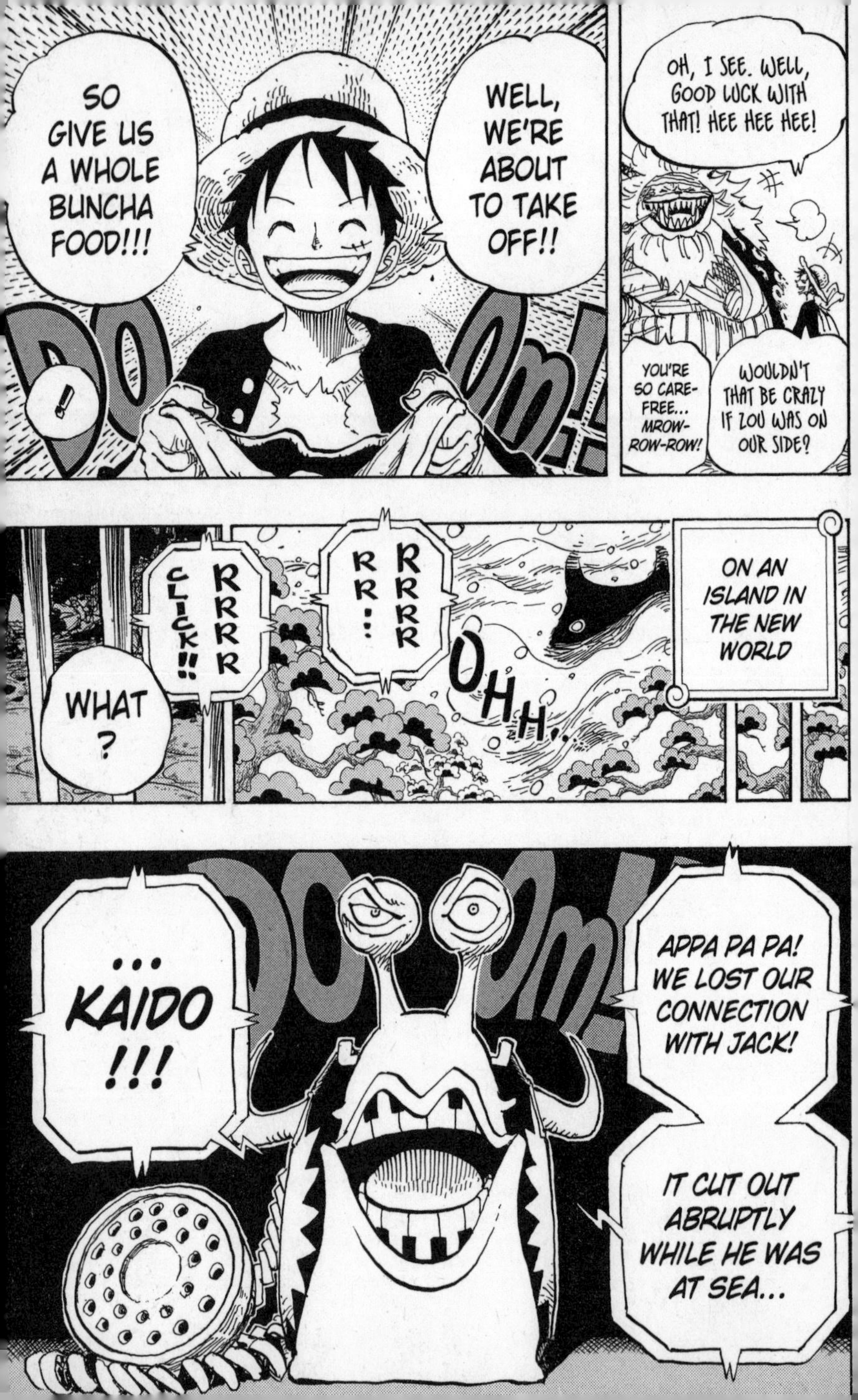
OH, I SEE. WELL, GOOD LUCK WITH THAT! HEE HEE HEE!
WOULDN'T THAT BE CRAZY IF ZOU WAS ON OUR SIDE?
YOU'RE SO CAREFREE... MROW-ROW-ROW!
WELL, WE'RE ABOUT TO TAKE OFF!!
SO GIVE US A WHOLE BUNCHA FOOD!!!
DOOM!!
!
ON AN ISLAND IN THE NEW WORLD
OHH
RRRR RR!!
RRRR CLICK!!
WHAT?
APPA PA PA! WE LOST OUR CONNECTION WITH JACK!
IT CUT OUT ABRUPTLY WHILE HE WAS AT SEA...
DOOM!
...KAIDO!!!

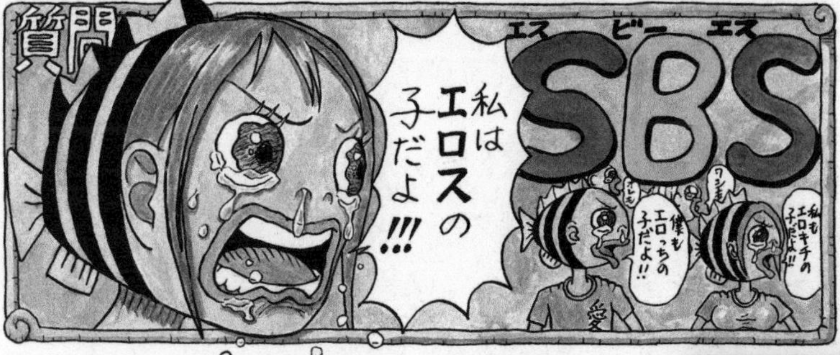
質問
エス ビー エス
SBS
私はエロスの子だよ!!!
私もエロキチの子だよ!!
ワシも
僕もエロっちの子だよ!!
オレも
愛

(Igarashi, Oita)

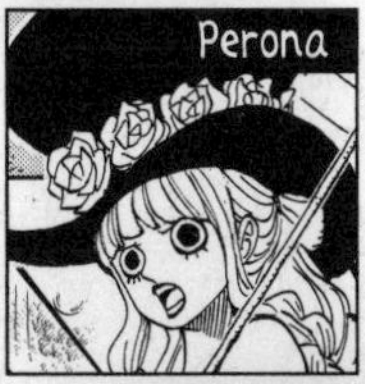
Perona

Q: I have a question for you. I'm currently in a fight with my little sister over Perona's age. Please bring an end to the hostilities. And tell us her height too. Please.

--Cherrypop, Age 12, 6th Grade

A: Perona is currently 25 years old, and she's 5'3" tall. That means she was 23 when the Straw Hats fought her. Moria took her in when she was a child, so she looks up him like a father. She believes that Moria's alive somewhere today, after his disappearance in the Paramount War.

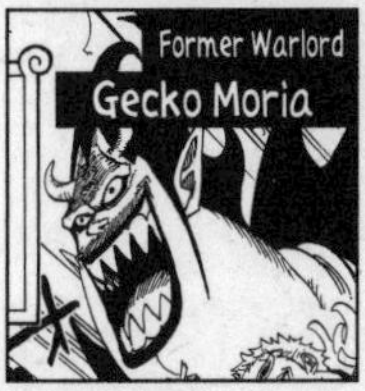
Former Warlord
Gecko Moria

Q: Which is more powerful, King Punch or Happiness Punch?

--Captain Nobuo

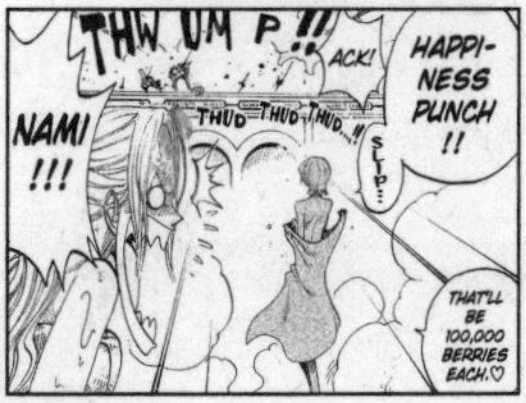
THW UM P !!
HAPPI-NESS PUNCH !!
ACK!
NAMI !!!
THUD THUD THUD
SLIP...
THAT'LL BE 100,000 BERRIES EACH.♡

A: Well, Happiness Punch knocked out Cobra, king of Alabasta, so I doubt Elizabello stands a chance against it.

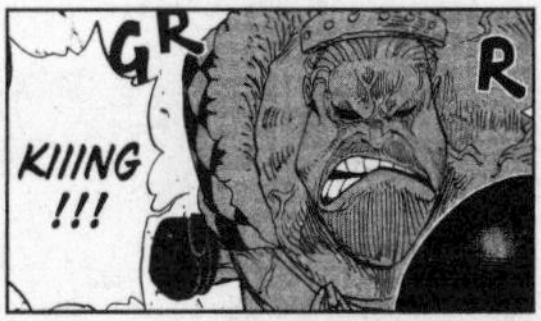
GR
R
KIIING !!!

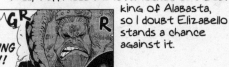

Q: The other day, this funky dude came to my house, claiming to be the missionary of a something-or-other club. He was mighty suspicious, so I called the cops on him at once, but then I wondered...was that Gambia? If so, I feel kind of bad about that.

--The Chimney Lasts Until You Get Home

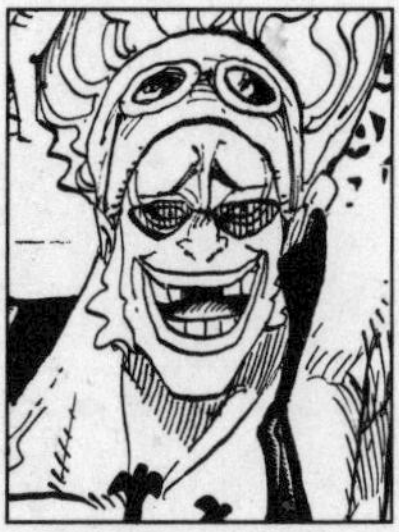

A: That was a close one, actually. Gambia from the Barto Club is a missionary for the religion of "Mister-Luffyanity." He was about to give you a sermon about the miracles created by Mister Luffy and his crew of pirate disciples.

Chapter 822:
DESCENDING THE ELEPHANT

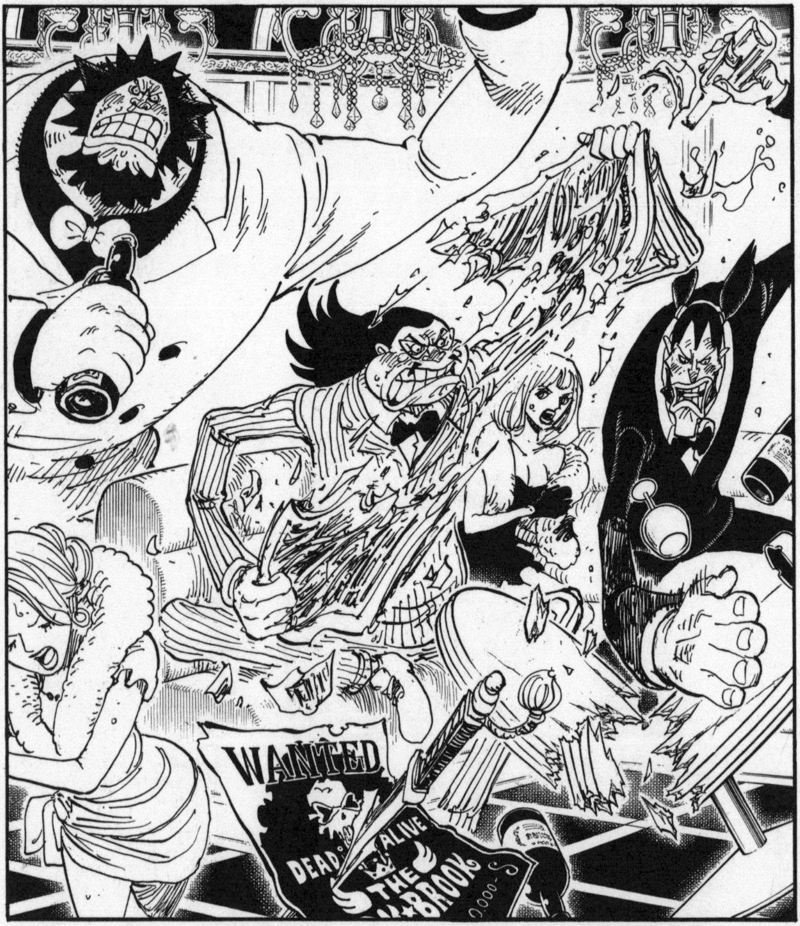
WANTED
DEAD ALIVE
THE BROOK

DECKS OF THE WORLD, 500-MILLION-MAN ARC, VOL. 14:
"SABAODY ARCHIPELAGO--ANGRY MANAGEMENT"

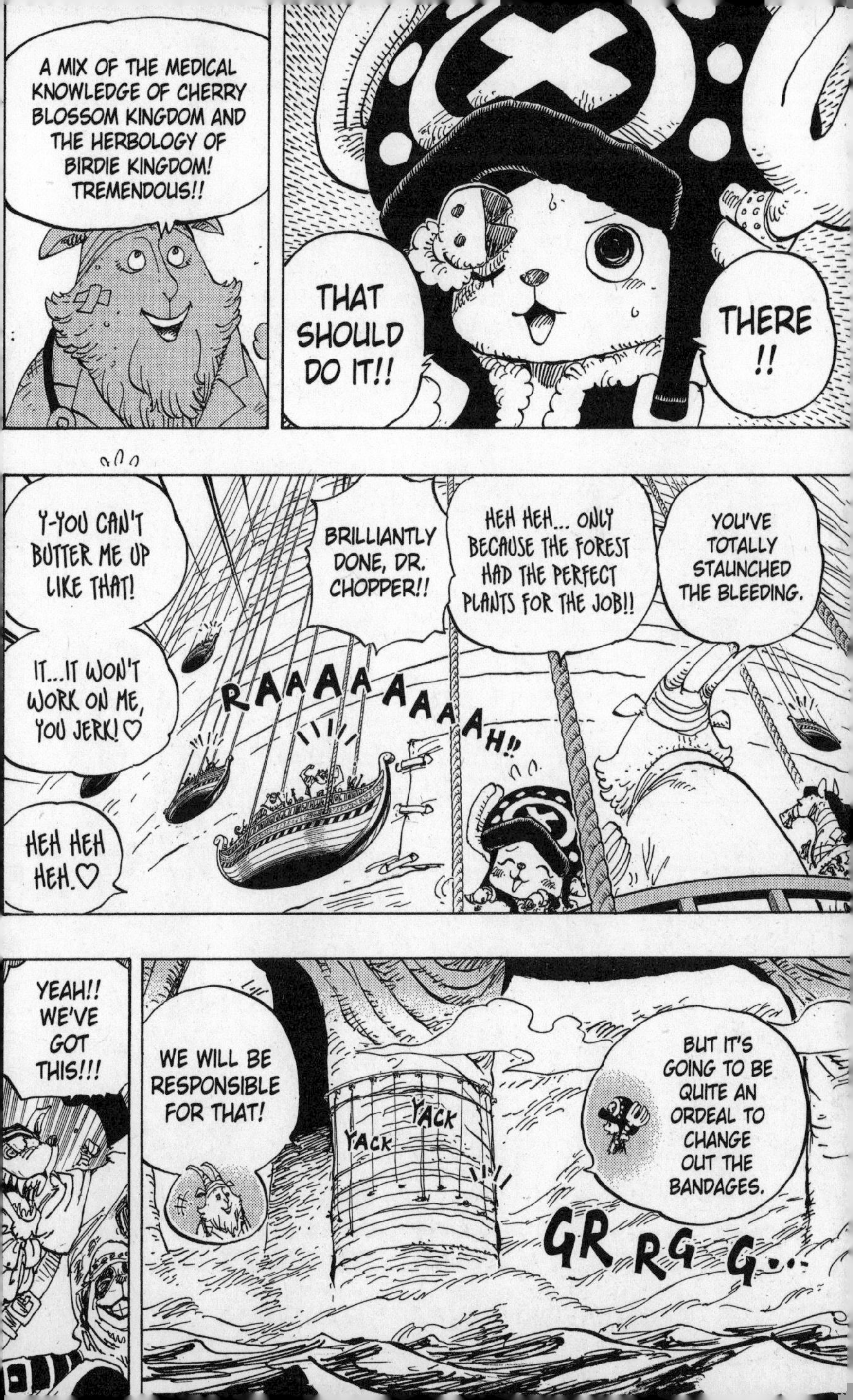
THERE!!
THAT SHOULD DO IT!!
A MIX OF THE MEDICAL KNOWLEDGE OF CHERRY BLOSSOM KINGDOM AND THE HERBOLOGY OF BIRDIE KINGDOM! TREMENDOUS!!
YOU'VE TOTALLY STAUNCHED THE BLEEDING.
HEH HEH... ONLY BECAUSE THE FOREST HAD THE PERFECT PLANTS FOR THE JOB!!
BRILLIANTLY DONE, DR. CHOPPER!!
RAAAAAAAAAH!!
Y-YOU CAN'T BUTTER ME UP LIKE THAT!
IT...IT WON'T WORK ON ME, YOU JERK! ♡
HEH HEH HEH. ♡
BUT IT'S GOING TO BE QUITE AN ORDEAL TO CHANGE OUT THE BANDAGES.
YACK
YACK
GRRGG...
WE WILL BE RESPONSIBLE FOR THAT!
YEAH!! WE'VE GOT THIS!!!

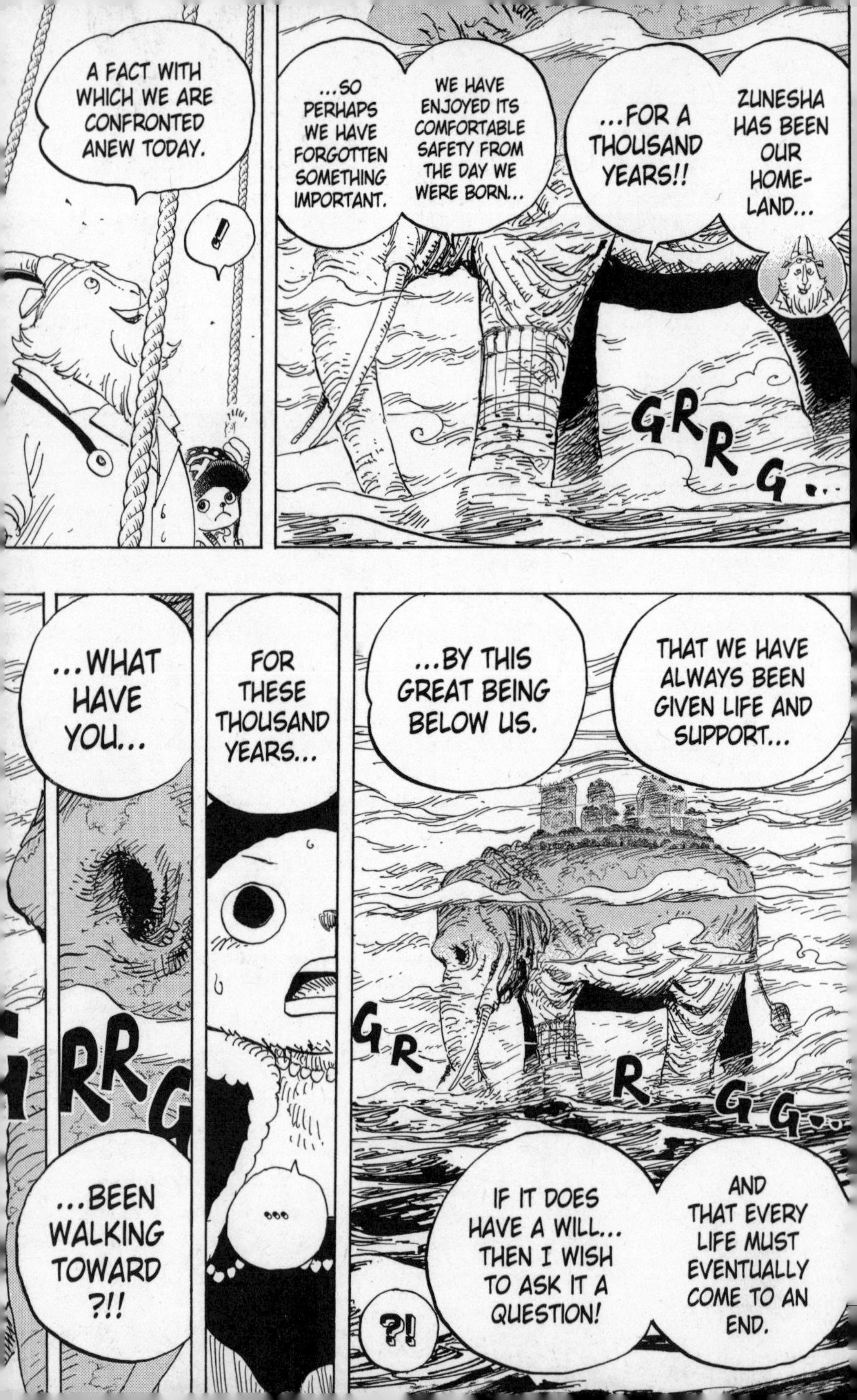
ZUNESHA HAS BEEN OUR HOMELAND...
...FOR A THOUSAND YEARS!!
WE HAVE ENJOYED ITS COMFORTABLE SAFETY FROM THE DAY WE WERE BORN...
...SO PERHAPS WE HAVE FORGOTTEN SOMETHING IMPORTANT.
GRRRG...
A FACT WITH WHICH WE ARE CONFRONTED ANEW TODAY.
!
THAT WE HAVE ALWAYS BEEN GIVEN LIFE AND SUPPORT...
...BY THIS GREAT BEING BELOW US.
GRRGG...
AND THAT EVERY LIFE MUST EVENTUALLY COME TO AN END.
IF IT DOES HAVE A WILL... THEN I WISH TO ASK IT A QUESTION!
?!
FOR THESE THOUSAND YEARS...
...
...WHAT HAVE YOU...
RRG
...BEEN WALKING TOWARD ?!!

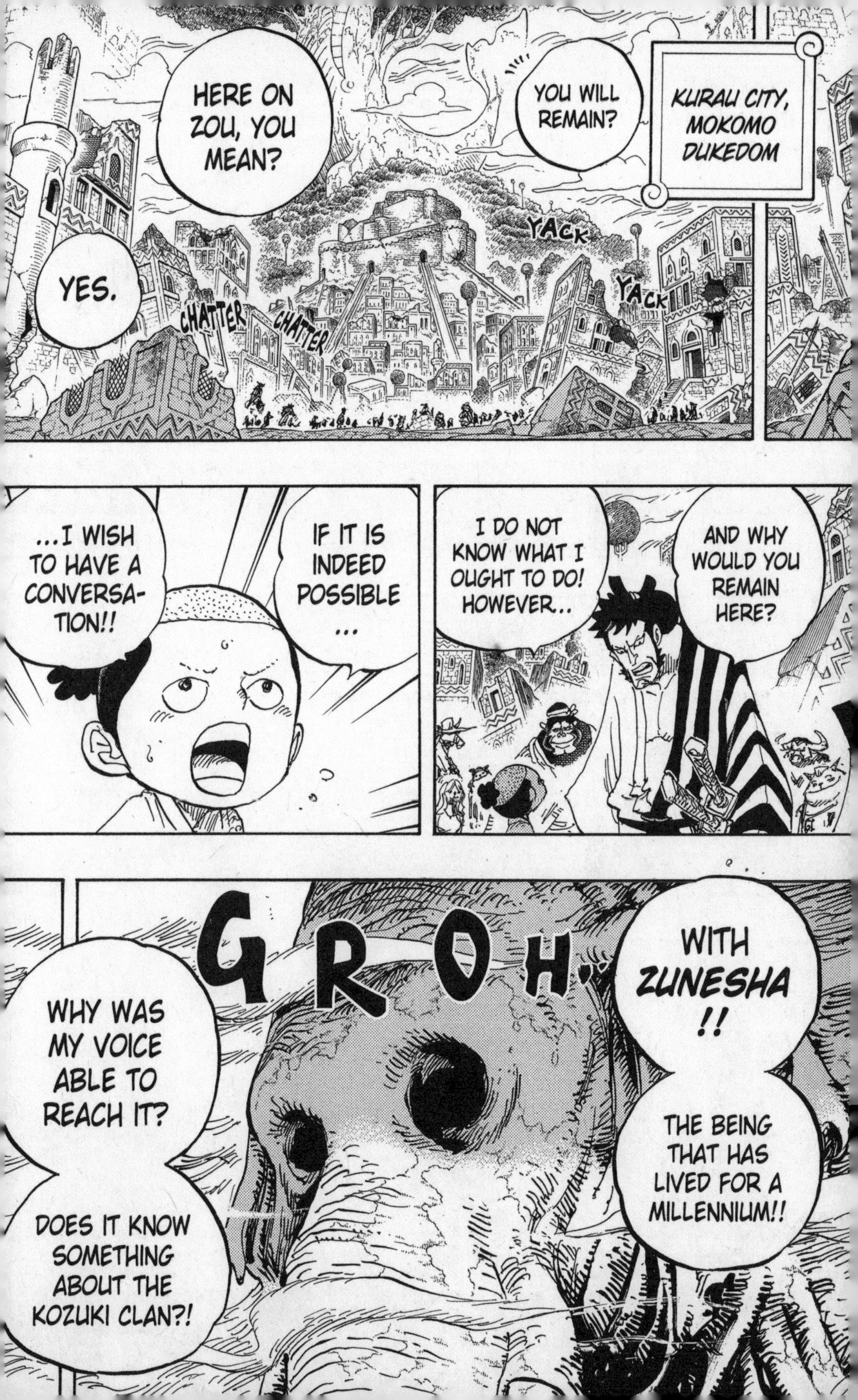
KURAU CITY, MOKOMO DUKEDOM
YOU WILL REMAIN?
HERE ON ZOU, YOU MEAN?
YES.
YACK
YACK
CHATTER
CHATTER
AND WHY WOULD YOU REMAIN HERE?
I DO NOT KNOW WHAT I OUGHT TO DO! HOWEVER...
IF IT IS INDEED POSSIBLE ...
...I WISH TO HAVE A CONVERSATION!!
WITH ZUNESHA !!
THE BEING THAT HAS LIVED FOR A MILLENNIUM!!
GROH..
WHY WAS MY VOICE ABLE TO REACH IT?
DOES IT KNOW SOMETHING ABOUT THE KOZUKI CLAN?!

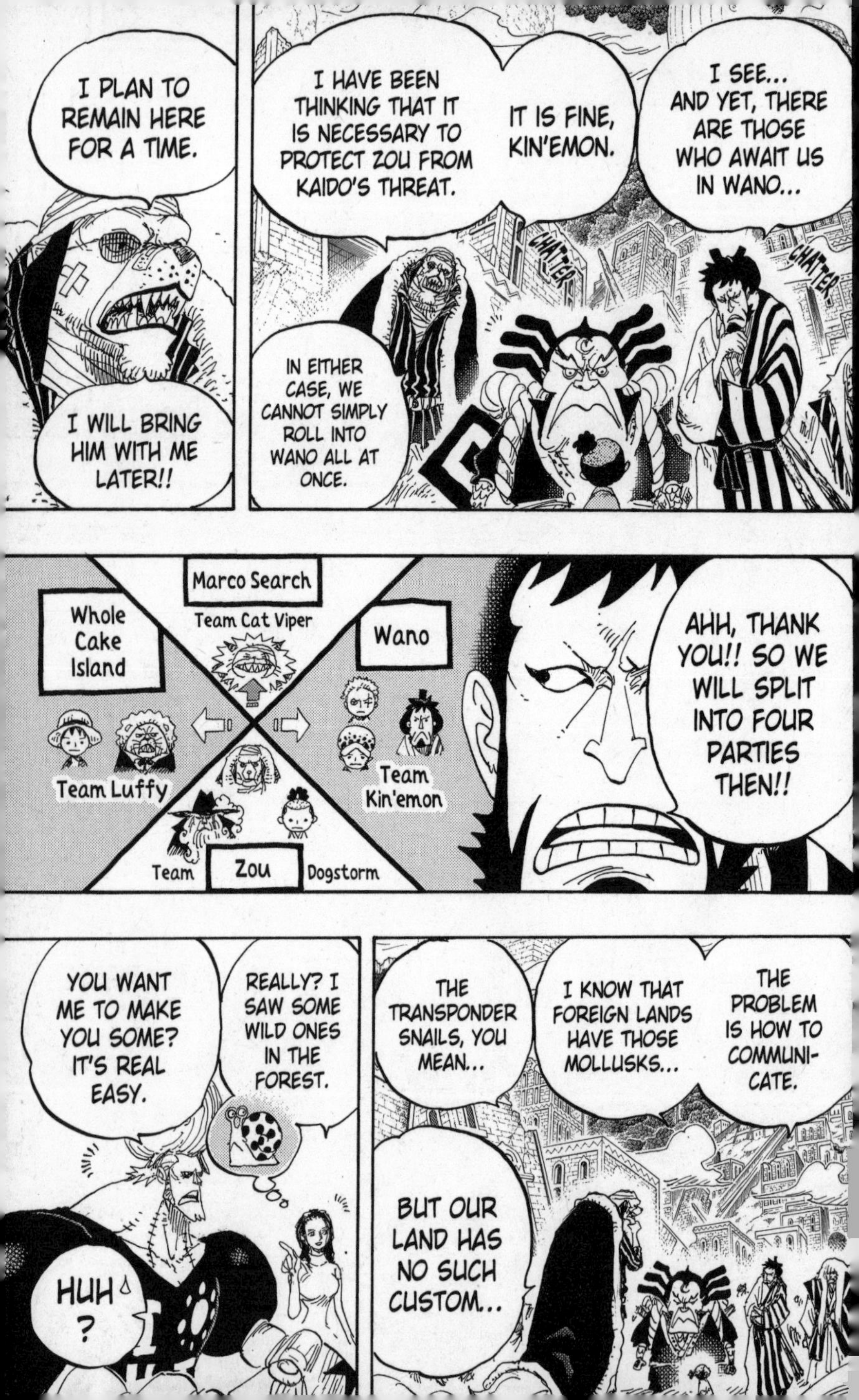
I SEE... AND YET, THERE ARE THOSE WHO AWAIT US IN WANO...
IT IS FINE, KIN'EMON.
I HAVE BEEN THINKING THAT IT IS NECESSARY TO PROTECT ZOU FROM KAIDO'S THREAT.
CHATTER
CHATTER
IN EITHER CASE, WE CANNOT SIMPLY ROLL INTO WANO ALL AT ONCE.
I PLAN TO REMAIN HERE FOR A TIME.
I WILL BRING HIM WITH ME LATER!!
AHH, THANK YOU!! SO WE WILL SPLIT INTO FOUR PARTIES THEN!!
Marco Search
Team Cat Viper
Wano
Team Kin'emon
Whole Cake Island
Team Luffy
Zou
Team Dogstorm
THE PROBLEM IS HOW TO COMMUNICATE.
I KNOW THAT FOREIGN LANDS HAVE THOSE MOLLUSKS...
THE TRANSPONDER SNAILS, YOU MEAN...
BUT OUR LAND HAS NO SUCH CUSTOM...
REALLY? I SAW SOME WILD ONES IN THE FOREST.
YOU WANT ME TO MAKE YOU SOME? IT'S REAL EASY.
HUH?

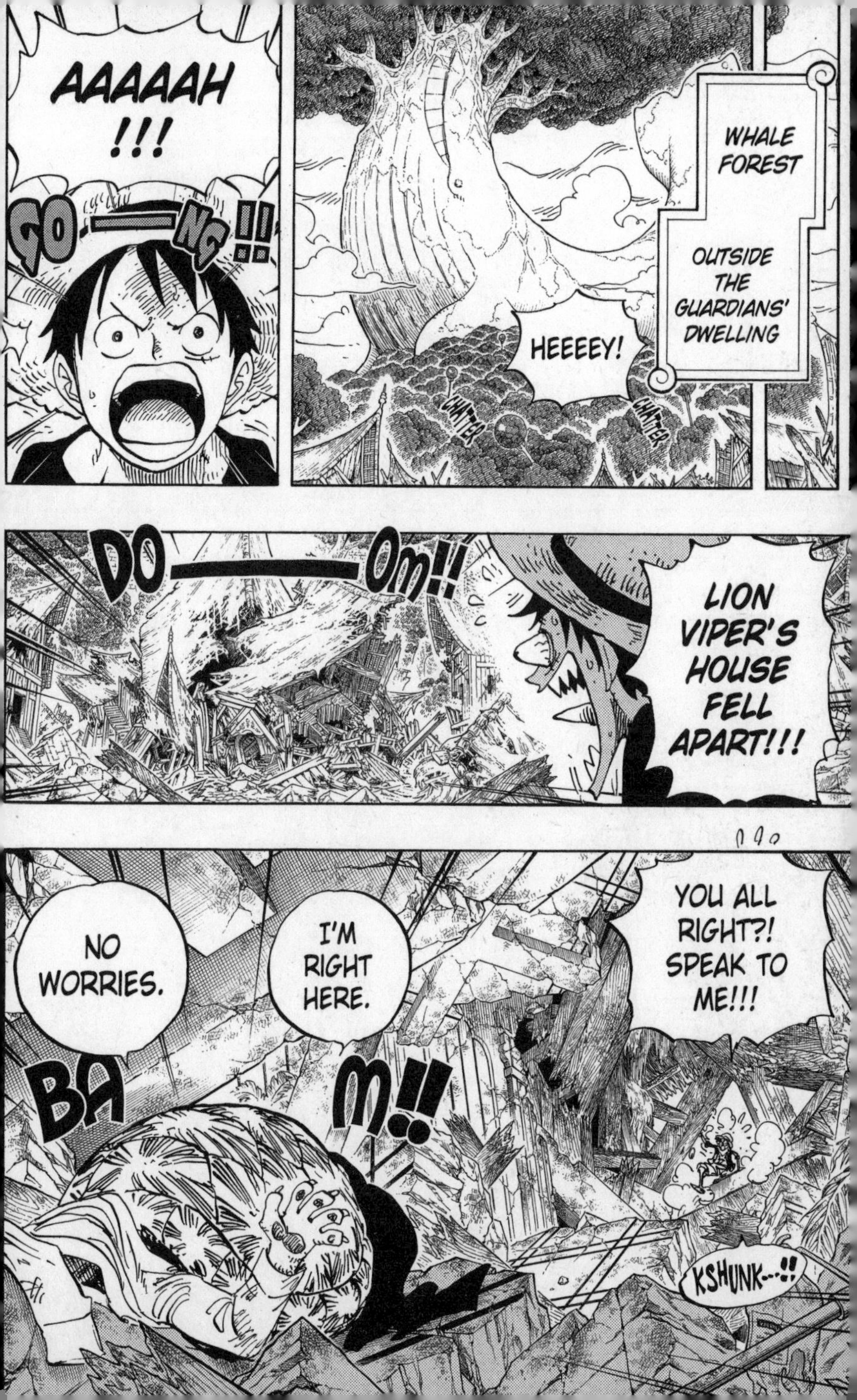
WHALE FOREST
OUTSIDE THE GUARDIANS' DWELLING
HEEEEY!
CHATTER
CHATTER
GO——NG!!
AAAAAH!!!
LION VIPER'S HOUSE FELL APART!!!
DO——Om!!
YOU ALL RIGHT?! SPEAK TO ME!!!
I'M RIGHT HERE.
NO WORRIES.
BAM!!
KSHUNK--!!

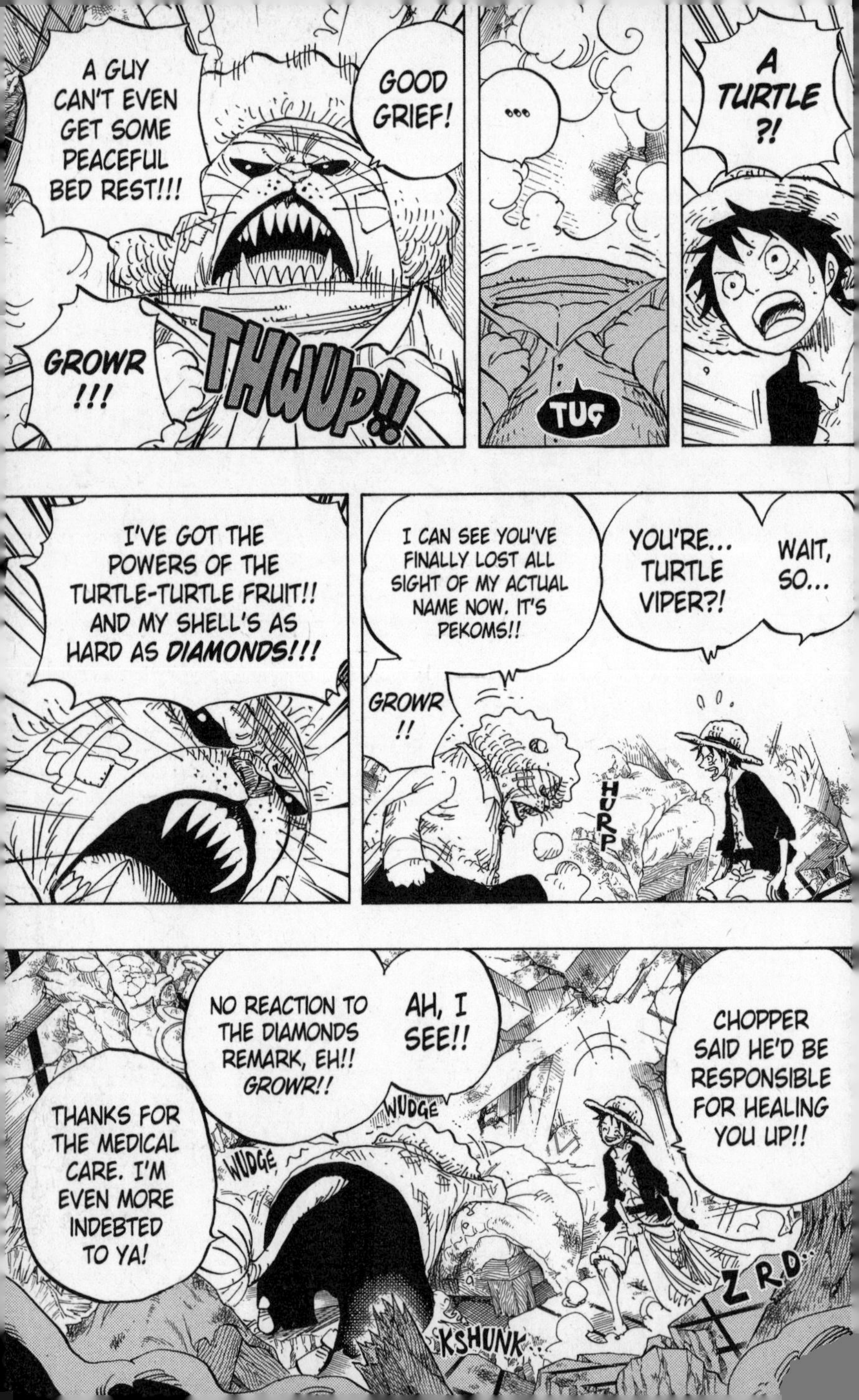
A TURTLE ?!
...
TUG
GOOD GRIEF!
A GUY CAN'T EVEN GET SOME PEACEFUL BED REST!!!
THWUP!!
GROWR !!!
WAIT, SO...
YOU'RE... TURTLE VIPER?!
I CAN SEE YOU'VE FINALLY LOST ALL SIGHT OF MY ACTUAL NAME NOW. IT'S PEKOMS!!
GROWR !!
HURP
I'VE GOT THE POWERS OF THE TURTLE-TURTLE FRUIT!! AND MY SHELL'S AS HARD AS DIAMONDS!!!
CHOPPER SAID HE'D BE RESPONSIBLE FOR HEALING YOU UP!!
AH, I SEE!!
NO REACTION TO THE DIAMONDS REMARK, EH!! GROWR!!
WUDGE
ZRD
THANKS FOR THE MEDICAL CARE. I'M EVEN MORE INDEBTED TO YA!
WUDGE
KSHUNK

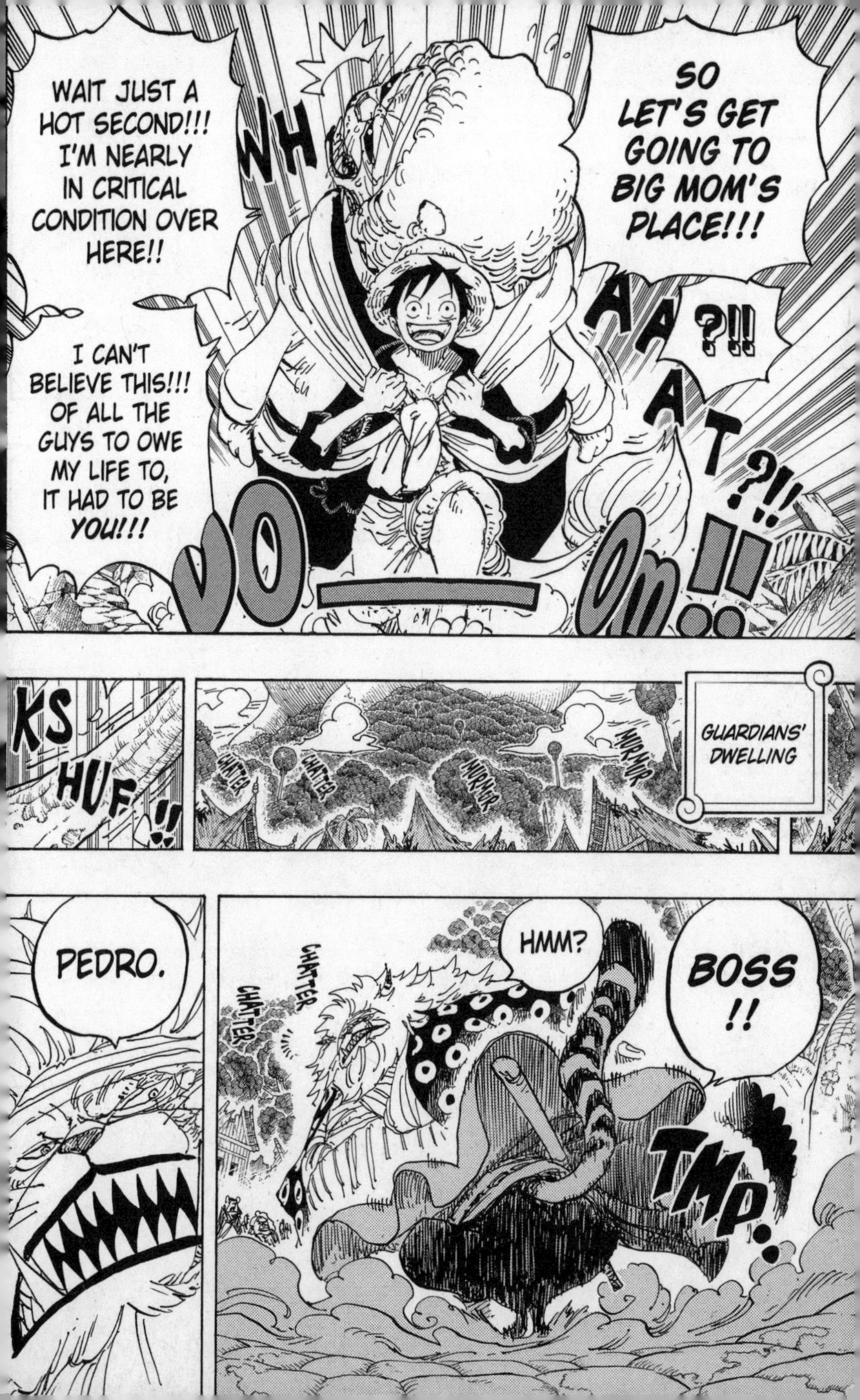
SO LET'S GET GOING TO BIG MOM'S PLACE!!!
?!!
WHAAAT?!!
WAIT JUST A HOT SECOND!!! I'M NEARLY IN CRITICAL CONDITION OVER HERE!!
I CAN'T BELIEVE THIS!!! OF ALL THE GUYS TO OWE MY LIFE TO, IT HAD TO BE YOU!!!
VO—OM!!
GUARDIANS' DWELLING
MURMUR
MURMUR
CHATTER
CHATTER
KS
HUF!!
BOSS!!
HMM?
CHATTER
CHATTER
TMP...
PEDRO.

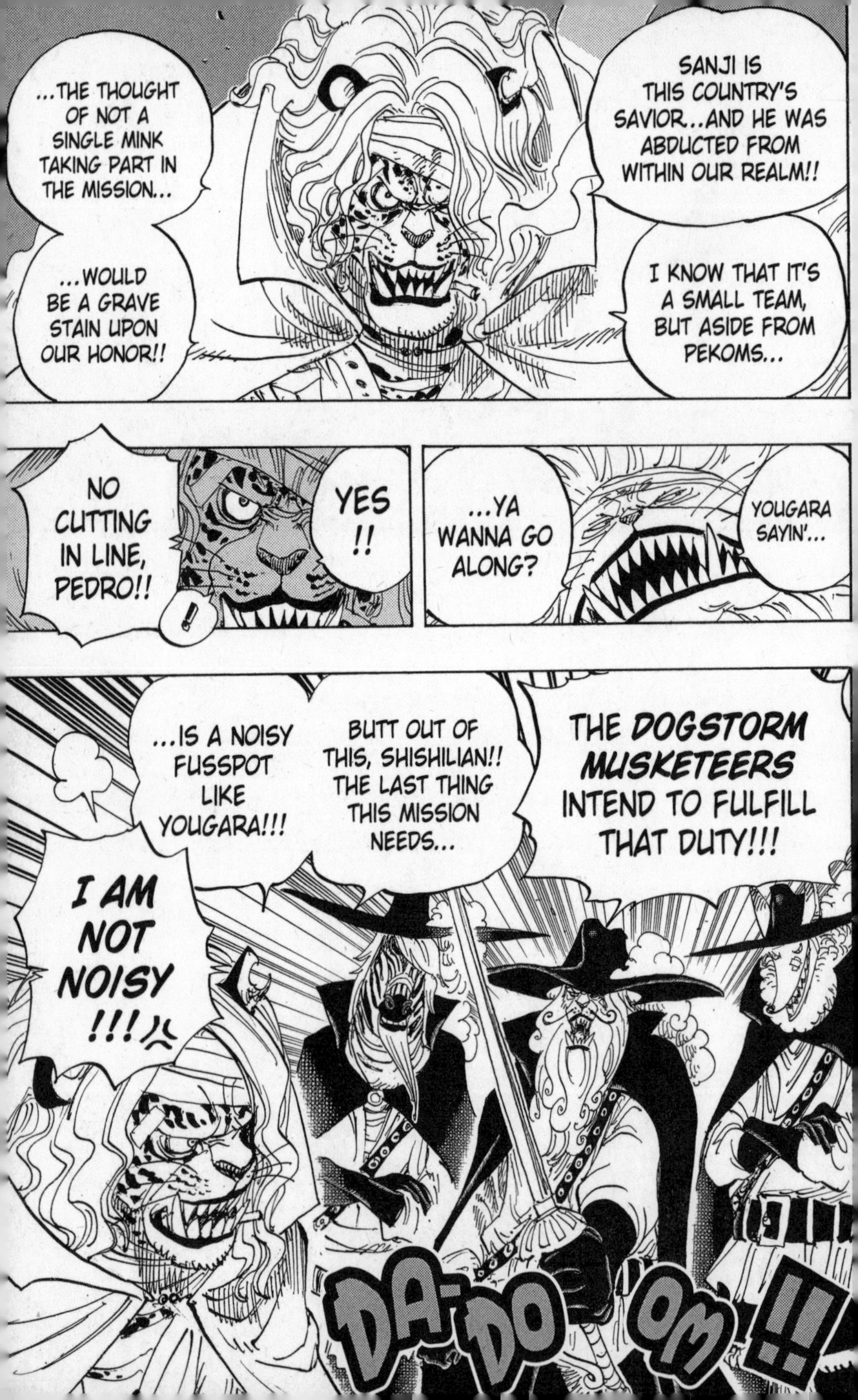
SANJI IS THIS COUNTRY'S SAVIOR...AND HE WAS ABDUCTED FROM WITHIN OUR REALM!!
I KNOW THAT IT'S A SMALL TEAM, BUT ASIDE FROM PEKOMS...
...THE THOUGHT OF NOT A SINGLE MINK TAKING PART IN THE MISSION...
...WOULD BE A GRAVE STAIN UPON OUR HONOR!!
YOUGARA SAYIN'...
...YA WANNA GO ALONG?
YES!!
!
NO CUTTING IN LINE, PEDRO!!
THE *DOGSTORM MUSKETEERS* INTEND TO FULFILL THAT DUTY!!!
BUTT OUT OF THIS, SHISHILIAN!! THE LAST THING THIS MISSION NEEDS...
...IS A NOISY FUSSPOT LIKE YOUGARA!!!
I AM NOT NOISY!!!
DA-DO-OM!!

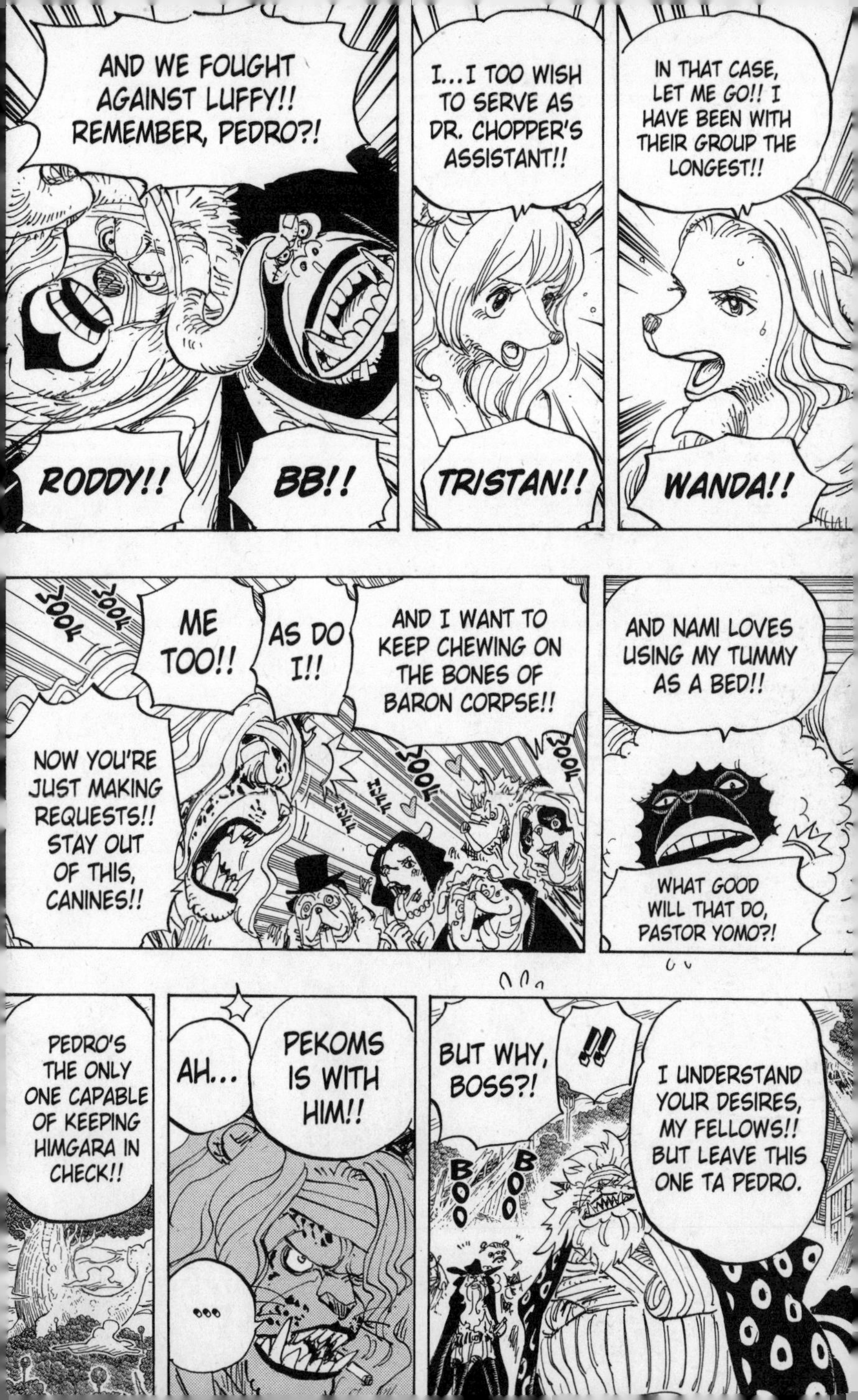
IN THAT CASE, LET ME GO!! I HAVE BEEN WITH THEIR GROUP THE LONGEST!!
WANDA!!
I...I TOO WISH TO SERVE AS DR. CHOPPER'S ASSISTANT!!
TRISTAN!!
AND WE FOUGHT AGAINST LUFFY!! REMEMBER, PEDRO?!
BB!!
RODDY!!
AND NAMI LOVES USING MY TUMMY AS A BED!!
WHAT GOOD WILL THAT DO, PASTOR YOMO?!
AND I WANT TO KEEP CHEWING ON THE BONES OF BARON CORPSE!!
AS DO I!!
ME TOO!!
WOOF
WOOF
WOOF
WOOF
HUFF
HUFF
NOW YOU'RE JUST MAKING REQUESTS!! STAY OUT OF THIS, CANINES!!
I UNDERSTAND YOUR DESIRES, MY FELLOWS!! BUT LEAVE THIS ONE TA PEDRO.
!!
BUT WHY, BOSS?!
BOO
BOO
PEKOMS IS WITH HIM!!
AH...
...
PEDRO'S THE ONLY ONE CAPABLE OF KEEPING HIMGARA IN CHECK!!

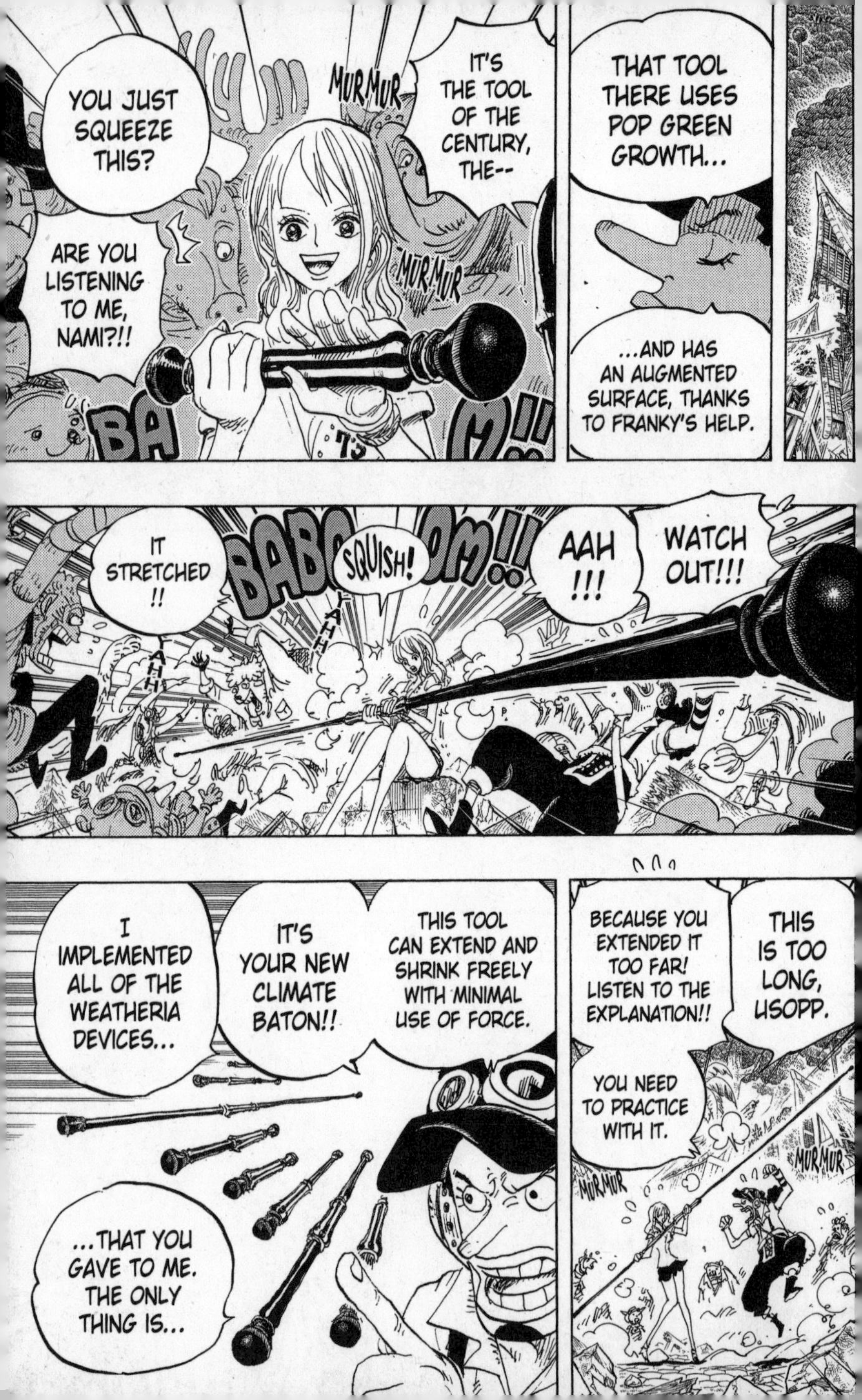
THAT TOOL THERE USES POP GREEN GROWTH...
...AND HAS AN AUGMENTED SURFACE, THANKS TO FRANKY'S HELP.
IT'S THE TOOL OF THE CENTURY, THE--
MURMUR
YOU JUST SQUEEZE THIS?
MURMUR
ARE YOU LISTENING TO ME, NAMI?!!
M!!
BA
WATCH OUT!!!
AAH!!!
OM!!
SQUISH!
BABO
YAHH
IT STRETCHED!!
AHH
THIS IS TOO LONG, USOPP.
BECAUSE YOU EXTENDED IT TOO FAR! LISTEN TO THE EXPLANATION!!
YOU NEED TO PRACTICE WITH IT.
MURMUR
MURMUR
THIS TOOL CAN EXTEND AND SHRINK FREELY WITH MINIMAL USE OF FORCE.
IT'S YOUR NEW CLIMATE BATON!!
I IMPLEMENTED ALL OF THE WEATHERIA DEVICES...
...THAT YOU GAVE TO ME. THE ONLY THING IS...

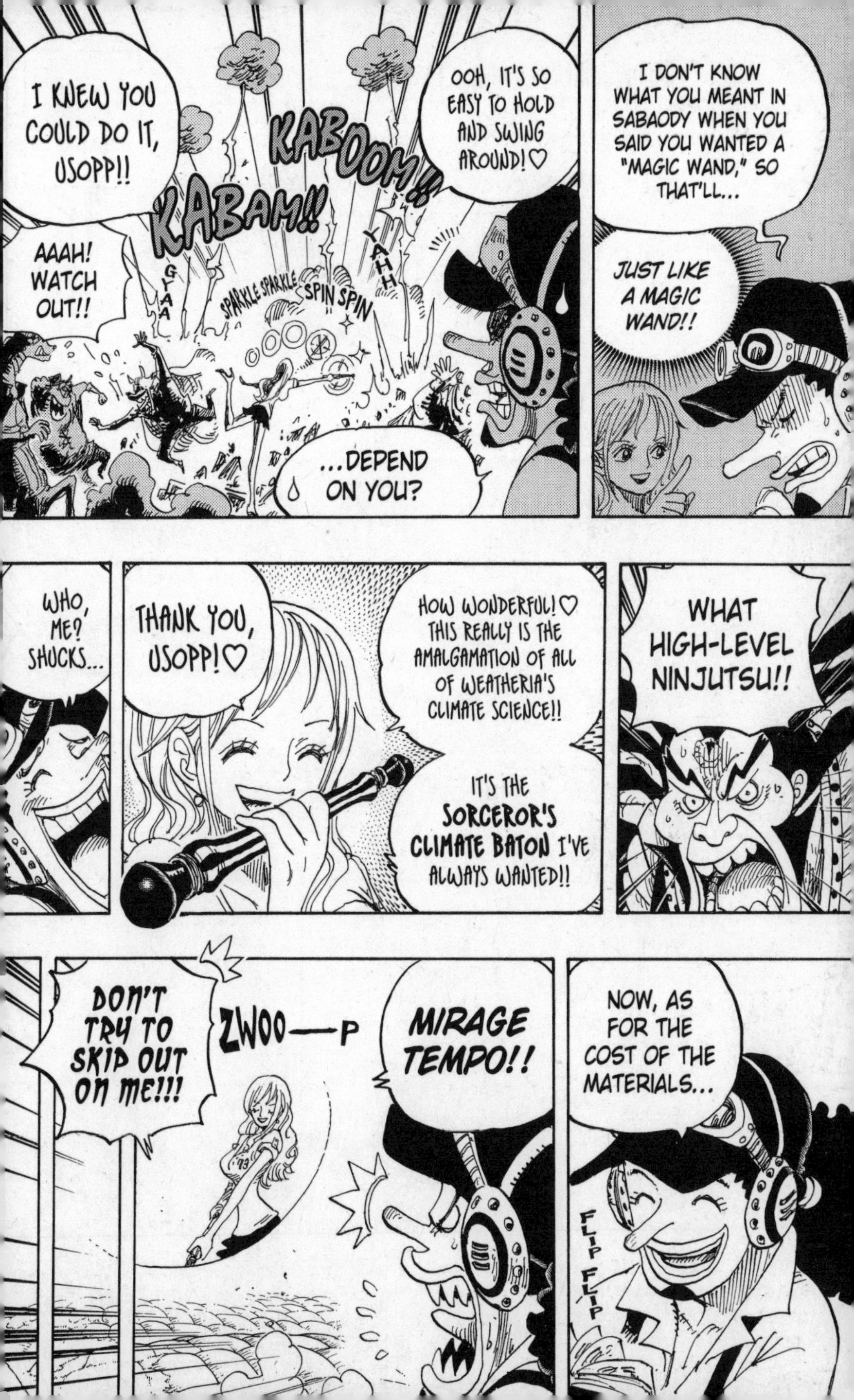
I DON'T KNOW WHAT YOU MEANT IN SABAODY WHEN YOU SAID YOU WANTED A "MAGIC WAND," SO THAT'LL...
JUST LIKE A MAGIC WAND!!
OOH, IT'S SO EASY TO HOLD AND SWING AROUND!♡
KABOOM!!
YAHH
KABAM!!
I KNEW YOU COULD DO IT, USOPP!!
SPIN SPIN
SPARKLE SPARKLE
GYAA
AAAH! WATCH OUT!!
...DEPEND ON YOU?
WHAT HIGH-LEVEL NINJUTSU!!
HOW WONDERFUL!♡ THIS REALLY IS THE AMALGAMATION OF ALL OF WEATHERIA'S CLIMATE SCIENCE!!
IT'S THE SORCEROR'S CLIMATE BATON I'VE ALWAYS WANTED!!
THANK YOU, USOPP!♡
WHO, ME? SHUCKS...
NOW, AS FOR THE COST OF THE MATERIALS...
FLIP FLIP
MIRAGE TEMPO!!
ZWOO—P
DON'T TRY TO SKIP OUT ON ME!!!

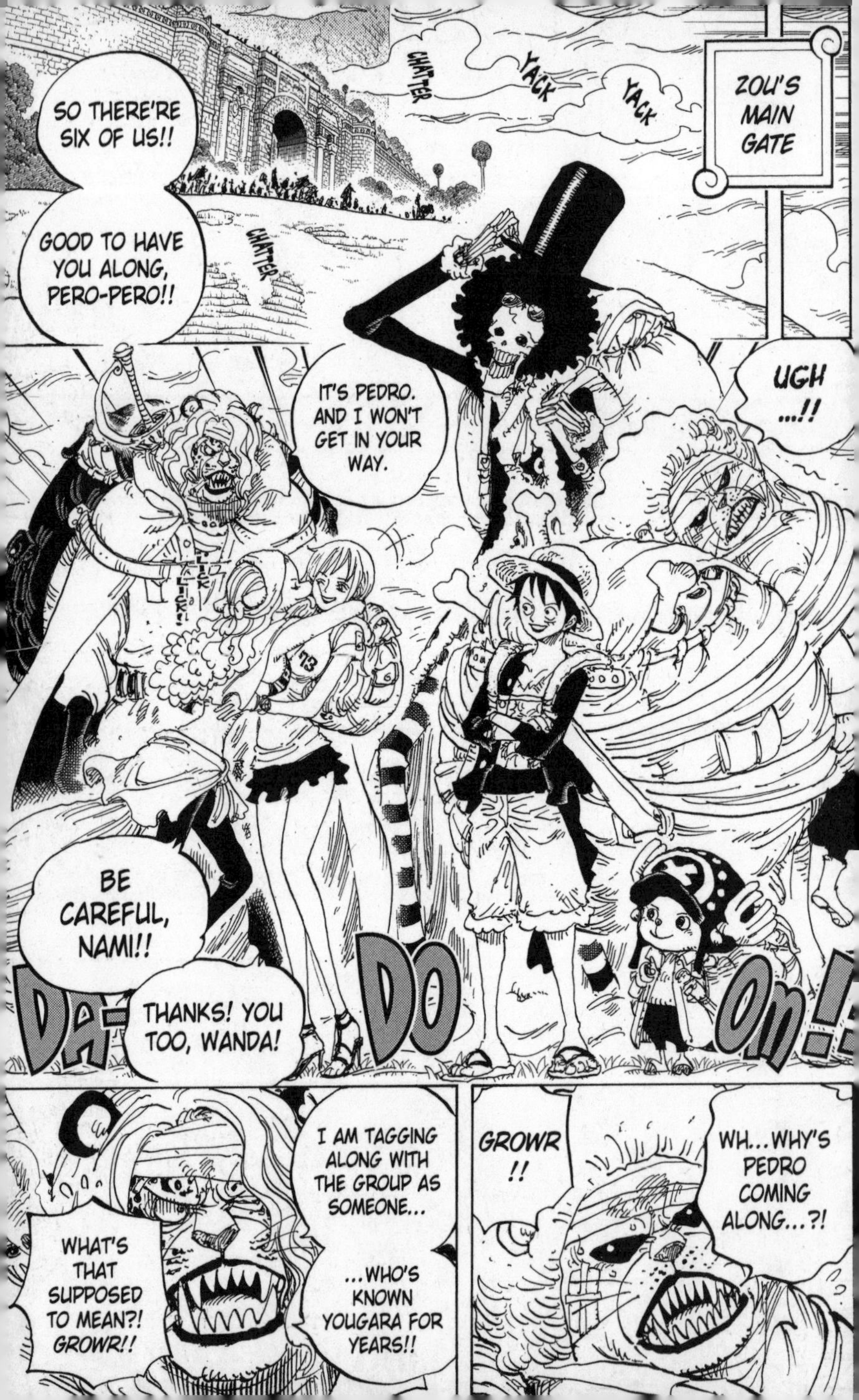
ZOU'S MAIN GATE
YACK
YACK
CHATTER
SO THERE'RE SIX OF US!!
GOOD TO HAVE YOU ALONG, PERO-PERO!!
CHATTER
UGH ...!!
IT'S PEDRO. AND I WON'T GET IN YOUR WAY.
LICK LICK
BE CAREFUL, NAMI!!
THANKS! YOU TOO, WANDA!
DA-DO-OM!!
WH...WHY'S PEDRO COMING ALONG...?!
GROWR!!
I AM TAGGING ALONG WITH THE GROUP AS SOMEONE...
...WHO'S KNOWN YOUGARA FOR YEARS!!
WHAT'S THAT SUPPOSED TO MEAN?! GROWR!!

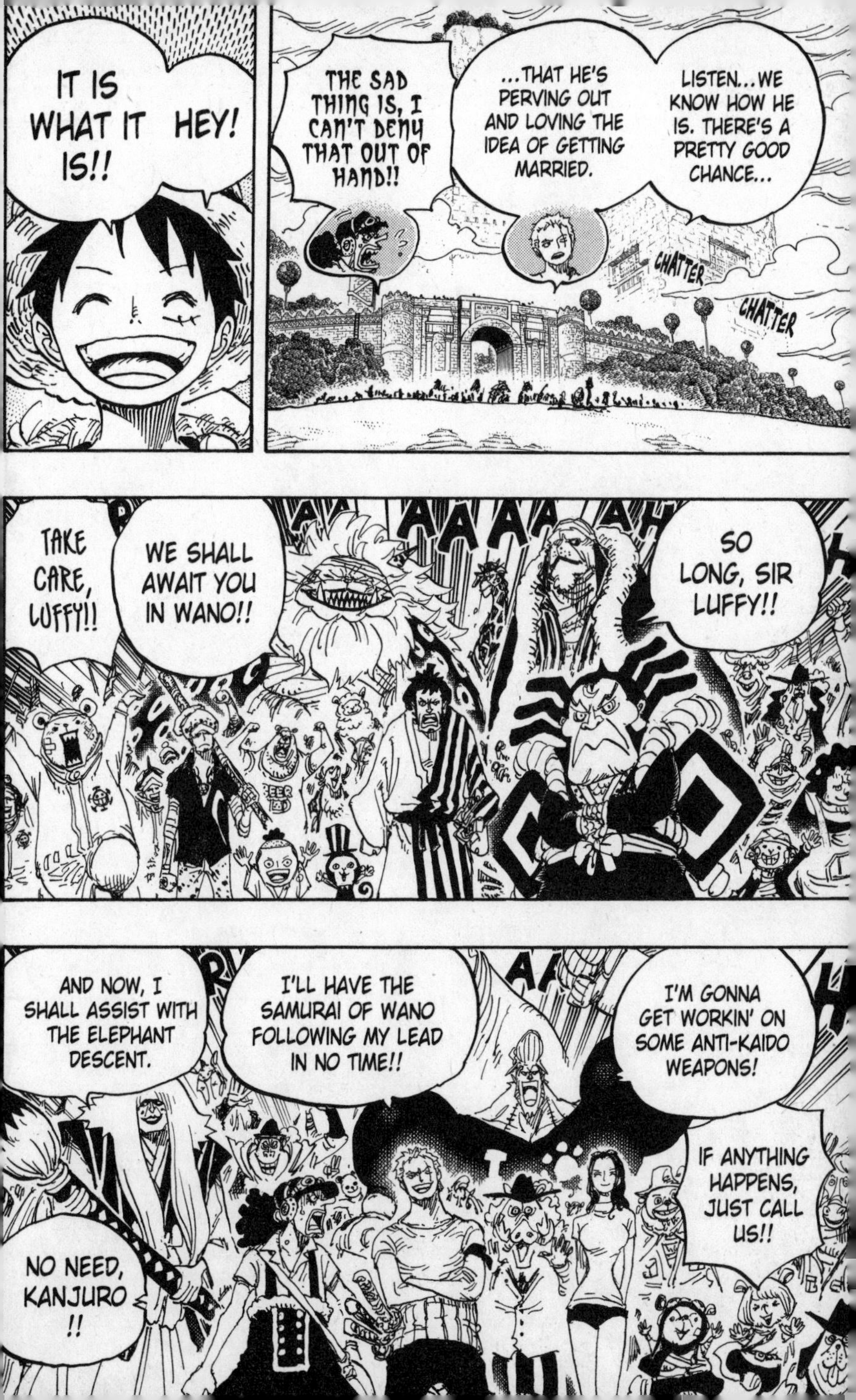
LISTEN...WE KNOW HOW HE IS. THERE'S A PRETTY GOOD CHANCE...
...THAT HE'S PERVING OUT AND LOVING THE IDEA OF GETTING MARRIED.
THE SAD THING IS, I CAN'T DENY THAT OUT OF HAND!!
CHATTER
CHATTER
HEY!
IT IS WHAT IT IS!!
SO LONG, SIR LUFFY!!
WE SHALL AWAIT YOU IN WANO!!
TAKE CARE, LUFFY!!
I'M GONNA GET WORKIN' ON SOME ANTI-KAIDO WEAPONS!
I'LL HAVE THE SAMURAI OF WANO FOLLOWING MY LEAD IN NO TIME!!
AND NOW, I SHALL ASSIST WITH THE ELEPHANT DESCENT.
IF ANYTHING HAPPENS, JUST CALL US!!
NO NEED, KANJURO!!

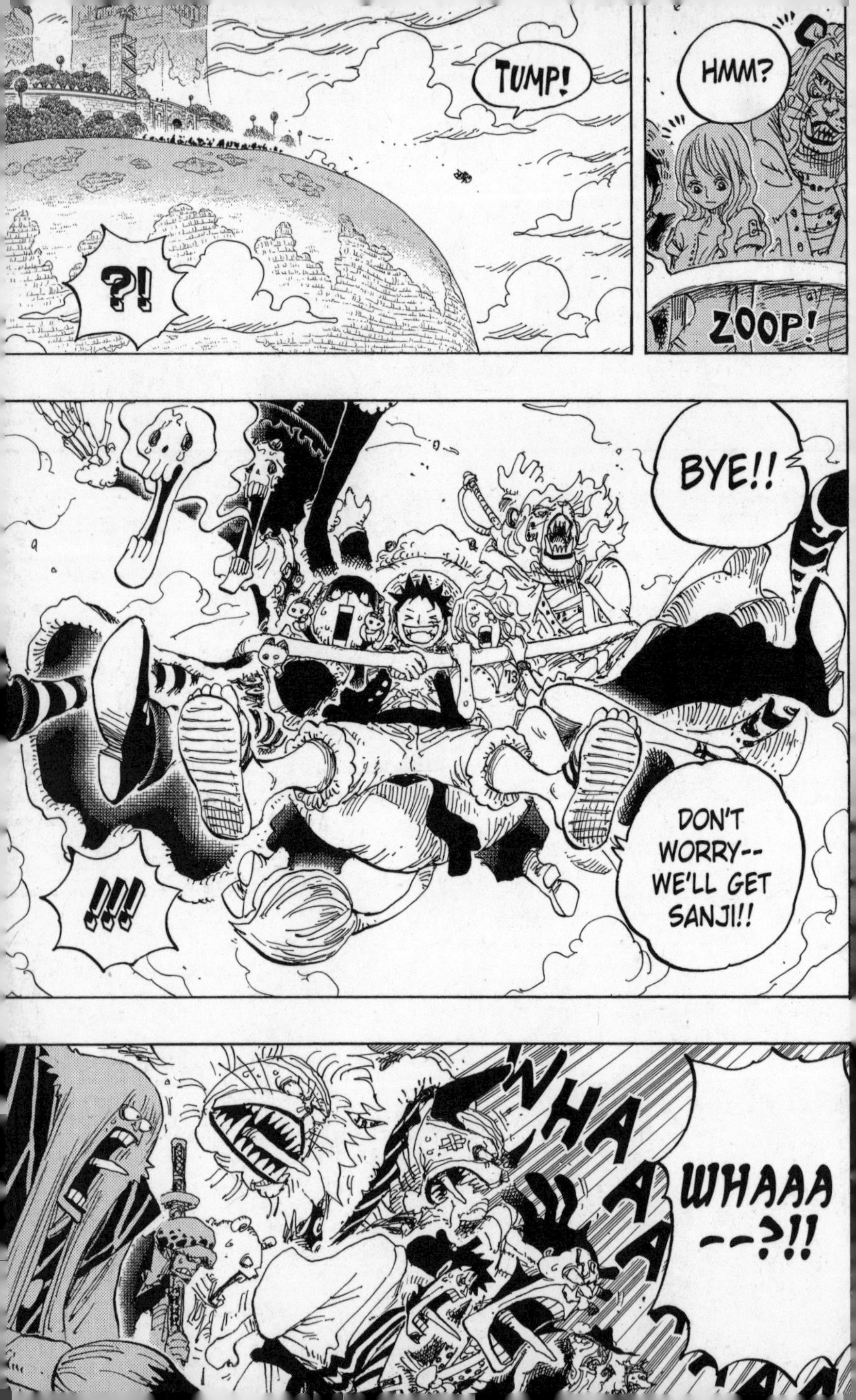
HMM?
ZOOP!
TUMP!
?!
BYE!!
DON'T WORRY-- WE'LL GET SANJI!!
!!!
WHAAAA --?!!

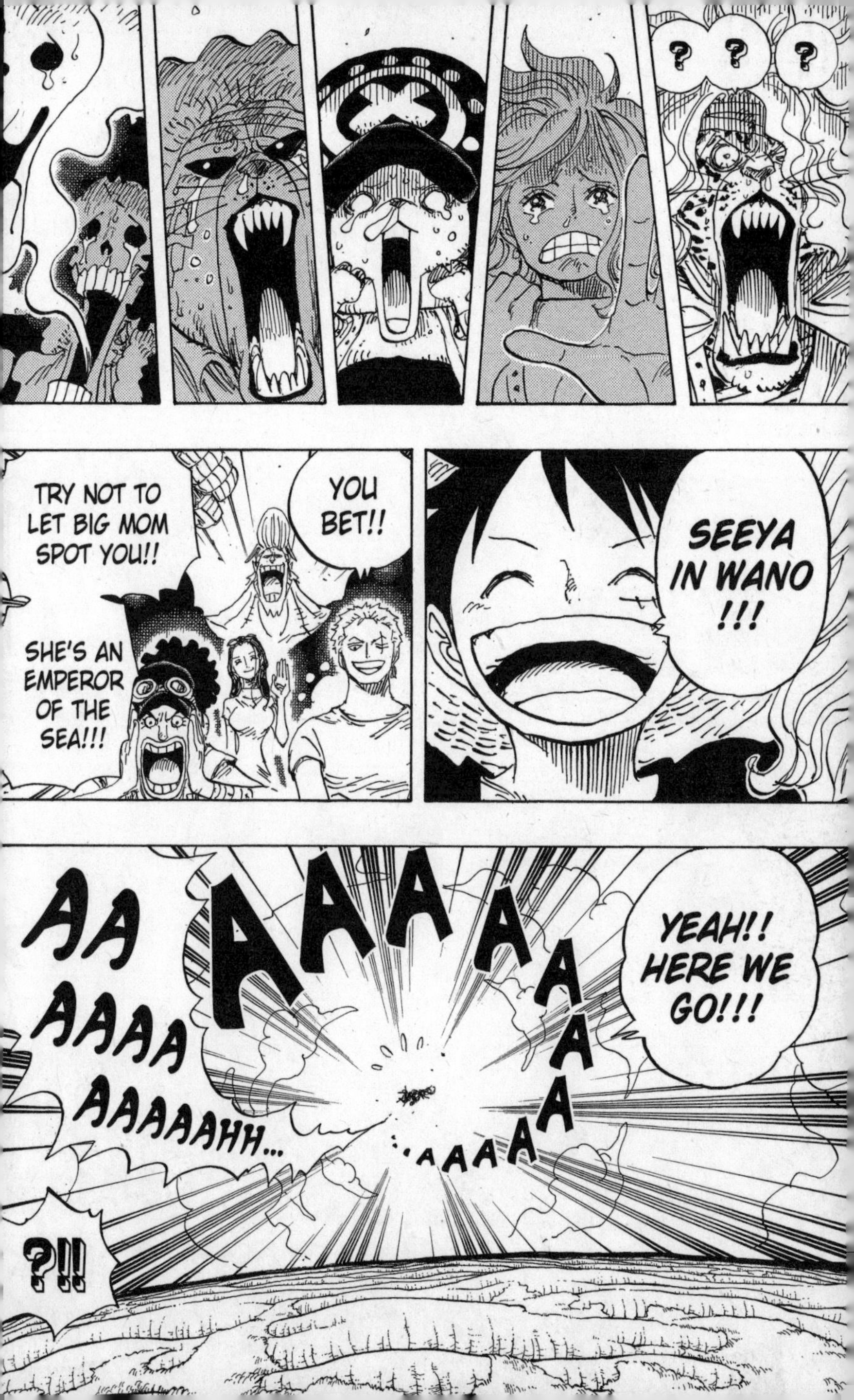
? ? ?
SEEYA IN WANO!!!
YOU BET!!
TRY NOT TO LET BIG MOM SPOT YOU!!
SHE'S AN EMPEROR OF THE SEA!!!
YEAH!! HERE WE GO!!!
AAAAAAAAAA...AAAA
AA AAAA AAAAAAHH...
?!!

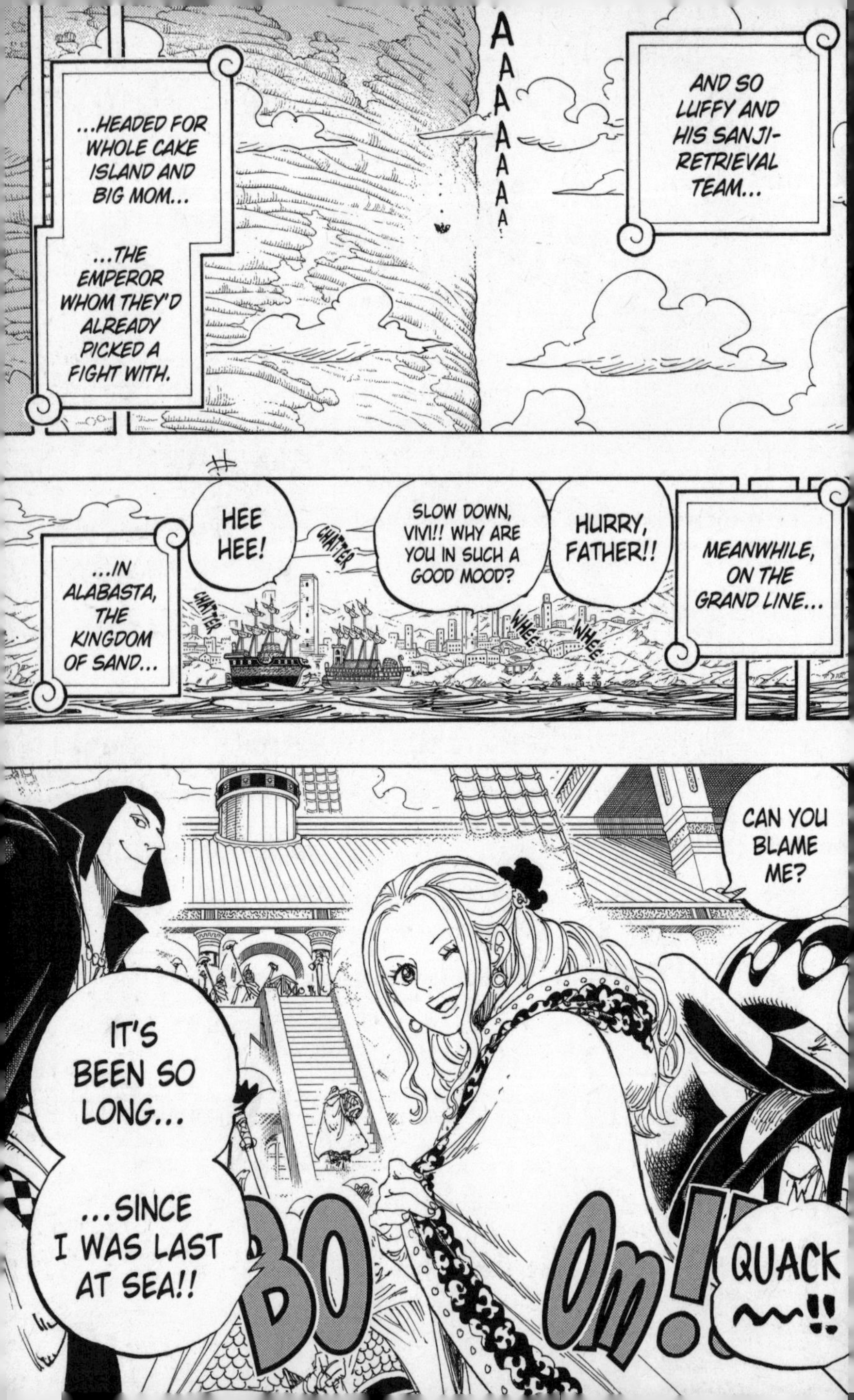

AND SO LUFFY AND HIS SANJI-RETRIEVAL TEAM...
AAAAAAAA
...HEADED FOR WHOLE CAKE ISLAND AND BIG MOM...
...THE EMPEROR WHOM THEY'D ALREADY PICKED A FIGHT WITH.
MEANWHILE, ON THE GRAND LINE...
HURRY, FATHER!!
WHEE
WHEE
SLOW DOWN, VIVI!! WHY ARE YOU IN SUCH A GOOD MOOD?
CHATTER
CHATTER
HEE HEE!
...IN ALABASTA, THE KINGDOM OF SAND...
CAN YOU BLAME ME?
QUACK ~~!!
BOOM!!
IT'S BEEN SO LONG...
...SINCE I WAS LAST AT SEA!!

SBS Question Corner

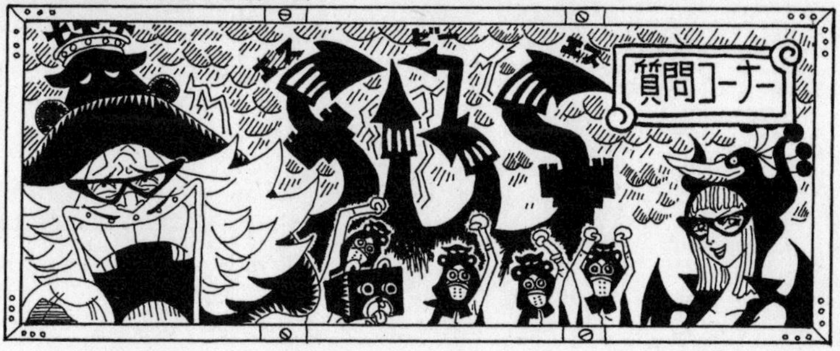
質問コーナー

(Pekoms, Miyagi)

Q: Hello, Oda Sensei!! When the Straw Hats' bounty posters got updated, I was so excited! By the way...where and how did Nami's bounty picture get taken? It's so sexy… ha ha ha.

--Yutiko Loves Nami's Voice

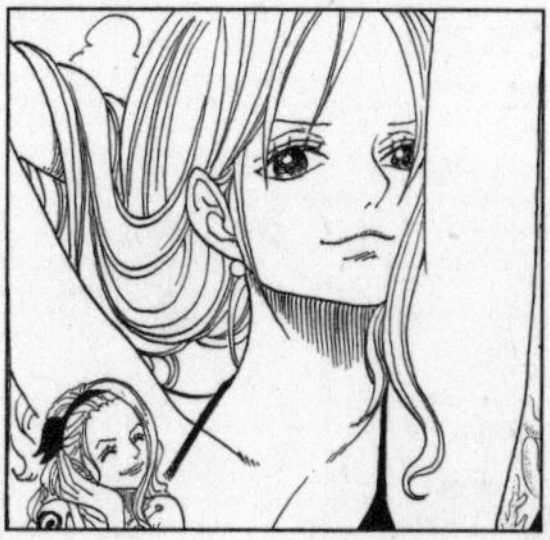

A: It's the second time in a row she's been doing a centerfold pose. In both cases, the situation went like this:
"Hello, I'm a writer for Blah-Blah Weekly (this part is a lie)! Wow, you're gorgeous!! May I take your photograph to put on the cover of our magazine?"
"Well, if you insist. As long as you make me look good!♡"
"Click!!"

Q: Personally, everything about Nami in the New World is right up my alley. I'm all about enjoying my Nami love through anime, merchandise, figures, game DLC, and so on. As the author, do you think it's sleazy that this is one my main sources of enjoyment for the series?

--B.S.L.

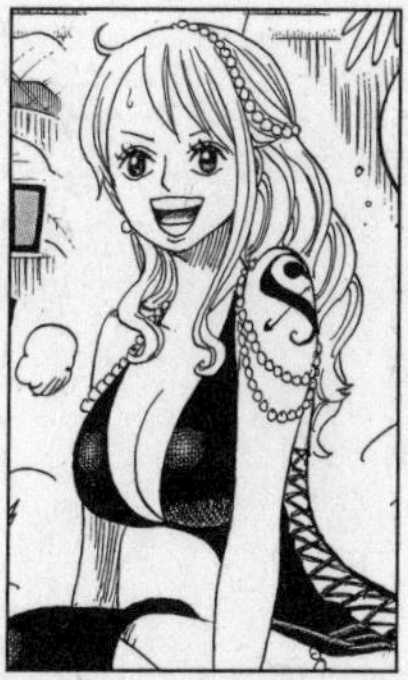

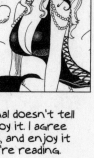

A: I feel like Nami's gotten more popular lately. Maybe it's because she hasn't been around for a bit? Anyway, you're feeling guilty about thinking of the characters in a naughty manner, aren't you? (*laughs*) Well, I have no problems with this--for any of my characters. A teacher of mine said that your manga world is a product to be sold, and a real professional doesn't tell the customer who bought it how they should enjoy it. I agree with that philosophy. You may interpret, fantasize, and enjoy it however you wish. I'm just happy knowing that you're reading.

Q: Was Nami named for her dy*nami*c breast size?

--Hiromu

A: Umm, don't parents usually name their children when they're newborns?!

Chapter 823:
THE WORLD IS RESTLESS

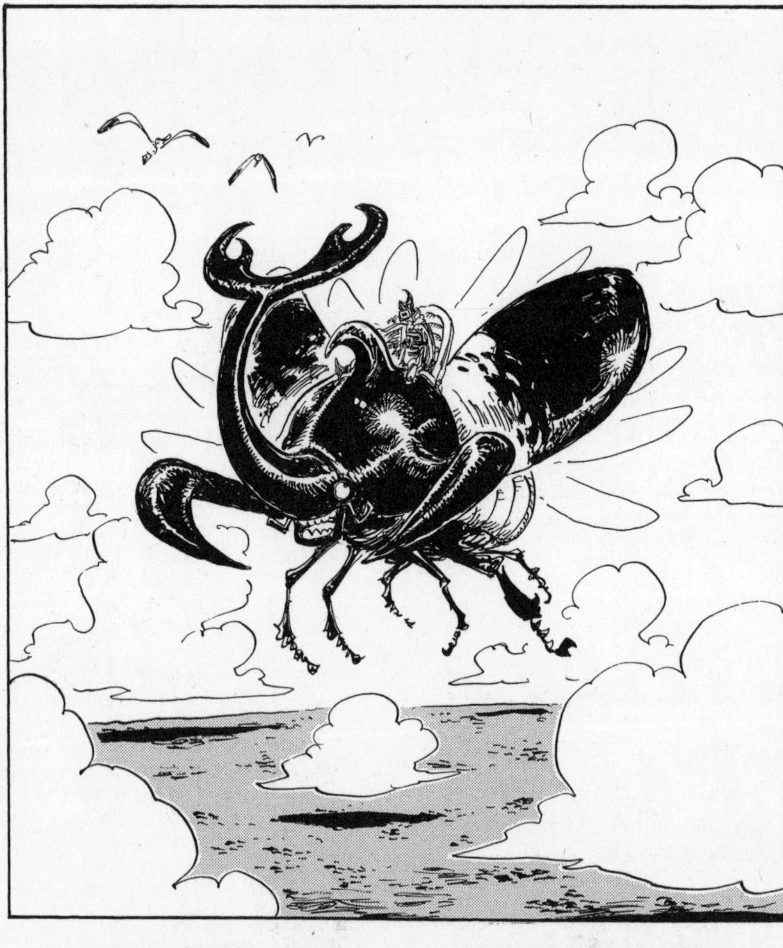

DECKS OF THE WORLD, 500-MILLION-MAN ARC, VOL. 15:
"NOT GOING BACK TO THE BOWIN ISLANDS YET"

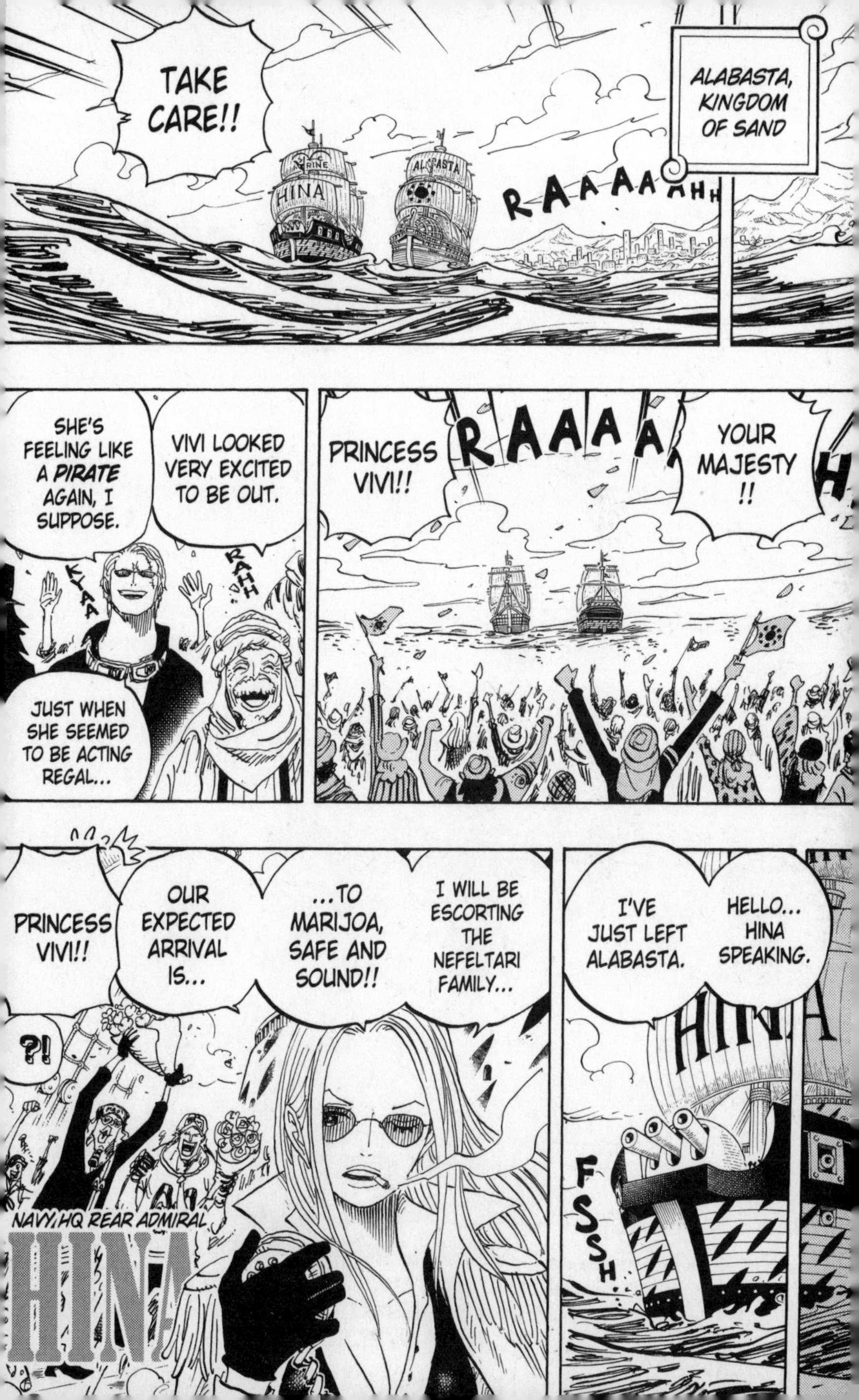
ALABASTA, KINGDOM OF SAND
RAAAAAAHH
TAKE CARE!!
YOUR MAJESTY!!
RAAAAAH
PRINCESS VIVI!!
VIVI LOOKED VERY EXCITED TO BE OUT.
SHE'S FEELING LIKE A PIRATE AGAIN, I SUPPOSE.
RAHH
KYAA
JUST WHEN SHE SEEMED TO BE ACTING REGAL...
HELLO... HINA SPEAKING.
I'VE JUST LEFT ALABASTA.
HINA
FSSH
I WILL BE ESCORTING THE NEFELTARI FAMILY...
...TO MARIJOA, SAFE AND SOUND!!
OUR EXPECTED ARRIVAL IS...
PRINCESS VIVI!!
?!
NAVY HQ REAR ADMIRAL
HINA

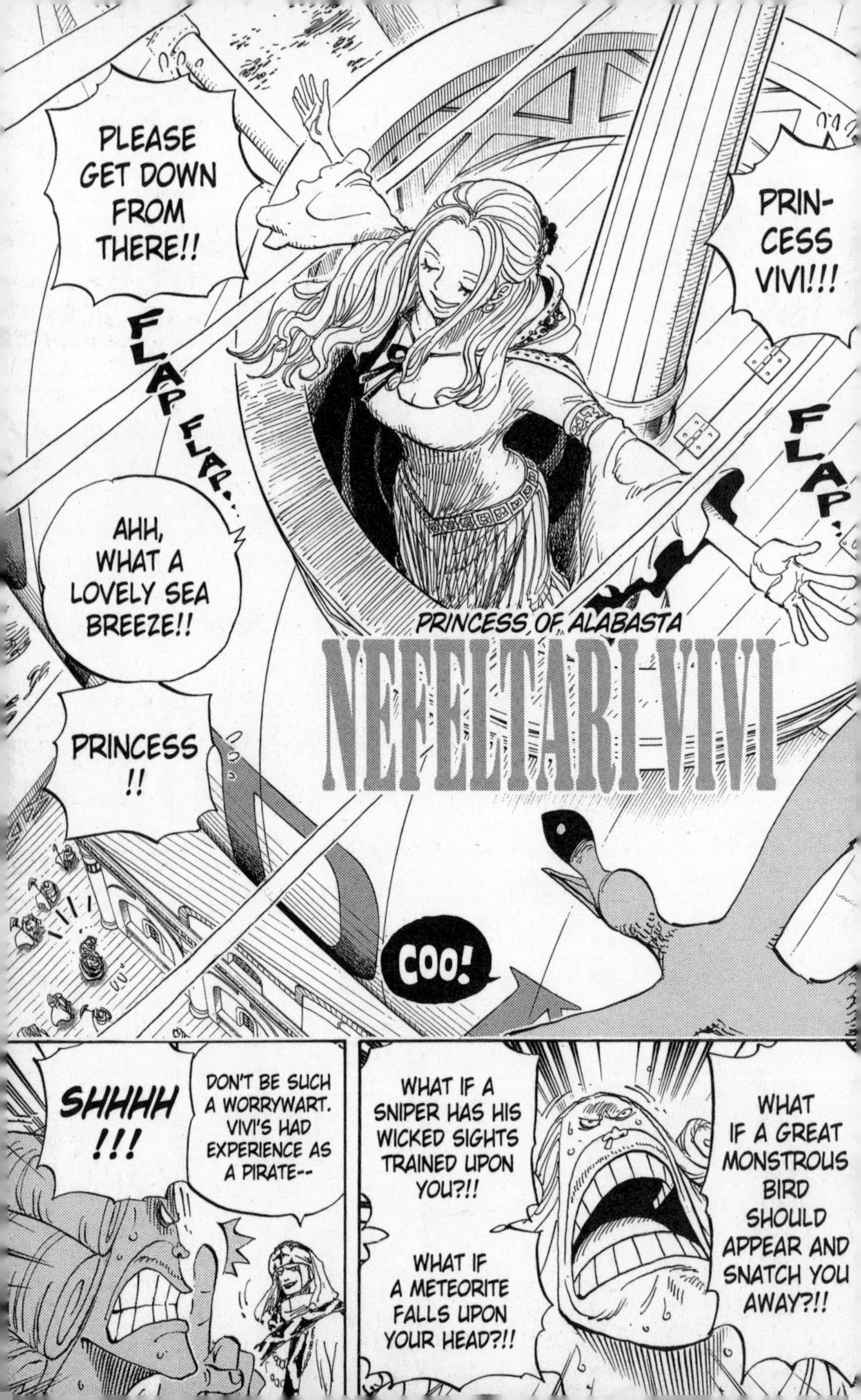
PRINCESS VIVI!!!
FLAP FLAP...
PLEASE GET DOWN FROM THERE!!
FLAP FLAP...
AHH, WHAT A LOVELY SEA BREEZE!!
PRINCESS OF ALABASTA
NEFELTARI VIVI
PRINCESS!!
COO!
WHAT IF A GREAT MONSTROUS BIRD SHOULD APPEAR AND SNATCH YOU AWAY?!!
WHAT IF A SNIPER HAS HIS WICKED SIGHTS TRAINED UPON YOU?!!
WHAT IF A METEORITE FALLS UPON YOUR HEAD?!!
DON'T BE SUCH A WORRYWART. VIVI'S HAD EXPERIENCE AS A PIRATE--
SHHHH!!!

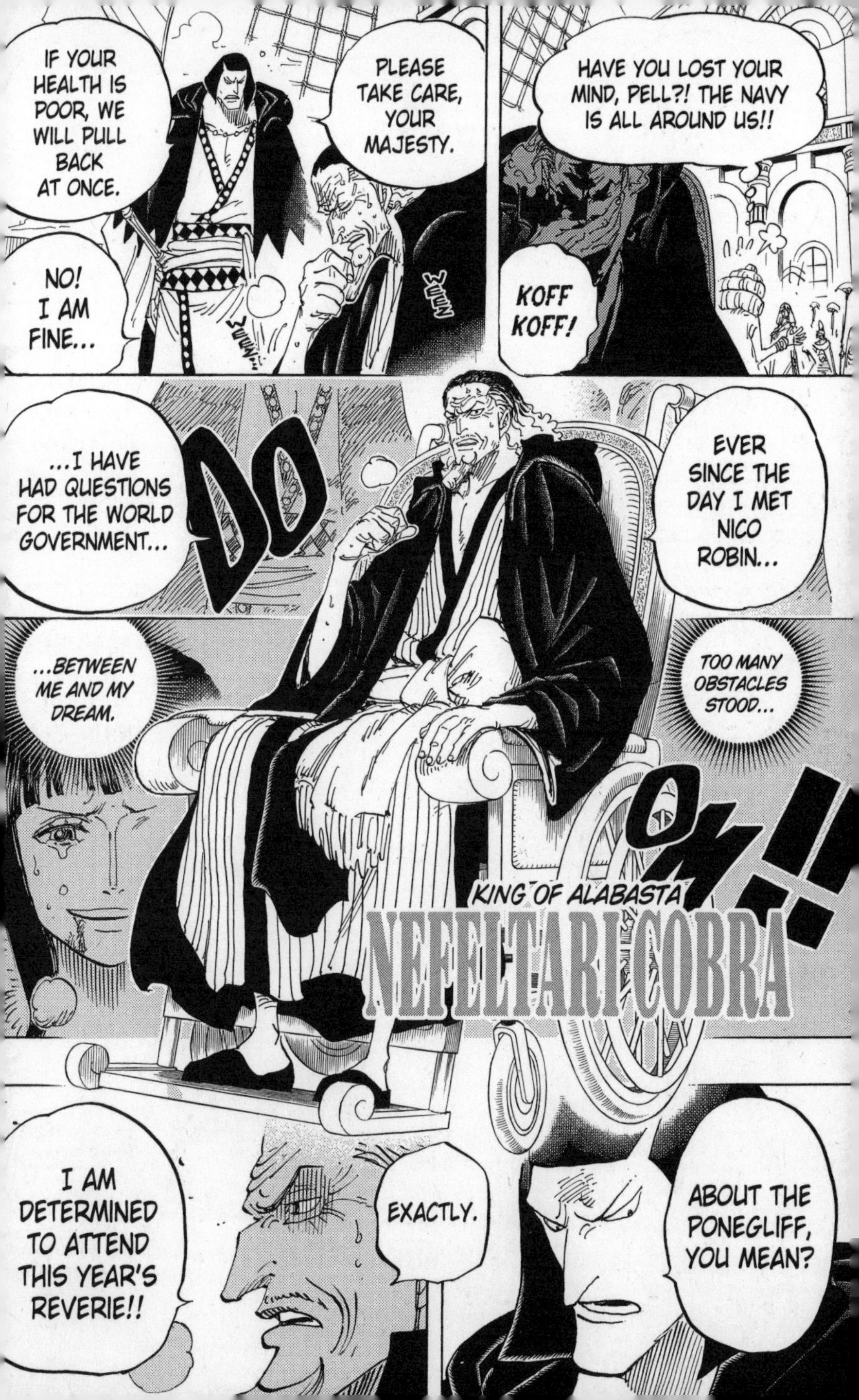
HAVE YOU LOST YOUR MIND, PELL?! THE NAVY IS ALL AROUND US!!
KOFF KOFF!
PLEASE TAKE CARE, YOUR MAJESTY.
IF YOUR HEALTH IS POOR, WE WILL PULL BACK AT ONCE.
NO! I AM FINE...
EVER SINCE THE DAY I MET NICO ROBIN...
...I HAVE HAD QUESTIONS FOR THE WORLD GOVERNMENT...
DO
ON!!
TOO MANY OBSTACLES STOOD...
...BETWEEN ME AND MY DREAM.
KING OF ALABASTA
NEFELTARI COBRA
ABOUT THE PONEGLIFF, YOU MEAN?
EXACTLY.
I AM DETERMINED TO ATTEND THIS YEAR'S REVERIE!!

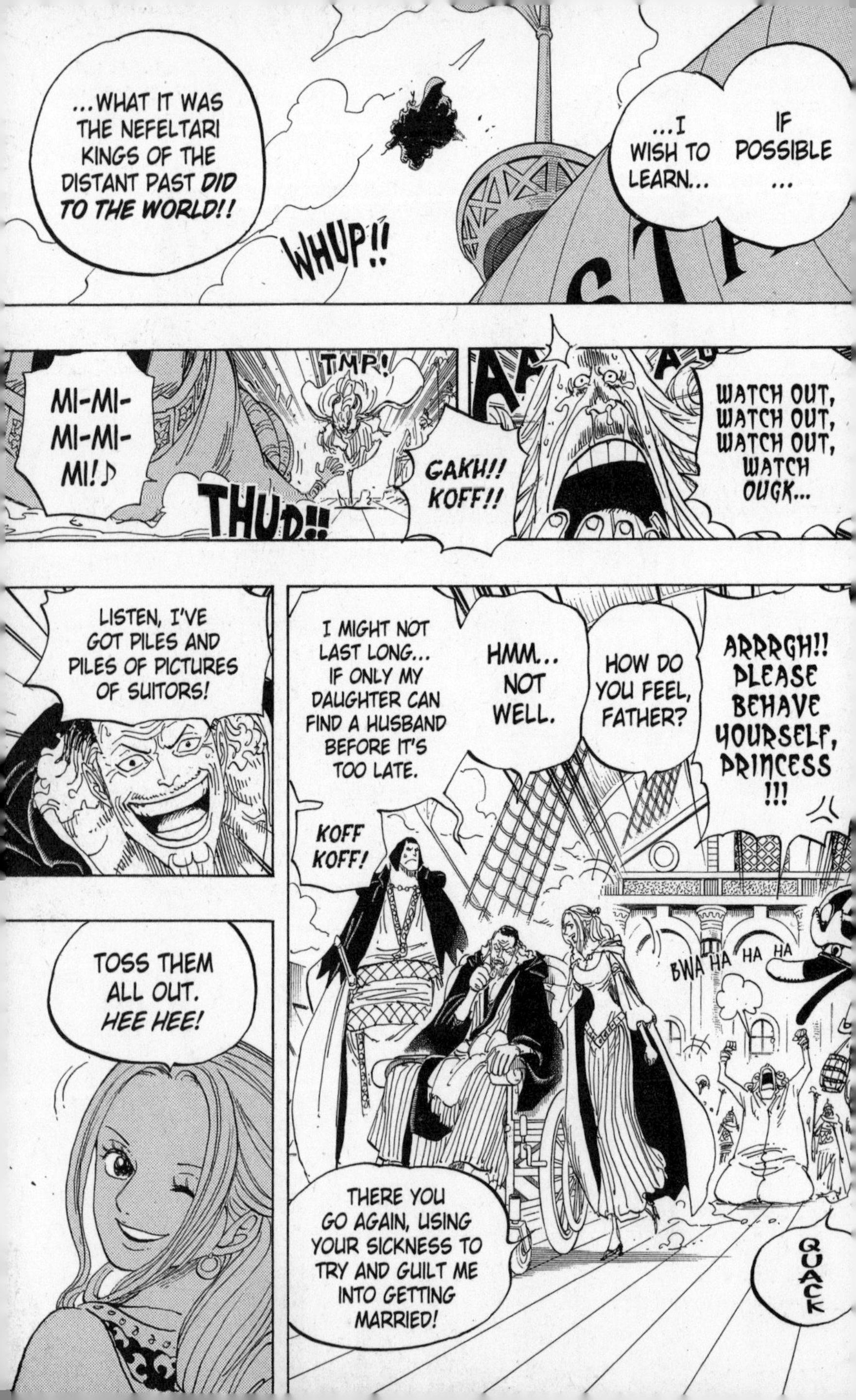
IF POSSIBLE ...
...I WISH TO LEARN...
...WHAT IT WAS THE NEFELTARI KINGS OF THE DISTANT PAST *DID TO THE WORLD!!*
WHUP!!
WATCH OUT, WATCH OUT, WATCH OUT, WATCH OUGK...
GAKH!! KOFF!!
TMP!
MI-MI-MI-MI-MI!♪
THUD!!
ARRRGH!! PLEASE BEHAVE YOURSELF, PRINCESS!!!
HOW DO YOU FEEL, FATHER?
HMM... NOT WELL.
I MIGHT NOT LAST LONG... IF ONLY MY DAUGHTER CAN FIND A HUSBAND BEFORE IT'S TOO LATE.
KOFF KOFF!
BWA HA HA HA
QUACK
THERE YOU GO AGAIN, USING YOUR SICKNESS TO TRY AND GUILT ME INTO GETTING MARRIED!
LISTEN, I'VE GOT PILES AND PILES OF PICTURES OF SUITORS!
TOSS THEM ALL OUT. *HEE HEE!*

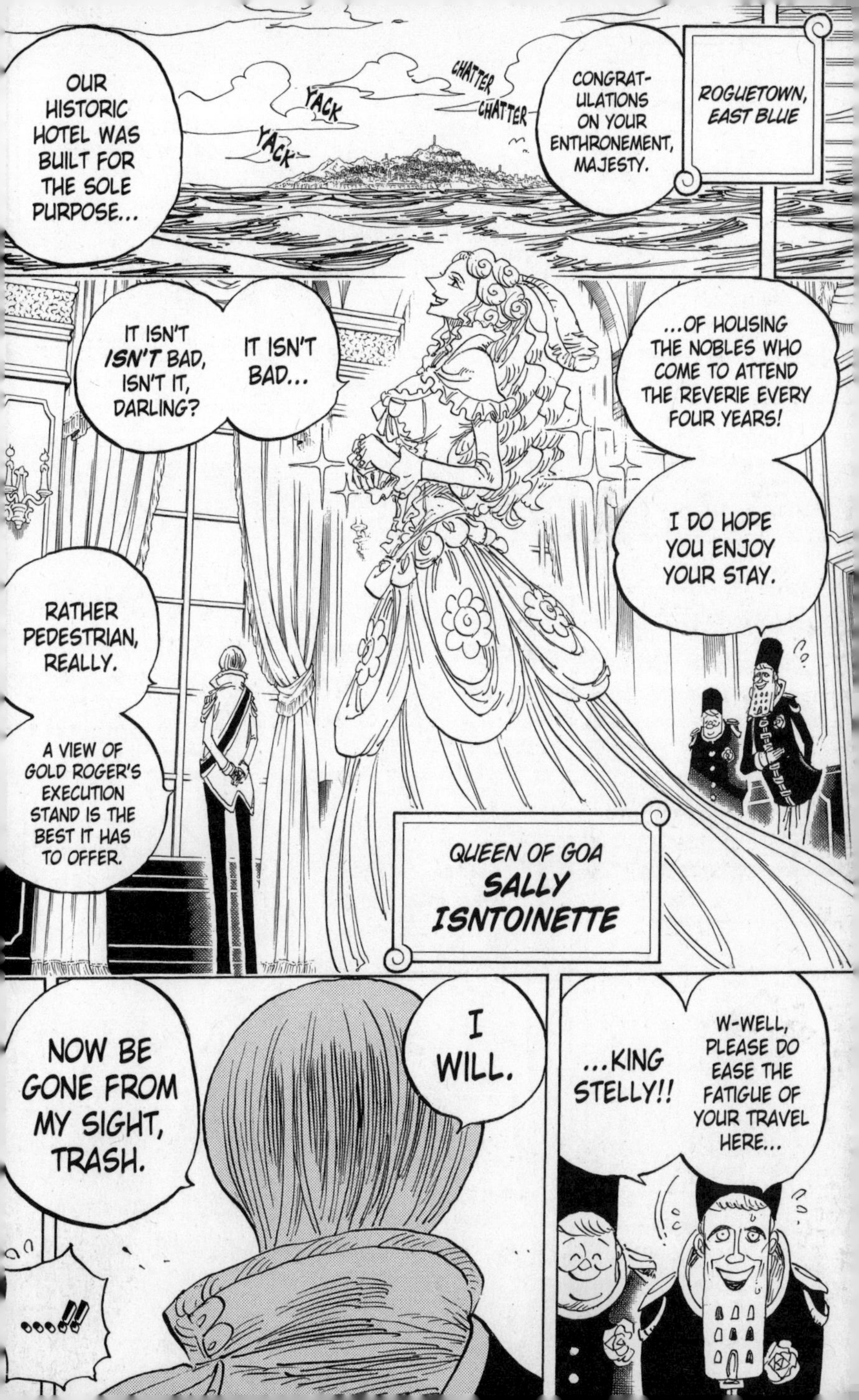
ROGUETOWN, EAST BLUE
CONGRATULATIONS ON YOUR ENTHRONEMENT, MAJESTY.
CHATTER CHATTER
YACK YACK
OUR HISTORIC HOTEL WAS BUILT FOR THE SOLE PURPOSE...
...OF HOUSING THE NOBLES WHO COME TO ATTEND THE REVERIE EVERY FOUR YEARS!
I DO HOPE YOU ENJOY YOUR STAY.
IT ISN'T BAD...
IT ISN'T *ISN'T* BAD, ISN'T IT, DARLING?
RATHER PEDESTRIAN, REALLY.
A VIEW OF GOLD ROGER'S EXECUTION STAND IS THE BEST IT HAS TO OFFER.
QUEEN OF GOA
SALLY ISNTOINETTE
W-WELL, PLEASE DO EASE THE FATIGUE OF YOUR TRAVEL HERE...
...KING STELLY!!
I WILL.
NOW BE GONE FROM MY SIGHT, TRASH.
....!!

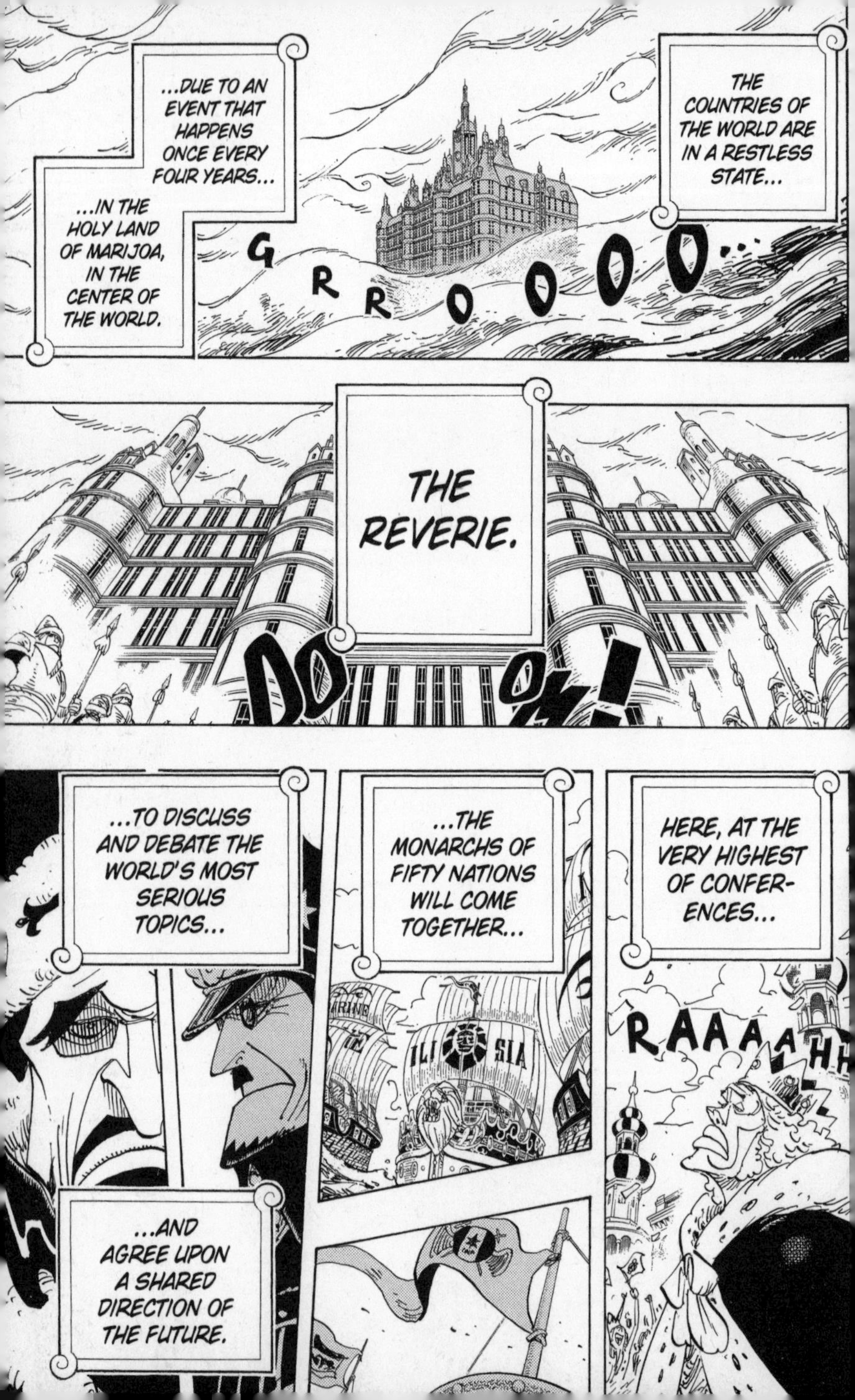

THE COUNTRIES OF THE WORLD ARE IN A RESTLESS STATE...
...DUE TO AN EVENT THAT HAPPENS ONCE EVERY FOUR YEARS...
...IN THE HOLY LAND OF MARIJOA, IN THE CENTER OF THE WORLD.
GRROOOO...
THE REVERIE.
DOOOM!
HERE, AT THE VERY HIGHEST OF CONFER-ENCES...
RAAAAHH
...THE MONARCHS OF FIFTY NATIONS WILL COME TOGETHER...
...TO DISCUSS AND DEBATE THE WORLD'S MOST SERIOUS TOPICS...
...AND AGREE UPON A SHARED DIRECTION OF THE FUTURE.

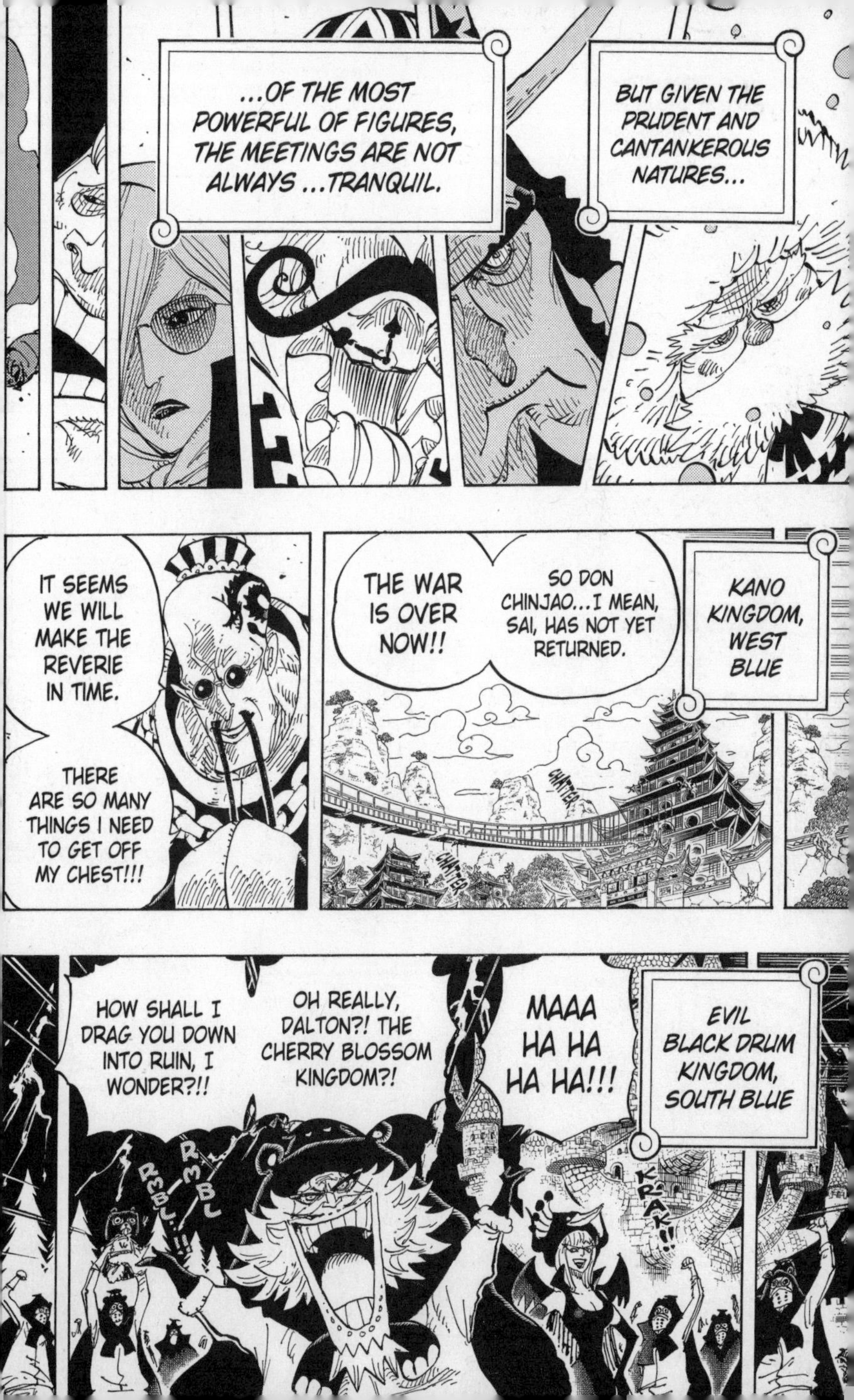
BUT GIVEN THE PRUDENT AND CANTANKEROUS NATURES...
...OF THE MOST POWERFUL OF FIGURES, THE MEETINGS ARE NOT ALWAYS ...TRANQUIL.
KANO KINGDOM, WEST BLUE
SO DON CHINJAO...I MEAN, SAI, HAS NOT YET RETURNED.
THE WAR IS OVER NOW!!
CHATTER
CHATTER
IT SEEMS WE WILL MAKE THE REVERIE IN TIME.
THERE ARE SO MANY THINGS I NEED TO GET OFF MY CHEST!!!
EVIL BLACK DRUM KINGDOM, SOUTH BLUE
KRAK!!
MAAA HA HA HA HA!!!
OH REALLY, DALTON?! THE CHERRY BLOSSOM KINGDOM?!
HOW SHALL I DRAG YOU DOWN INTO RUIN, I WONDER?!!
RMBL
RMBL!!

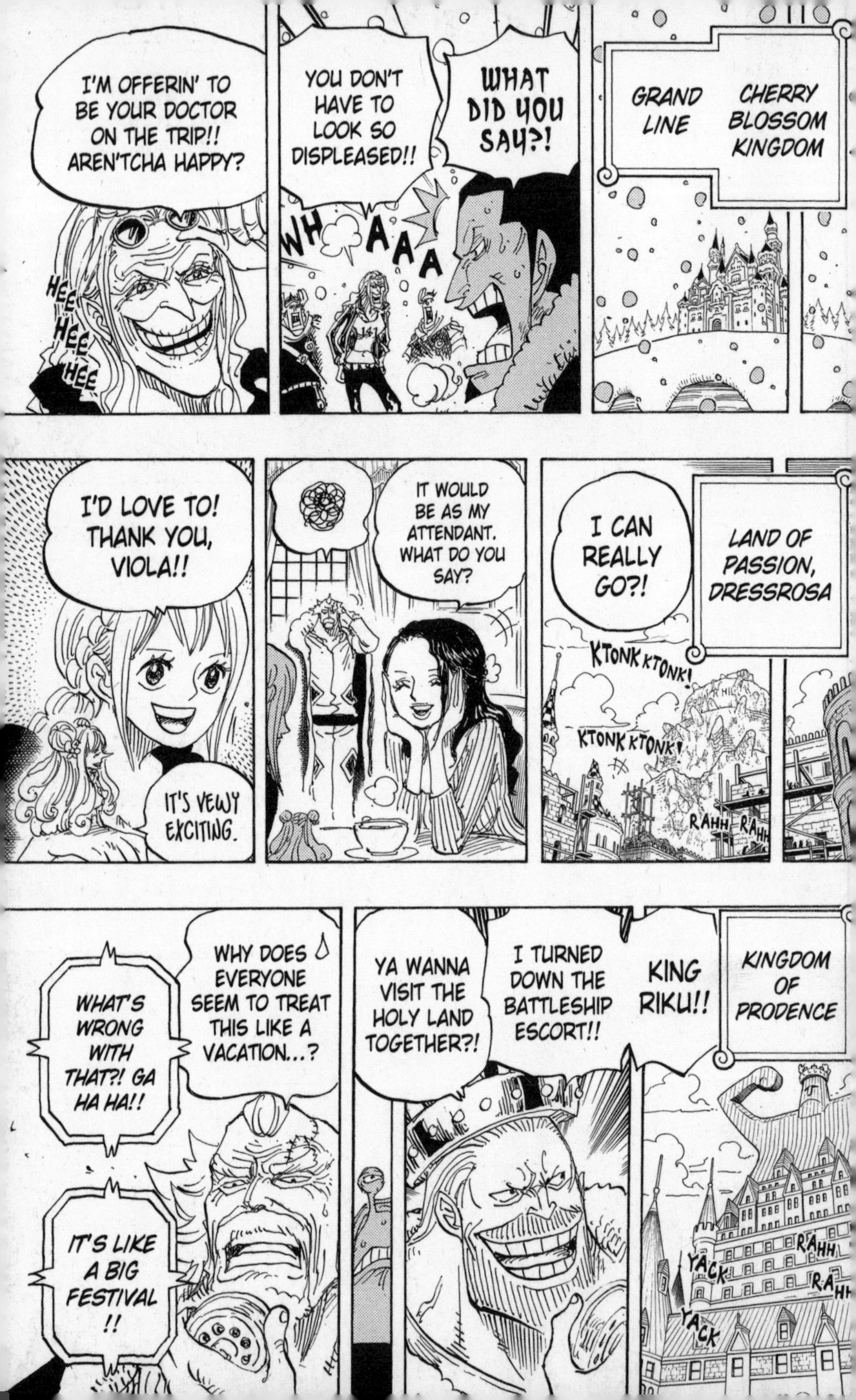
GRAND LINE
CHERRY BLOSSOM KINGDOM
WHAT DID YOU SAY?!
YOU DON'T HAVE TO LOOK SO DISPLEASED!!
WHAAA
I'M OFFERIN' TO BE YOUR DOCTOR ON THE TRIP!! AREN'TCHA HAPPY?
HEE HEE HEE HEE
LAND OF PASSION, DRESSROSA
I CAN REALLY GO?!
KTONK KTONK!
KTONK KTONK!
RAHH RAHH
IT WOULD BE AS MY ATTENDANT. WHAT DO YOU SAY?
I'D LOVE TO! THANK YOU, VIOLA!!
IT'S VEWY EXCITING.
KINGDOM OF PRODENCE
RAHH
RAHH
YACK
YACK
KING RIKU!!
I TURNED DOWN THE BATTLESHIP ESCORT!!
YA WANNA VISIT THE HOLY LAND TOGETHER?!
WHY DOES EVERYONE SEEM TO TREAT THIS LIKE A VACATION...?
WHAT'S WRONG WITH THAT?! GA HA HA!!
IT'S LIKE A BIG FESTIVAL!!

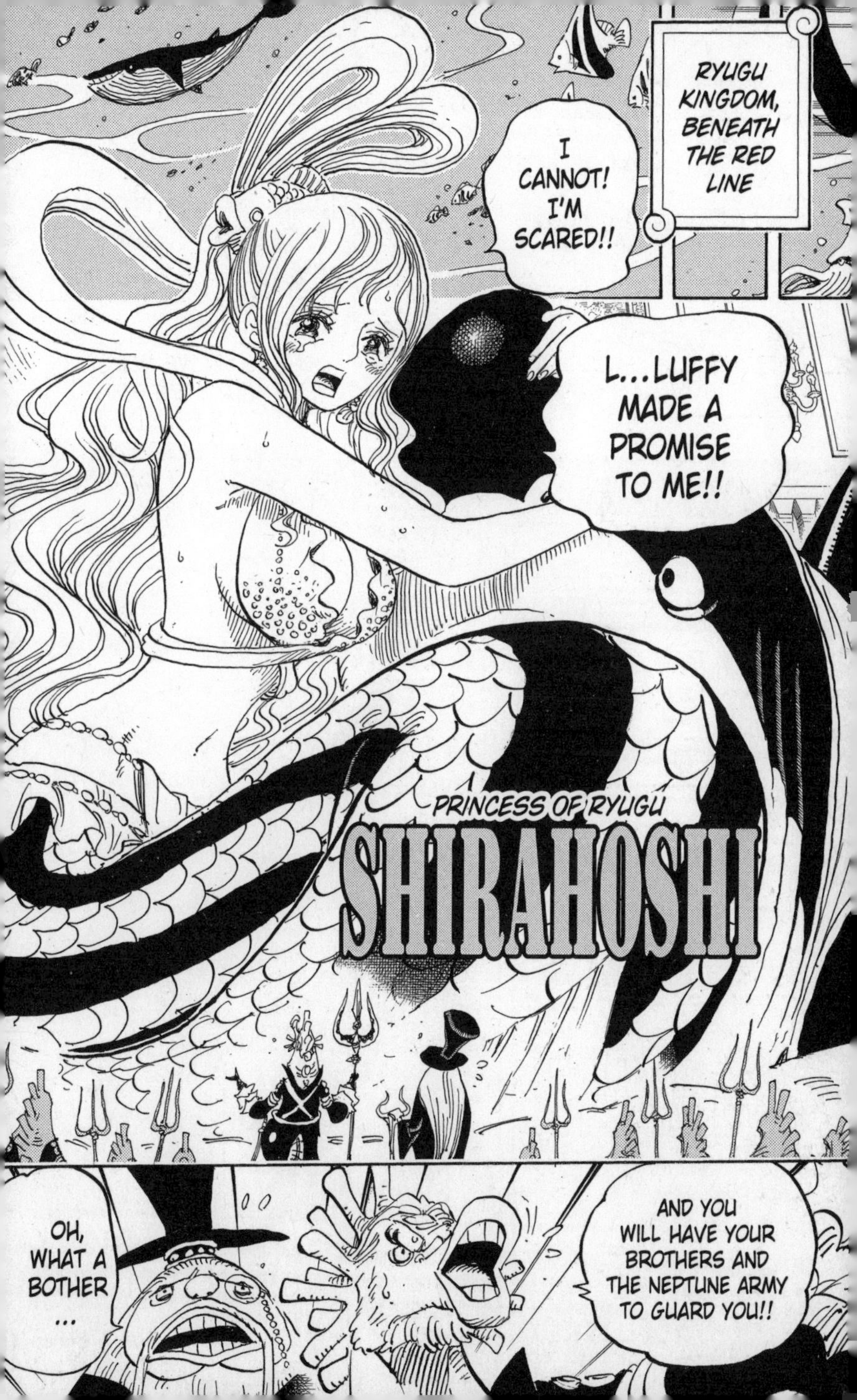
RYUGU KINGDOM, BENEATH THE RED LINE
I CANNOT! I'M SCARED!!
L...LUFFY MADE A PROMISE TO ME!!
PRINCESS OF RYUGU
SHIRAHOSHI
AND YOU WILL HAVE YOUR BROTHERS AND THE NEPTUNE ARMY TO GUARD YOU!!
OH, WHAT A BOTHER ...

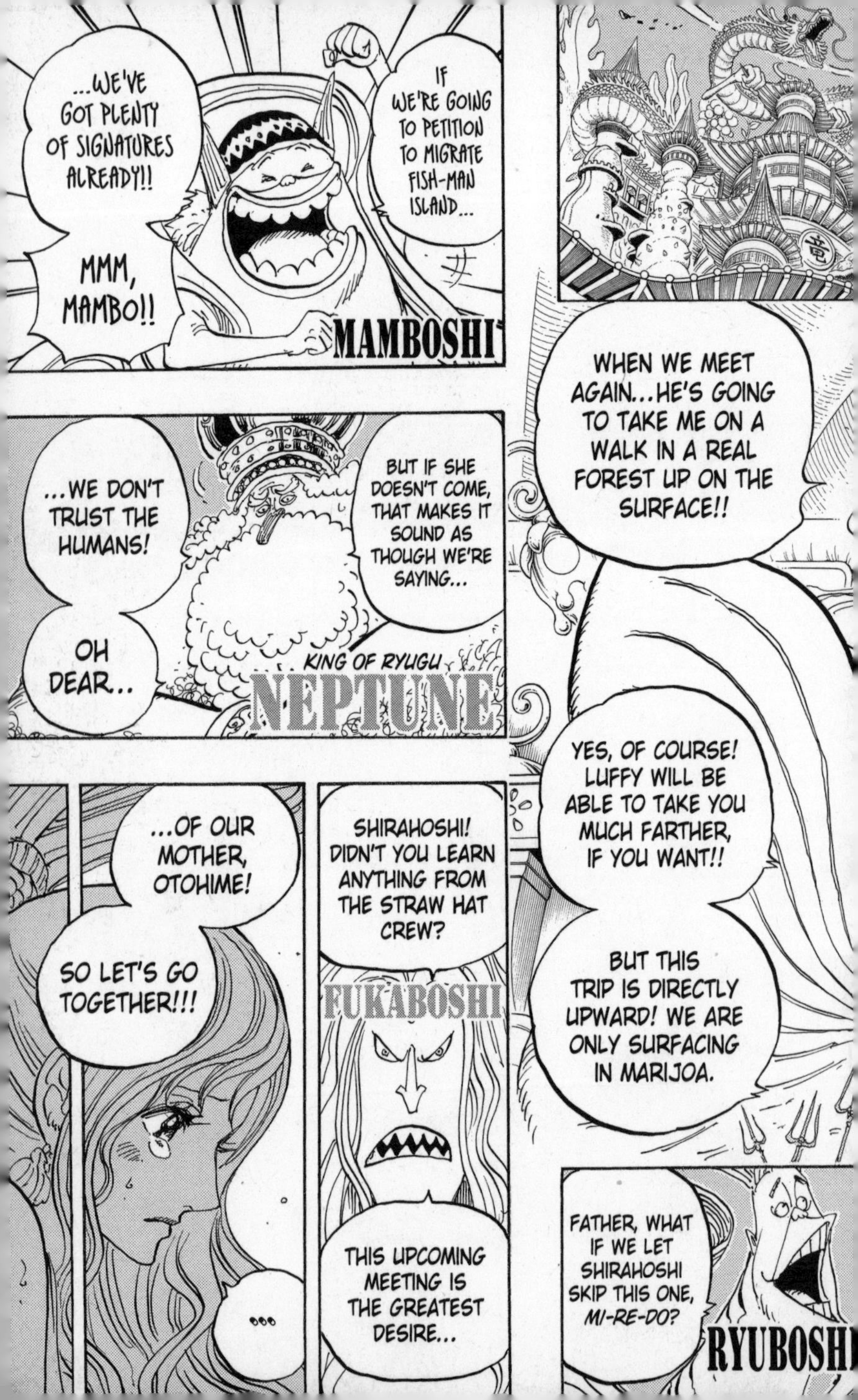
WHEN WE MEET AGAIN...HE'S GOING TO TAKE ME ON A WALK IN A REAL FOREST UP ON THE SURFACE!!
YES, OF COURSE! LUFFY WILL BE ABLE TO TAKE YOU MUCH FARTHER, IF YOU WANT!!
BUT THIS TRIP IS DIRECTLY UPWARD! WE ARE ONLY SURFACING IN MARIJOA.
FATHER, WHAT IF WE LET SHIRAHOSHI SKIP THIS ONE, *MI-RE-DO*?
RYUBOSHI
IF WE'RE GOING TO PETITION TO MIGRATE FISH-MAN ISLAND...
...WE'VE GOT PLENTY OF SIGNATURES ALREADY!!
MMM, MAMBO!!
MAMBOSHI
BUT IF SHE DOESN'T COME, THAT MAKES IT SOUND AS THOUGH WE'RE SAYING...
...WE DON'T TRUST THE HUMANS!
OH DEAR...
KING OF RYUGU
NEPTUNE
SHIRAHOSHI! DIDN'T YOU LEARN ANYTHING FROM THE STRAW HAT CREW?
FUKABOSHI
THIS UPCOMING MEETING IS THE GREATEST DESIRE...
...OF OUR MOTHER, OTOHIME!
SO LET'S GO TOGETHER!!!
...

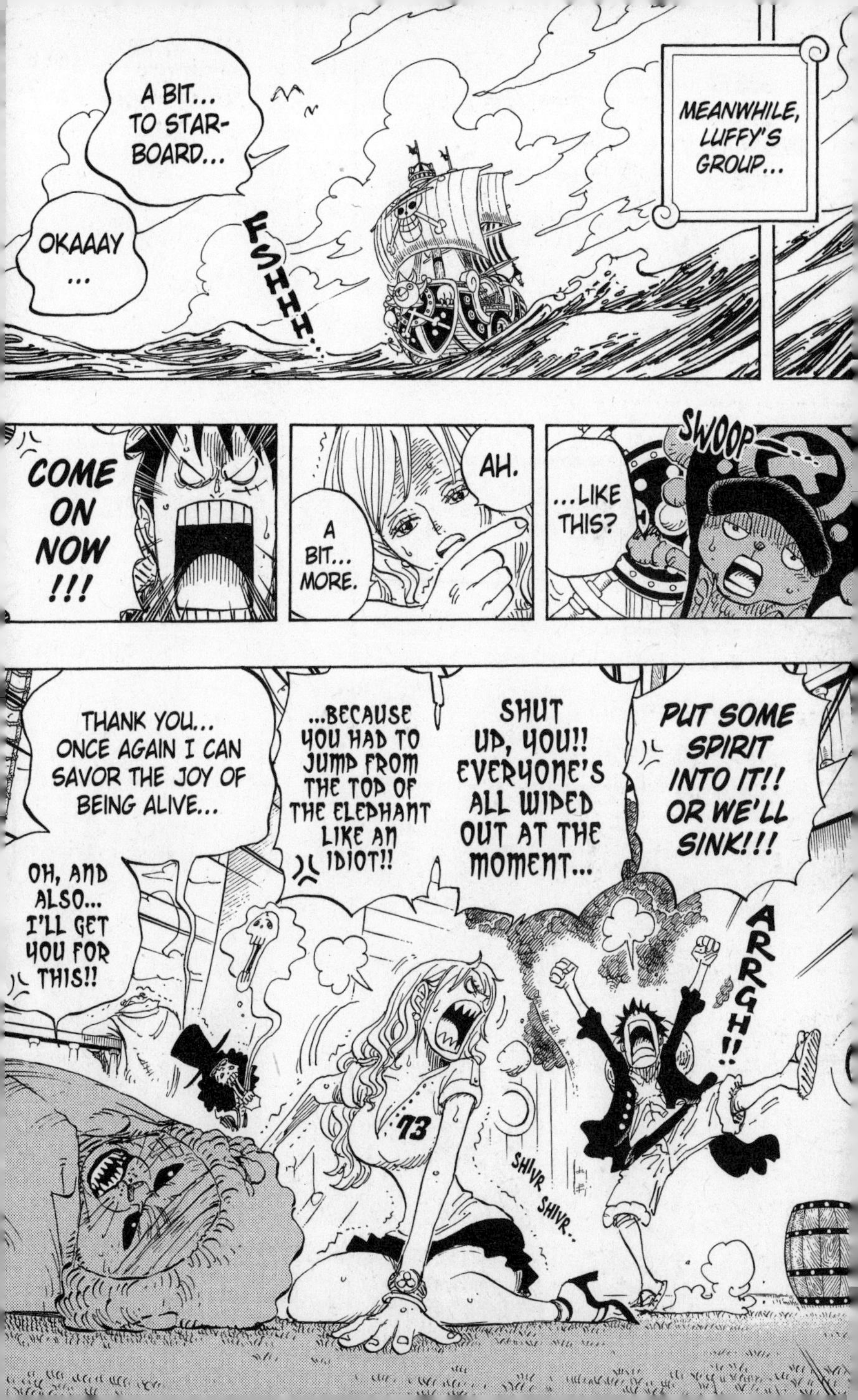
MEANWHILE, LUFFY'S GROUP...
A BIT... TO STAR-BOARD...
OKAAAY ...
FSHHH...
SWOOP
...LIKE THIS?
AH.
A BIT... MORE.
COME ON NOW !!!
PUT SOME SPIRIT INTO IT!! OR WE'LL SINK!!!
ARRGH!!
SHUT UP, YOU!! EVERYONE'S ALL WIPED OUT AT THE MOMENT...
...BECAUSE YOU HAD TO JUMP FROM THE TOP OF THE ELEPHANT LIKE AN IDIOT!!
THANK YOU... ONCE AGAIN I CAN SAVOR THE JOY OF BEING ALIVE...
OH, AND ALSO... I'LL GET YOU FOR THIS!!
SHIVR SHIVR...

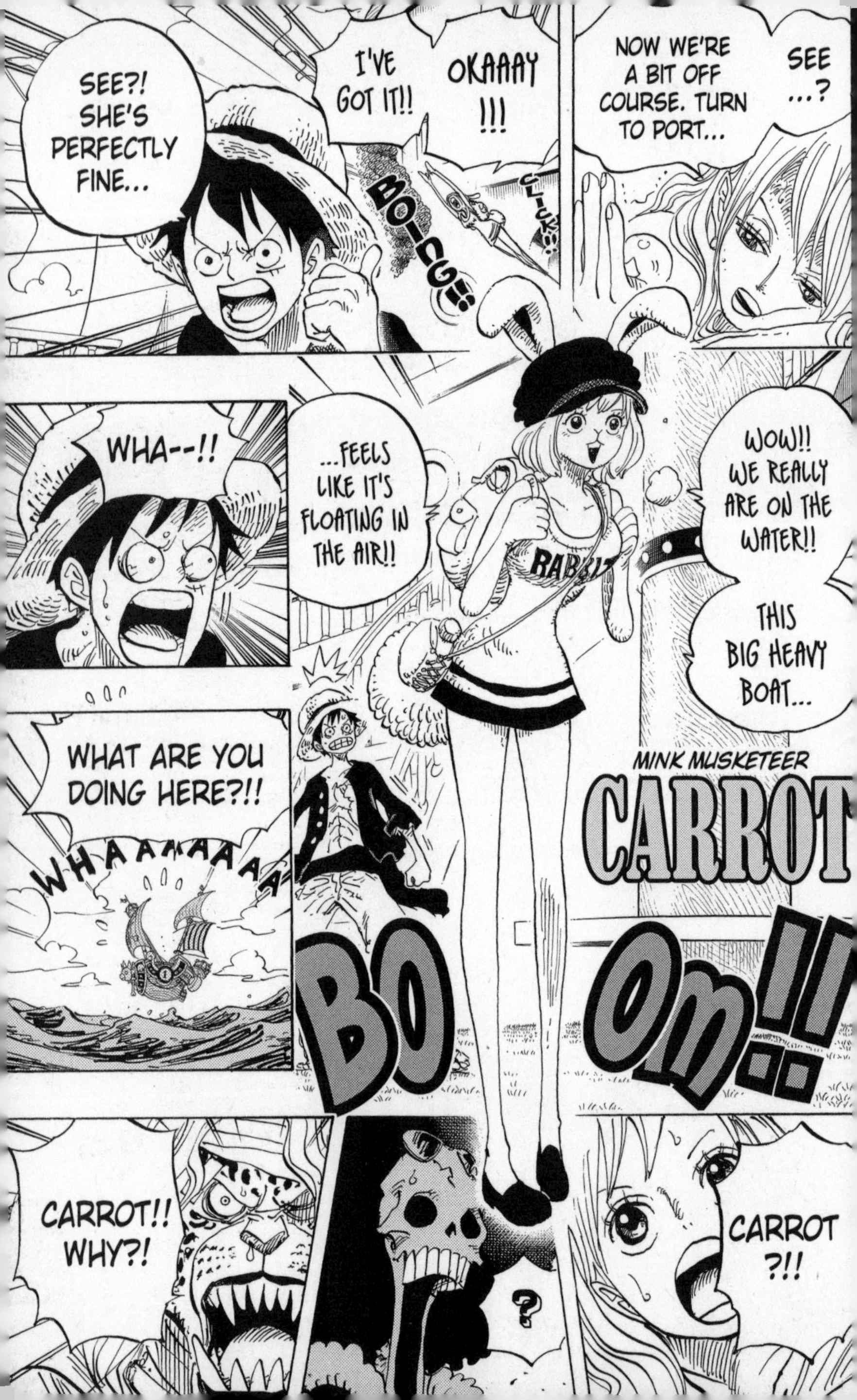
SEE ...?
NOW WE'RE A BIT OFF COURSE. TURN TO PORT...
OKAAAY !!!
I'VE GOT IT!!
BOING!!
CLICK!!
SEE?! SHE'S PERFECTLY FINE...
WOW!! WE REALLY ARE ON THE WATER!!
THIS BIG HEAVY BOAT...
...FEELS LIKE IT'S FLOATING IN THE AIR!!
WHA--!!
RABBIT
MINK MUSKETEER
CARROT
BOOM!!
WHAT ARE YOU DOING HERE?!!
WHAAAAAAAA
CARROT ?!!
?
CARROT!! WHY?!

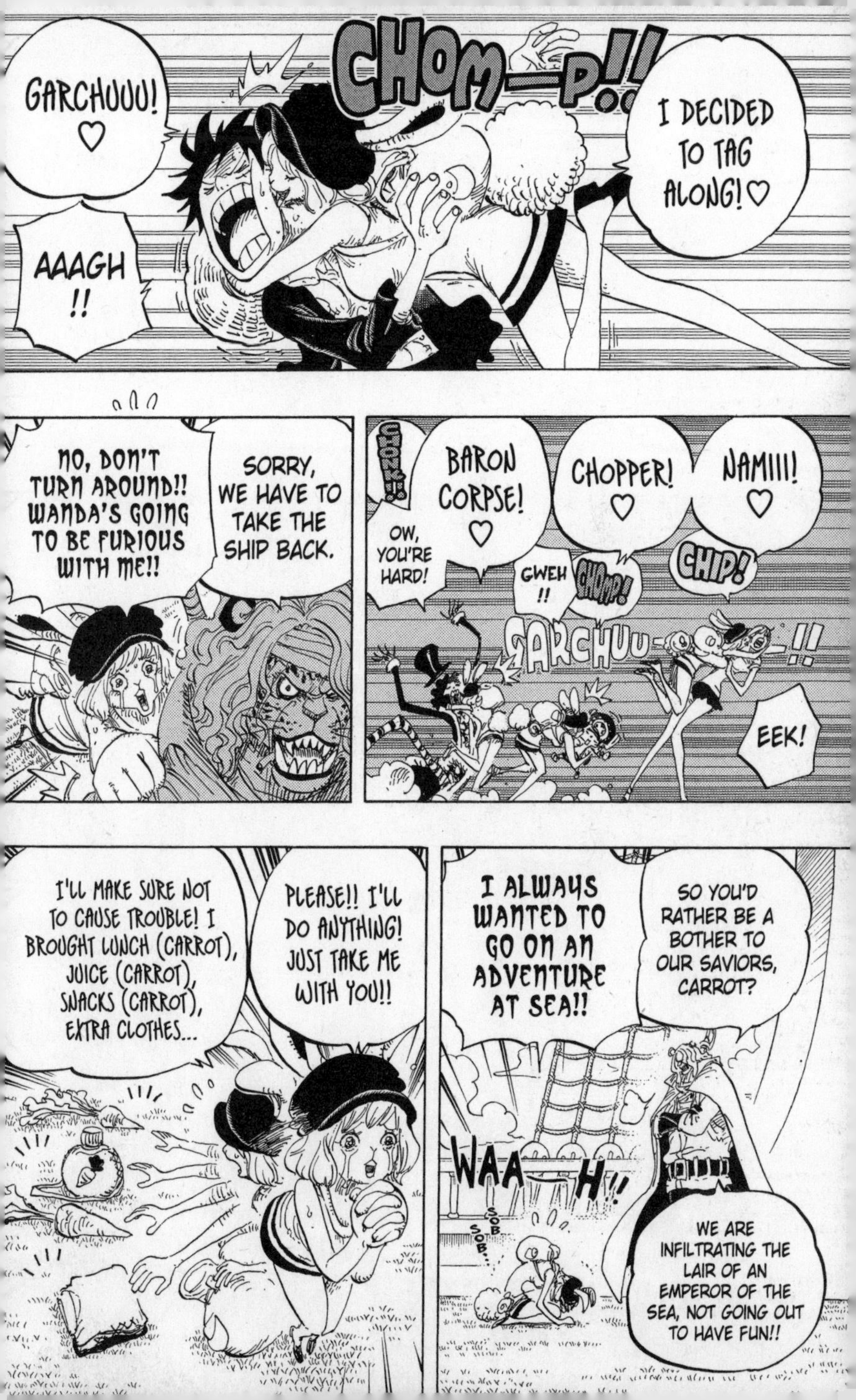
CHOM-P!!
I DECIDED TO TAG ALONG!♡
GARCHUUU! ♡
AAAGH!!
NAMIIII! ♡
CHOPPER! ♡
BARON CORPSE! ♡
CHONK!!
CHIP!
CHOMP!
OW, YOU'RE HARD!
GWEH!!
GARCHUU-!!
EEK!
SORRY, WE HAVE TO TAKE THE SHIP BACK.
NO, DON'T TURN AROUND!! WANDA'S GOING TO BE FURIOUS WITH ME!!
SO YOU'D RATHER BE A BOTHER TO OUR SAVIORS, CARROT?
I ALWAYS WANTED TO GO ON AN ADVENTURE AT SEA!!
WAA-H!!
SOB SOB...
WE ARE INFILTRATING THE LAIR OF AN EMPEROR OF THE SEA, NOT GOING OUT TO HAVE FUN!!
PLEASE!! I'LL DO ANYTHING! JUST TAKE ME WITH YOU!!
I'LL MAKE SURE NOT TO CAUSE TROUBLE! I BROUGHT LUNCH (CARROT), JUICE (CARROT), SNACKS (CARROT), EXTRA CLOTHES...

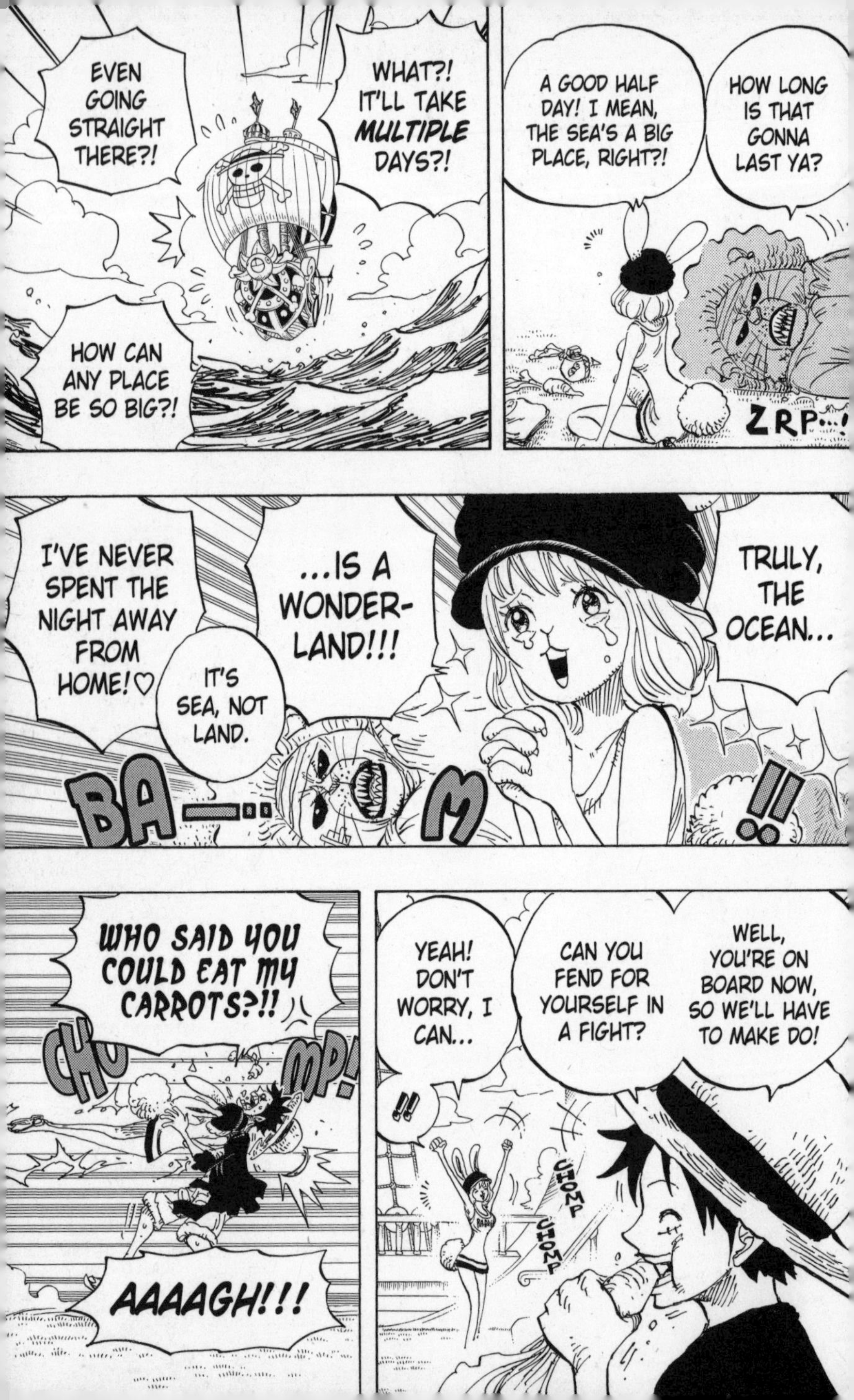
HOW LONG IS THAT GONNA LAST YA?
A GOOD HALF DAY! I MEAN, THE SEA'S A BIG PLACE, RIGHT?!
ZRP...!
WHAT?! IT'LL TAKE *MULTIPLE* DAYS?!
EVEN GOING STRAIGHT THERE?!
HOW CAN ANY PLACE BE SO BIG?!
TRULY, THE OCEAN...
...IS A WONDERLAND!!!
I'VE NEVER SPENT THE NIGHT AWAY FROM HOME!♡
IT'S SEA, NOT LAND.
BA—...M
!!
WELL, YOU'RE ON BOARD NOW, SO WE'LL HAVE TO MAKE DO!
CAN YOU FEND FOR YOURSELF IN A FIGHT?
YEAH! DON'T WORRY, I CAN...
!!
CHOMP
CHOMP
WHO SAID YOU COULD EAT MY CARROTS?!!
CHOMP!
AAAAGH!!!

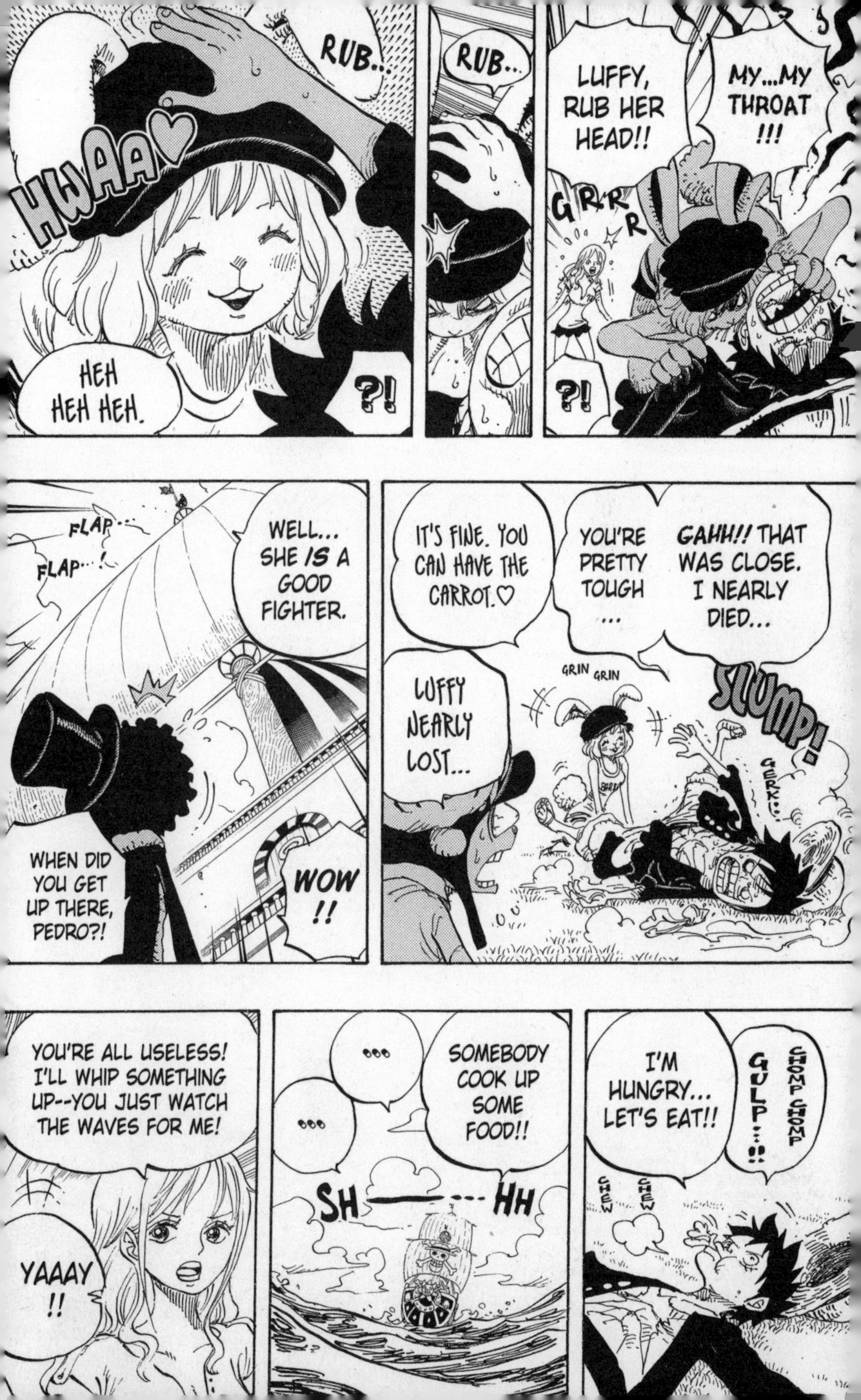

MY...MY THROAT !!!
LUFFY, RUB HER HEAD!!
GRRR
?!
RUB...
?!
RUB...
HWAA♡
HEH HEH HEH.
GAHH!! THAT WAS CLOSE. I NEARLY DIED...
YOU'RE PRETTY TOUGH ...
IT'S FINE. YOU CAN HAVE THE CARROT.♡
SLUMP!
GRIN GRIN
GERK!...
LUFFY NEARLY LOST...
WELL... SHE IS A GOOD FIGHTER.
FLAP...
FLAP...!
WOW !!
WHEN DID YOU GET UP THERE, PEDRO?!
CHOMP CHOMP
GULP...!!
I'M HUNGRY... LET'S EAT!!
CHEW CHEW
SOMEBODY COOK UP SOME FOOD!!
...
...
SH———...HH
YOU'RE ALL USELESS! I'LL WHIP SOMETHING UP--YOU JUST WATCH THE WAVES FOR ME!
YAAAY !!

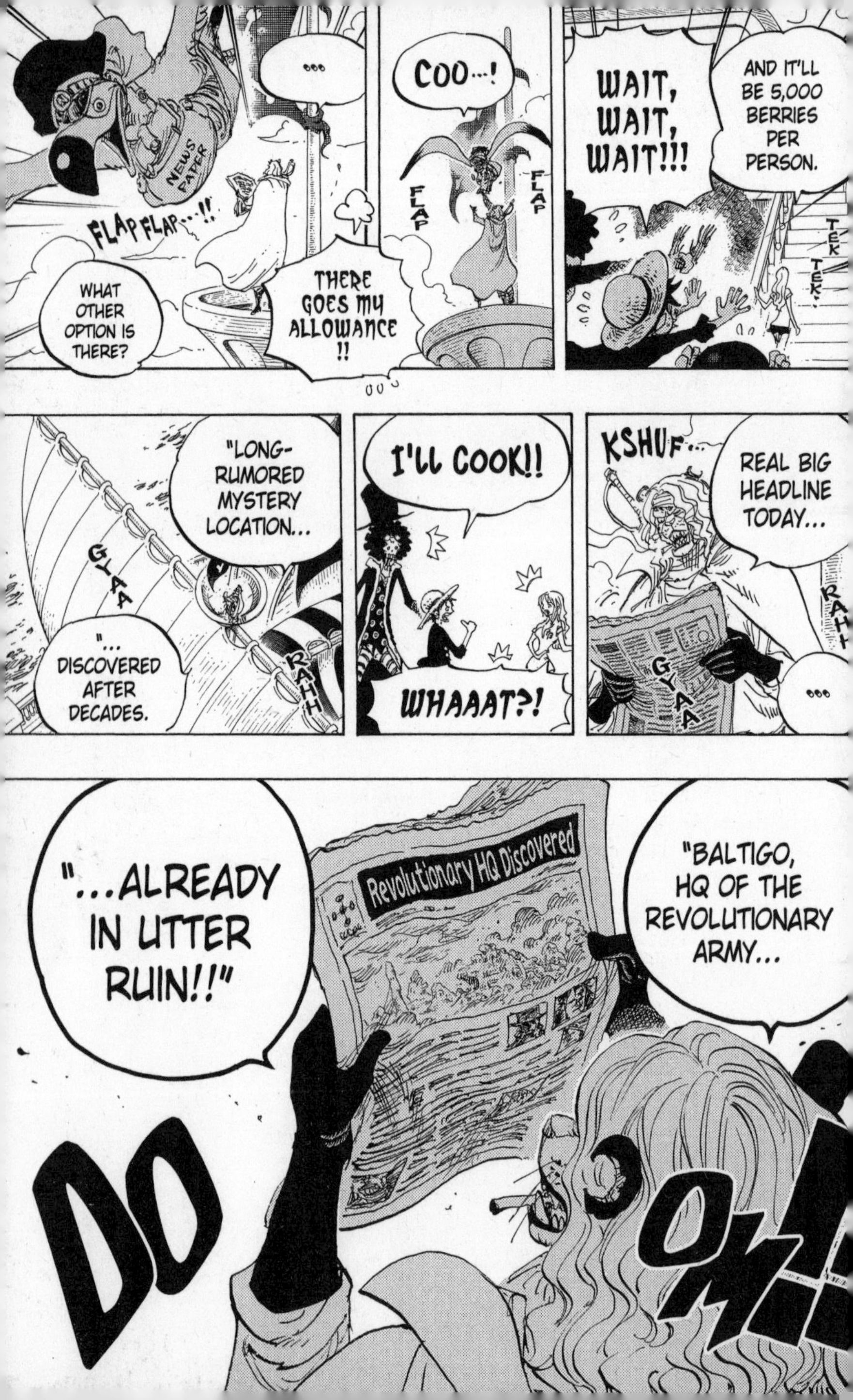
AND IT'LL BE 5,000 BERRIES PER PERSON.
WAIT, WAIT, WAIT!!!
TEK
TEK
COO...!
FLAP
FLAP
THERE GOES MY ALLOWANCE!!
...
FLAP FLAP...!!
WHAT OTHER OPTION IS THERE?
KSHUF...
REAL BIG HEADLINE TODAY...
RAHH
GYAA
...
I'LL COOK!!
WHAAAT?!
"LONG-RUMORED MYSTERY LOCATION...
GYAA
"...DISCOVERED AFTER DECADES.
RAHH
"BALTIGO, HQ OF THE REVOLUTIONARY ARMY...
Revolutionary HQ Discovered
"...ALREADY IN UTTER RUIN!!"
DOOM!!

PLAYING PIRATES

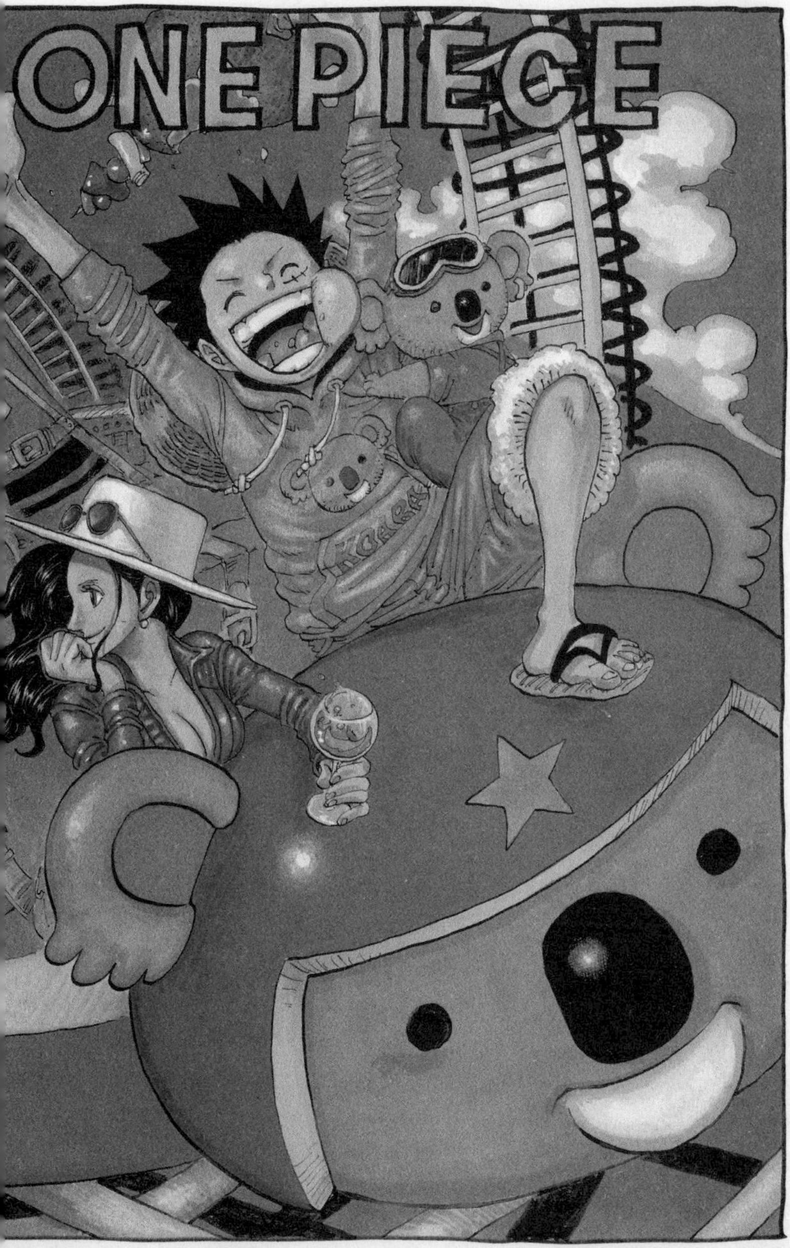
ONE PIECE

Chapter 824:

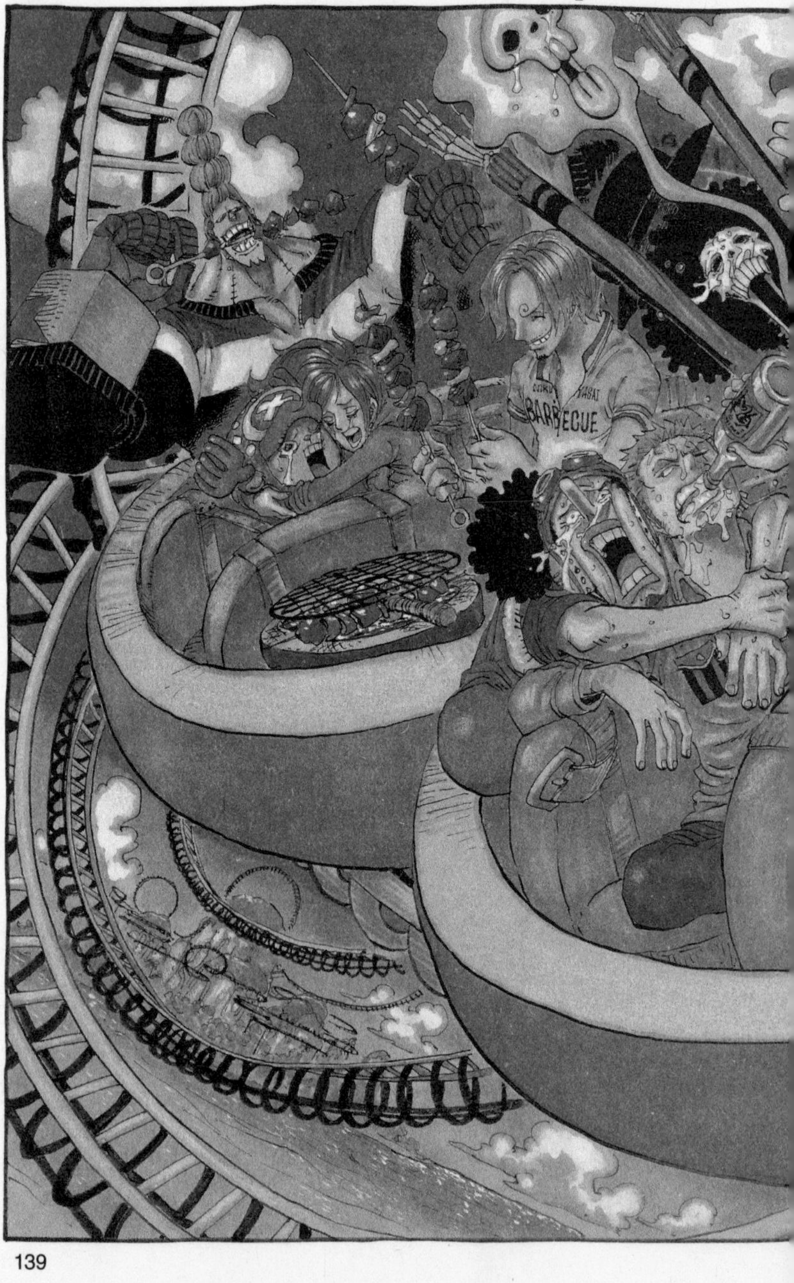
BARBECUE

vol. 82
ONE PIECE

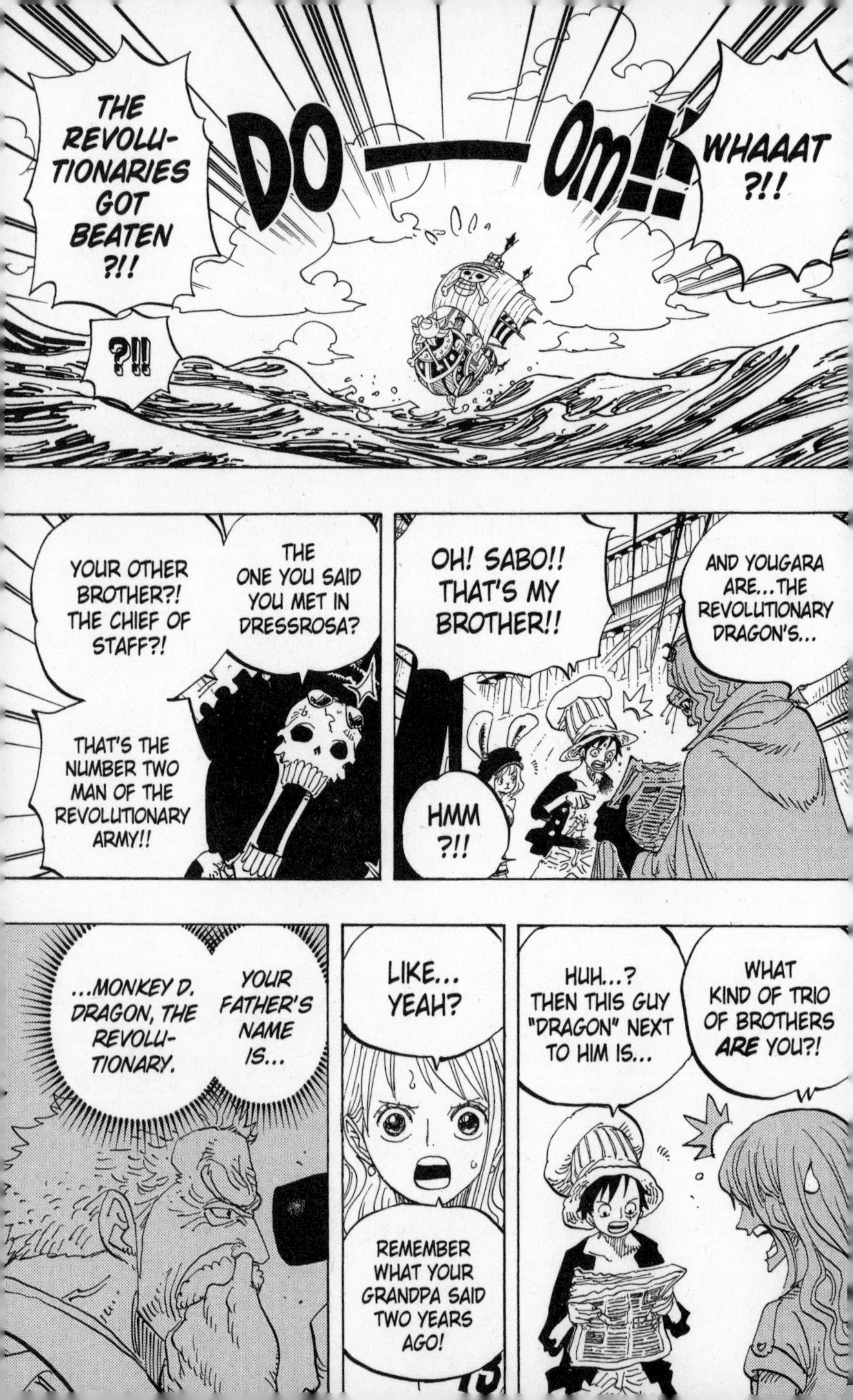
WHAAAT ?!!
DO—OM!!
THE REVOLUTIONARIES GOT BEATEN ?!!
?!!
AND YOUGARA ARE...THE REVOLUTIONARY DRAGON'S...
OH! SABO!! THAT'S MY BROTHER!!
HMM ?!!
THE ONE YOU SAID YOU MET IN DRESSROSA?
YOUR OTHER BROTHER?! THE CHIEF OF STAFF?!
THAT'S THE NUMBER TWO MAN OF THE REVOLUTIONARY ARMY!!
WHAT KIND OF TRIO OF BROTHERS **ARE** YOU?!
HUH...? THEN THIS GUY "DRAGON" NEXT TO HIM IS...
LIKE... YEAH?
REMEMBER WHAT YOUR GRANDPA SAID TWO YEARS AGO!
YOUR FATHER'S NAME IS...
...MONKEY D. DRAGON, THE REVOLUTIONARY.

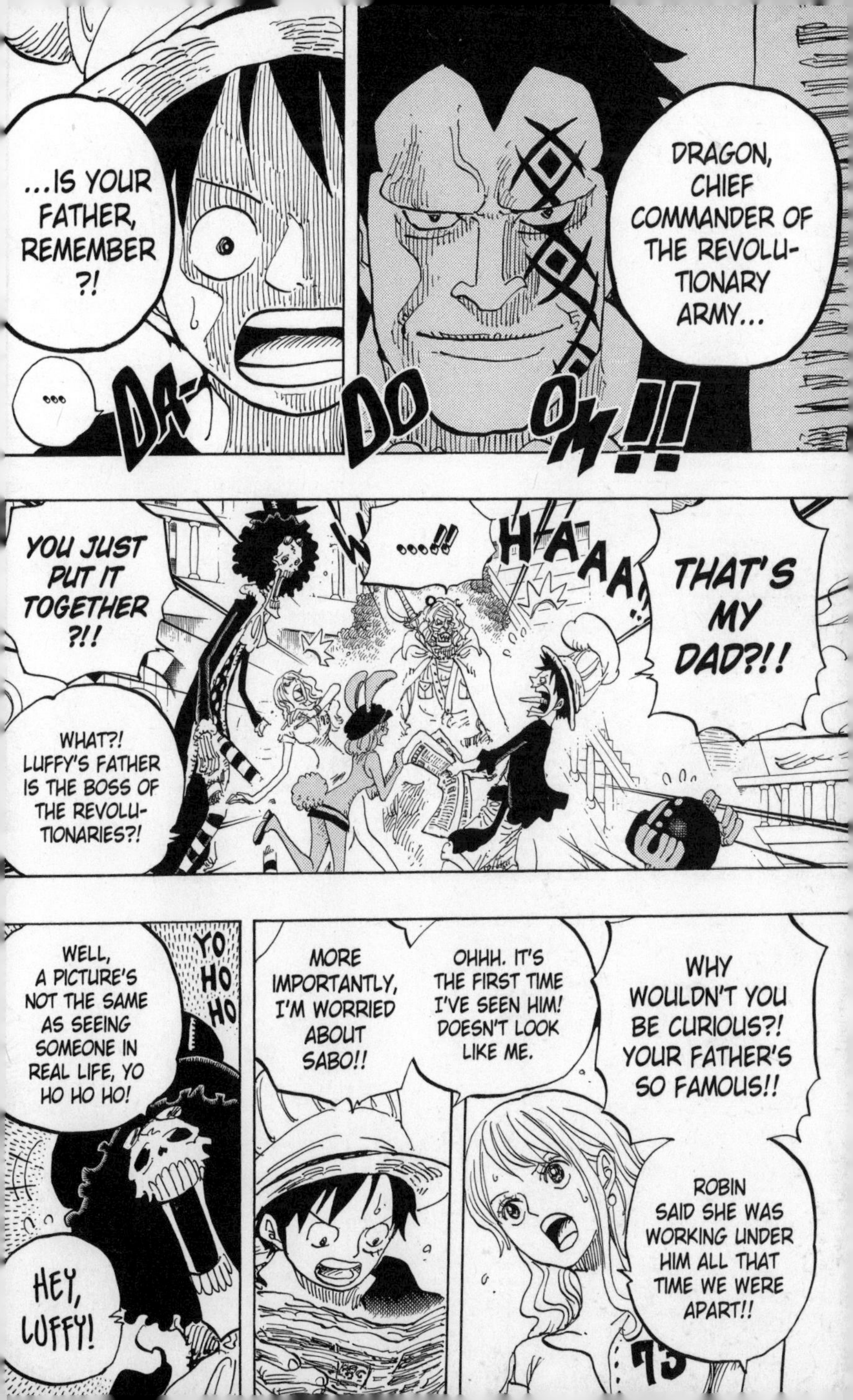
DRAGON, CHIEF COMMANDER OF THE REVOLUTIONARY ARMY...
...IS YOUR FATHER, REMEMBER?!
...
DA-DOOM!!
THAT'S MY DAD?!!
...!!
WHAAA
YOU JUST PUT IT TOGETHER?!!
WHAT?! LUFFY'S FATHER IS THE BOSS OF THE REVOLUTIONARIES?!
WHY WOULDN'T YOU BE CURIOUS?! YOUR FATHER'S SO FAMOUS!!
ROBIN SAID SHE WAS WORKING UNDER HIM ALL THAT TIME WE WERE APART!!
OHHH. IT'S THE FIRST TIME I'VE SEEN HIM! DOESN'T LOOK LIKE ME.
MORE IMPORTANTLY, I'M WORRIED ABOUT SABO!!
YO HO HO
WELL, A PICTURE'S NOT THE SAME AS SEEING SOMEONE IN REAL LIFE, YO HO HO HO!
HEY, LUFFY!

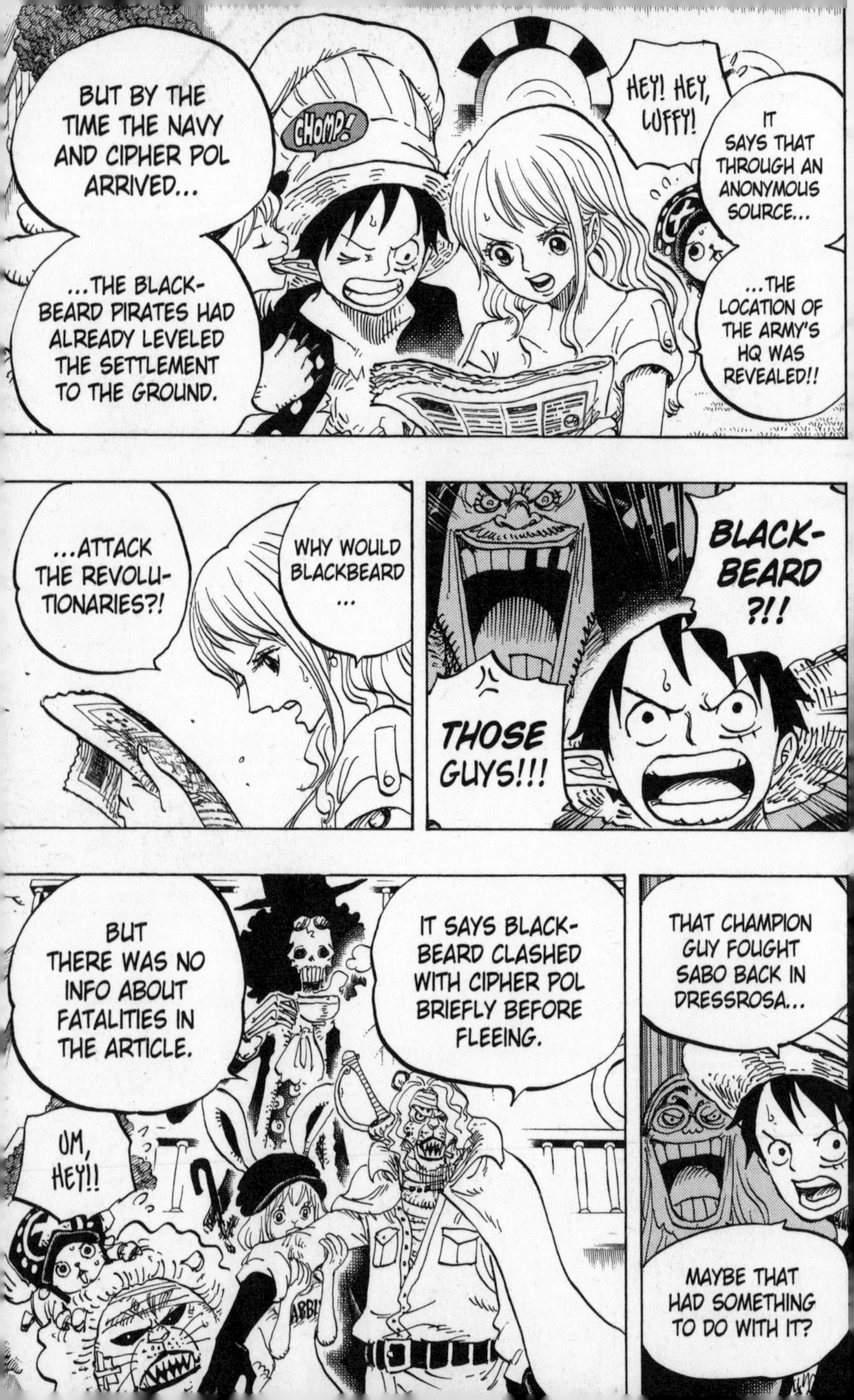
HEY! HEY, LUFFY!
IT SAYS THAT THROUGH AN ANONYMOUS SOURCE...
...THE LOCATION OF THE ARMY'S HQ WAS REVEALED!!
CHOMP!
BUT BY THE TIME THE NAVY AND CIPHER POL ARRIVED...
...THE BLACK-BEARD PIRATES HAD ALREADY LEVELED THE SETTLEMENT TO THE GROUND.
BLACK-BEARD?!!
THOSE GUYS!!!
WHY WOULD BLACKBEARD...
...ATTACK THE REVOLU-TIONARIES?!
THAT CHAMPION GUY FOUGHT SABO BACK IN DRESSROSA...
MAYBE THAT HAD SOMETHING TO DO WITH IT?
IT SAYS BLACK-BEARD CLASHED WITH CIPHER POL BRIEFLY BEFORE FLEEING.
BUT THERE WAS NO INFO ABOUT FATALITIES IN THE ARTICLE.
UM, HEY!!

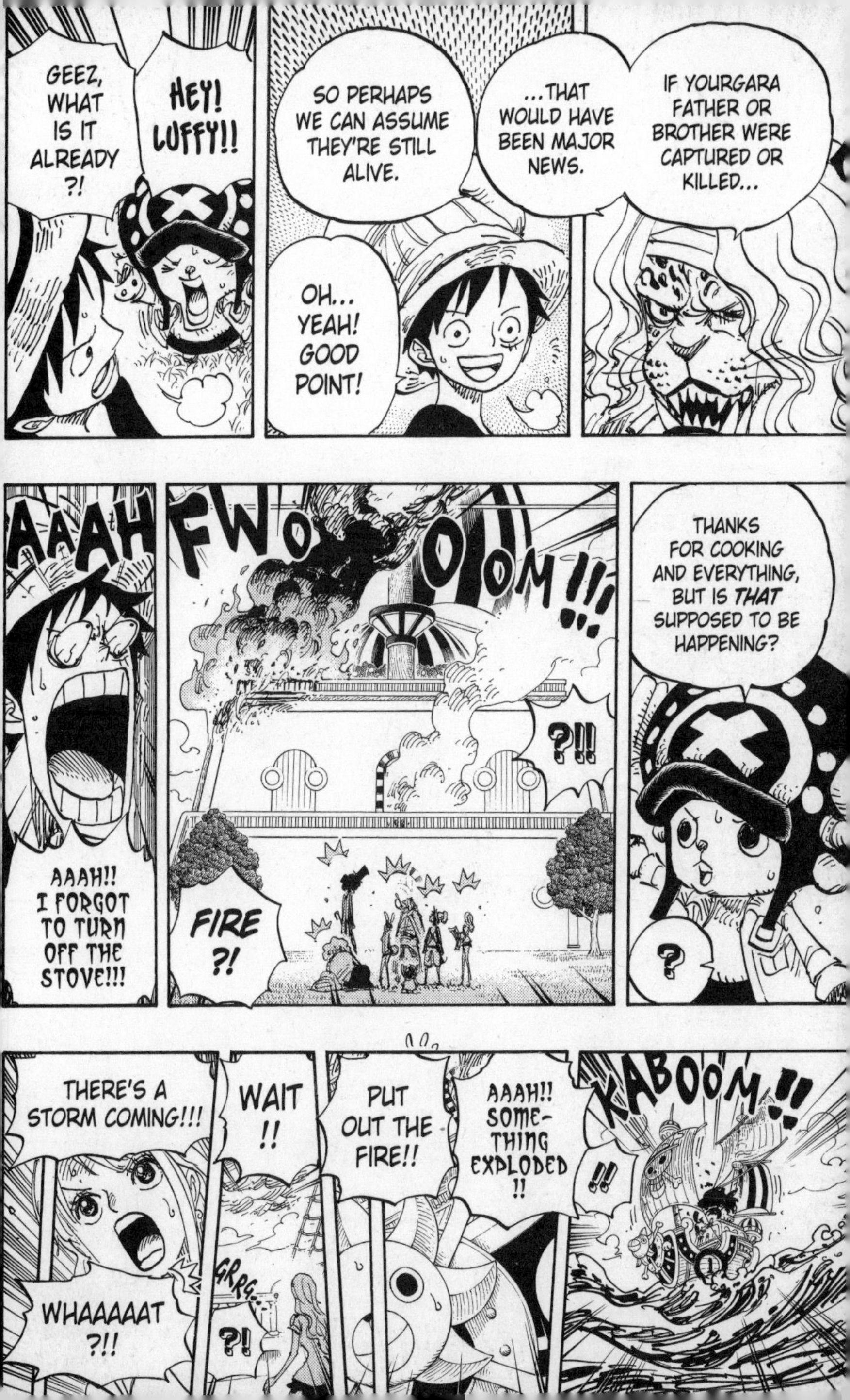
IF YOURGARA FATHER OR BROTHER WERE CAPTURED OR KILLED...
...THAT WOULD HAVE BEEN MAJOR NEWS.
SO PERHAPS WE CAN ASSUME THEY'RE STILL ALIVE.
OH... YEAH! GOOD POINT!
HEY! LUFFY!!
GEEZ, WHAT IS IT ALREADY ?!
THANKS FOR COOKING AND EVERYTHING, BUT IS THAT SUPPOSED TO BE HAPPENING?
?
FWOOOM!!!
?!!
FIRE ?!
AAAH
AAAH!! I FORGOT TO TURN OFF THE STOVE!!!
KABOOM!!
AAAH!! SOME-THING EXPLODED !!
!!
PUT OUT THE FIRE!!
WAIT !!
GRRG...
?!
THERE'S A STORM COMING!!!
WHAAAAAT ?!!

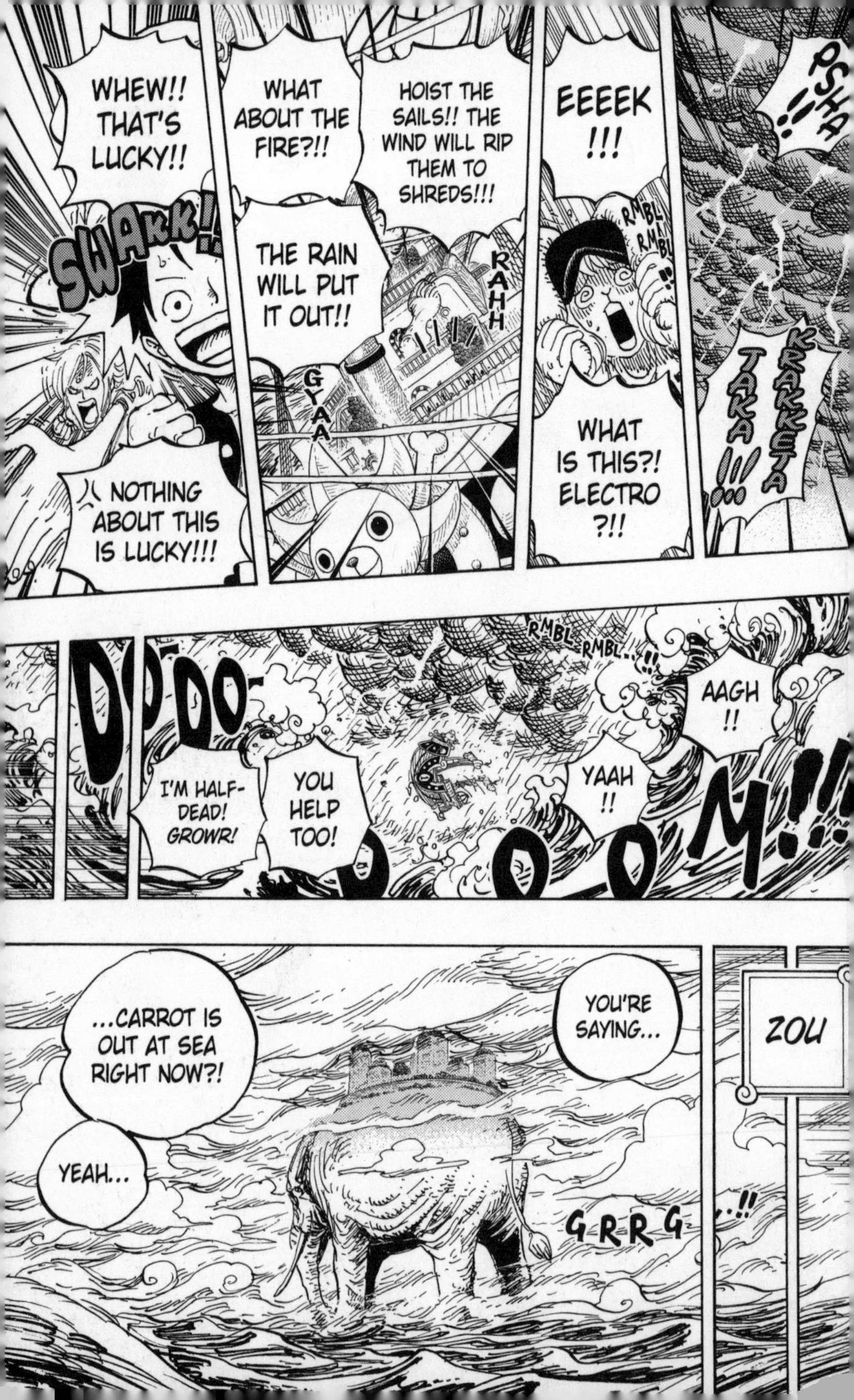
PSHA!!!
KRAKKETA TAKA!!!...
EEEEK!!!
RMBL RMBL!!
WHAT IS THIS?! ELECTRO?!!
HOIST THE SAILS!! THE WIND WILL RIP THEM TO SHREDS!!!
WHAT ABOUT THE FIRE?!!
RAHH
THE RAIN WILL PUT IT OUT!!
GYAA
WHEW!! THAT'S LUCKY!!
SWAKK!!
NOTHING ABOUT THIS IS LUCKY!!!
RMBL RMBL..!!
AAGH!!
YAAH!!
DO-DO-O-O-OM!!!
YOU HELP TOO!
I'M HALF-DEAD! GROWR!
ZOU
YOU'RE SAYING...
...CARROT IS OUT AT SEA RIGHT NOW?!
YEAH...
GRRRG..!!

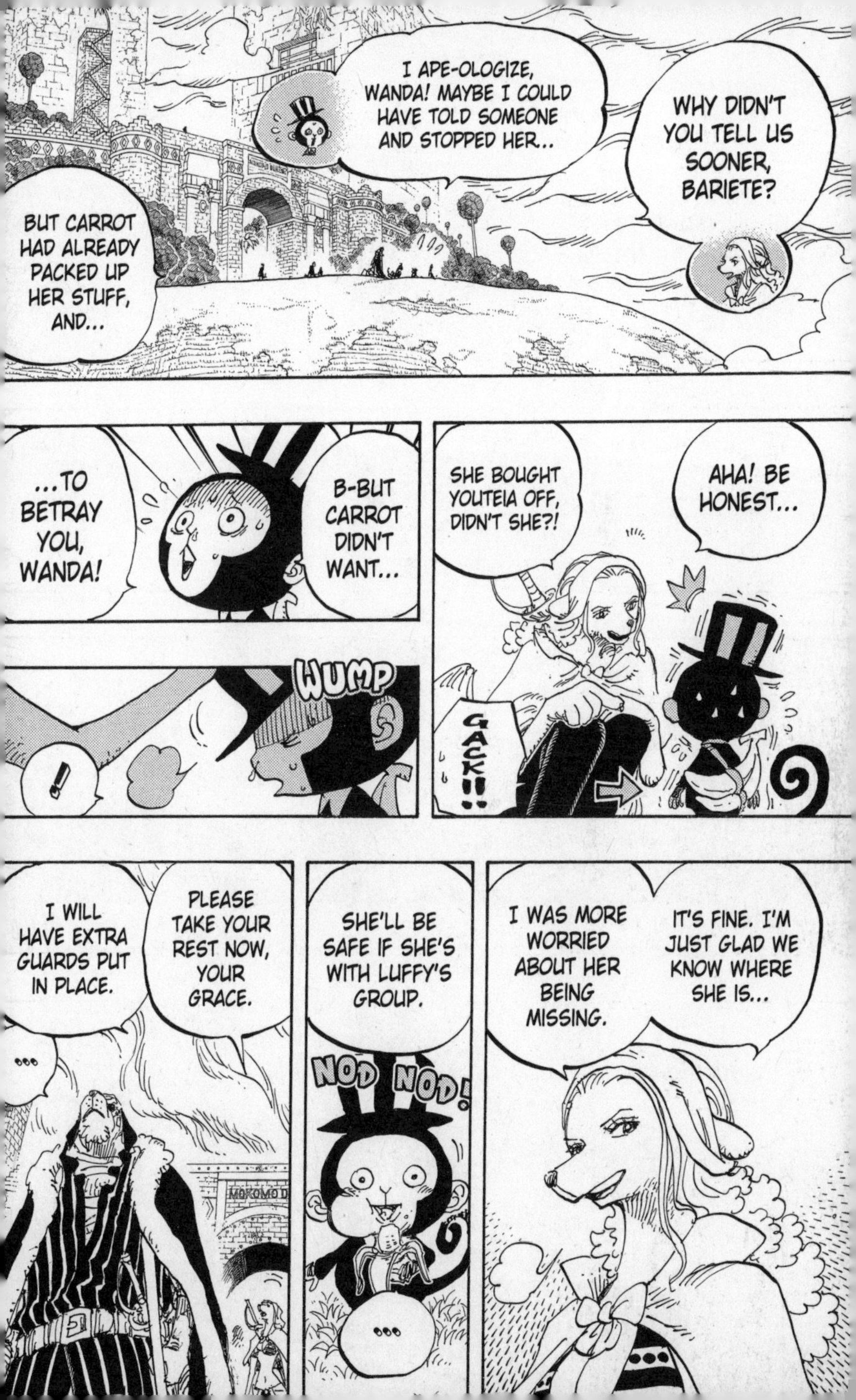
WHY DIDN'T YOU TELL US SOONER, BARIETE?
I APE-OLOGIZE, WANDA! MAYBE I COULD HAVE TOLD SOMEONE AND STOPPED HER...
BUT CARROT HAD ALREADY PACKED UP HER STUFF, AND...
AHA! BE HONEST...
SHE BOUGHT YOUTEIA OFF, DIDN'T SHE?!
GACK!!
B-BUT CARROT DIDN'T WANT...
...TO BETRAY YOU, WANDA!
WUMP
!
IT'S FINE. I'M JUST GLAD WE KNOW WHERE SHE IS...
I WAS MORE WORRIED ABOUT HER BEING MISSING.
SHE'LL BE SAFE IF SHE'S WITH LUFFY'S GROUP.
NOD NOD!
...
PLEASE TAKE YOUR REST NOW, YOUR GRACE.
I WILL HAVE EXTRA GUARDS PUT IN PLACE.
...

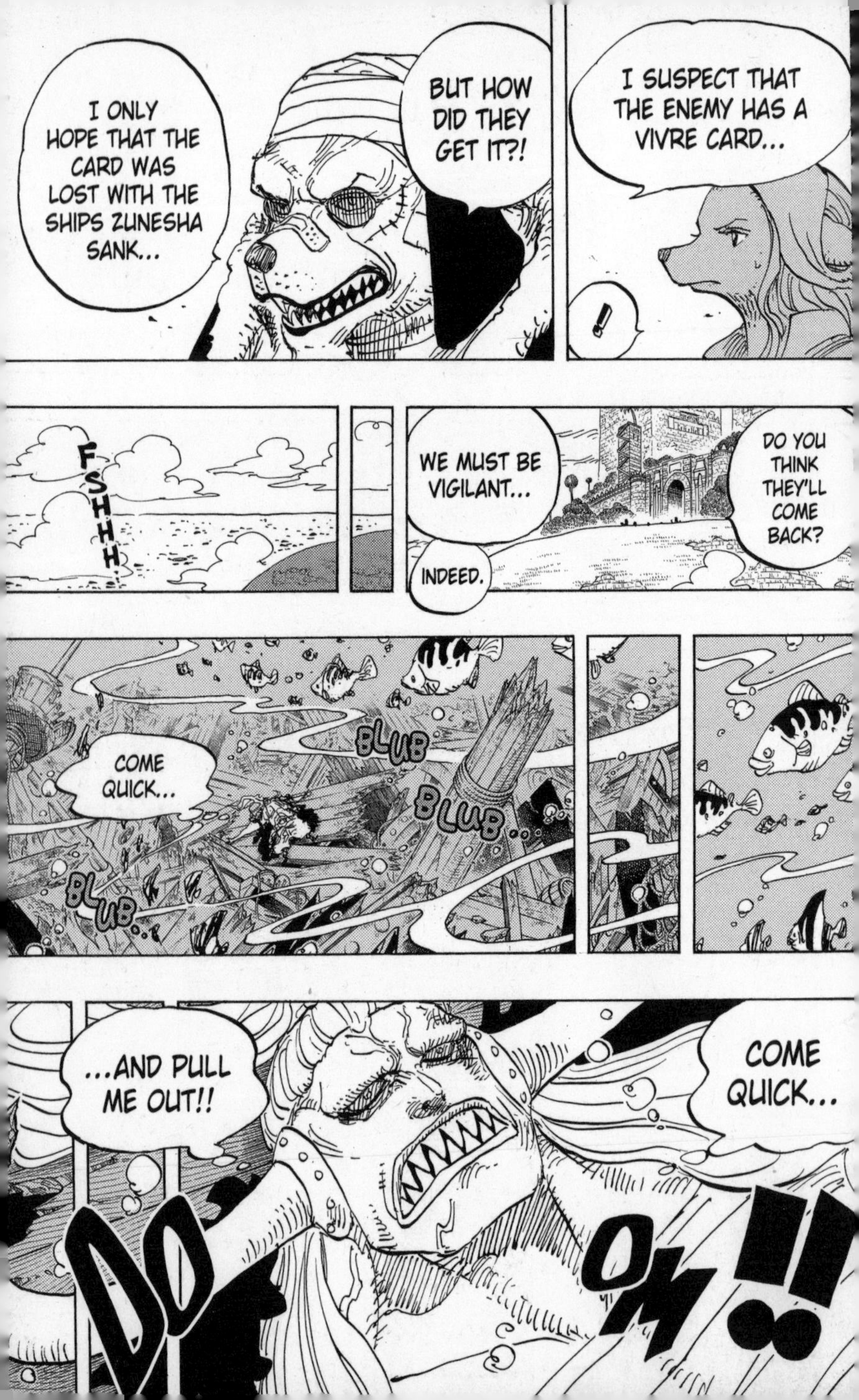
I SUSPECT THAT THE ENEMY HAS A VIVRE CARD...
!
BUT HOW DID THEY GET IT?!
I ONLY HOPE THAT THE CARD WAS LOST WITH THE SHIPS ZUNESHA SANK...
DO YOU THINK THEY'LL COME BACK?
WE MUST BE VIGILANT...
INDEED.
FSHHH
BLUB
BLUB..
COME QUICK...
BLUB..
COME QUICK...
...AND PULL ME OUT!!
DO
OM!!

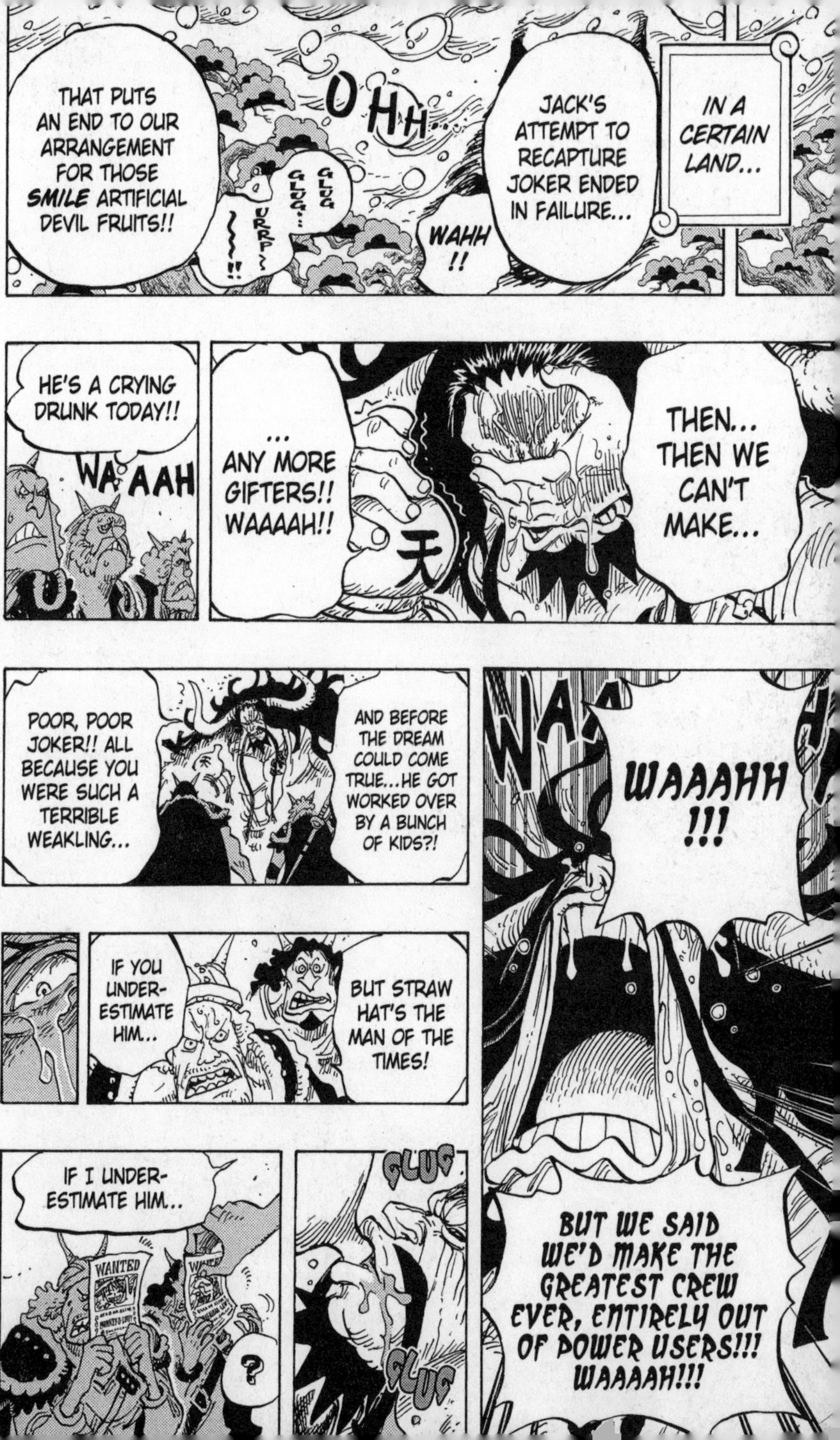
IN A CERTAIN LAND...
JACK'S ATTEMPT TO RECAPTURE JOKER ENDED IN FAILURE...
OHHH
WAHH!!
GLUG GLUG...
URRP~ ~~~!!
THAT PUTS AN END TO OUR ARRANGEMENT FOR THOSE **SMILE** ARTIFICIAL DEVIL FRUITS!!
THEN... THEN WE CAN'T MAKE...
... ANY MORE GIFTERS!! WAAAAH!!
HE'S A CRYING DRUNK TODAY!!
WA AAH
WAAAHH!!!
BUT WE SAID WE'D MAKE THE GREATEST CREW EVER, ENTIRELY OUT OF POWER USERS!!! WAAAAH!!!
AND BEFORE THE DREAM COULD COME TRUE...HE GOT WORKED OVER BY A BUNCH OF KIDS?!
POOR, POOR JOKER!! ALL BECAUSE YOU WERE SUCH A TERRIBLE WEAKLING...
BUT STRAW HAT'S THE MAN OF THE TIMES!
IF YOU UNDER-ESTIMATE HIM...
GLUG
GLUG
IF I UNDER-ESTIMATE HIM...
WANTED
?

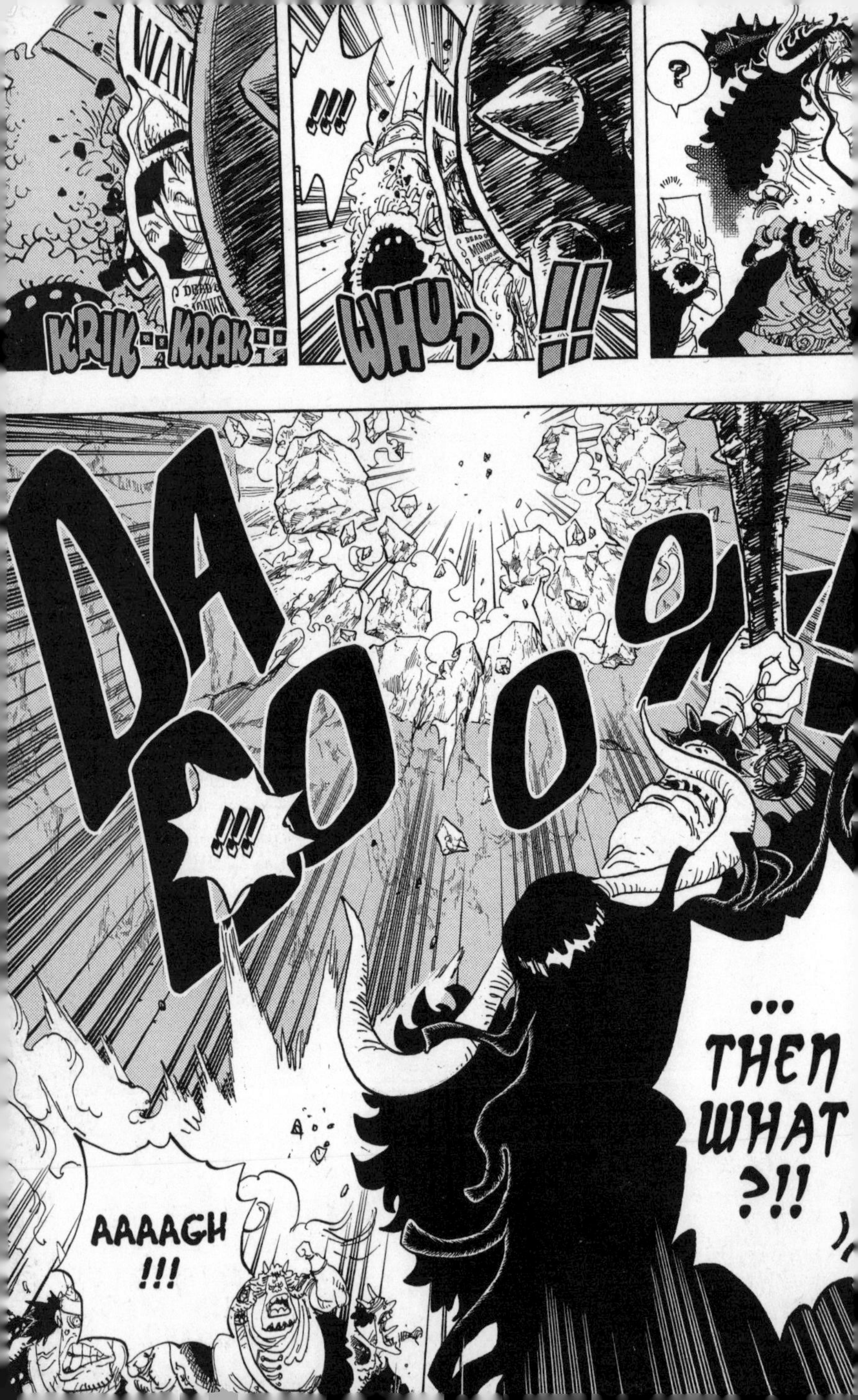
?
!!!
WHUD!!
KRIK...KRAK...
!!!
...THEN WHAT ?!!
AAAAGH !!!

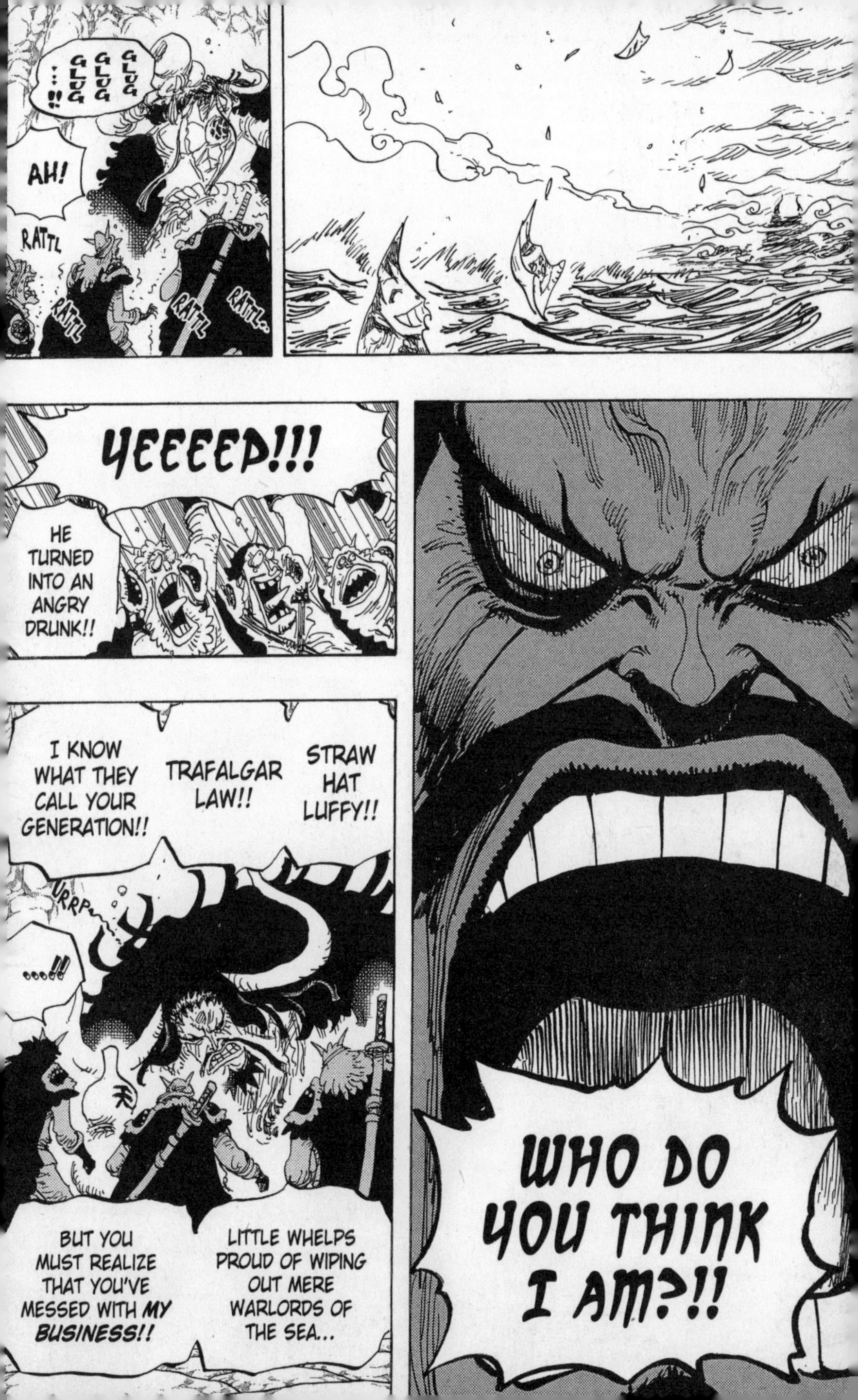
GLUG GLUG GLUG ...!!
AH!
RATTL
RATTL
RATTL
RATTL...
WHO DO YOU THINK I AM?!!
YEEEEP!!!
HE TURNED INTO AN ANGRY DRUNK!!
STRAW HAT LUFFY!!
TRAFALGAR LAW!!
I KNOW WHAT THEY CALL YOUR GENERATION!!
URRP...
....!!
LITTLE WHELPS PROUD OF WIPING OUT MERE WARLORDS OF THE SEA...
BUT YOU MUST REALIZE THAT YOU'VE MESSED WITH *MY BUSINESS!!*

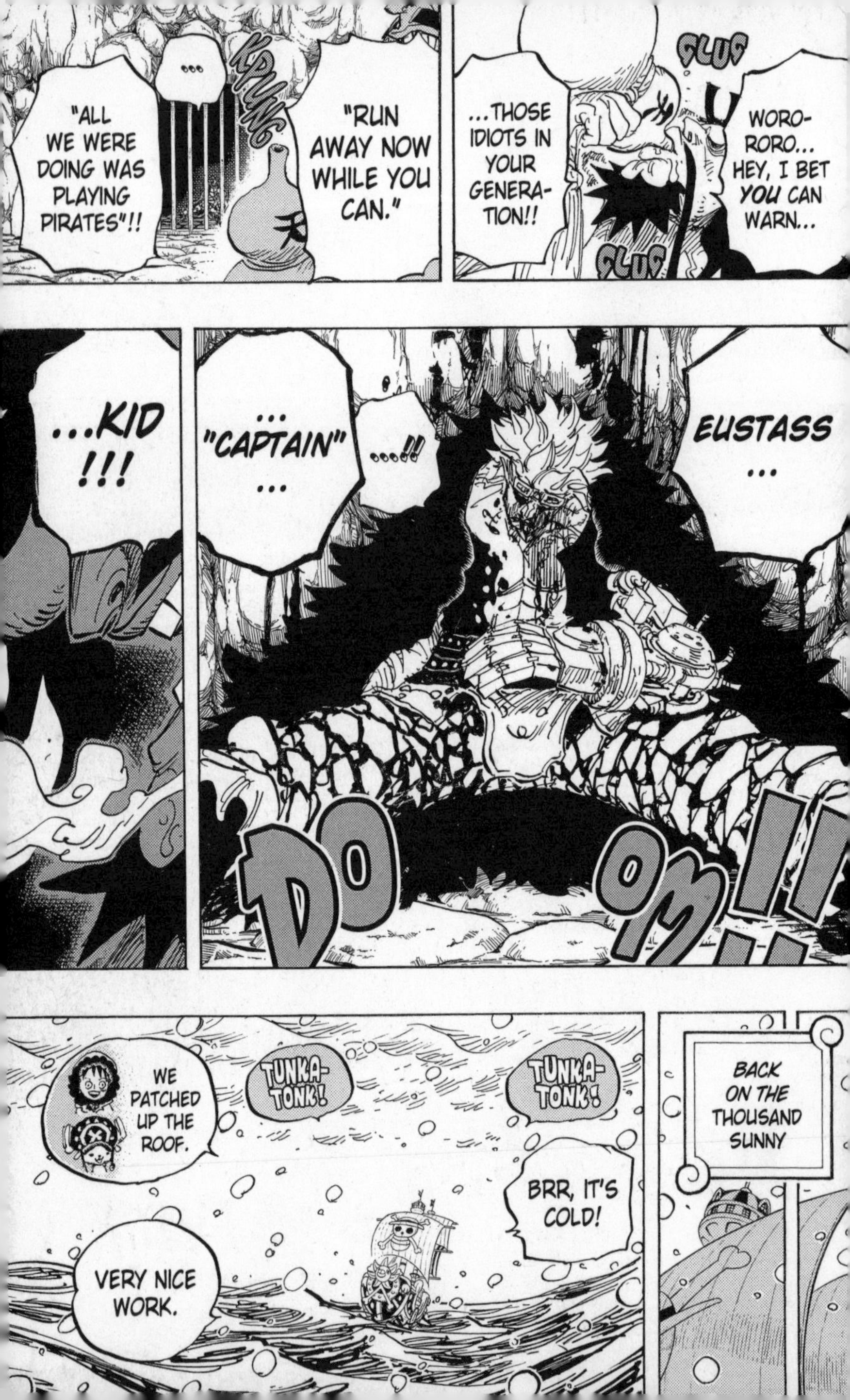
GLUG
WORO-RORO... HEY, I BET YOU CAN WARN...
GLUG
...THOSE IDIOTS IN YOUR GENERATION!!
"RUN AWAY NOW WHILE YOU CAN."
KRUNG
...
"ALL WE WERE DOING WAS PLAYING PIRATES"!!
EUSTASS ...
...!!
... "CAPTAIN" ...
DOOM!!!
...KID !!!
BACK ON THE THOUSAND SUNNY
TUNKA-TONK!
BRR, IT'S COLD!
TUNKA-TONK!
WE PATCHED UP THE ROOF.
VERY NICE WORK.

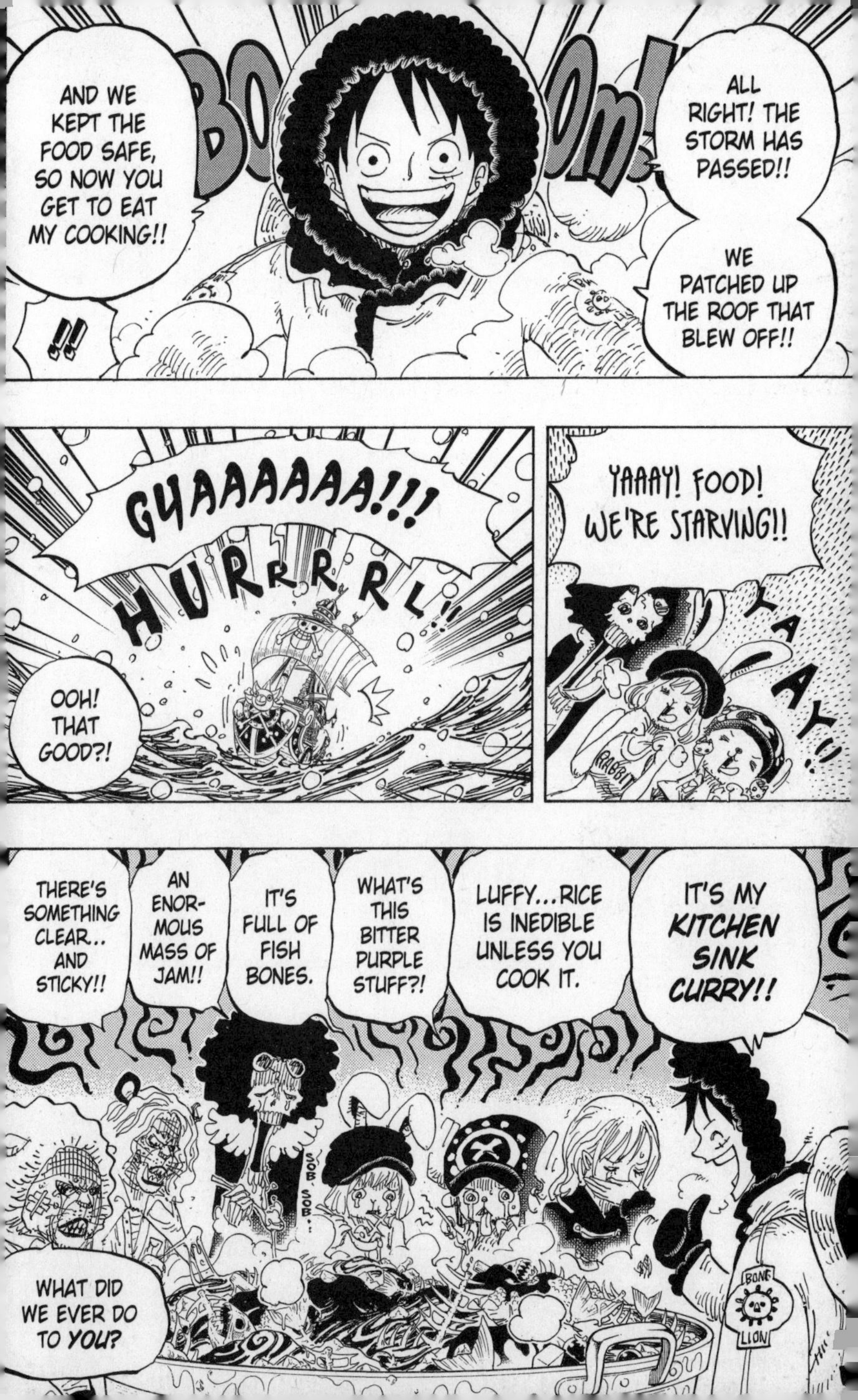
ALL RIGHT! THE STORM HAS PASSED!!
WE PATCHED UP THE ROOF THAT BLEW OFF!!
AND WE KEPT THE FOOD SAFE, SO NOW YOU GET TO EAT MY COOKING!!
!!
YAAAY! FOOD! WE'RE STARVING!!
YAAY!!
GUAAAAAAA!!!
HURRRRL!!
OOH! THAT GOOD?!
IT'S MY *KITCHEN SINK CURRY!!*
LUFFY...RICE IS INEDIBLE UNLESS YOU COOK IT.
WHAT'S THIS BITTER PURPLE STUFF?!
IT'S FULL OF FISH BONES.
AN ENORMOUS MASS OF JAM!!
THERE'S SOMETHING CLEAR... AND STICKY!!
SOB SOB
WHAT DID WE EVER DO TO *YOU?*

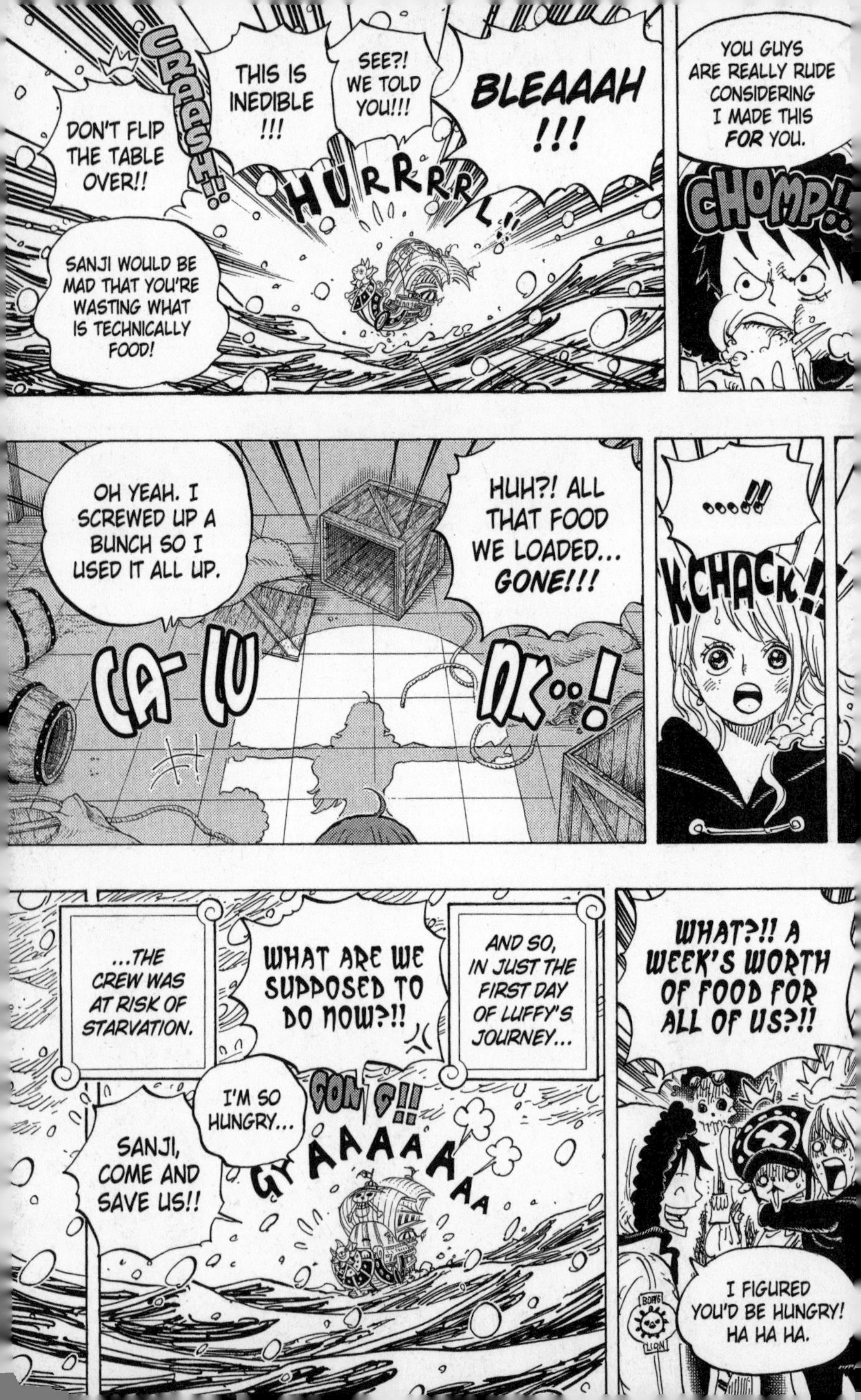
YOU GUYS ARE REALLY RUDE CONSIDERING I MADE THIS FOR YOU.
CHOMP!!
BLEAAAH!!!
SEE?! WE TOLD YOU!!!
THIS IS INEDIBLE!!!
CRAASH!!
DON'T FLIP THE TABLE OVER!!
HURRRRL!!
SANJI WOULD BE MAD THAT YOU'RE WASTING WHAT IS TECHNICALLY FOOD!
....!!
KCHACK!!
HUH?! ALL THAT FOOD WE LOADED... GONE!!!
OH YEAH. I SCREWED UP A BUNCH SO I USED IT ALL UP.
CA-LUNK..!
WHAT?!! A WEEK'S WORTH OF FOOD FOR ALL OF US?!!
I FIGURED YOU'D BE HUNGRY! HA HA HA.
AND SO, IN JUST THE FIRST DAY OF LUFFY'S JOURNEY...
WHAT ARE WE SUPPOSED TO DO NOW?!!
...THE CREW WAS AT RISK OF STARVATION.
GONG!!
I'M SO HUNGRY...
GYAAAAAAAA
SANJI, COME AND SAVE US!!

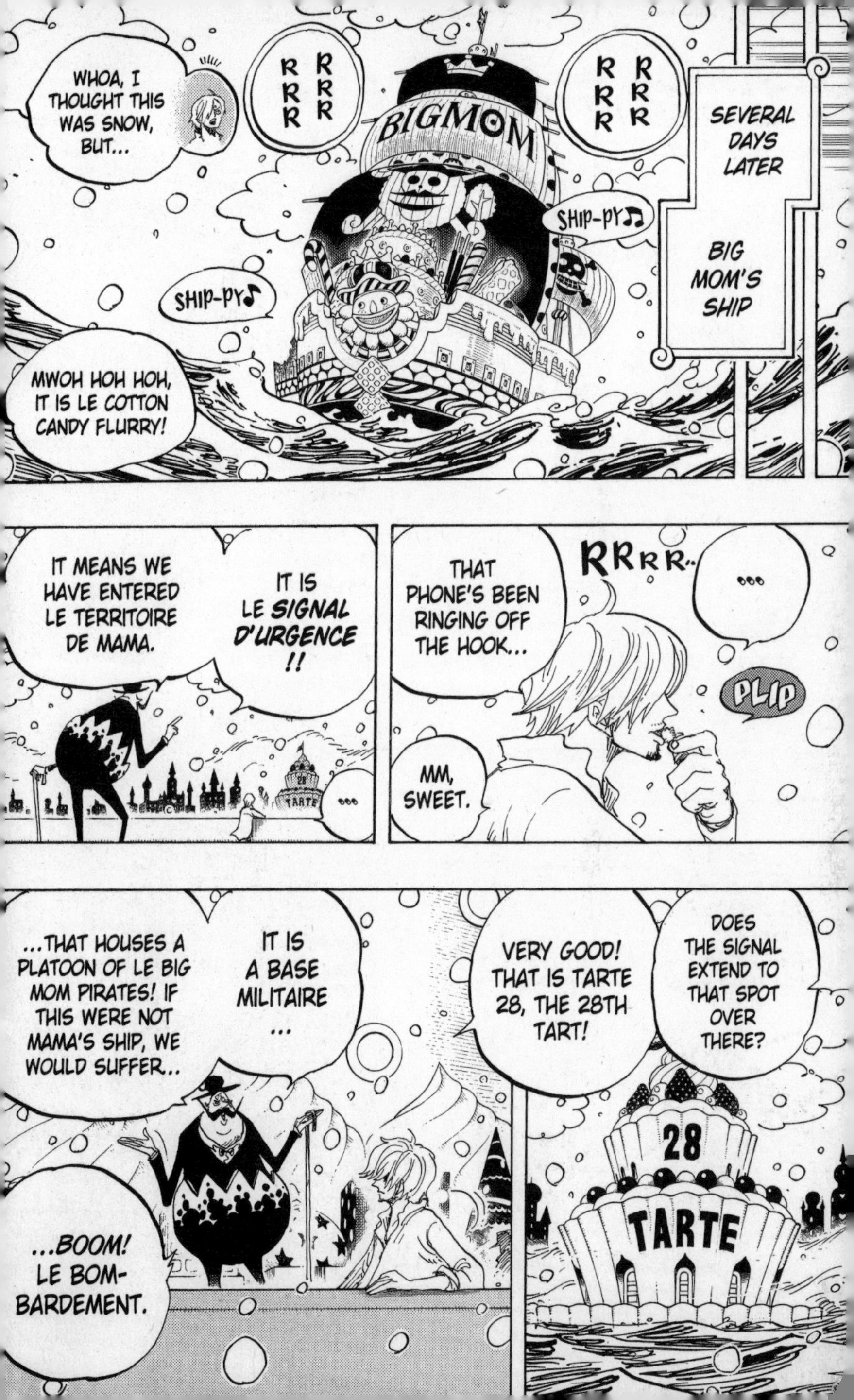

SEVERAL DAYS LATER
BIG MOM'S SHIP
RRR RRR
SHIP-PY♫
BIGMOM
RRR RRR
WHOA, I THOUGHT THIS WAS SNOW, BUT...
SHIP-PY♪
MWOH HOH HOH, IT IS LE COTTON CANDY FLURRY!
RRRR..
...
PLIP
THAT PHONE'S BEEN RINGING OFF THE HOOK...
MM, SWEET.
IT IS LE SIGNAL D'URGENCE!!
IT MEANS WE HAVE ENTERED LE TERRITOIRE DE MAMA.
...
DOES THE SIGNAL EXTEND TO THAT SPOT OVER THERE?
VERY GOOD! THAT IS TARTE 28, THE 28TH TART!
28
TARTE
IT IS A BASE MILITAIRE...
...THAT HOUSES A PLATOON OF LE BIG MOM PIRATES! IF THIS WERE NOT MAMA'S SHIP, WE WOULD SUFFER...
...BOOM! LE BOMBARDEMENT.

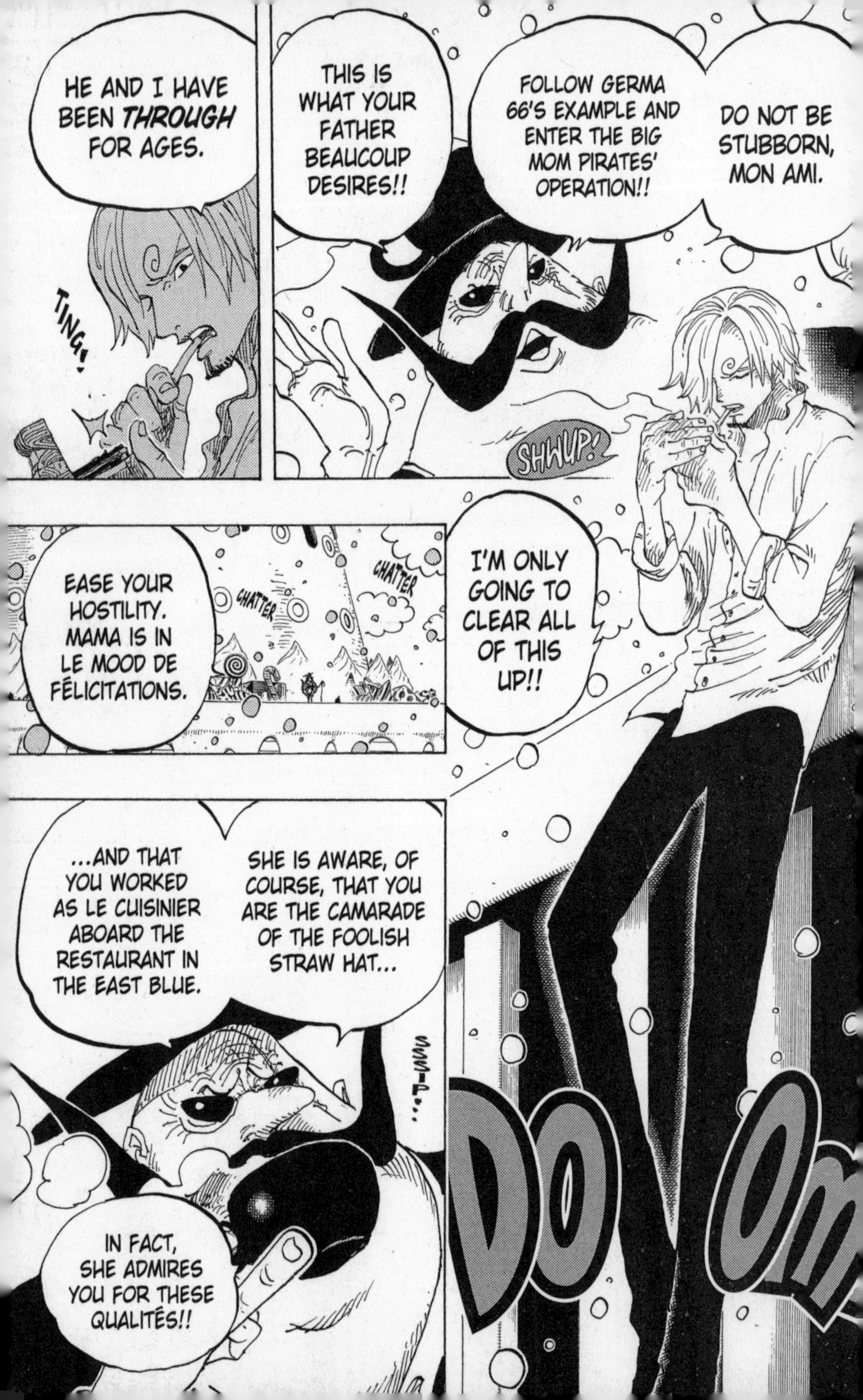
DO NOT BE STUBBORN, MON AMI.
FOLLOW GERMA 66'S EXAMPLE AND ENTER THE BIG MOM PIRATES' OPERATION!!
THIS IS WHAT YOUR FATHER BEAUCOUP DESIRES!!
HE AND I HAVE BEEN *THROUGH* FOR AGES.
TING!
SHWUP!
I'M ONLY GOING TO CLEAR ALL OF THIS UP!!
CHATTER
CHATTER
EASE YOUR HOSTILITY. MAMA IS IN LE MOOD DE FÉLICITATIONS.
SHE IS AWARE, OF COURSE, THAT YOU ARE THE CAMARADE OF THE FOOLISH STRAW HAT...
...AND THAT YOU WORKED AS LE CUISINIER ABOARD THE RESTAURANT IN THE EAST BLUE.
SSSIP...
IN FACT, SHE ADMIRES YOU FOR THESE QUALITÉS!!
DOOOM

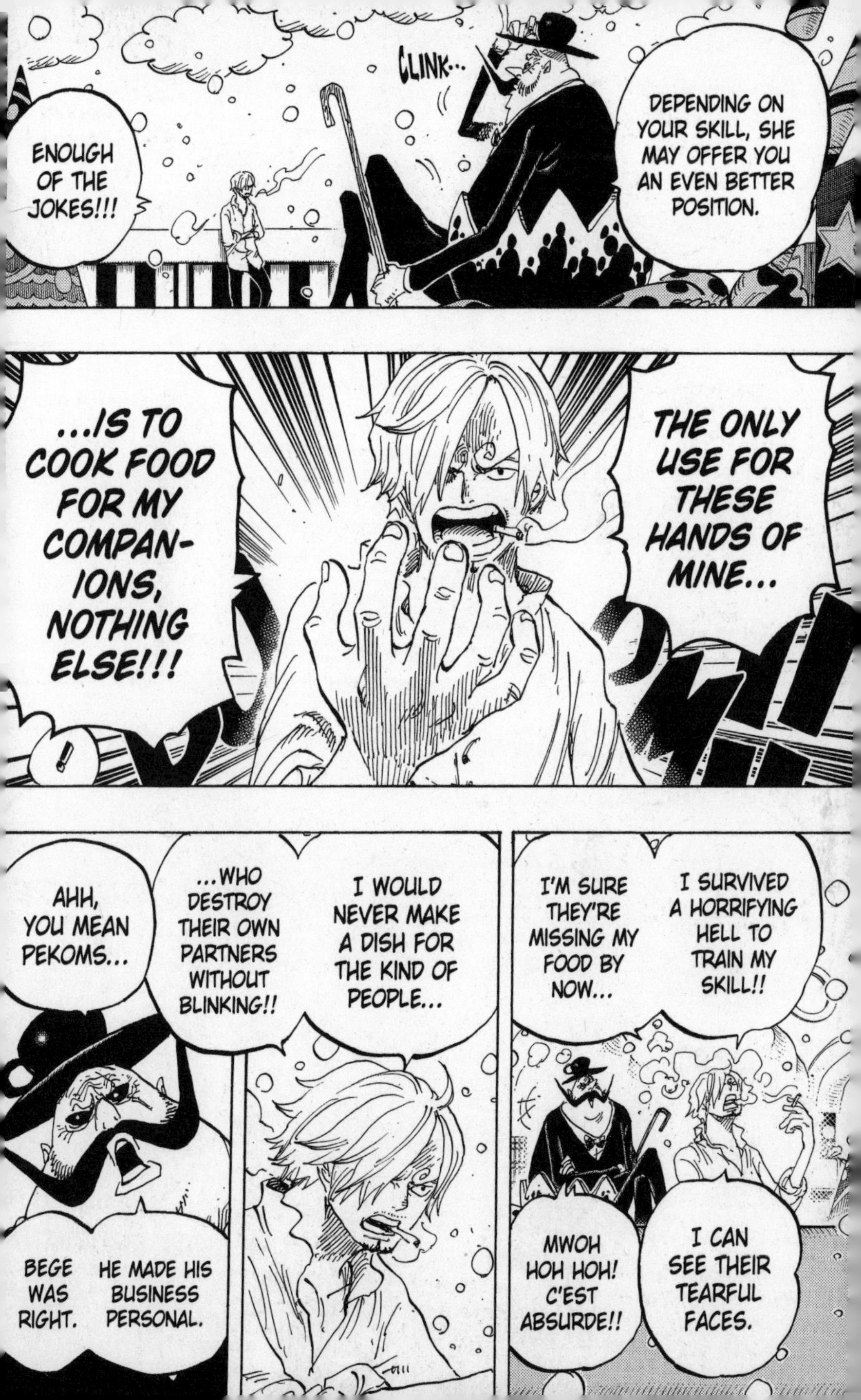
DEPENDING ON YOUR SKILL, SHE MAY OFFER YOU AN EVEN BETTER POSITION.
CLINK...
ENOUGH OF THE JOKES!!!
THE ONLY USE FOR THESE HANDS OF MINE...
...IS TO COOK FOOD FOR MY COMPAN-IONS, NOTHING ELSE!!!
!
I SURVIVED A HORRIFYING HELL TO TRAIN MY SKILL!!
I'M SURE THEY'RE MISSING MY FOOD BY NOW...
I CAN SEE THEIR TEARFUL FACES.
MWOH HOH HOH! C'EST ABSURDE!!
I WOULD NEVER MAKE A DISH FOR THE KIND OF PEOPLE...
...WHO DESTROY THEIR OWN PARTNERS WITHOUT BLINKING!!
AHH, YOU MEAN PEKOMS...
HE MADE HIS BUSINESS PERSONAL.
BEGE WAS RIGHT.

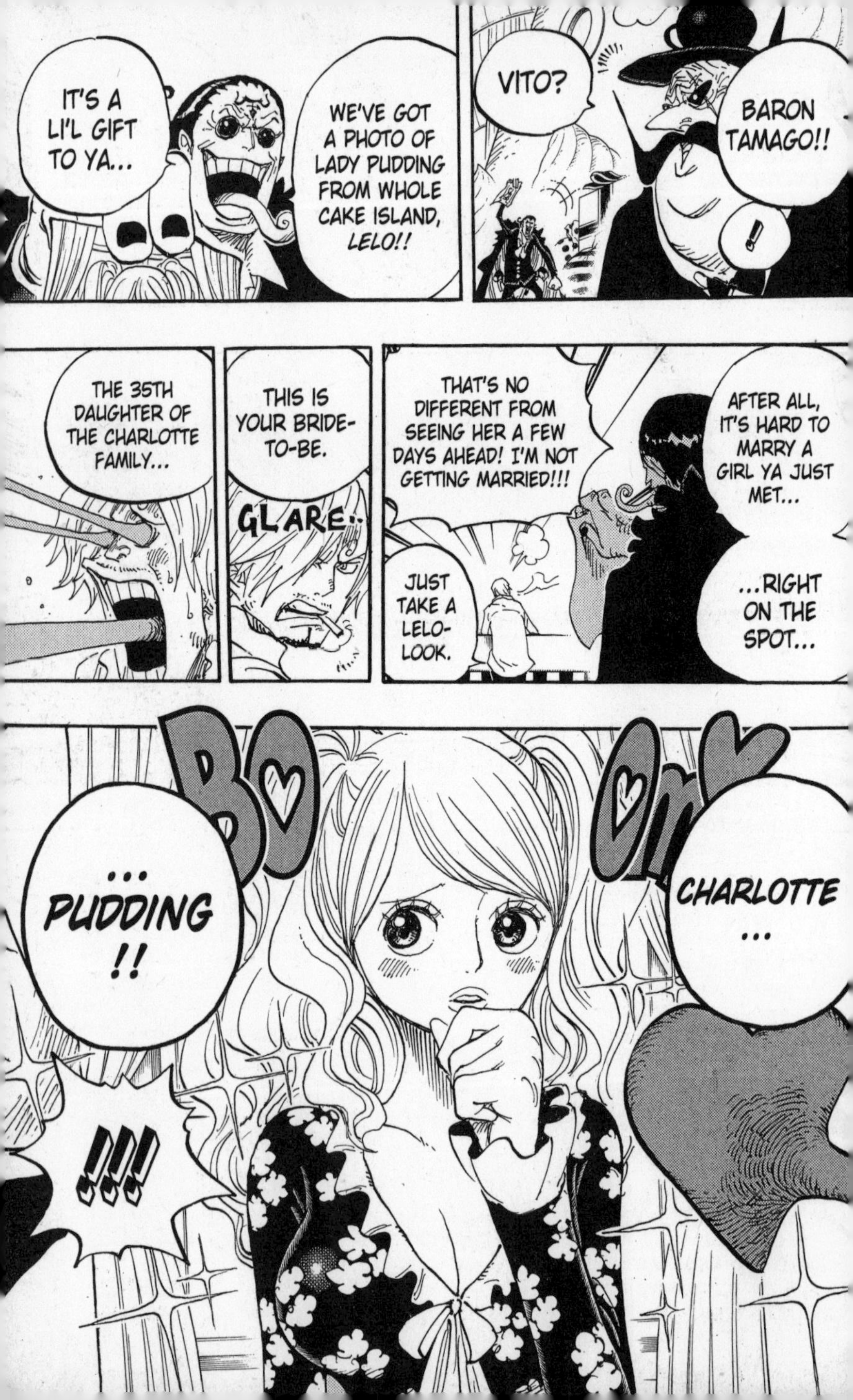

BARON TAMAGO!!
VITO?
!
WE'VE GOT A PHOTO OF LADY PUDDING FROM WHOLE CAKE ISLAND, LELO!!
IT'S A LI'L GIFT TO YA...
AFTER ALL, IT'S HARD TO MARRY A GIRL YA JUST MET...
...RIGHT ON THE SPOT...
THAT'S NO DIFFERENT FROM SEEING HER A FEW DAYS AHEAD! I'M NOT GETTING MARRIED!!!
JUST TAKE A LELO-LOOK.
THIS IS YOUR BRIDE-TO-BE.
GLARE..
THE 35TH DAUGHTER OF THE CHARLOTTE FAMILY...
CHARLOTTE ...
BOOM
... PUDDING !!
!!!!

SBS Question Corner

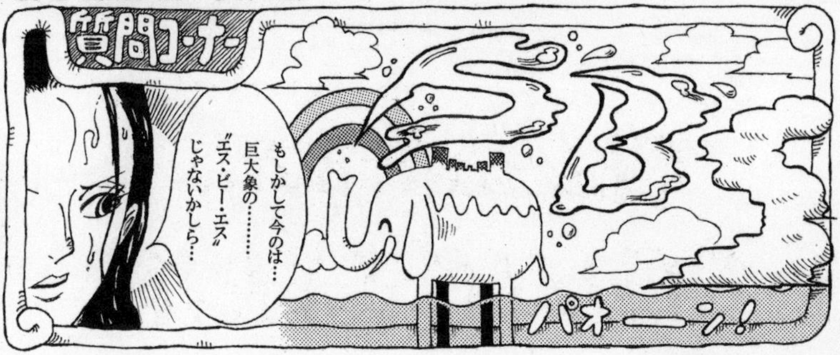
質問コーナー
SBS
もしかして今のは…巨大象の………"エス・ビー・エス"じゃないかしら…
パオーン!

(Hiramegu, Kagoshima)

Q: Hello, Oda Sensei. Doflamingo certainly grew to a very large size. What are his favorite and least favorite foods? Does he like apples? Does he hate green peppers?

--Donuts

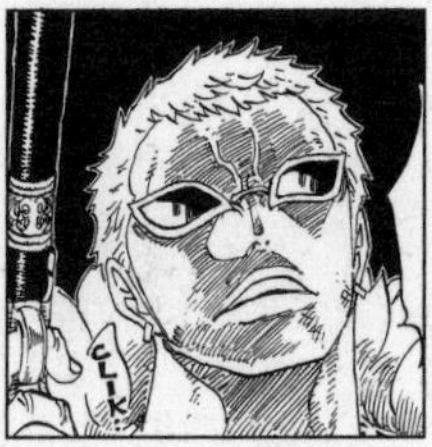
CLIK

A: Let me guess: you like apples and hate peppers? Doflamingo's favorite food is lobster. His least favorite is barbecue. Too bad, barbecue's really tasty and fun. I guess he has some bad memories about it. Go figure!

Q: I noticed that the reindeer mink Chopper fell in love with is also on a T-shirt worn by another mink. He's a rival!

--Takataka

A: Yup, there she is on the shirt. You'll notice it says "Milky." Milky is the madonna of the Guardians!! You're correct that she's a reindeer; that's the only species of deer in which the females grow horns too. It's a chance Chopper might never get again. Think he'll make a move on her?

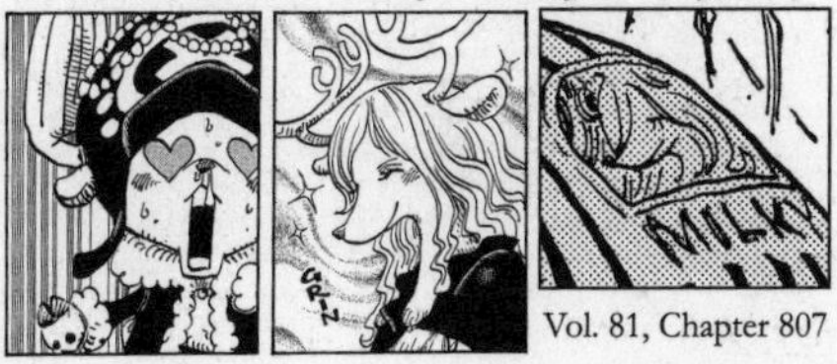
MILKY
GRIN

Vol. 81, Chapter 807

Q: Odacchi, I ask thee: why doth Sabo grow out his hair? Select any and all that applyeth. 1. To copy Ace. 2. To show off his blond hair. 3. To look cool for Koala. 4. For fashion. (Personally, the third option wouldst make me happiest.)

--Sweat Ninja

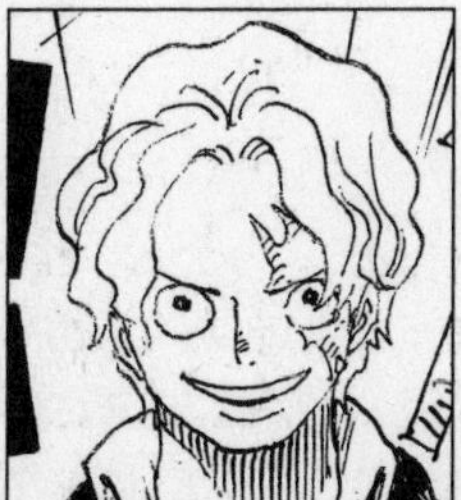

A: The answer is: 5. To hide the large scar on his face. If you look closely, you'll notice that when facing him, the part is slightly to the left, leaving more hair to fall over the right side of his face. In his case, the scar isn't exactly a badge of honor.

Chapter 825:
COMIC STRIP

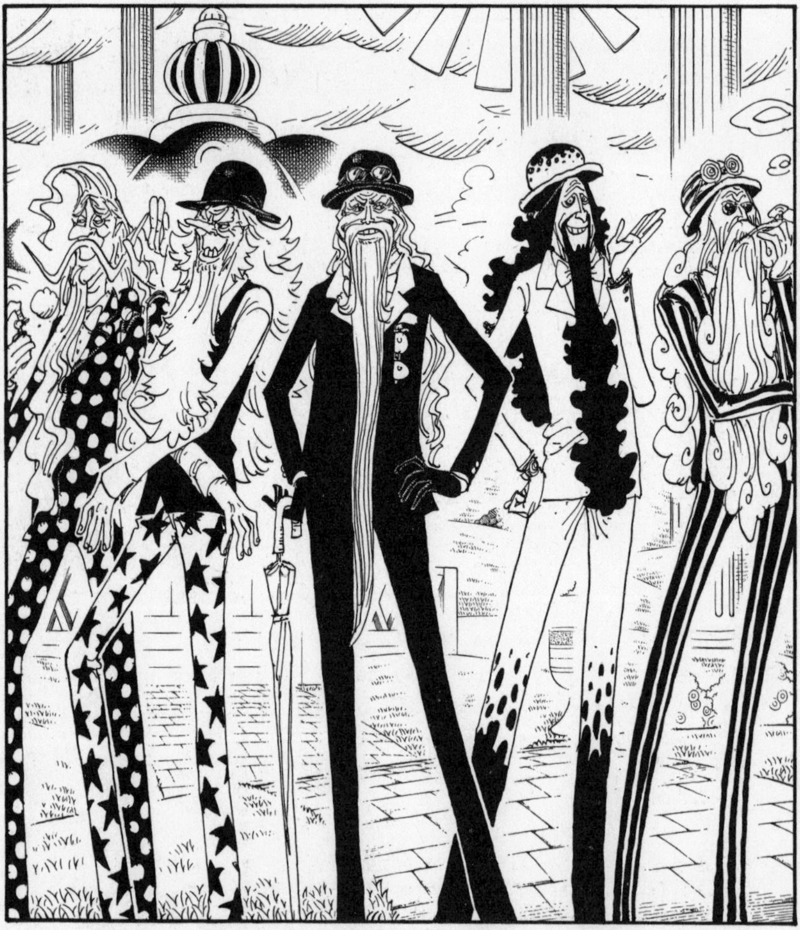

DECKS OF THE WORLD, 500-MILLION-MAN ARC, VOL. 16: "WEATHERIA--GOTTA DRESS TO IMPRESS FOR WHEN NAMI VISITS AGAIN"

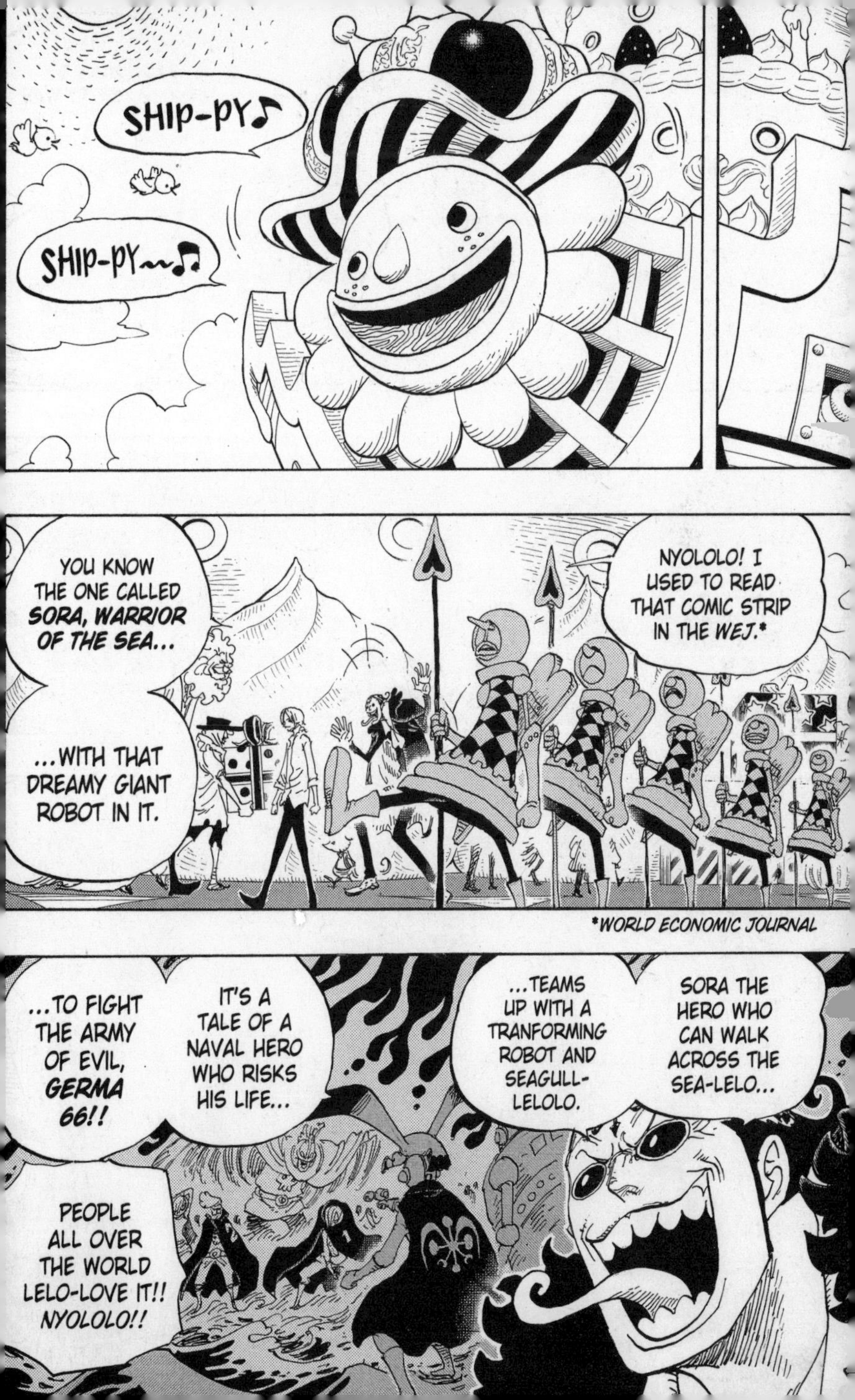
SHIP-PY♪
SHIP-PY~~♪
NYOLOLO! I USED TO READ THAT COMIC STRIP IN THE WEJ.*
YOU KNOW THE ONE CALLED SORA, WARRIOR OF THE SEA...
...WITH THAT DREAMY GIANT ROBOT IN IT.
*WORLD ECONOMIC JOURNAL
SORA THE HERO WHO CAN WALK ACROSS THE SEA-LELO...
...TEAMS UP WITH A TRANFORMING ROBOT AND SEAGULL-LELOLO.
IT'S A TALE OF A NAVAL HERO WHO RISKS HIS LIFE...
...TO FIGHT THE ARMY OF EVIL, GERMA 66!!
PEOPLE ALL OVER THE WORLD LELO-LOVE IT!! NYOLOLO!!

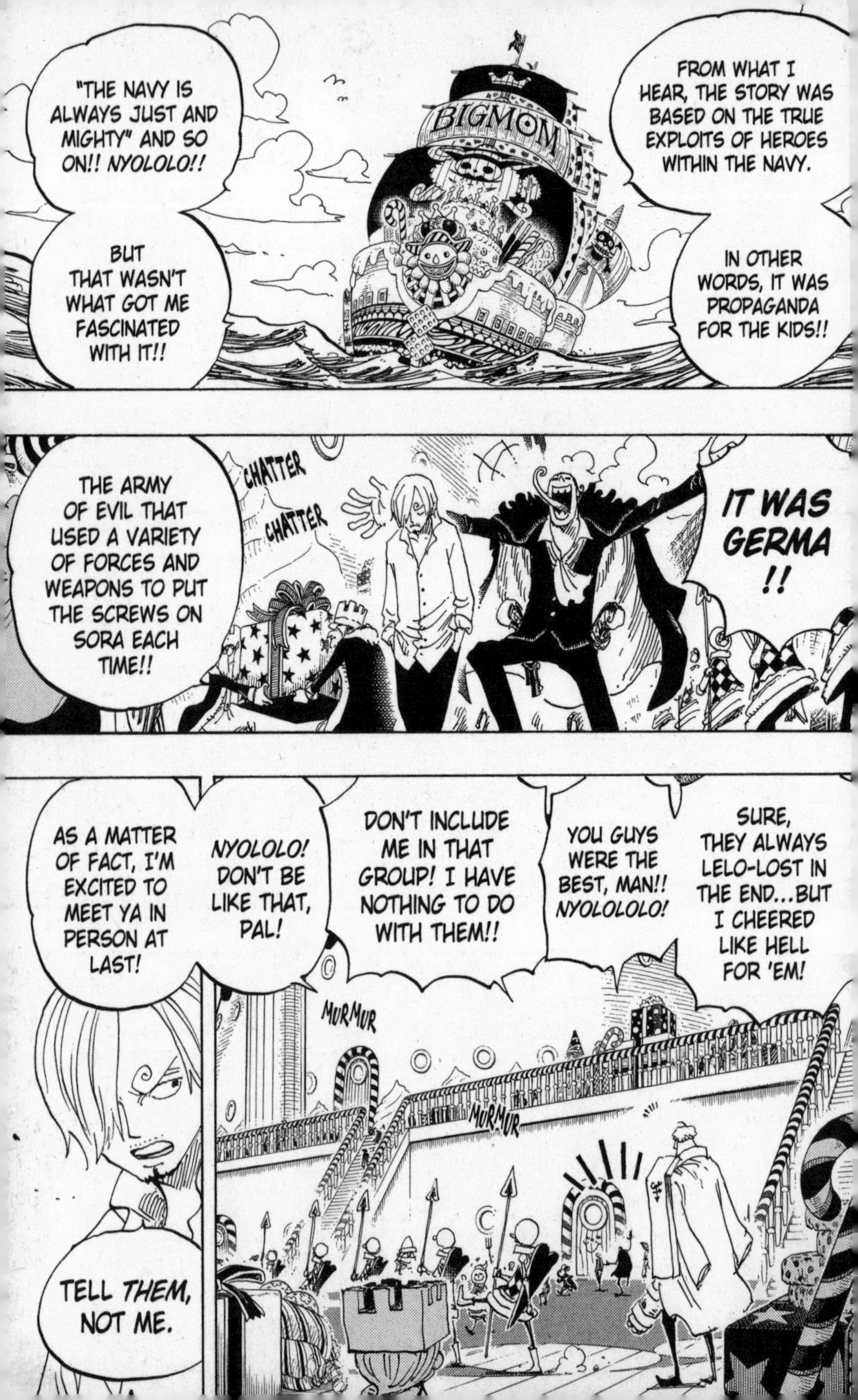
FROM WHAT I HEAR, THE STORY WAS BASED ON THE TRUE EXPLOITS OF HEROES WITHIN THE NAVY.
IN OTHER WORDS, IT WAS PROPAGANDA FOR THE KIDS!!
BIGMOM
"THE NAVY IS ALWAYS JUST AND MIGHTY" AND SO ON!! *NYOLOLO!!*
BUT THAT WASN'T WHAT GOT ME FASCINATED WITH IT!!
IT WAS GERMA!!
CHATTER
CHATTER
THE ARMY OF EVIL THAT USED A VARIETY OF FORCES AND WEAPONS TO PUT THE SCREWS ON SORA EACH TIME!!
SURE, THEY ALWAYS LELO-LOST IN THE END...BUT I CHEERED LIKE HELL FOR 'EM!
YOU GUYS WERE THE BEST, MAN!! *NYOLOLOLO!*
DON'T INCLUDE ME IN THAT GROUP! I HAVE NOTHING TO DO WITH THEM!!
NYOLOLO! DON'T BE LIKE THAT, PAL!
AS A MATTER OF FACT, I'M EXCITED TO MEET YA IN PERSON AT LAST!
MURMUR
MURMUR
TELL *THEM*, NOT ME.

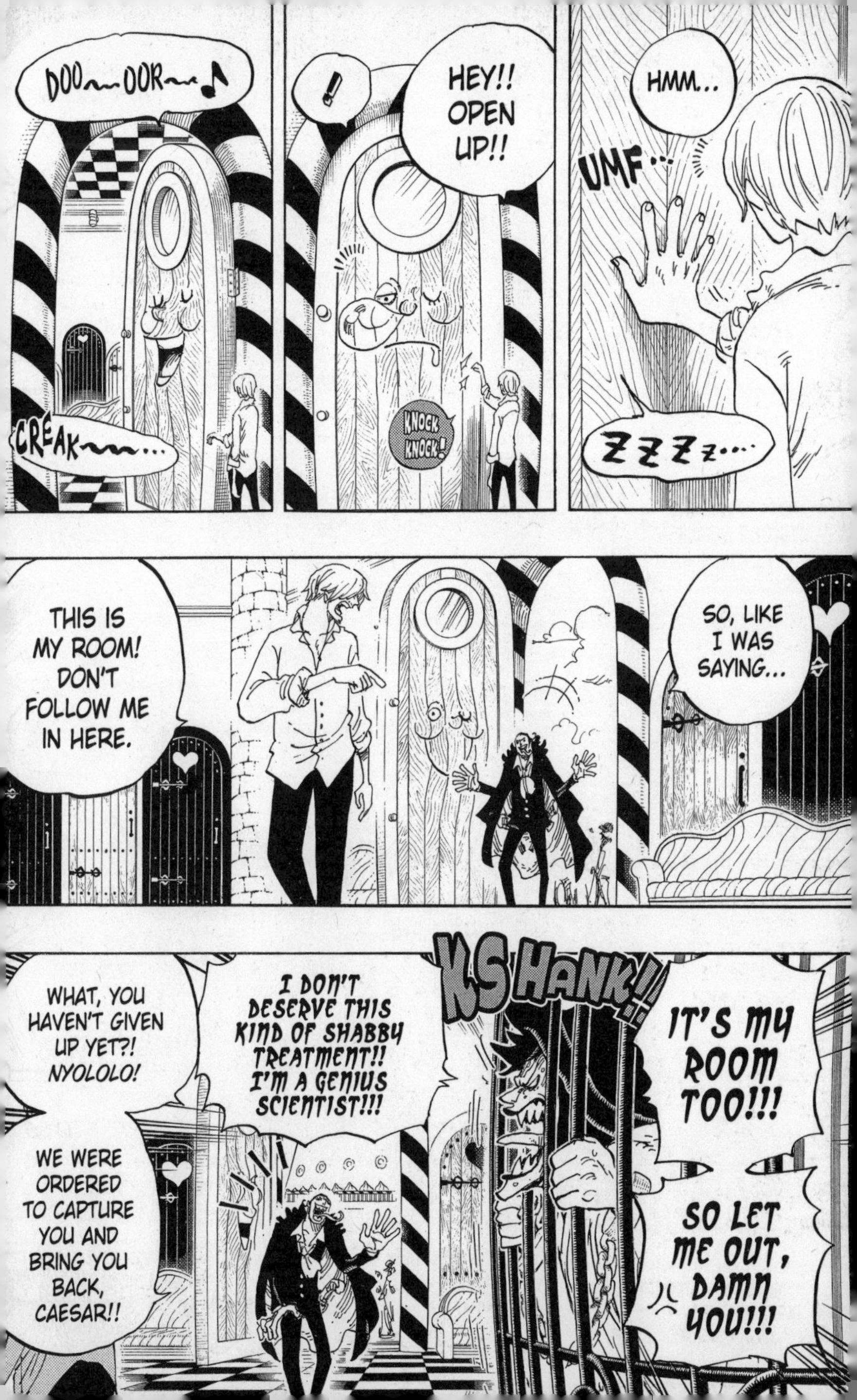
HMM...
UMF...
ZZZz...
!
HEY!! OPEN UP!!
KNOCK KNOCK!
DOO~~OOR~~♪
CREAK~~...
SO, LIKE I WAS SAYING...
THIS IS MY ROOM! DON'T FOLLOW ME IN HERE.
KSHANK!!
IT'S MY ROOM TOO!!!
SO LET ME OUT, DAMN YOU!!!
I DON'T DESERVE THIS KIND OF SHABBY TREATMENT!! I'M A GENIUS SCIENTIST!!!
WHAT, YOU HAVEN'T GIVEN UP YET?! NYOLOLO!
WE WERE ORDERED TO CAPTURE YOU AND BRING YOU BACK, CAESAR!!

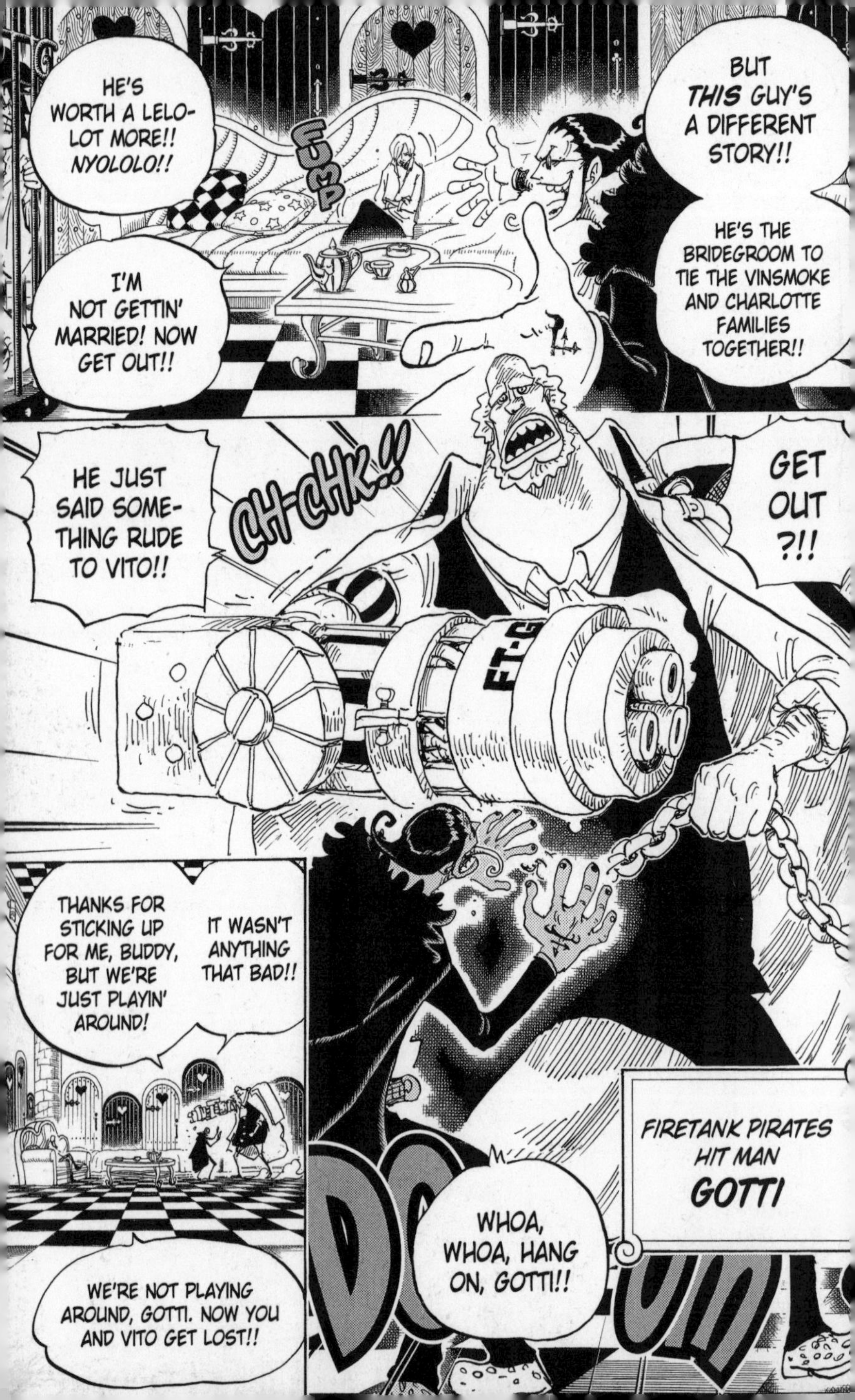
BUT THIS GUY'S A DIFFERENT STORY!!
HE'S THE BRIDEGROOM TO TIE THE VINSMOKE AND CHARLOTTE FAMILIES TOGETHER!!
HE'S WORTH A LELO-LOT MORE!! NYOLOLO!!
FUMP
I'M NOT GETTIN' MARRIED! NOW GET OUT!!
GET OUT?!!
CH-CHK..!!
HE JUST SAID SOME-THING RUDE TO VITO!!
FIRETANK PIRATES HIT MAN GOTTI
WHOA, WHOA, HANG ON, GOTTI!!
THANKS FOR STICKING UP FOR ME, BUDDY, BUT WE'RE JUST PLAYIN' AROUND!
IT WASN'T ANYTHING THAT BAD!!
WE'RE NOT PLAYING AROUND, GOTTI. NOW YOU AND VITO GET LOST!!

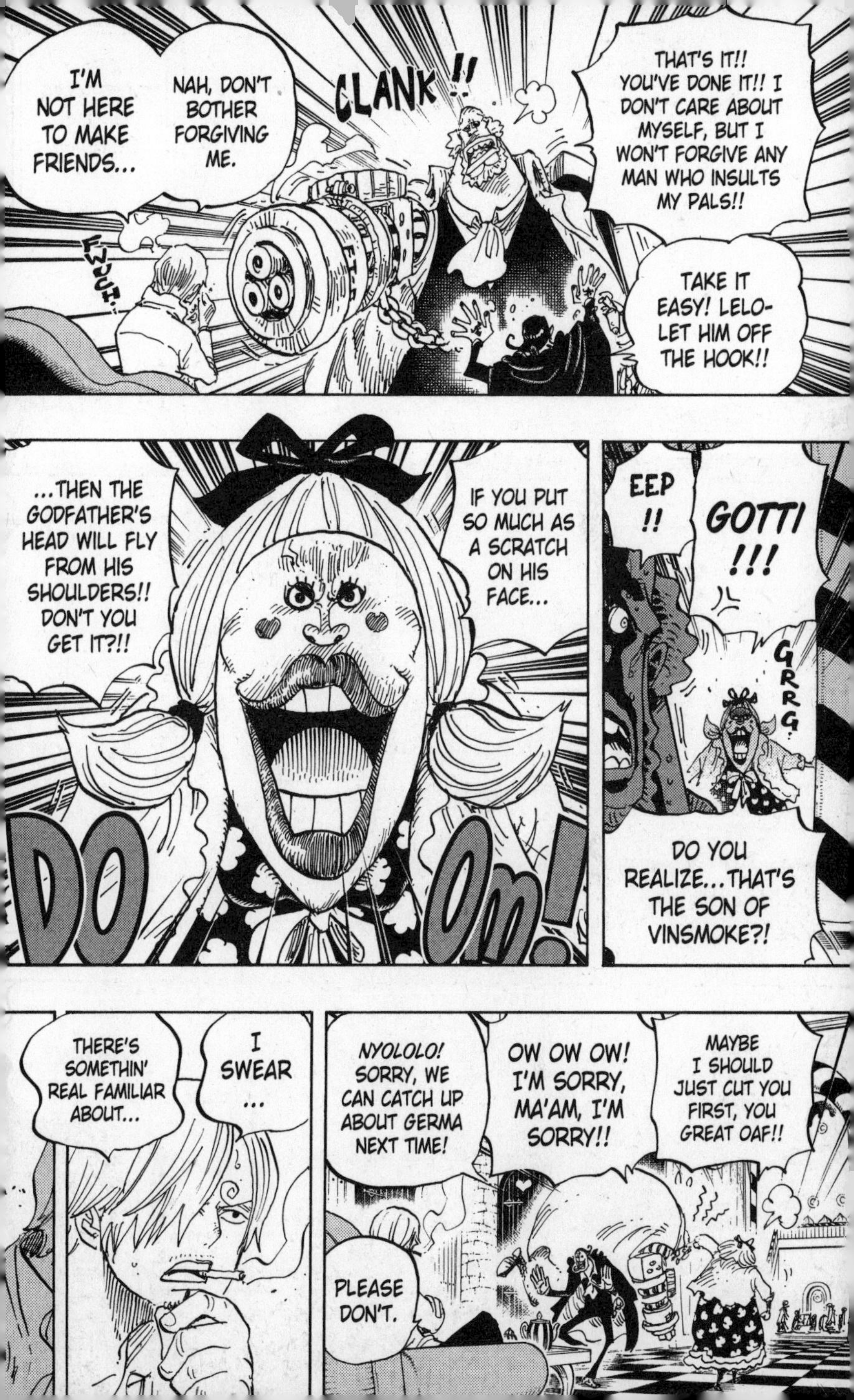
THAT'S IT!! YOU'VE DONE IT!! I DON'T CARE ABOUT MYSELF, BUT I WON'T FORGIVE ANY MAN WHO INSULTS MY PALS!!
TAKE IT EASY! LELO-LET HIM OFF THE HOOK!!
CLANK!!
NAH, DON'T BOTHER FORGIVING ME.
I'M NOT HERE TO MAKE FRIENDS...
FWUCH...
GOTTI!!!
EEP!!
GRRG
DO YOU REALIZE...THAT'S THE SON OF VINSMOKE?!
IF YOU PUT SO MUCH AS A SCRATCH ON HIS FACE...
...THEN THE GODFATHER'S HEAD WILL FLY FROM HIS SHOULDERS!! DON'T YOU GET IT?!!
DOOM!
MAYBE I SHOULD JUST CUT YOU FIRST, YOU GREAT OAF!!
OW OW OW! I'M SORRY, MA'AM, I'M SORRY!!
NYOLOLO! SORRY, WE CAN CATCH UP ABOUT GERMA NEXT TIME!
PLEASE DON'T.
I SWEAR...
THERE'S SOMETHIN' REAL FAMILIAR ABOUT...

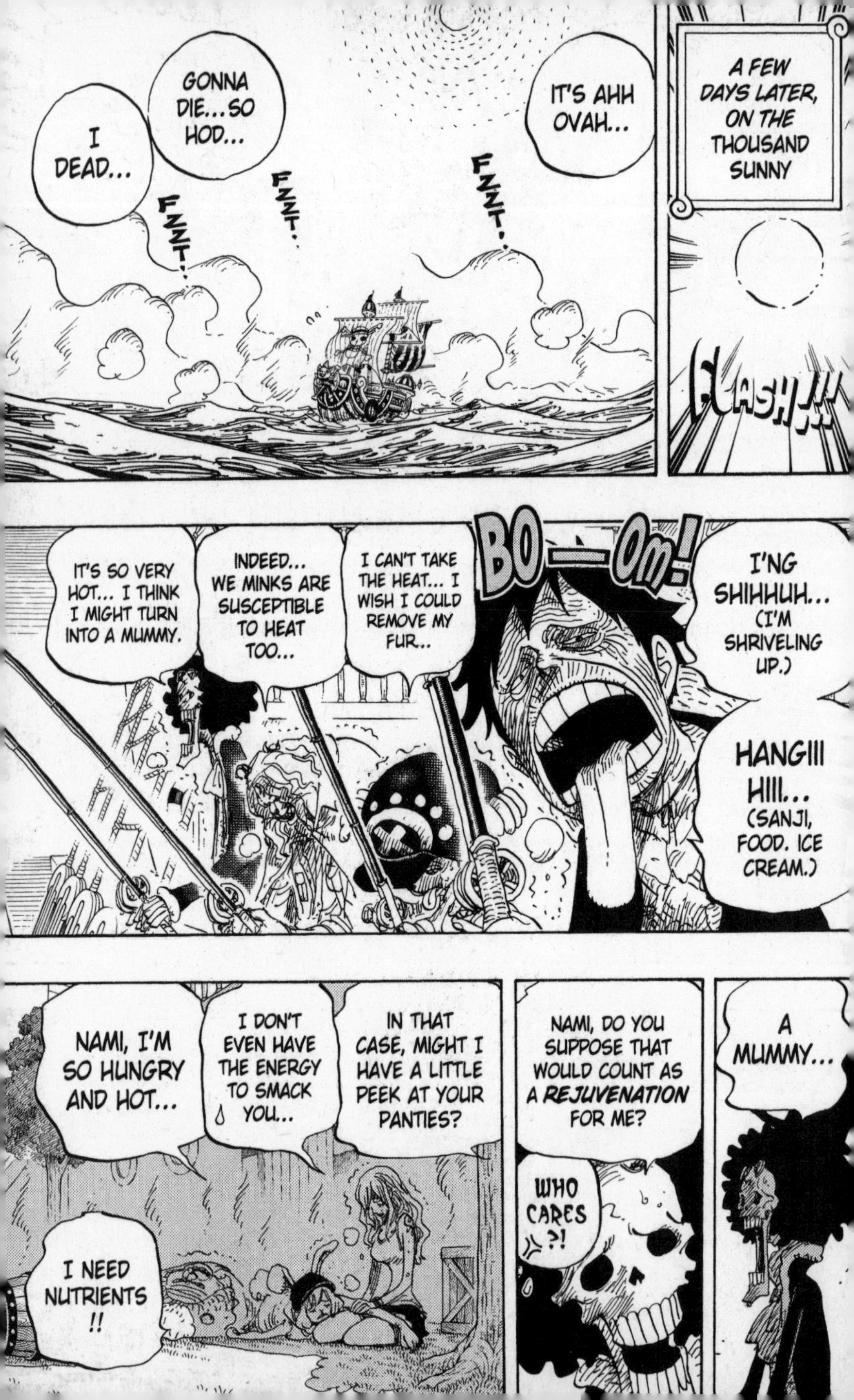
A FEW DAYS LATER, ON THE THOUSAND SUNNY
FLASH!!!
IT'S AHH OVAH...
FZZT...
FZZT...
GONNA DIE...SO HOD...
I DEAD...
FZZT...
I'NG SHIHHUH... (I'M SHRIVELING UP.)
HANGIII HIII... (SANJI, FOOD. ICE CREAM.)
BO—OM!
I CAN'T TAKE THE HEAT... I WISH I COULD REMOVE MY FUR...
INDEED... WE MINKS ARE SUSCEPTIBLE TO HEAT TOO...
IT'S SO VERY HOT... I THINK I MIGHT TURN INTO A MUMMY.
A MUMMY...
NAMI, DO YOU SUPPOSE THAT WOULD COUNT AS A *REJUVENATION* FOR ME?
WHO CARES ?!
IN THAT CASE, MIGHT I HAVE A LITTLE PEEK AT YOUR PANTIES?
I DON'T EVEN HAVE THE ENERGY TO SMACK YOU...
NAMI, I'M SO HUNGRY AND HOT...
I NEED NUTRIENTS !!

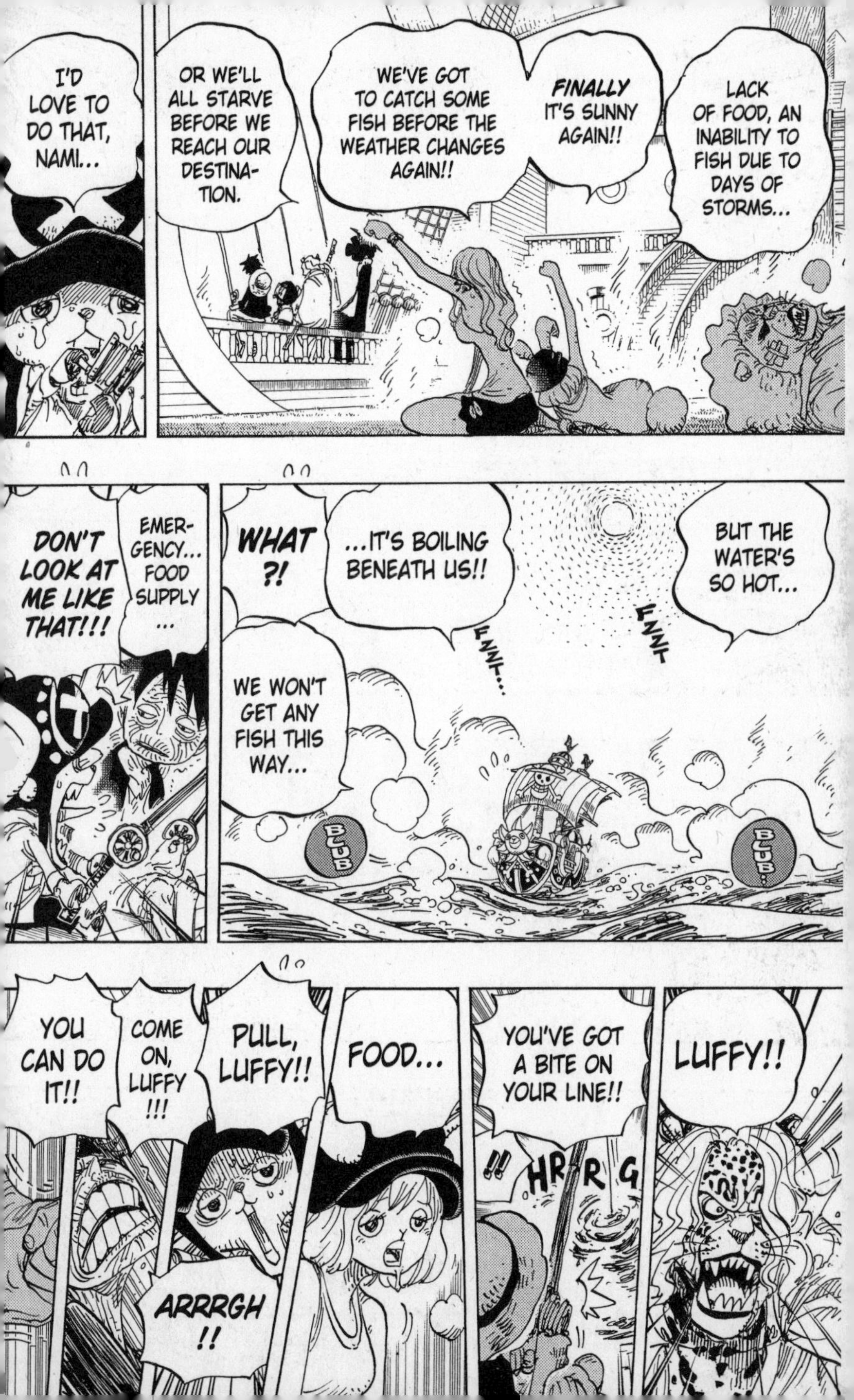
LACK OF FOOD, AN INABILITY TO FISH DUE TO DAYS OF STORMS...
FINALLY IT'S SUNNY AGAIN!!
WE'VE GOT TO CATCH SOME FISH BEFORE THE WEATHER CHANGES AGAIN!!
OR WE'LL ALL STARVE BEFORE WE REACH OUR DESTINATION.
I'D LOVE TO DO THAT, NAMI...
BUT THE WATER'S SO HOT...
FZZT
...IT'S BOILING BENEATH US!!
FZZT...
WHAT?!
WE WON'T GET ANY FISH THIS WAY...
BLUB
BLUB
EMERGENCY... FOOD SUPPLY...
DON'T LOOK AT ME LIKE THAT!!!
LUFFY!!
YOU'VE GOT A BITE ON YOUR LINE!!
!!
HRRG
FOOD...
PULL, LUFFY!!
COME ON, LUFFY!!!
ARRRGH!!
YOU CAN DO IT!!

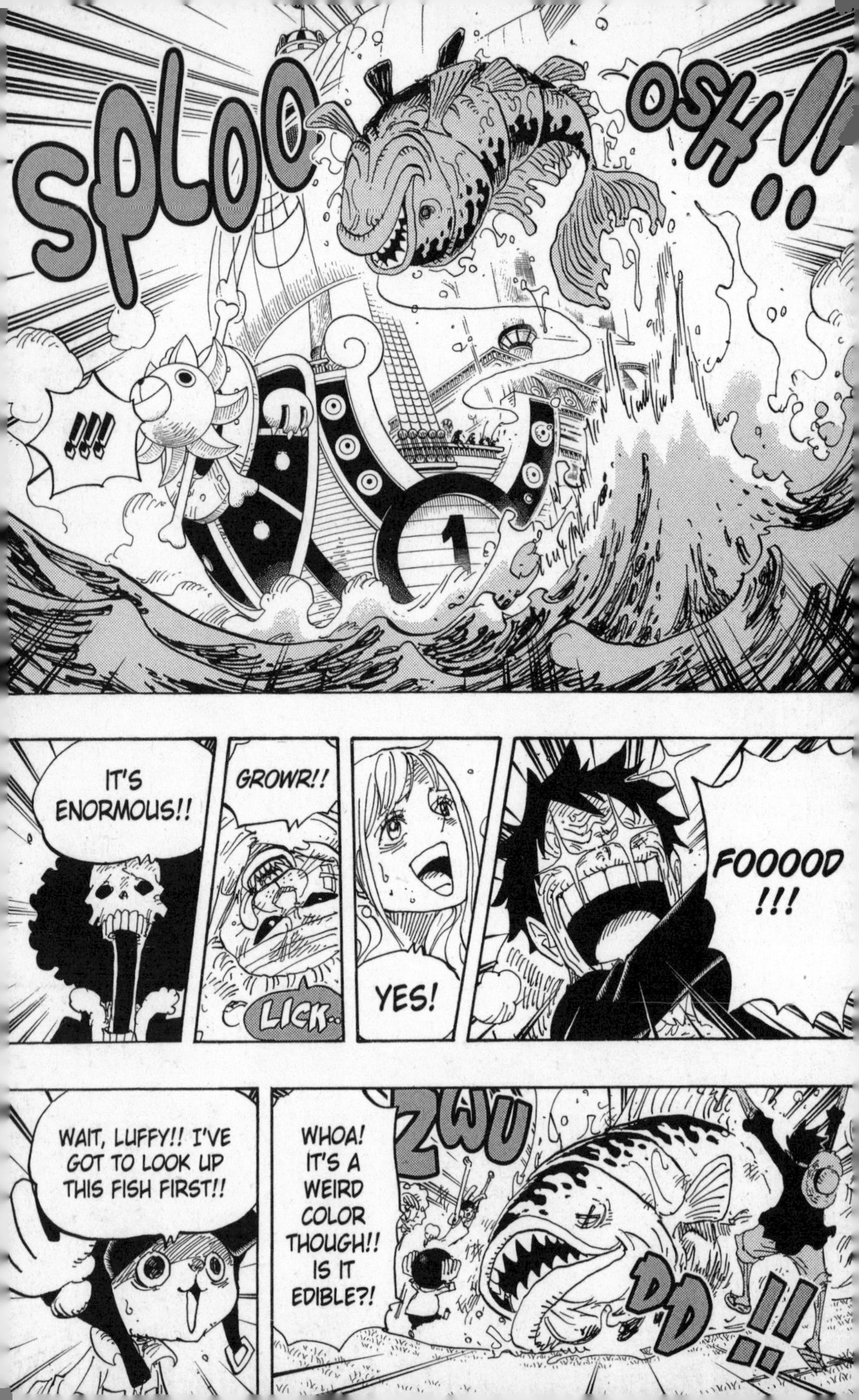
SPLOOOSH!!
!!!
FOOOOD!!!
YES!
GROWR!!
LICK..
IT'S ENORMOUS!!
ZWUDD!!
WHOA! IT'S A WEIRD COLOR THOUGH!! IS IT EDIBLE?!
WAIT, LUFFY!! I'VE GOT TO LOOK UP THIS FISH FIRST!!

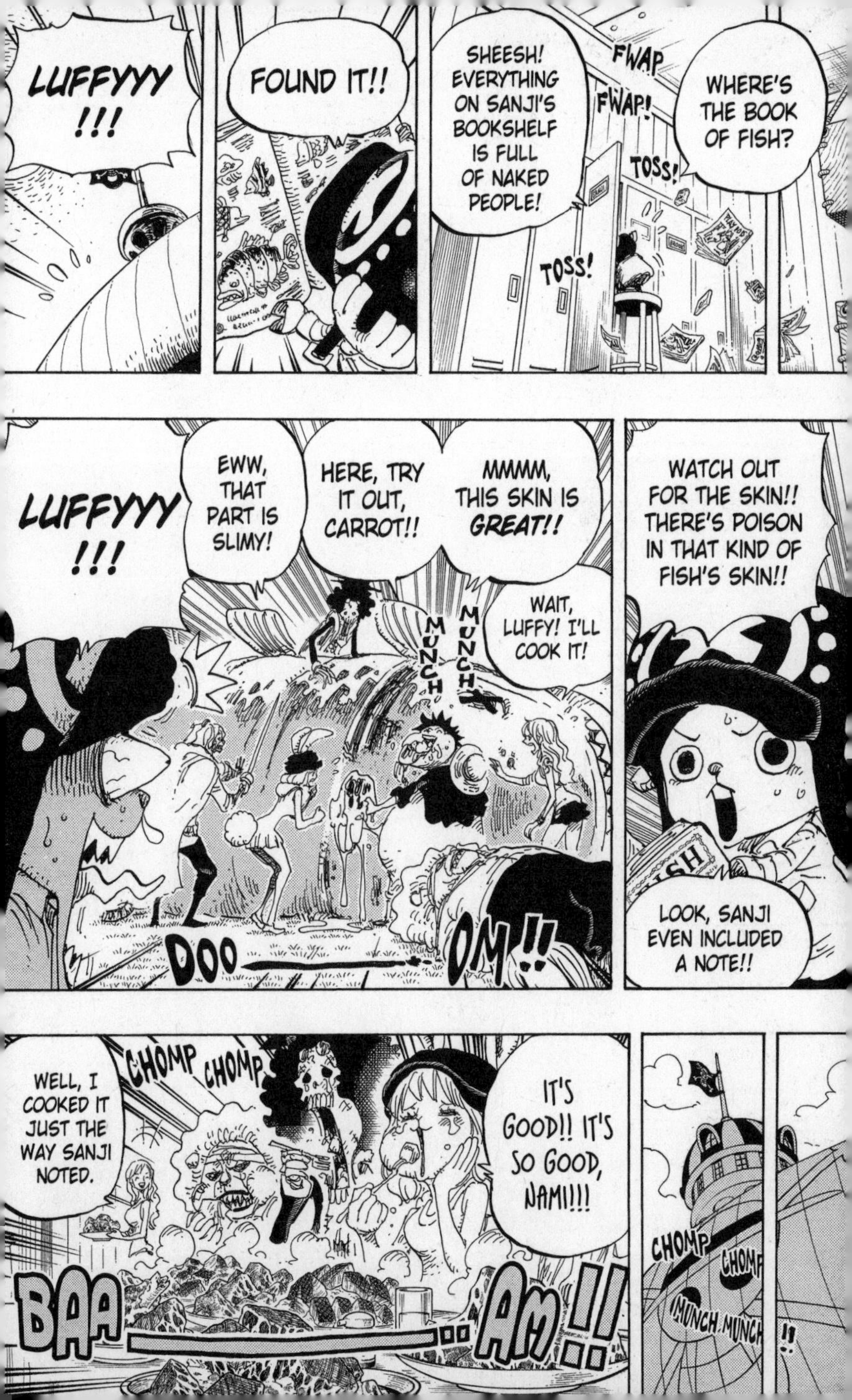
FWAP
WHERE'S THE BOOK OF FISH?
FWAP!
TOSS!
SHEESH! EVERYTHING ON SANJI'S BOOKSHELF IS FULL OF NAKED PEOPLE!
TOSS!
FOUND IT!!
LUFFYYY !!!
WATCH OUT FOR THE SKIN!! THERE'S POISON IN THAT KIND OF FISH'S SKIN!!
LOOK, SANJI EVEN INCLUDED A NOTE!!
MMMM, THIS SKIN IS GREAT!!
WAIT, LUFFY! I'LL COOK IT!
MUNCH MUNCH
HERE, TRY IT OUT, CARROT!!
EWW, THAT PART IS SLIMY!
LUFFYYY !!!
DOO——OM!!
CHOMP CHOMP
MUNCH MUNCH!!
IT'S GOOD!! IT'S SO GOOD, NAMI!!!
CHOMP CHOMP
WELL, I COOKED IT JUST THE WAY SANJI NOTED.
BAA——AM!!

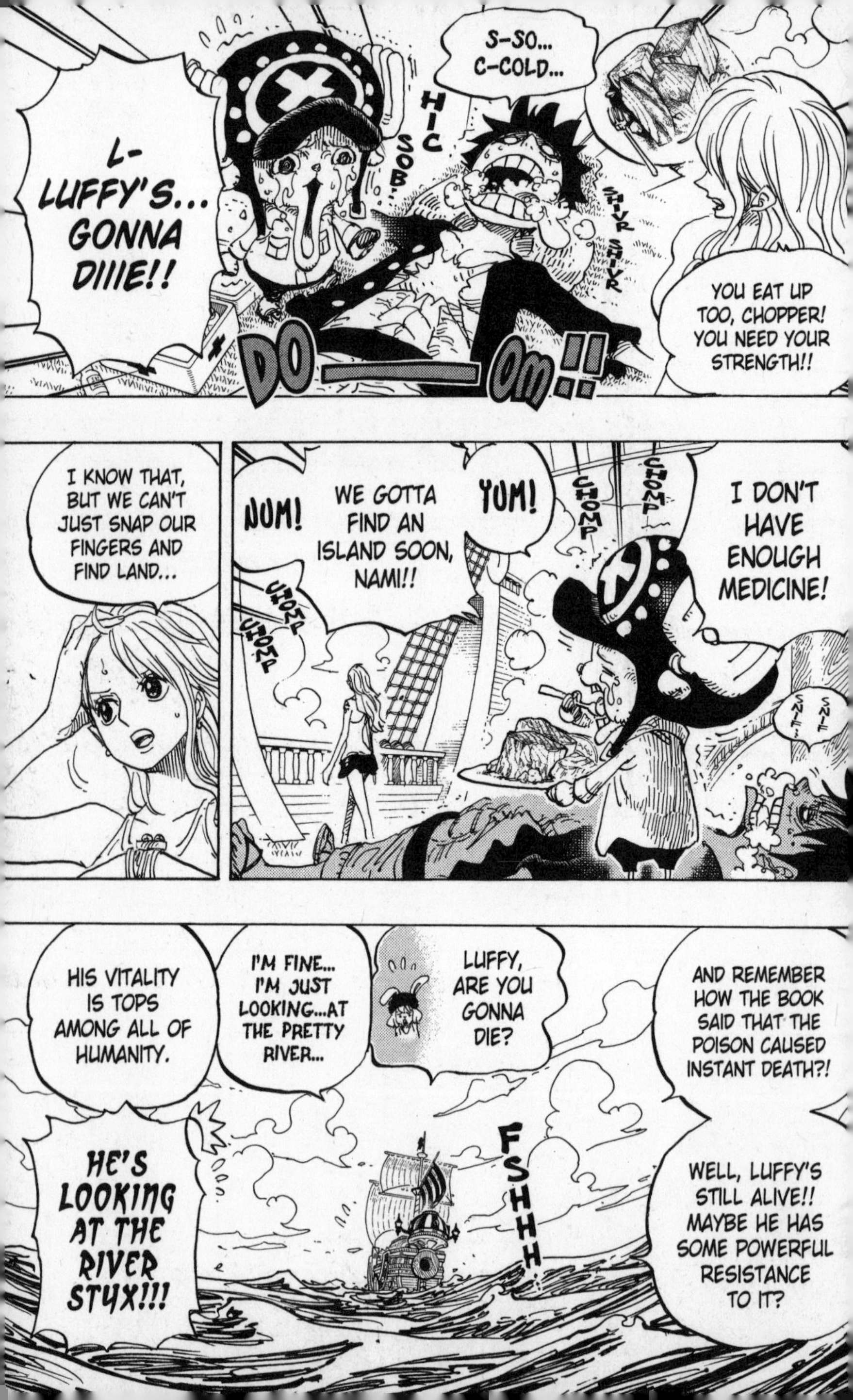
S-SO... C-COLD...
HIC
SOB
SHIVR SHIVR
L-LUFFY'S... GONNA DIIIE!!
YOU EAT UP TOO, CHOPPER! YOU NEED YOUR STRENGTH!!
DO—OM!!
I DON'T HAVE ENOUGH MEDICINE!
CHOMP
CHOMP
YUM!
WE GOTTA FIND AN ISLAND SOON, NAMI!!
NUM!
CHOMP
CHOMP
SNIF
SNIF
I KNOW THAT, BUT WE CAN'T JUST SNAP OUR FINGERS AND FIND LAND...
AND REMEMBER HOW THE BOOK SAID THAT THE POISON CAUSED INSTANT DEATH?!
WELL, LUFFY'S STILL ALIVE!! MAYBE HE HAS SOME POWERFUL RESISTANCE TO IT?
HIS VITALITY IS TOPS AMONG ALL OF HUMANITY.
LUFFY, ARE YOU GONNA DIE?
I'M FINE... I'M JUST LOOKING...AT THE PRETTY RIVER...
FSHHH
HE'S LOOKING AT THE RIVER STYX!!!

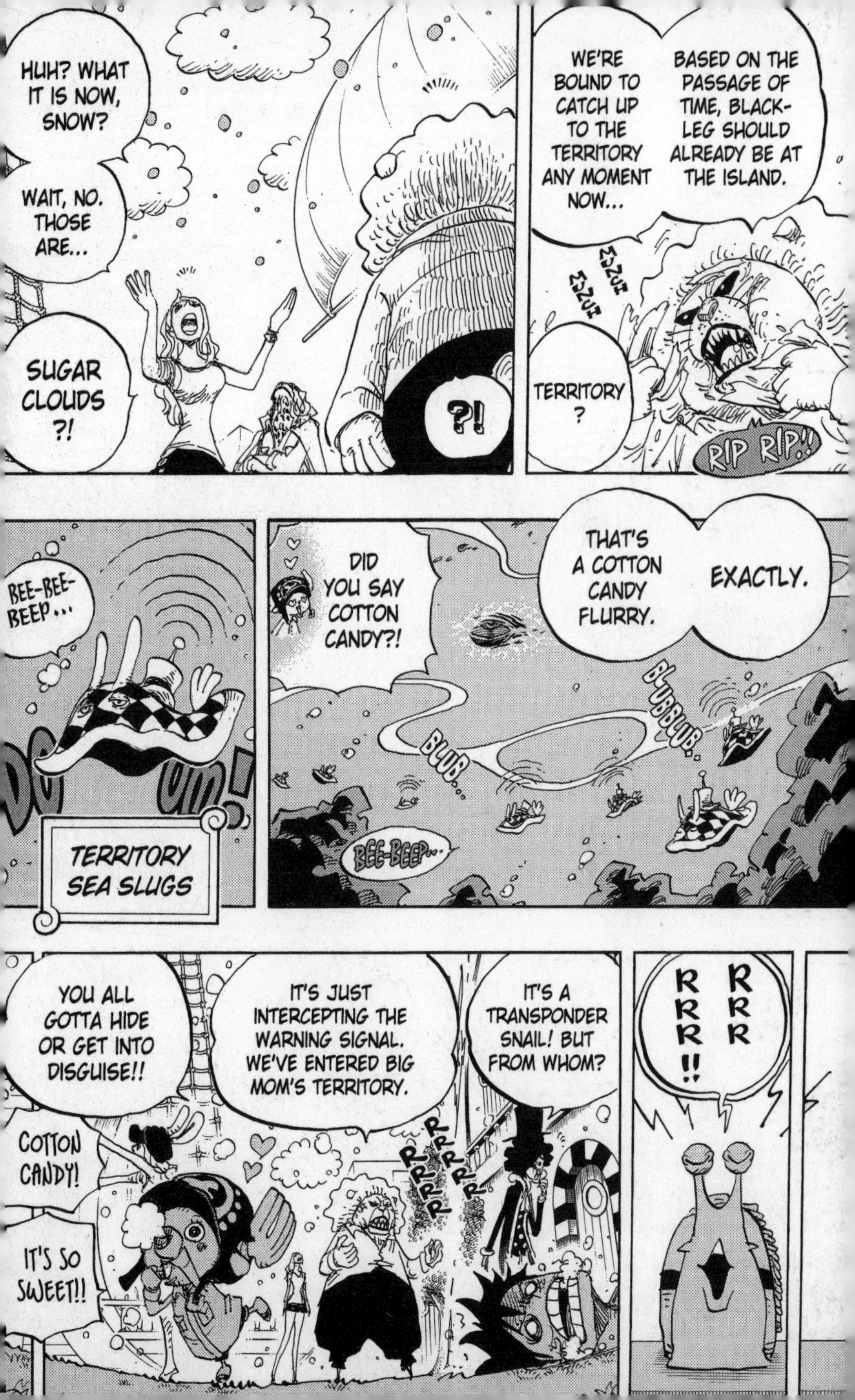
BASED ON THE PASSAGE OF TIME, BLACK-LEG SHOULD ALREADY BE AT THE ISLAND.
WE'RE BOUND TO CATCH UP TO THE TERRITORY ANY MOMENT NOW...
MUNCH MUNCH
TERRITORY?
RIP RIP!!
?!
HUH? WHAT IT IS NOW, SNOW?
WAIT, NO. THOSE ARE...
SUGAR CLOUDS?!
EXACTLY.
THAT'S A COTTON CANDY FLURRY.
DID YOU SAY COTTON CANDY?!
BLUBBLUB...
BLUB...
BEE-BEEP...
BEE-BEE-BEEP...
TERRITORY SEA SLUGS
RRR
RRR!!
IT'S A TRANSPONDER SNAIL! BUT FROM WHOM?
IT'S JUST INTERCEPTING THE WARNING SIGNAL. WE'VE ENTERED BIG MOM'S TERRITORY.
YOU ALL GOTTA HIDE OR GET INTO DISGUISE!!
RRRRR
COTTON CANDY!
IT'S SO SWEET!!

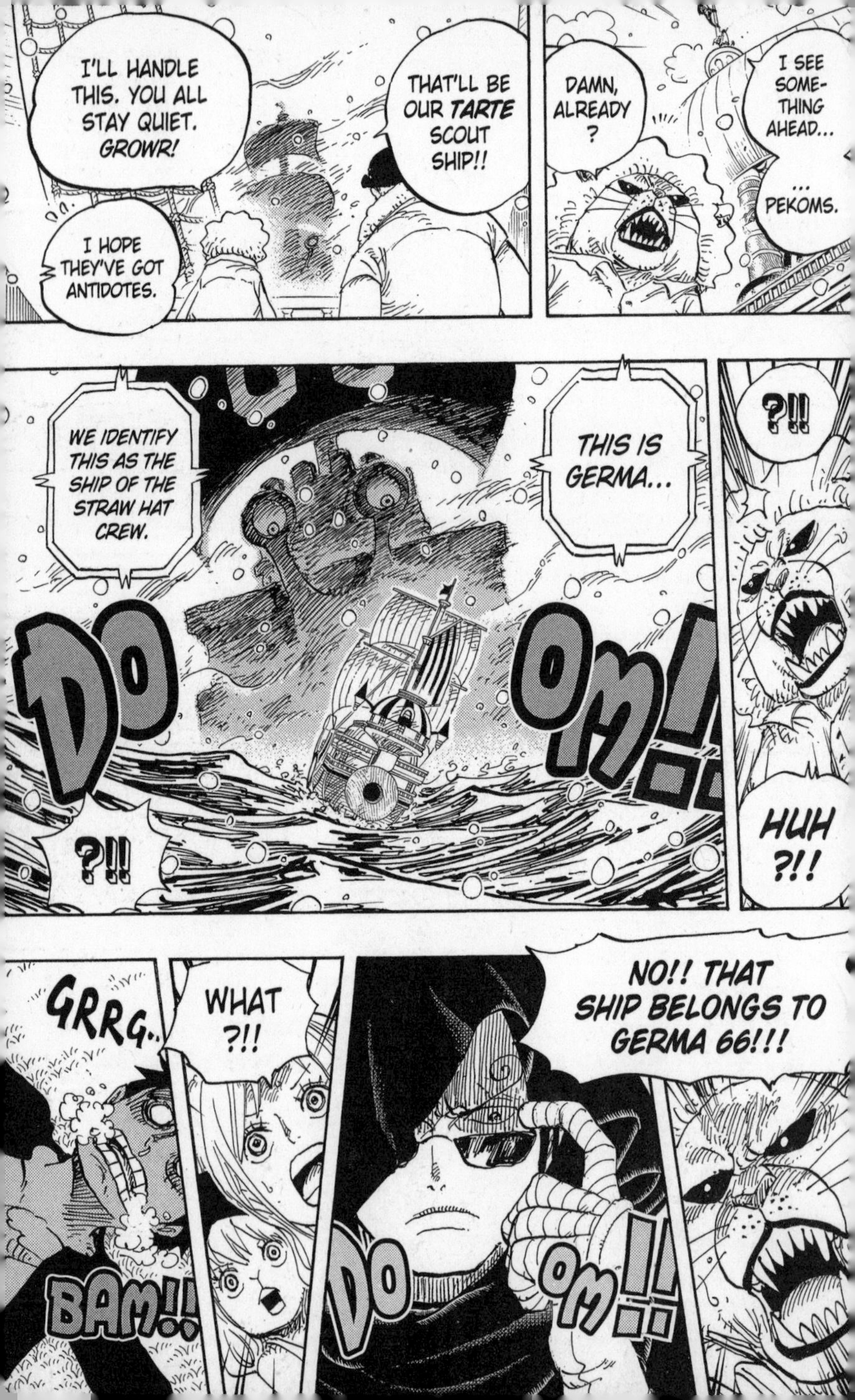
I SEE SOMETHING AHEAD...
... PEKOMS.
DAMN, ALREADY?
THAT'LL BE OUR TARTE SCOUT SHIP!!
I'LL HANDLE THIS. YOU ALL STAY QUIET. GROWR!
I HOPE THEY'VE GOT ANTIDOTES.
?!!
HUH ?!!
THIS IS GERMA...
WE IDENTIFY THIS AS THE SHIP OF THE STRAW HAT CREW.
DOOM!!
?!!
NO!! THAT SHIP BELONGS TO GERMA 66!!!
DOOM!!
WHAT ?!!
GRRG..
BAM!!

SBS Question Corner

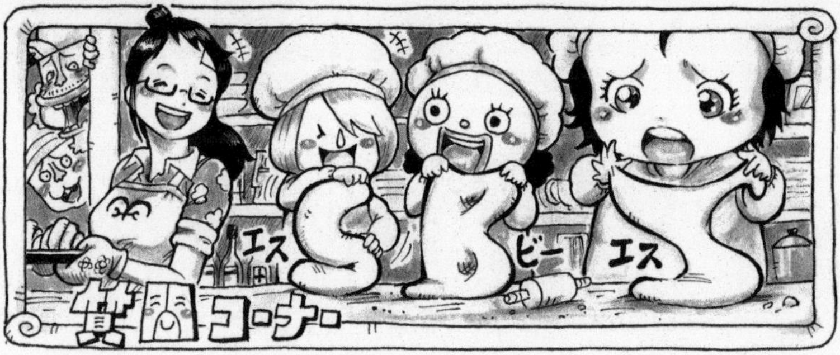
エス
ビー
エス
(Hippo Iron, Saitama)

Q: I want the Cat Viper's birthday to be November 22, since it can be interpreted as "Good Meow-Meow." Is that okay?

--I Love Cats

A: Whaaaat?! Okay.

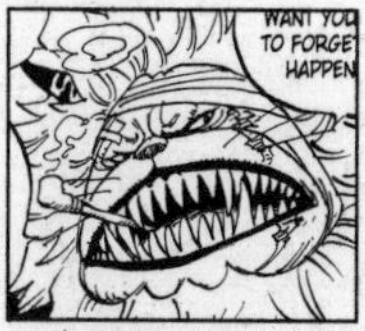
WANT YOU
TO FORGE
HAPPEN

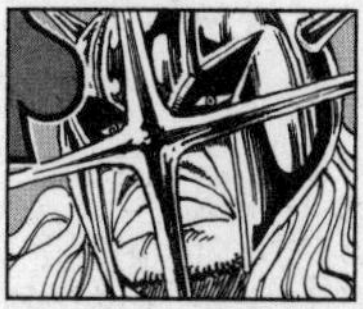

Q: Hey, Masao! The guy in the SBS of Volume 81 whose birthday was December 14!! I've come to make your dream come true!! Pica's birthday will be December 14, because it kind of sounds like "controls stone freely"! What say you, Odacchi?!

--Pitera

A: How kind! (laughs) Masao was upset that no characters shared his birthday! Well, there you go! You have to speak in a funny high-pitched voice from now on.

Q: Heso, Oda Sensei! I was checking the birthday list and noticed that none of the Alabastan characters aside from Vivi had birthdays, so I did my best to fill them in.

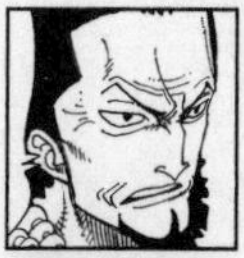
King Cobra (February 13)
Bu (Ko-bu-ra) is 2, the King card is 13

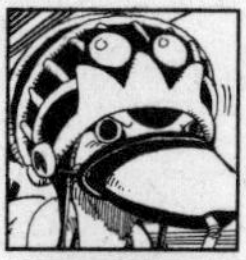
Karoo (November 8)
"Ka" and "u" are 118 on a phone keypad

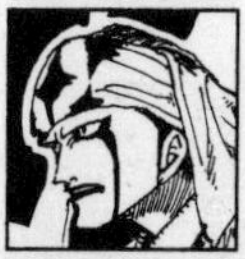
Pell (August 23)
Falcon is "Hayabusa," ha-bu-sa is "823"

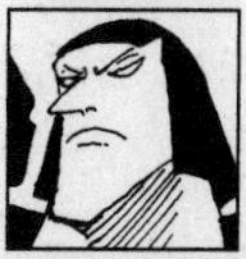
Chaka (April 26)
Jackal, ji-ka-ru is "426"

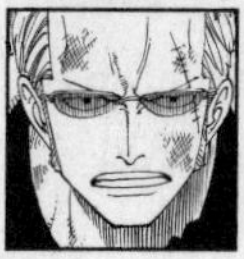
Koza (May 26)
Ko-za is 526 on a phone keypad

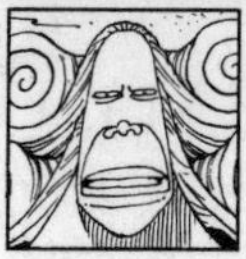
Igaram (December 6)
I-ga-mu is "126"

What do you think of that?

--Hii (Age 20)

A: Whaaaaaat?! Okay.

Chapter 826:
0 AND 4

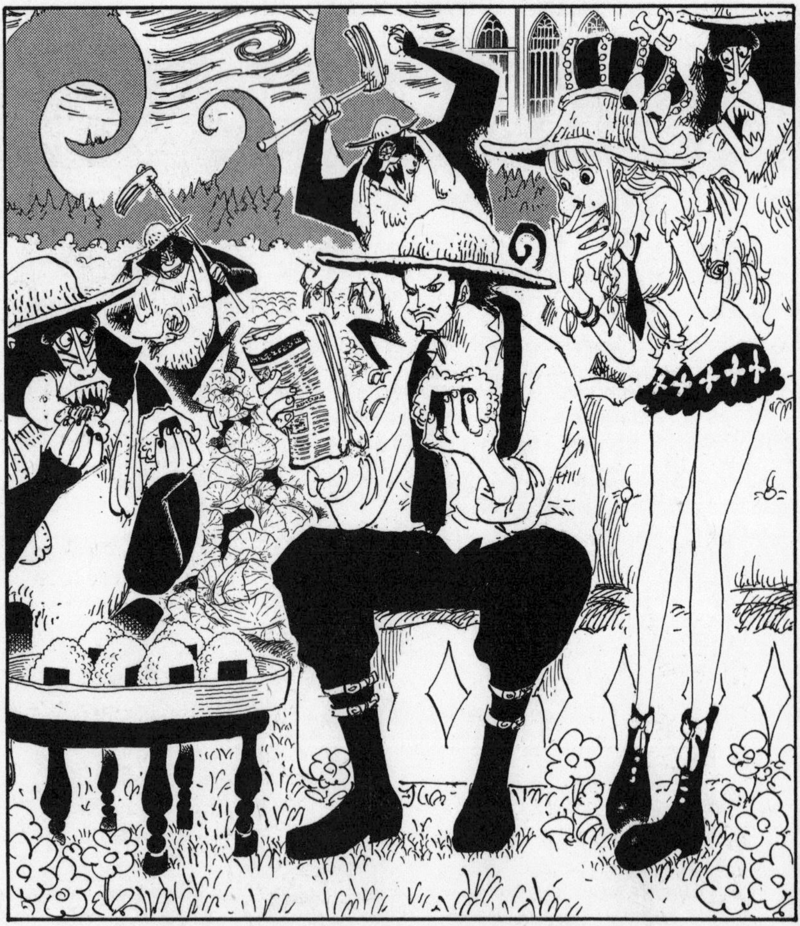

DECKS OF THE WORLD, 500-MILLION-MAN ARC, VOL. 17: "FORMER MUGGY KINGDOM-- TILLING THE OLD BATTLEGROUND"

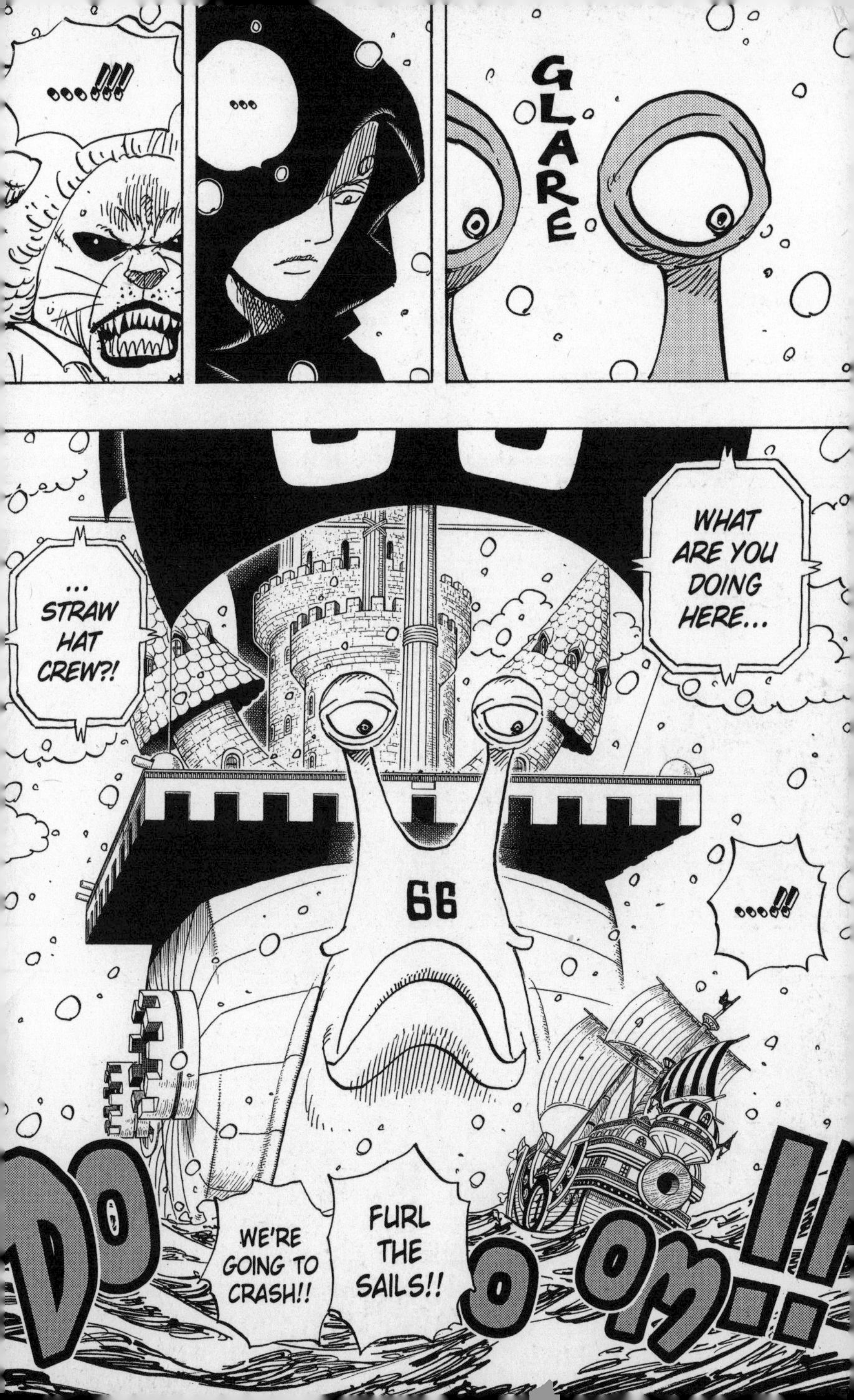
GLARE
...
...!!!
WHAT ARE YOU DOING HERE...
... STRAW HAT CREW?!
...!!
FURL THE SAILS!!
WE'RE GOING TO CRASH!!
DOOOM!!

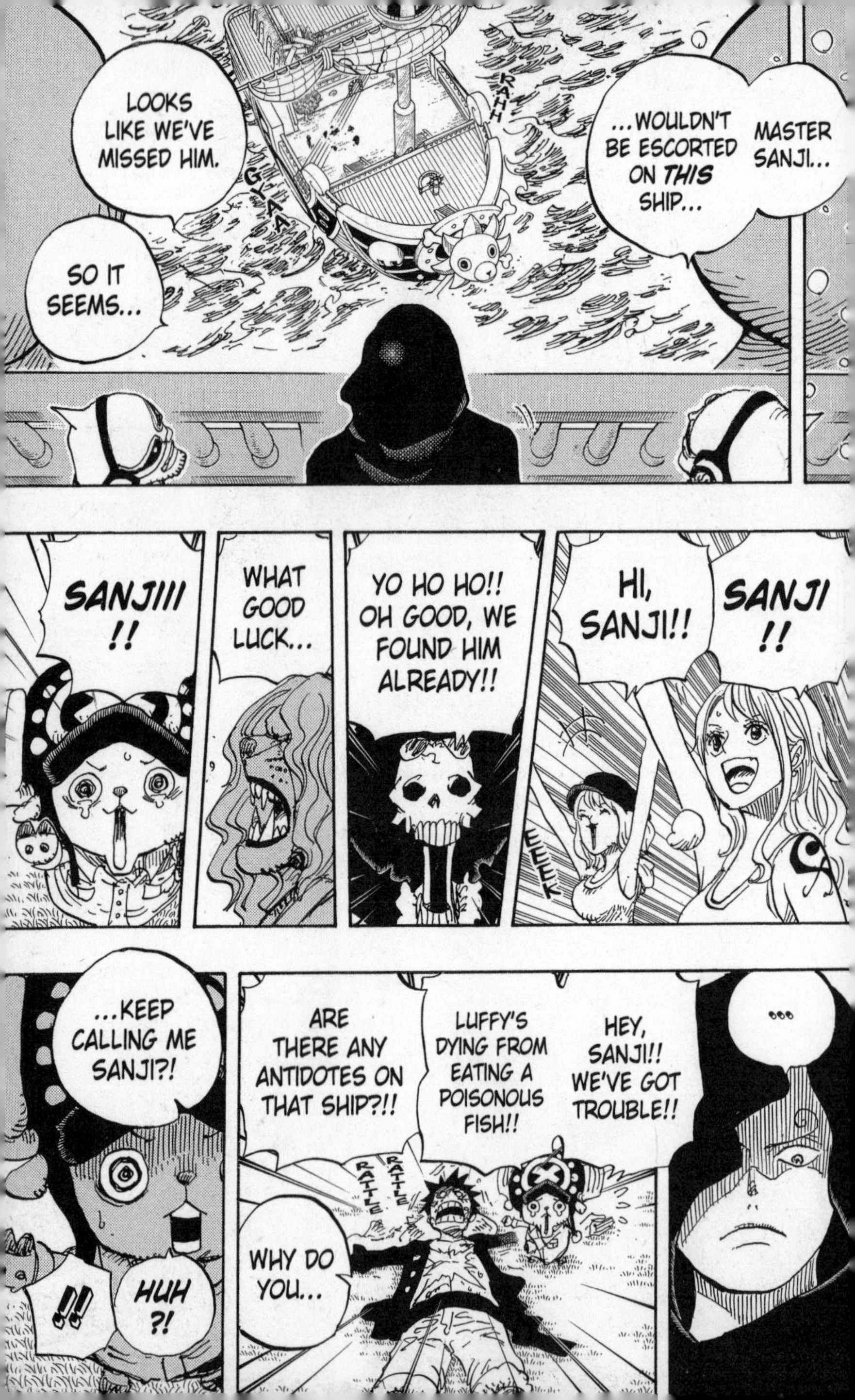
MASTER SANJI...
...WOULDN'T BE ESCORTED ON *THIS* SHIP...
RAHH
GYAA
LOOKS LIKE WE'VE MISSED HIM.
SO IT SEEMS...
SANJI !!
HI, SANJI!!
EEEK
YO HO HO!! OH GOOD, WE FOUND HIM ALREADY!!
WHAT GOOD LUCK...
SANJIII !!
...
HEY, SANJI!! WE'VE GOT TROUBLE!!
LUFFY'S DYING FROM EATING A POISONOUS FISH!!
ARE THERE ANY ANTIDOTES ON THAT SHIP?!!
RATTLE
RATTLE
WHY DO YOU...
...KEEP CALLING ME SANJI?!
HUH ?!
!!

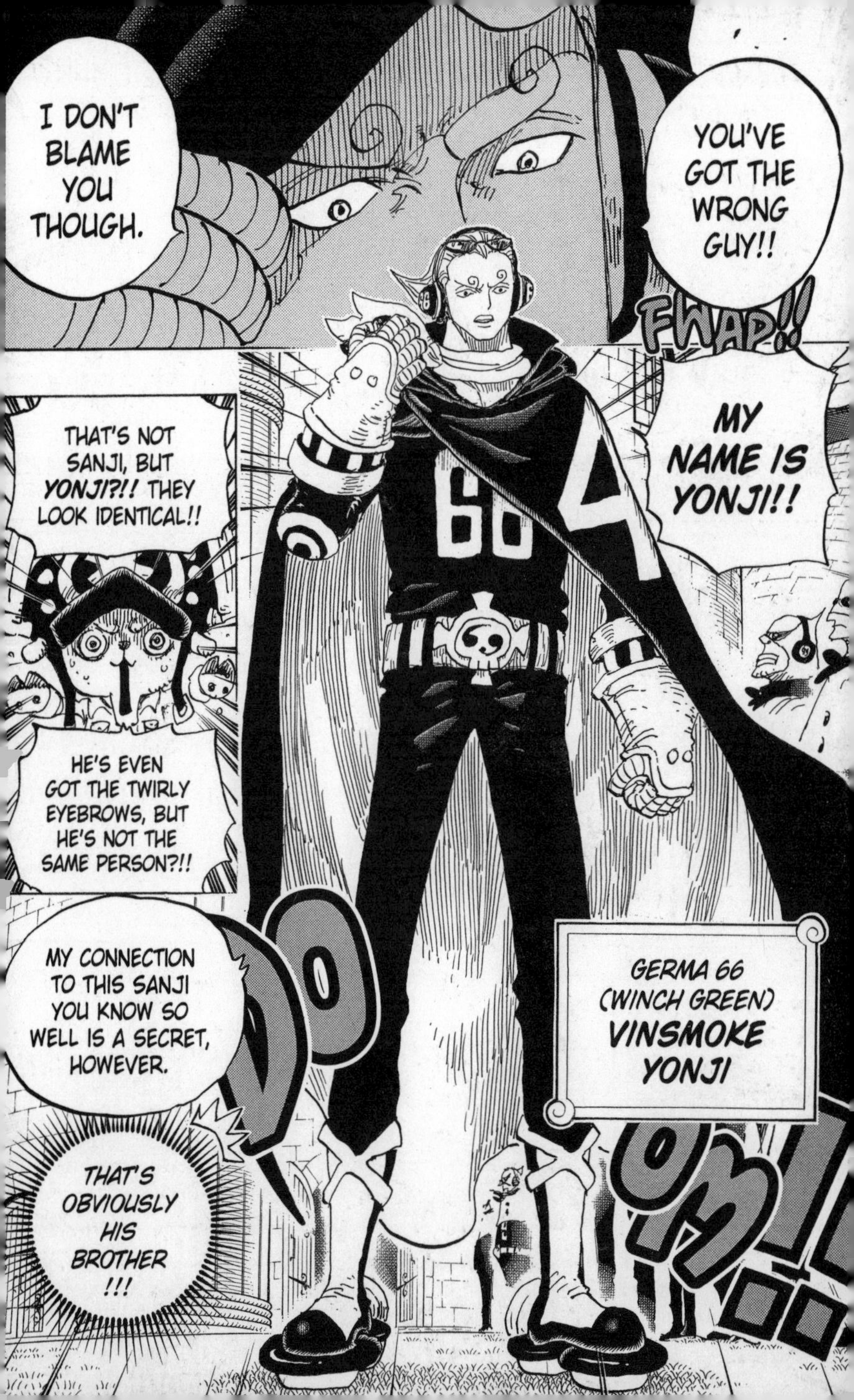
YOU'VE GOT THE WRONG GUY!!
I DON'T BLAME YOU THOUGH.
FWAP!!
MY NAME IS YONJI!!
GERMA 66 (WINCH GREEN) VINSMOKE YONJI
MY CONNECTION TO THIS SANJI YOU KNOW SO WELL IS A SECRET, HOWEVER.
THAT'S NOT SANJI, BUT YONJI?!! THEY LOOK IDENTICAL!!
HE'S EVEN GOT THE TWIRLY EYEBROWS, BUT HE'S NOT THE SAME PERSON?!!
THAT'S OBVIOUSLY HIS BROTHER!!!

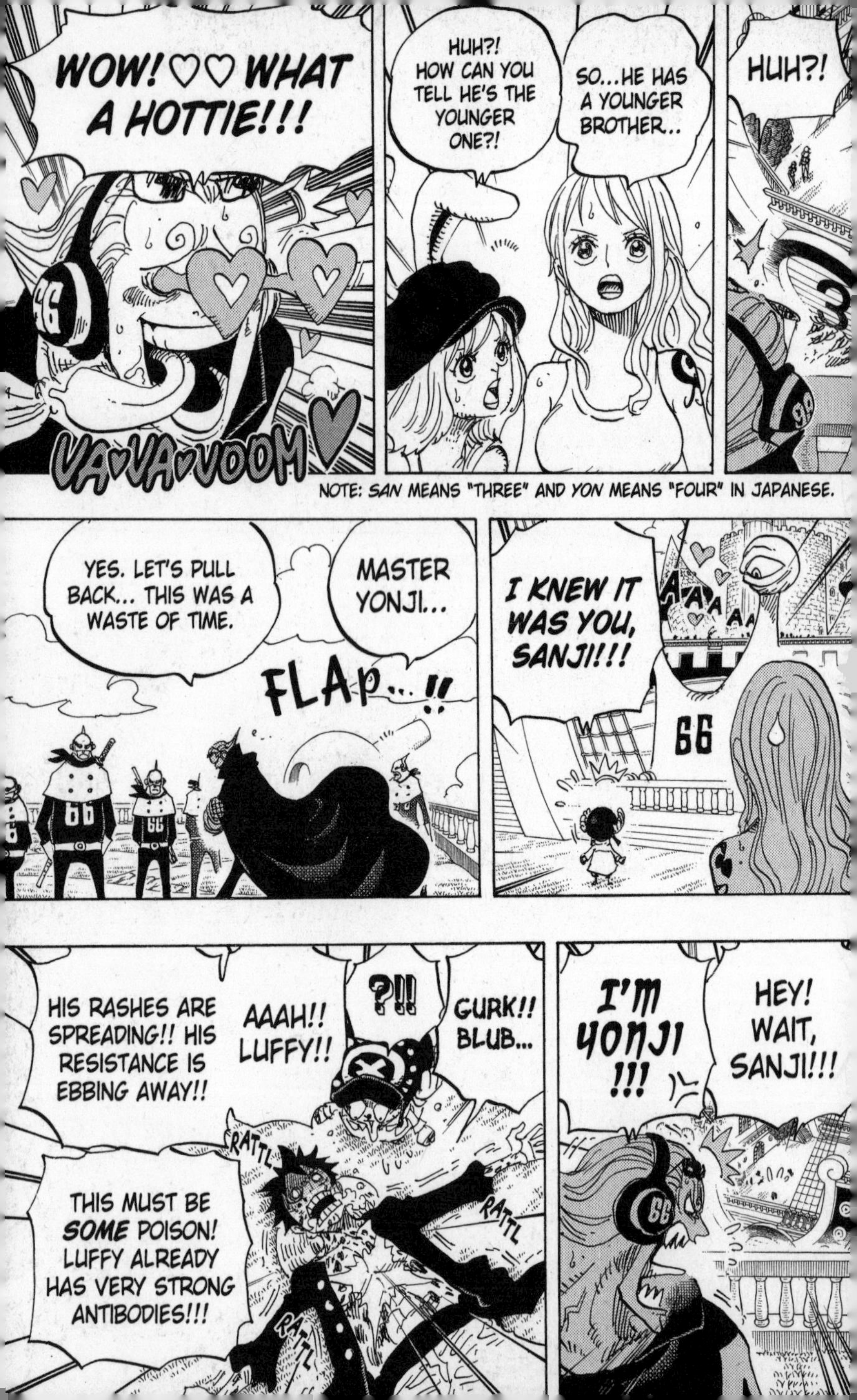
HUH?!
SO...HE HAS A YOUNGER BROTHER...
HUH?! HOW CAN YOU TELL HE'S THE YOUNGER ONE?!
WOW! ♡♡ WHAT A HOTTIE!!!
VA♥VA♥VOOM♥
NOTE: SAN MEANS "THREE" AND YON MEANS "FOUR" IN JAPANESE.
I KNEW IT WAS YOU, SANJI!!!
66
MASTER YONJI...
YES. LET'S PULL BACK... THIS WAS A WASTE OF TIME.
FLAp...!!
HEY! WAIT, SANJI!!!
I'M YONJI!!!
GURK!! BLUB...
?!!
AAAH!! LUFFY!!
HIS RASHES ARE SPREADING!! HIS RESISTANCE IS EBBING AWAY!!
RATTL
THIS MUST BE SOME POISON! LUFFY ALREADY HAS VERY STRONG ANTIBODIES!!!
RATTL
RATTL

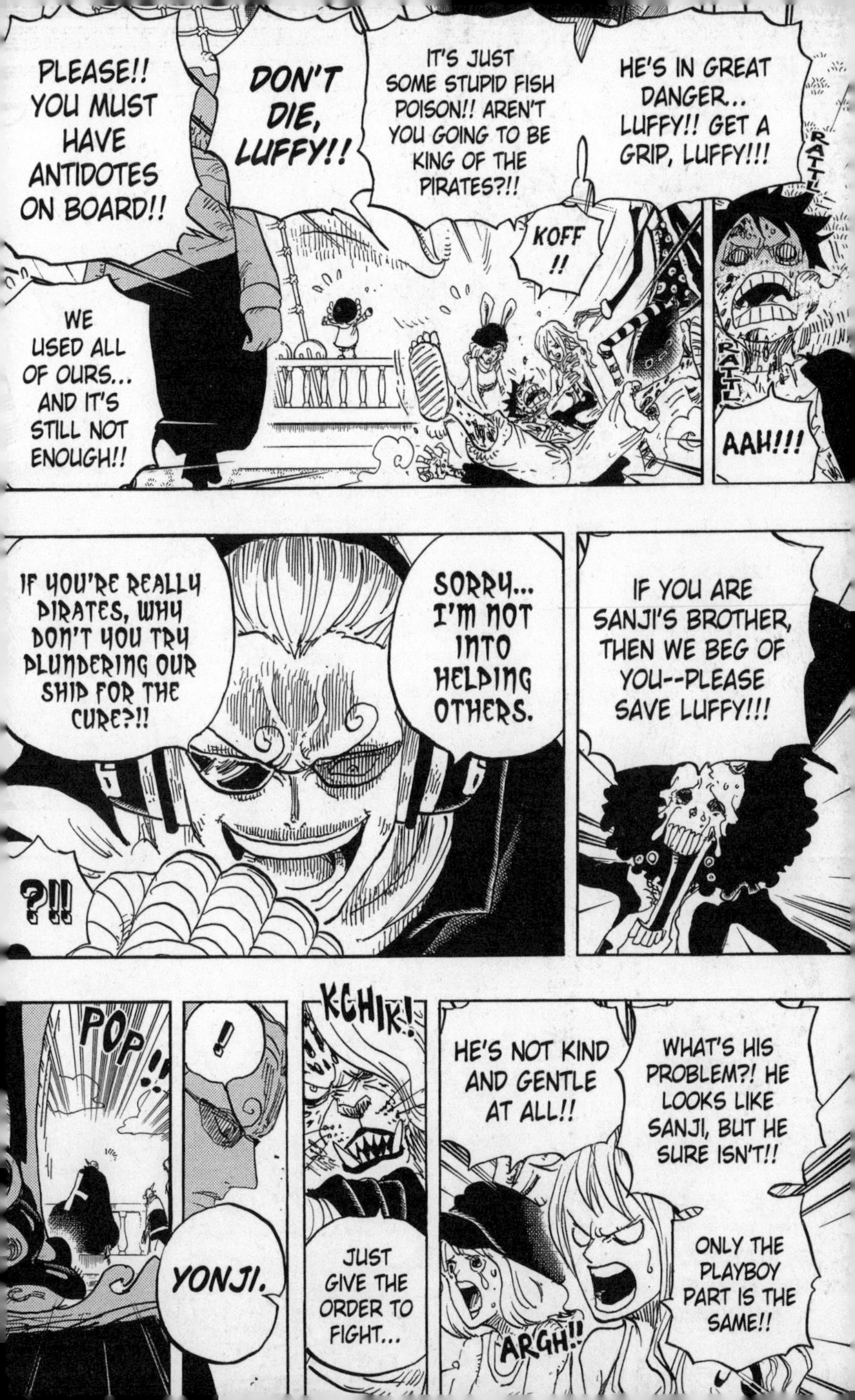
HE'S IN GREAT DANGER... LUFFY!! GET A GRIP, LUFFY!!!
RATTL
RATTL
AAH!!!
IT'S JUST SOME STUPID FISH POISON!! AREN'T YOU GOING TO BE KING OF THE PIRATES?!!
KOFF!!
DON'T DIE, LUFFY!!
PLEASE!! YOU MUST HAVE ANTIDOTES ON BOARD!!
WE USED ALL OF OURS... AND IT'S STILL NOT ENOUGH!!
IF YOU ARE SANJI'S BROTHER, THEN WE BEG OF YOU--PLEASE SAVE LUFFY!!!
SORRY... I'M NOT INTO HELPING OTHERS.
IF YOU'RE REALLY PIRATES, WHY DON'T YOU TRY PLUNDERING OUR SHIP FOR THE CURE?!!
?!!
WHAT'S HIS PROBLEM?! HE LOOKS LIKE SANJI, BUT HE SURE ISN'T!!
HE'S NOT KIND AND GENTLE AT ALL!!
ONLY THE PLAYBOY PART IS THE SAME!!
ARGH!!
K-CHIK!
JUST GIVE THE ORDER TO FIGHT...
!
YONJI.
POP!!

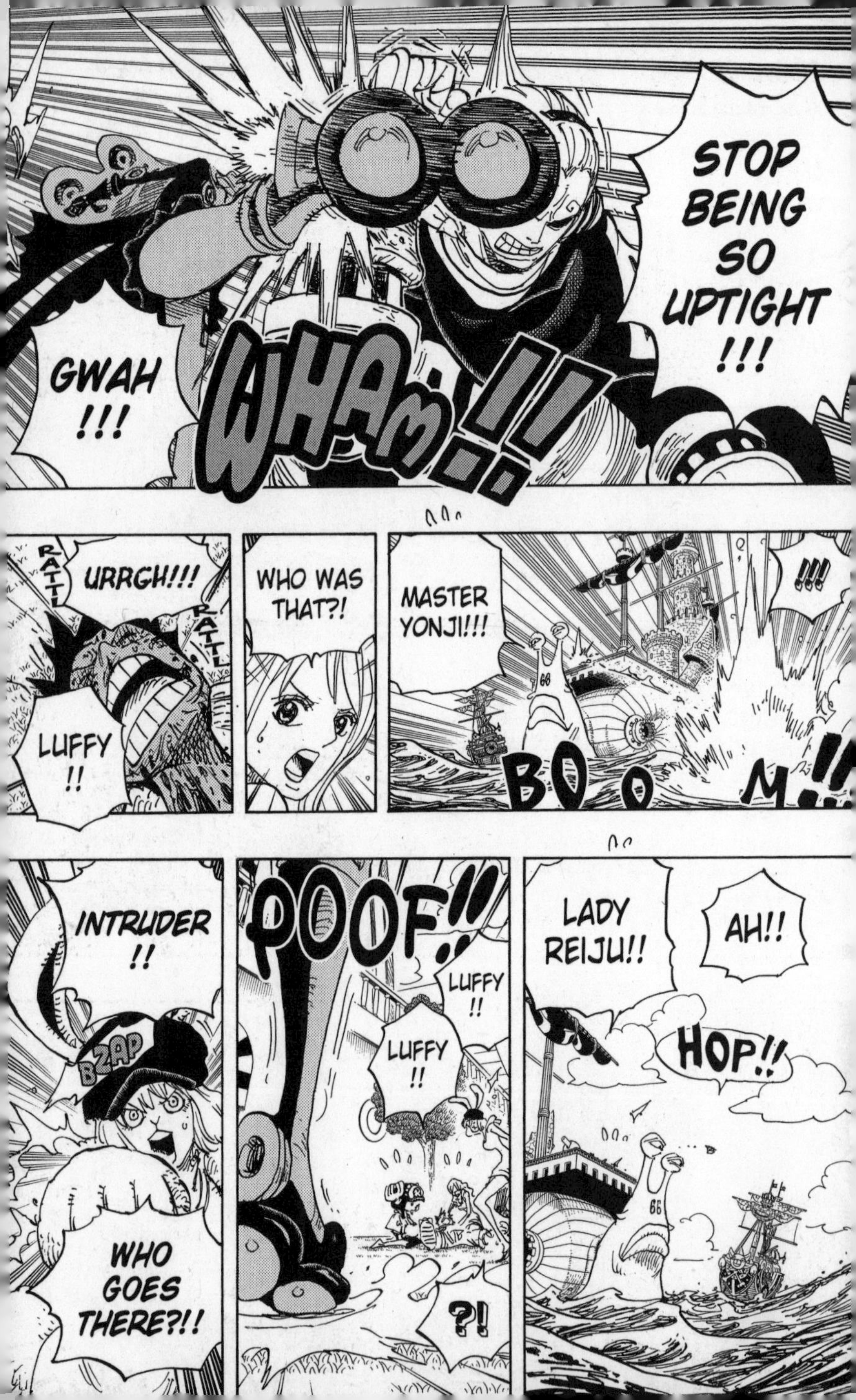
STOP BEING SO UPTIGHT!!!
WHAM!!
GWAH!!!
!!!
MASTER YONJI!!!
BOOM!!
WHO WAS THAT?!
URRGH!!!
RATTL
RATTL
LUFFY!!
AH!!
LADY REIJU!!
HOP!!
POOF!!
LUFFY!!
LUFFY!!
?!
INTRUDER!!
BZAP
WHO GOES THERE?!!

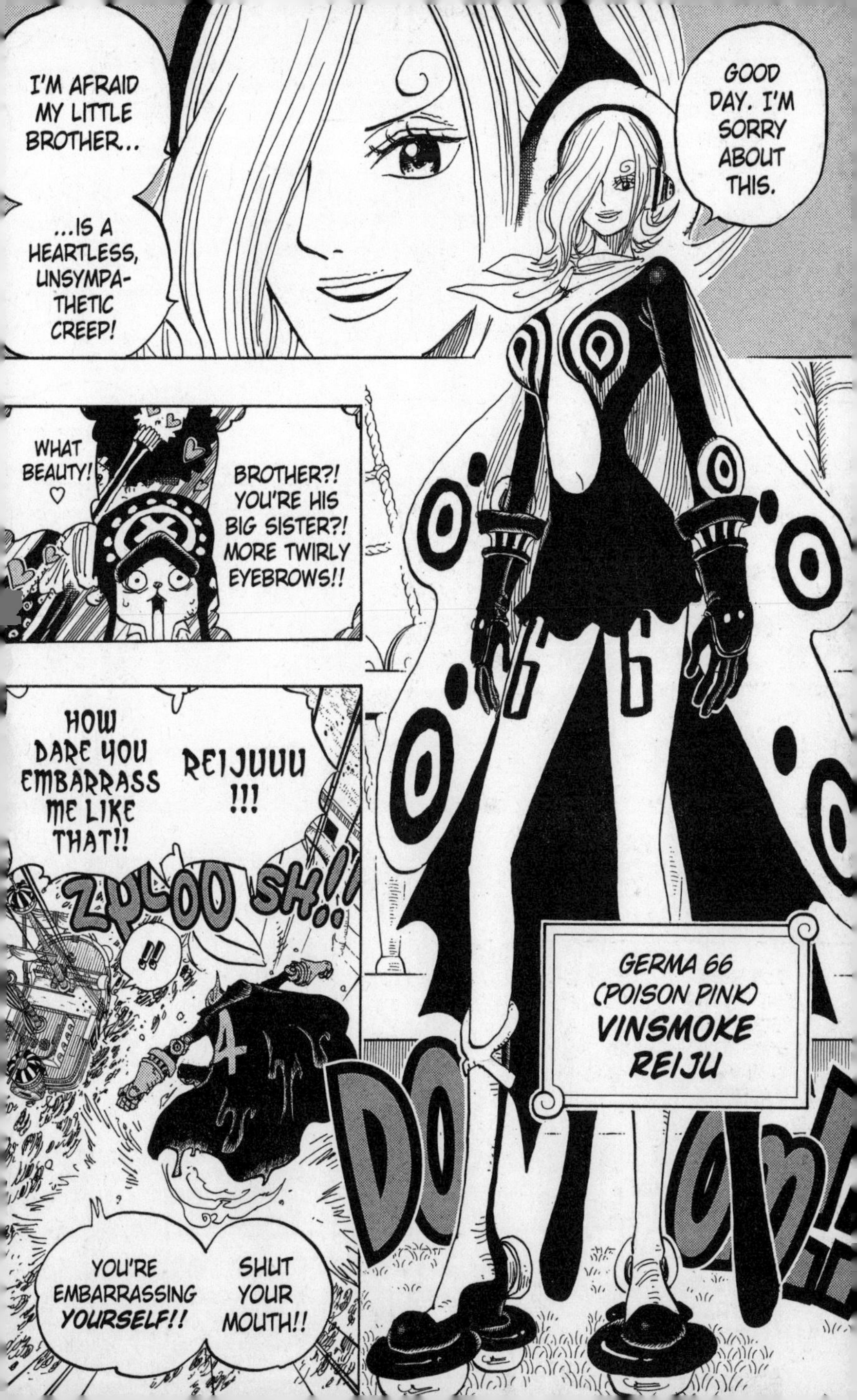
GOOD DAY. I'M SORRY ABOUT THIS.
GERMA 66 (POISON PINK) VINSMOKE REIJU
I'M AFRAID MY LITTLE BROTHER...
...IS A HEARTLESS, UNSYMPA-THETIC CREEP!
BROTHER?! YOU'RE HIS BIG SISTER?! MORE TWIRLY EYEBROWS!!
WHAT BEAUTY! ♡
REIJUUU!!!
HOW DARE YOU EMBARRASS ME LIKE THAT!!
ZPLOOSH!!
!!
SHUT YOUR MOUTH!!
YOU'RE EMBARRASSING YOURSELF!!

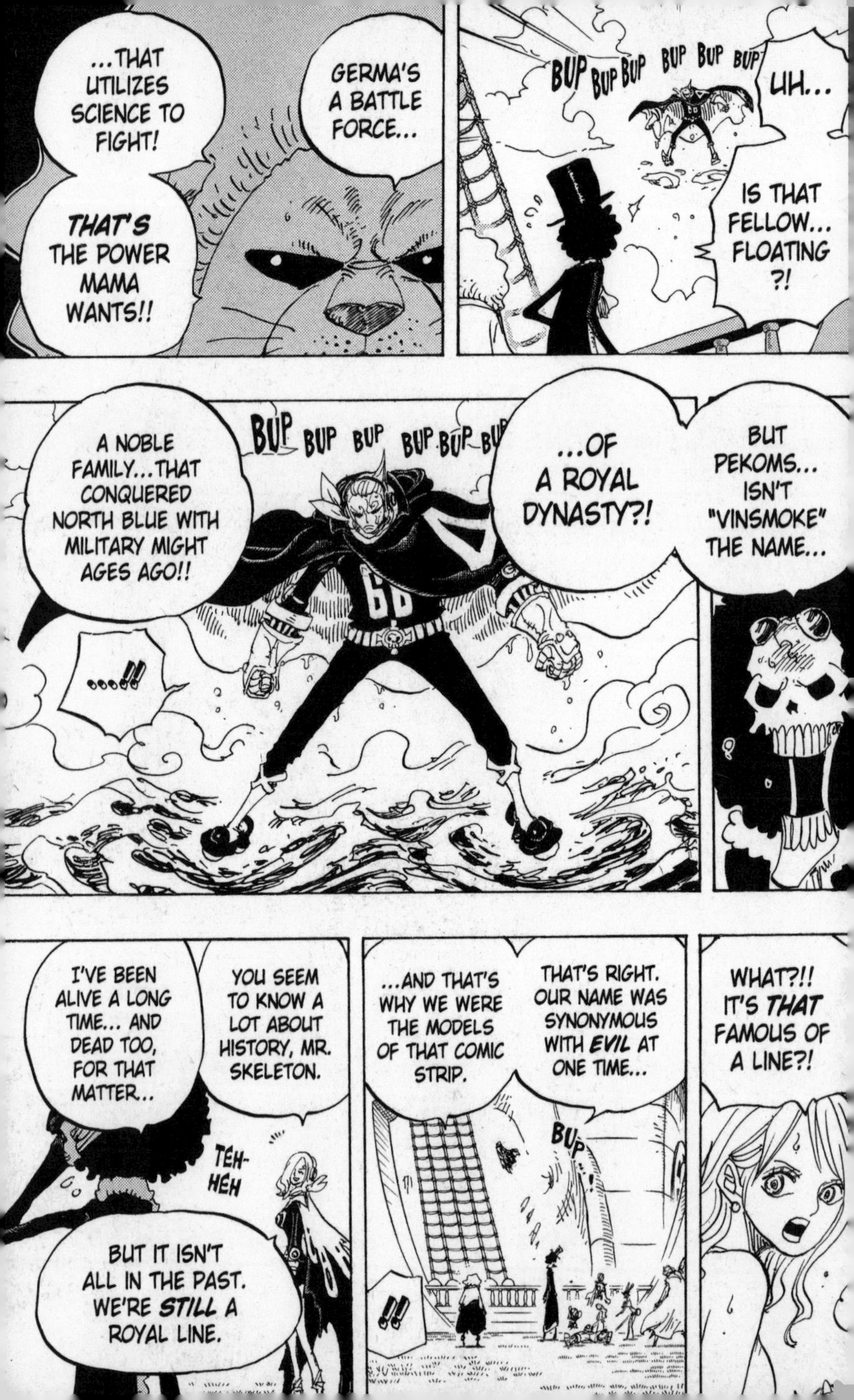
BUP BUP BUP BUP BUP BUP
UH...
IS THAT FELLOW... FLOATING?!
GERMA'S A BATTLE FORCE...
...THAT UTILIZES SCIENCE TO FIGHT!
THAT'S THE POWER MAMA WANTS!!
BUT PEKOMS... ISN'T "VINSMOKE" THE NAME...
...OF A ROYAL DYNASTY?!
BUP BUP BUP BUP BUP BUP
A NOBLE FAMILY...THAT CONQUERED NORTH BLUE WITH MILITARY MIGHT AGES AGO!!
....!!
WHAT?!! IT'S *THAT* FAMOUS OF A LINE?!
THAT'S RIGHT. OUR NAME WAS SYNONYMOUS WITH *EVIL* AT ONE TIME...
...AND THAT'S WHY WE WERE THE MODELS OF THAT COMIC STRIP.
BUP
!!
YOU SEEM TO KNOW A LOT ABOUT HISTORY, MR. SKELETON.
I'VE BEEN ALIVE A LONG TIME... AND DEAD TOO, FOR THAT MATTER...
TEH-HEH
BUT IT ISN'T ALL IN THE PAST. WE'RE *STILL* A ROYAL LINE.

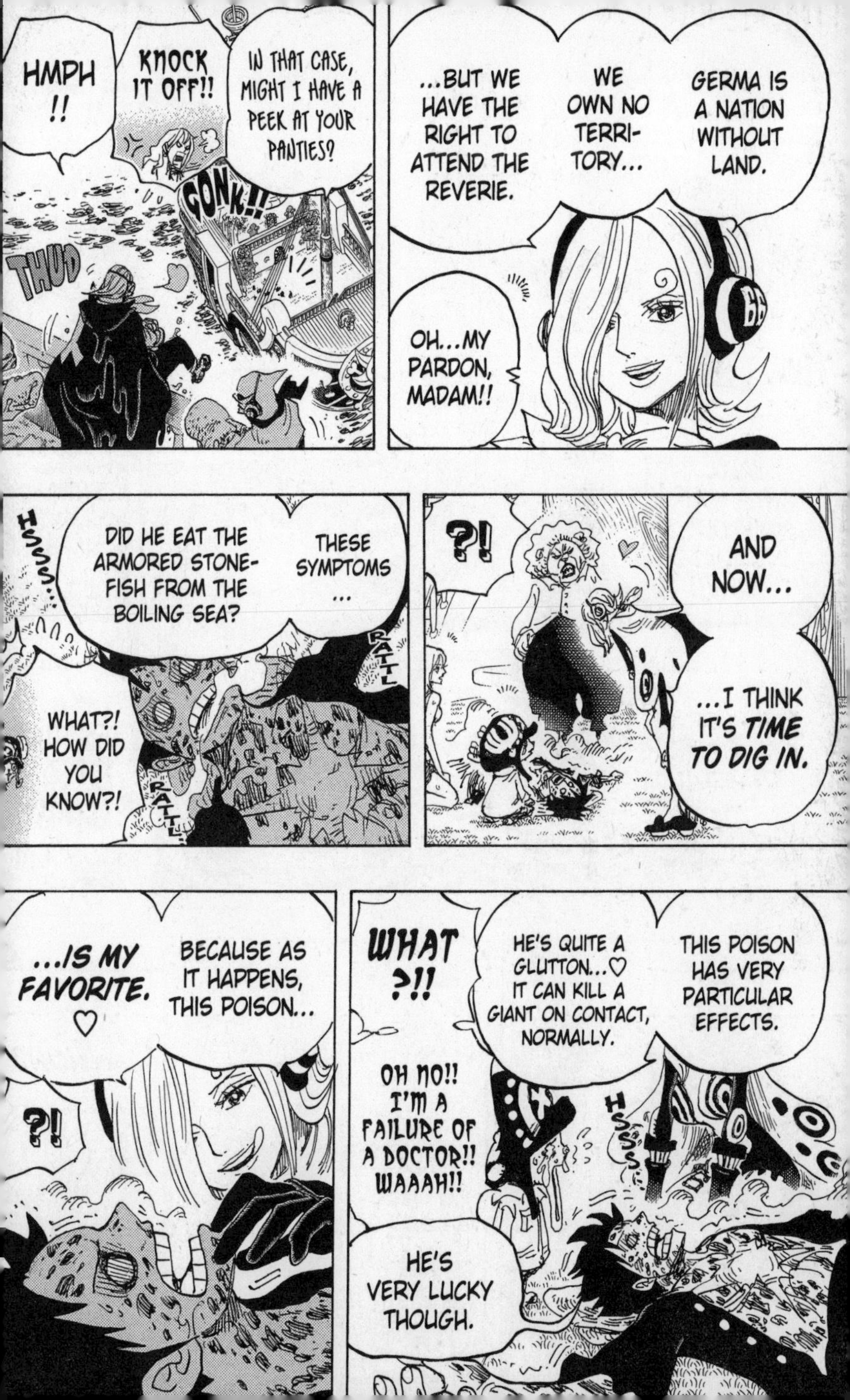
GERMA IS A NATION WITHOUT LAND.
WE OWN NO TERRITORY...
...BUT WE HAVE THE RIGHT TO ATTEND THE REVERIE.
OH...MY PARDON, MADAM!!
IN THAT CASE, MIGHT I HAVE A PEEK AT YOUR PANTIES?
KNOCK IT OFF!!
HMPH!!
GONK!!
THUD
?!
AND NOW...
...I THINK IT'S TIME TO DIG IN.
THESE SYMPTOMS...
DID HE EAT THE ARMORED STONE-FISH FROM THE BOILING SEA?
HSSS...
RATTL
WHAT?! HOW DID YOU KNOW?!
RATTL
THIS POISON HAS VERY PARTICULAR EFFECTS.
HE'S QUITE A GLUTTON...♡ IT CAN KILL A GIANT ON CONTACT, NORMALLY.
WHAT?!!
OH NO!! I'M A FAILURE OF A DOCTOR!! WAAAH!!
HSSS
HE'S VERY LUCKY THOUGH.
BECAUSE AS IT HAPPENS, THIS POISON...
...IS MY FAVORITE. ♡
?!

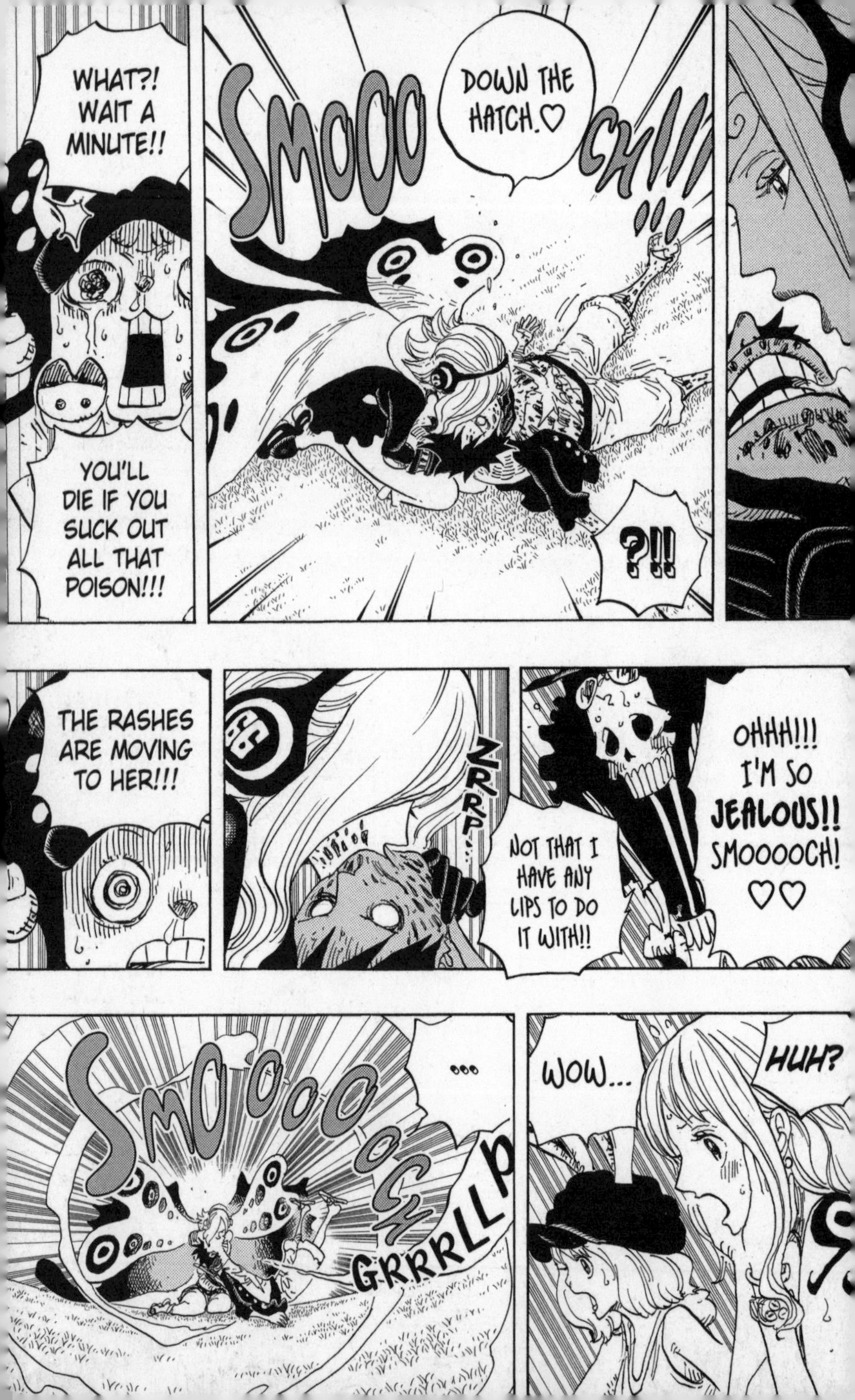
SMOOOCH!!!
DOWN THE HATCH.♡
?!!
WHAT?! WAIT A MINUTE!!
YOU'LL DIE IF YOU SUCK OUT ALL THAT POISON!!!
OHHH!!! I'M SO JEALOUS!! SMOOOOCH! ♡♡
NOT THAT I HAVE ANY LIPS TO DO IT WITH!!
ZRRP...
THE RASHES ARE MOVING TO HER!!!
HUH?
WOW...
...
SMOOOOOOCH
GRRRLLP

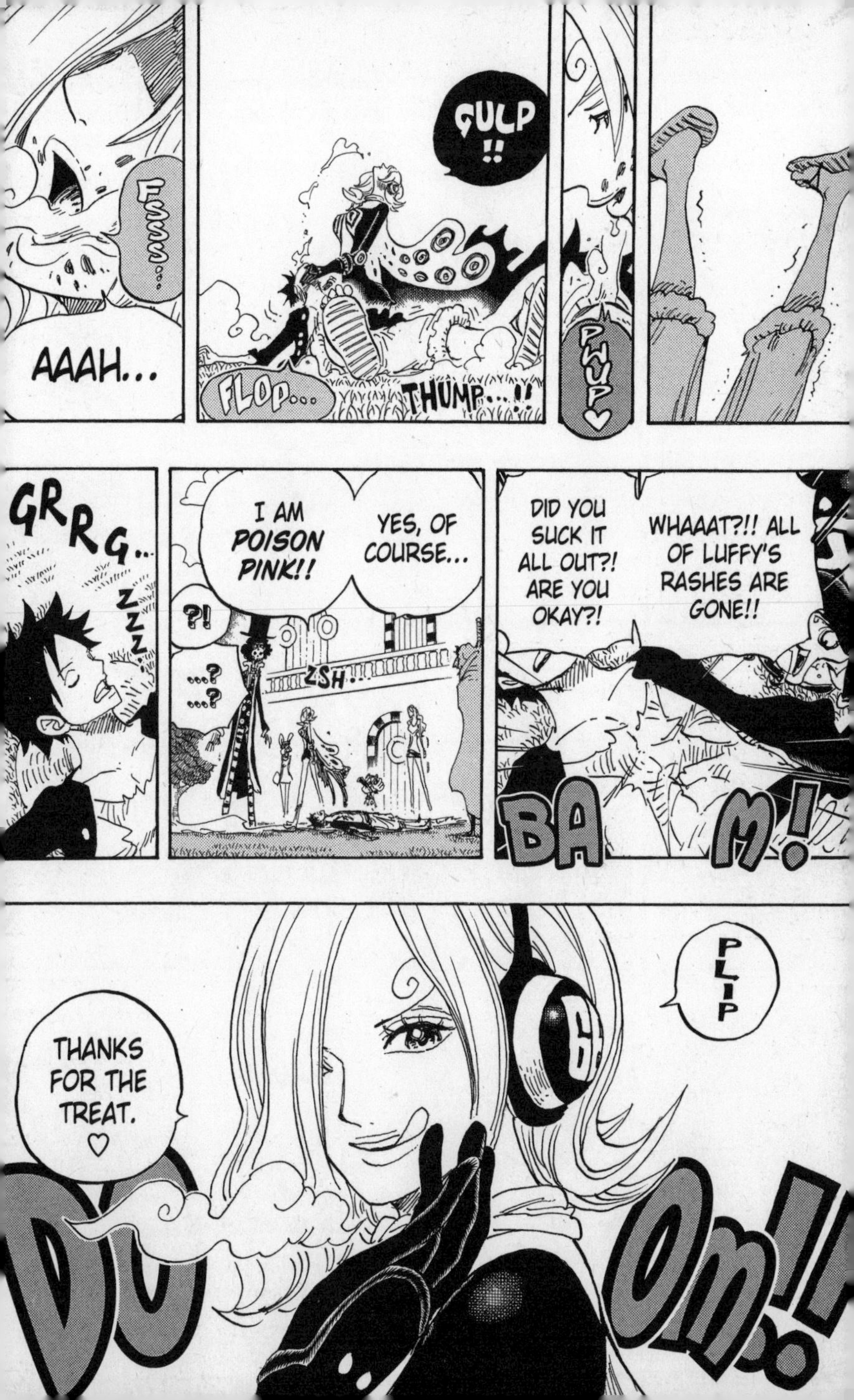
PHUP♥
GULP!!
FLOP...
THUMP...!!
FSSS...
AAAH...
WHAAAT?!! ALL OF LUFFY'S RASHES ARE GONE!!
DID YOU SUCK IT ALL OUT?! ARE YOU OKAY?!
BAM!
YES, OF COURSE...
I AM POISON PINK!!
?!
...?
...?
ZSH!...
GRRG...
ZZZ
PLIP
THANKS FOR THE TREAT. ♡
DOOM!!

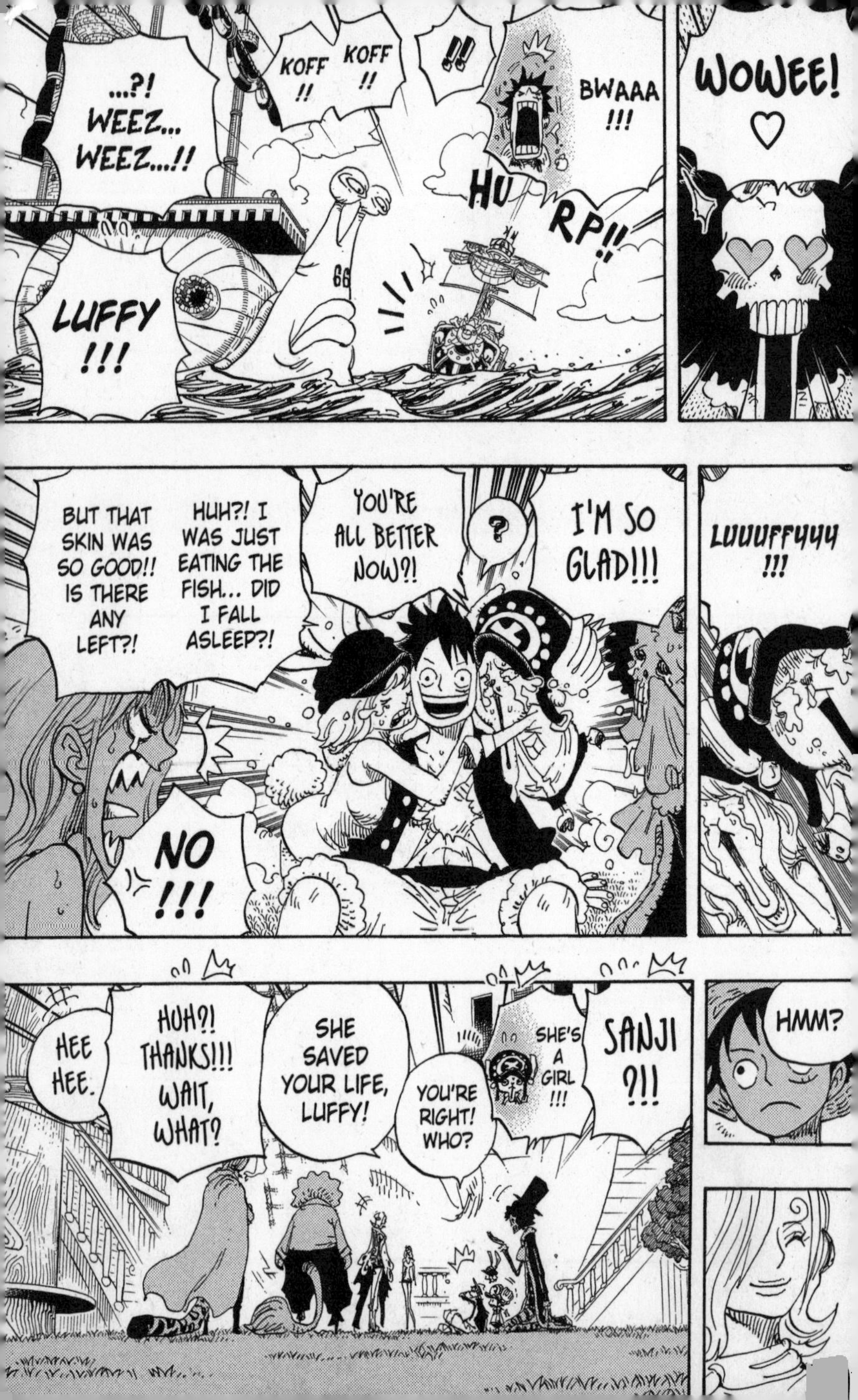
WOWEE! ♡
BWAAA !!!
!!
KOFF !!
KOFF !!
HURP!!
...?! WEEZ... WEEZ...!!
LUFFY !!!
LUUUFFYYY !!!
I'M SO GLAD!!!
?
YOU'RE ALL BETTER NOW?!
HUH?! I WAS JUST EATING THE FISH... DID I FALL ASLEEP?!
BUT THAT SKIN WAS SO GOOD!! IS THERE ANY LEFT?!
NO !!!
HMM?
SANJI ?!!
SHE'S A GIRL !!!
YOU'RE RIGHT! WHO?
SHE SAVED YOUR LIFE, LUFFY!
HUH?! THANKS!!! WAIT, WHAT?
HEE HEE.

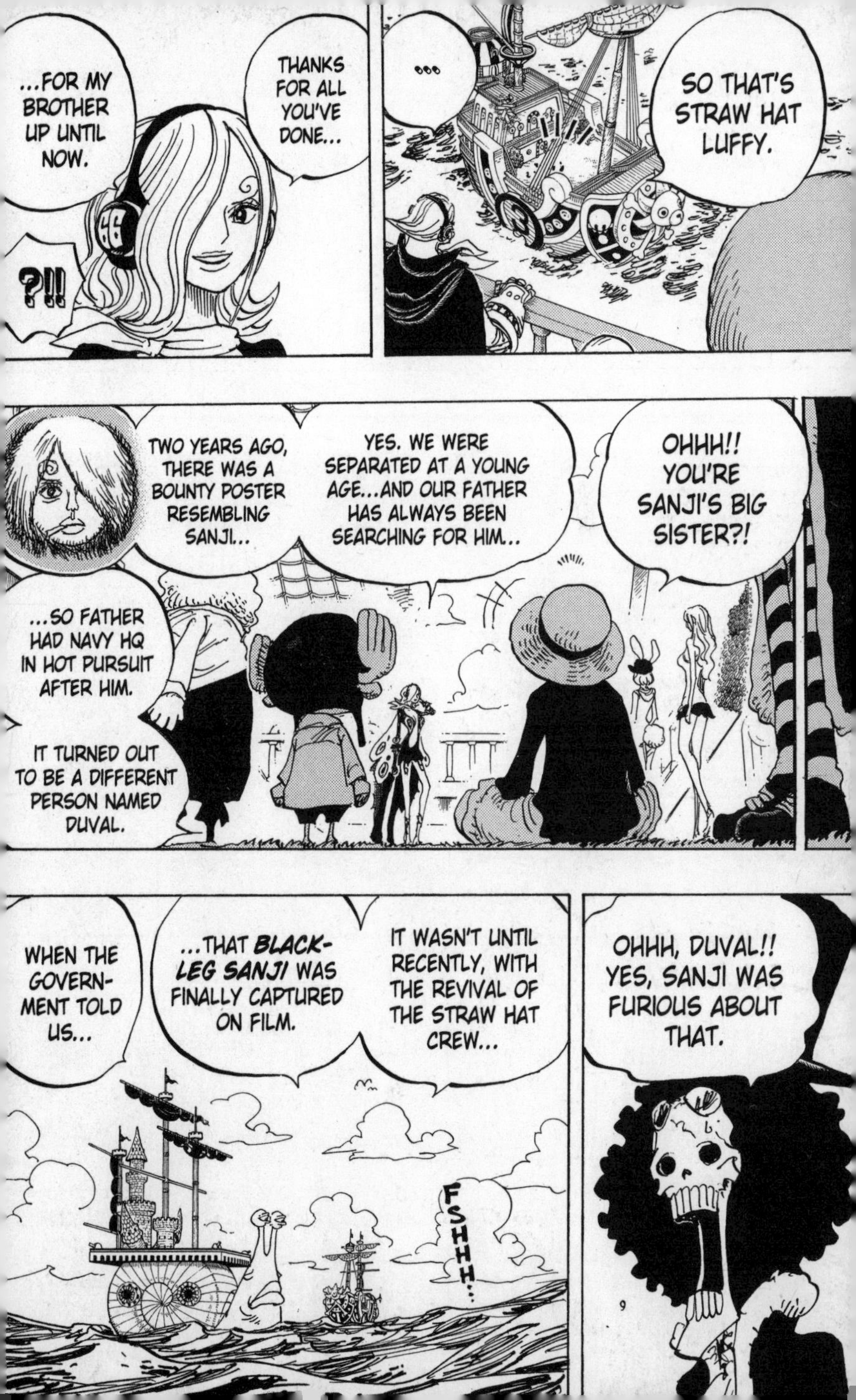
SO THAT'S STRAW HAT LUFFY.
...
THANKS FOR ALL YOU'VE DONE...
...FOR MY BROTHER UP UNTIL NOW.
?!!
OHHH!! YOU'RE SANJI'S BIG SISTER?!
YES. WE WERE SEPARATED AT A YOUNG AGE...AND OUR FATHER HAS ALWAYS BEEN SEARCHING FOR HIM...
TWO YEARS AGO, THERE WAS A BOUNTY POSTER RESEMBLING SANJI...
...SO FATHER HAD NAVY HQ IN HOT PURSUIT AFTER HIM.
IT TURNED OUT TO BE A DIFFERENT PERSON NAMED DUVAL.
OHHH, DUVAL!! YES, SANJI WAS FURIOUS ABOUT THAT.
IT WASN'T UNTIL RECENTLY, WITH THE REVIVAL OF THE STRAW HAT CREW...
...THAT ***BLACK-LEG SANJI*** WAS FINALLY CAPTURED ON FILM.
WHEN THE GOVERNMENT TOLD US...
FSHHH..

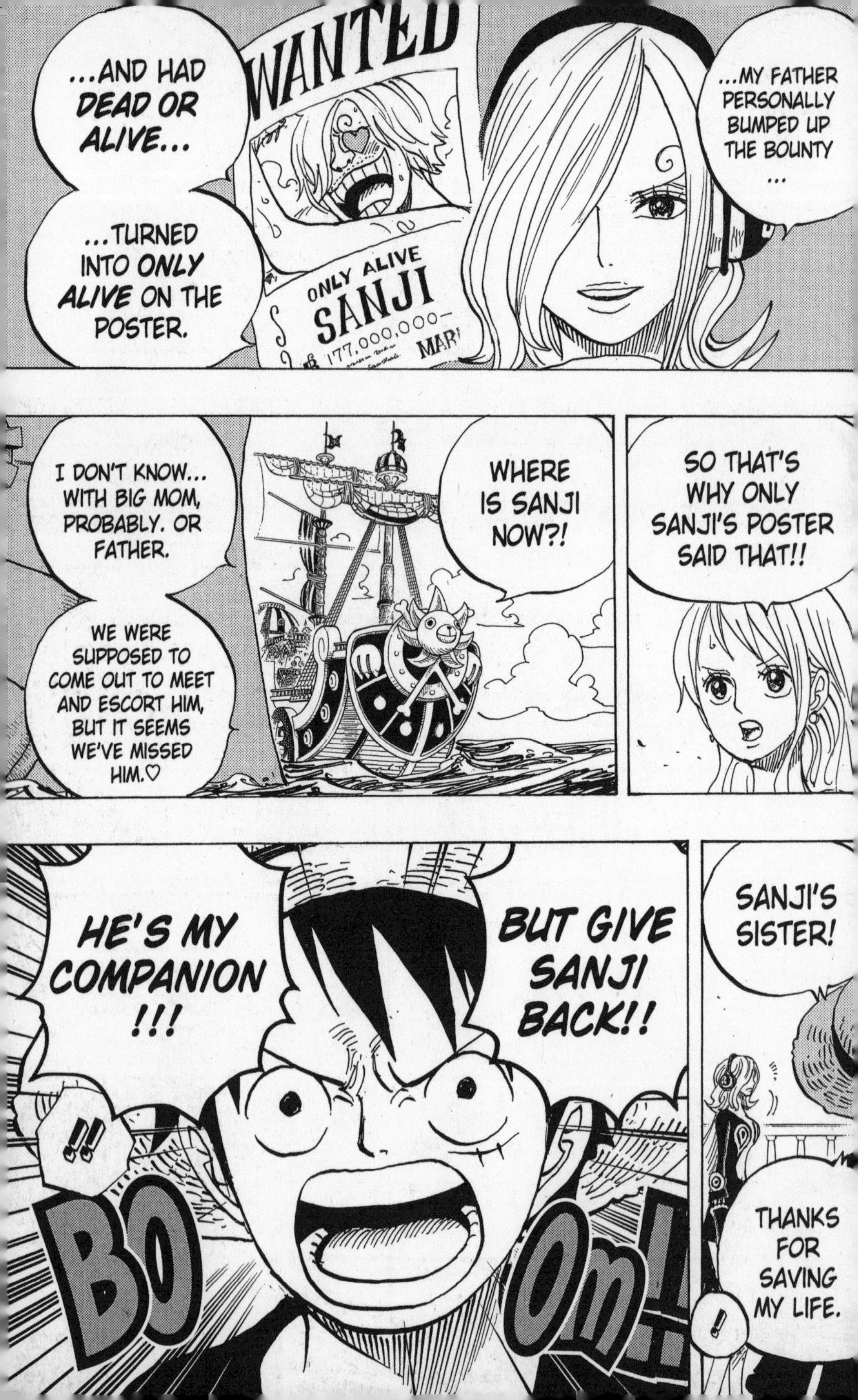
...MY FATHER PERSONALLY BUMPED UP THE BOUNTY ...
WANTED
ONLY ALIVE
SANJI
177,000,000-
...AND HAD DEAD OR ALIVE...
...TURNED INTO ONLY ALIVE ON THE POSTER.
SO THAT'S WHY ONLY SANJI'S POSTER SAID THAT!!
WHERE IS SANJI NOW?!
I DON'T KNOW... WITH BIG MOM, PROBABLY. OR FATHER.
WE WERE SUPPOSED TO COME OUT TO MEET AND ESCORT HIM, BUT IT SEEMS WE'VE MISSED HIM.♡
SANJI'S SISTER!
THANKS FOR SAVING MY LIFE.
!
BUT GIVE SANJI BACK!!
HE'S MY COMPANION !!!
!!
BOOM!!

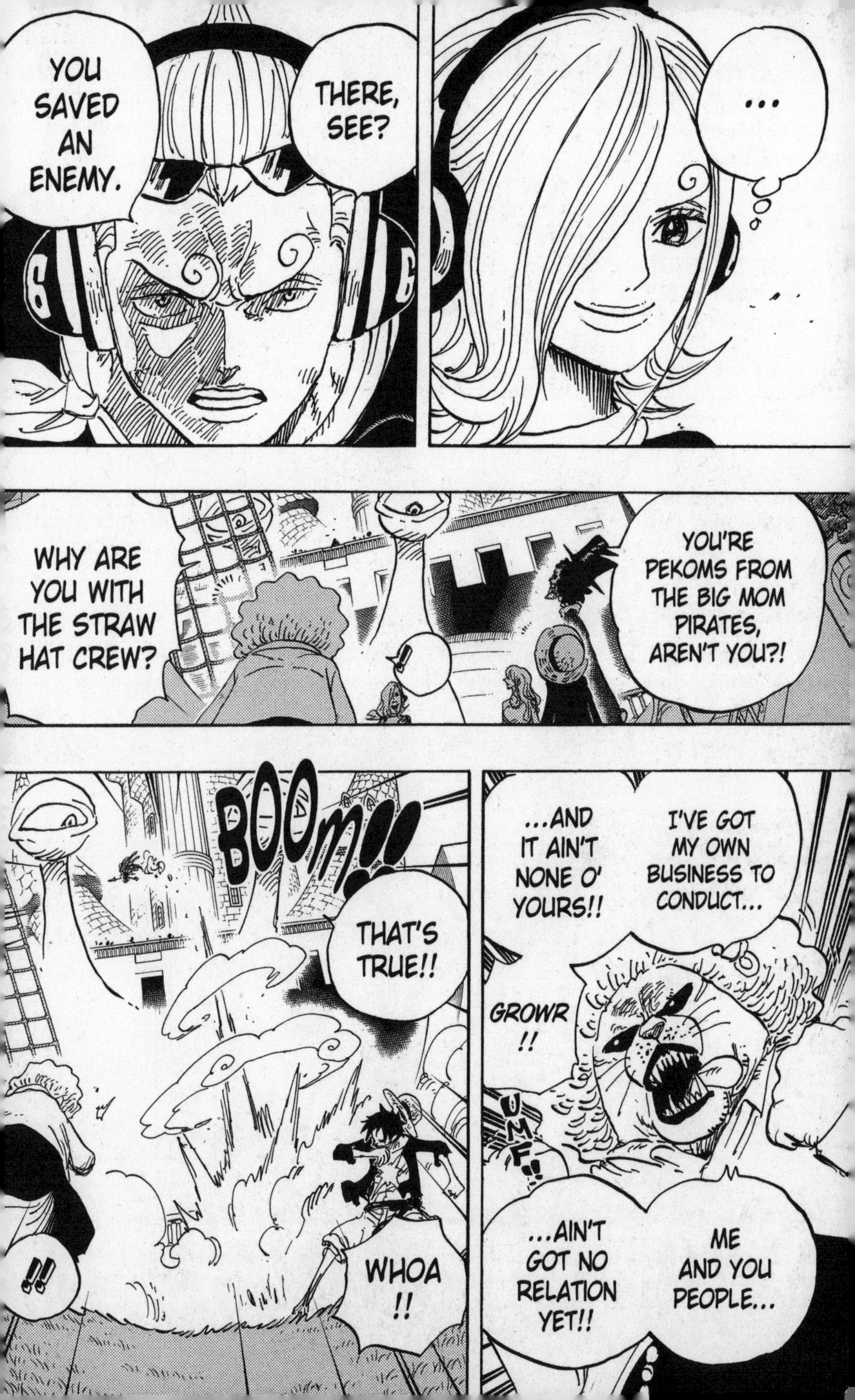
...
THERE, SEE?
YOU SAVED AN ENEMY.
YOU'RE PEKOMS FROM THE BIG MOM PIRATES, AREN'T YOU?!
WHY ARE YOU WITH THE STRAW HAT CREW?
I'VE GOT MY OWN BUSINESS TO CONDUCT...
...AND IT AIN'T NONE O' YOURS!!
GROWR !!
UMF!!
ME AND YOU PEOPLE...
...AIN'T GOT NO RELATION YET!!
BOOM!!
THAT'S TRUE!!
WHOA !!
!!

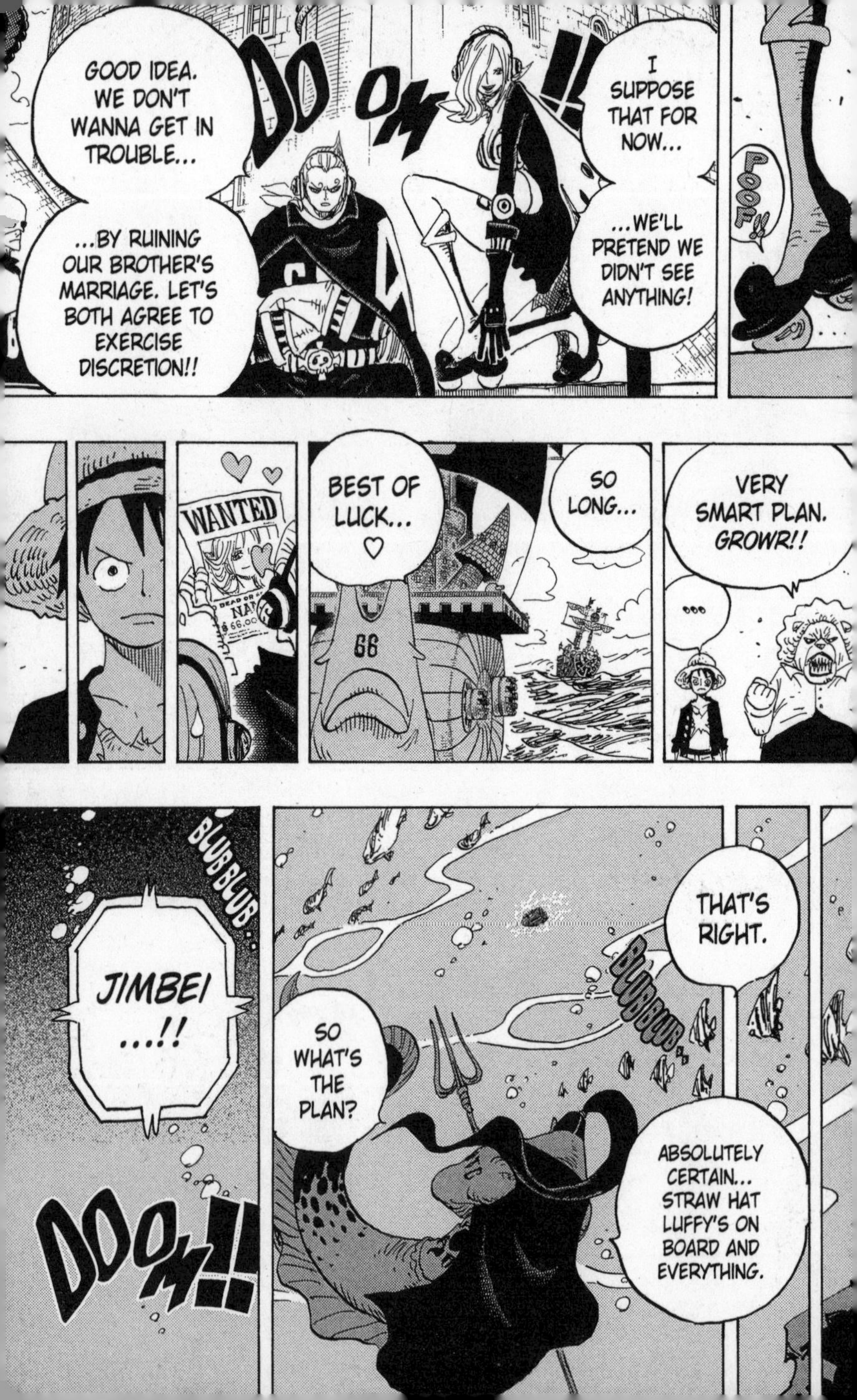
POOF!!
I SUPPOSE THAT FOR NOW...
...WE'LL PRETEND WE DIDN'T SEE ANYTHING!
DOOM!!
GOOD IDEA. WE DON'T WANNA GET IN TROUBLE...
...BY RUINING OUR BROTHER'S MARRIAGE. LET'S BOTH AGREE TO EXERCISE DISCRETION!!
VERY SMART PLAN. GROWR!!
•••
SO LONG...
BEST OF LUCK... ♡
WANTED
DEAD OR
THAT'S RIGHT.
BLUBBLUB
ABSOLUTELY CERTAIN... STRAW HAT LUFFY'S ON BOARD AND EVERYTHING.
SO WHAT'S THE PLAN?
BLUBBLUB
JIMBEI ...!!
DOOM!!

SBS Question Corner

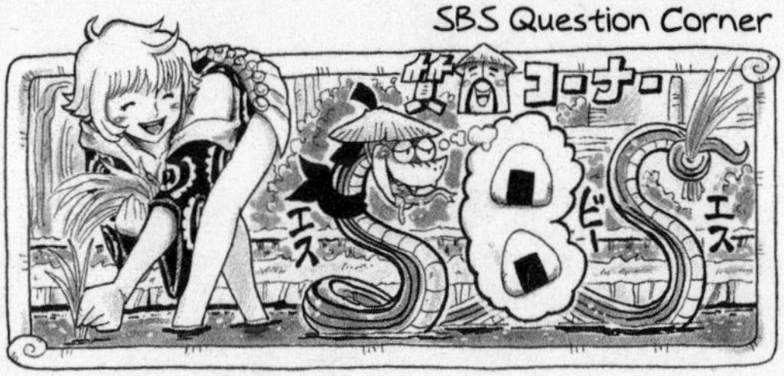

エス
ビー
エス

(Hippo Iron, Saitama)

Q: Oda Sensei, please draw the pirate captains who joined the Straw Hat Fleet as children! Please!!

--Thank You Pirates

A: Here you go.

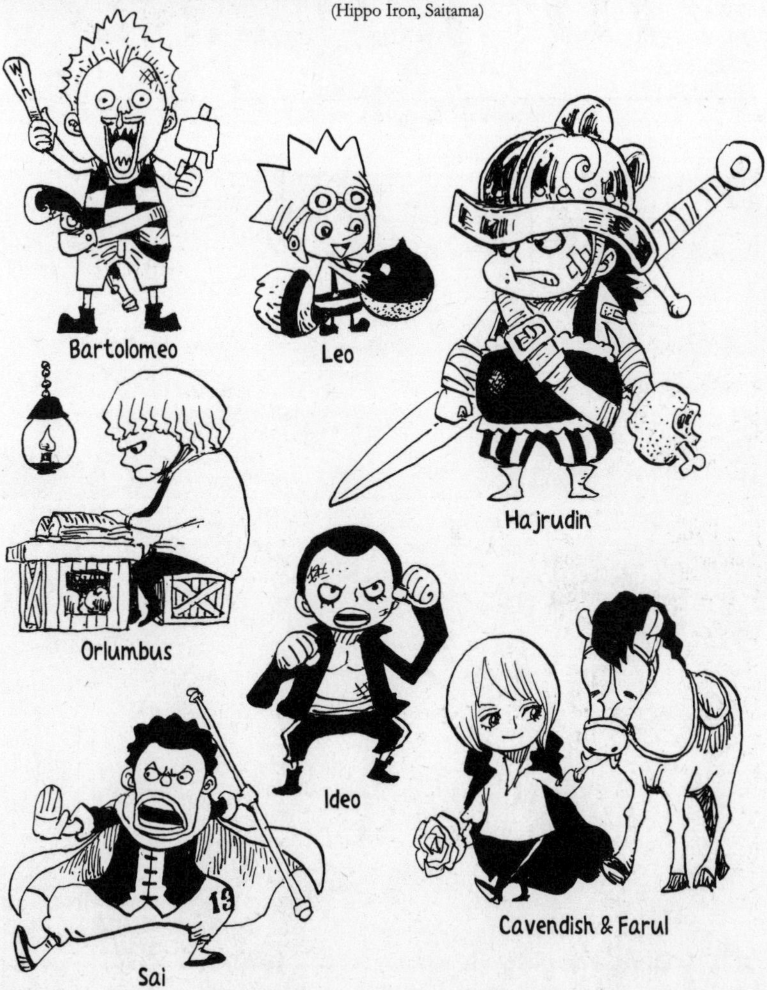

Bartolomeo
Leo
Hajrudin
Orlumbus
Ideo
Sai
Cavendish & Farul

That's it for the SBS! There's more info about the upcoming movie at the end of the book. See you next time!!

Chapter 827:
TOTTO LAND

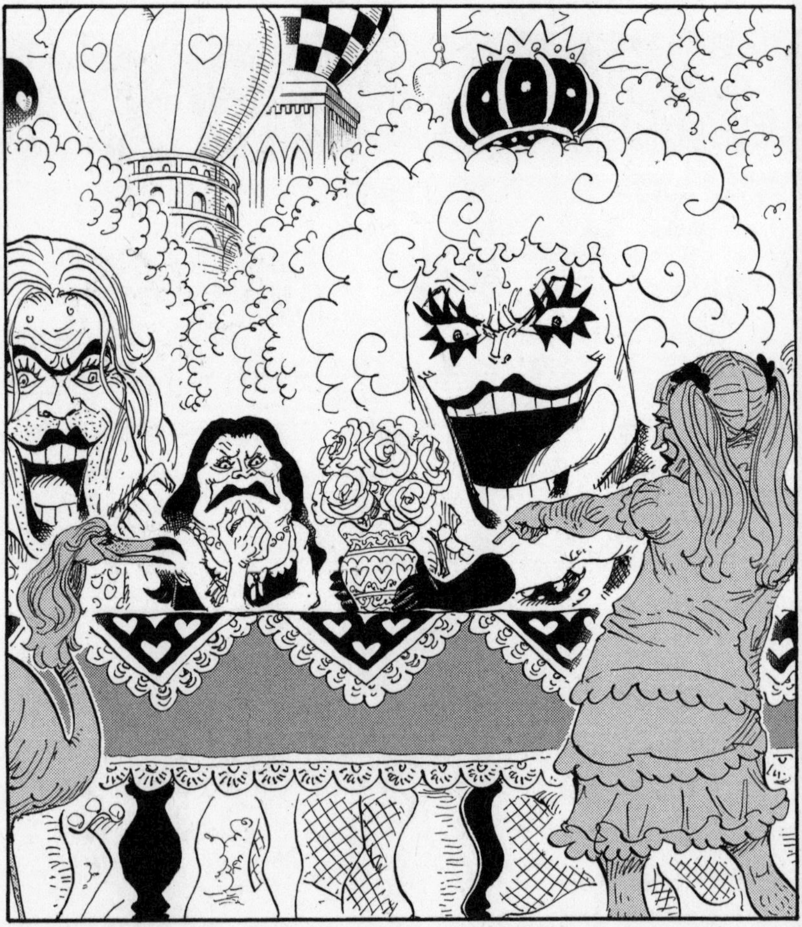

DECKS OF THE WORLD, 500-MILLION-MAN ARC, VOL. 18:
"KAMABAKKA QUEENDOM--MAKING PREPARATIONS"

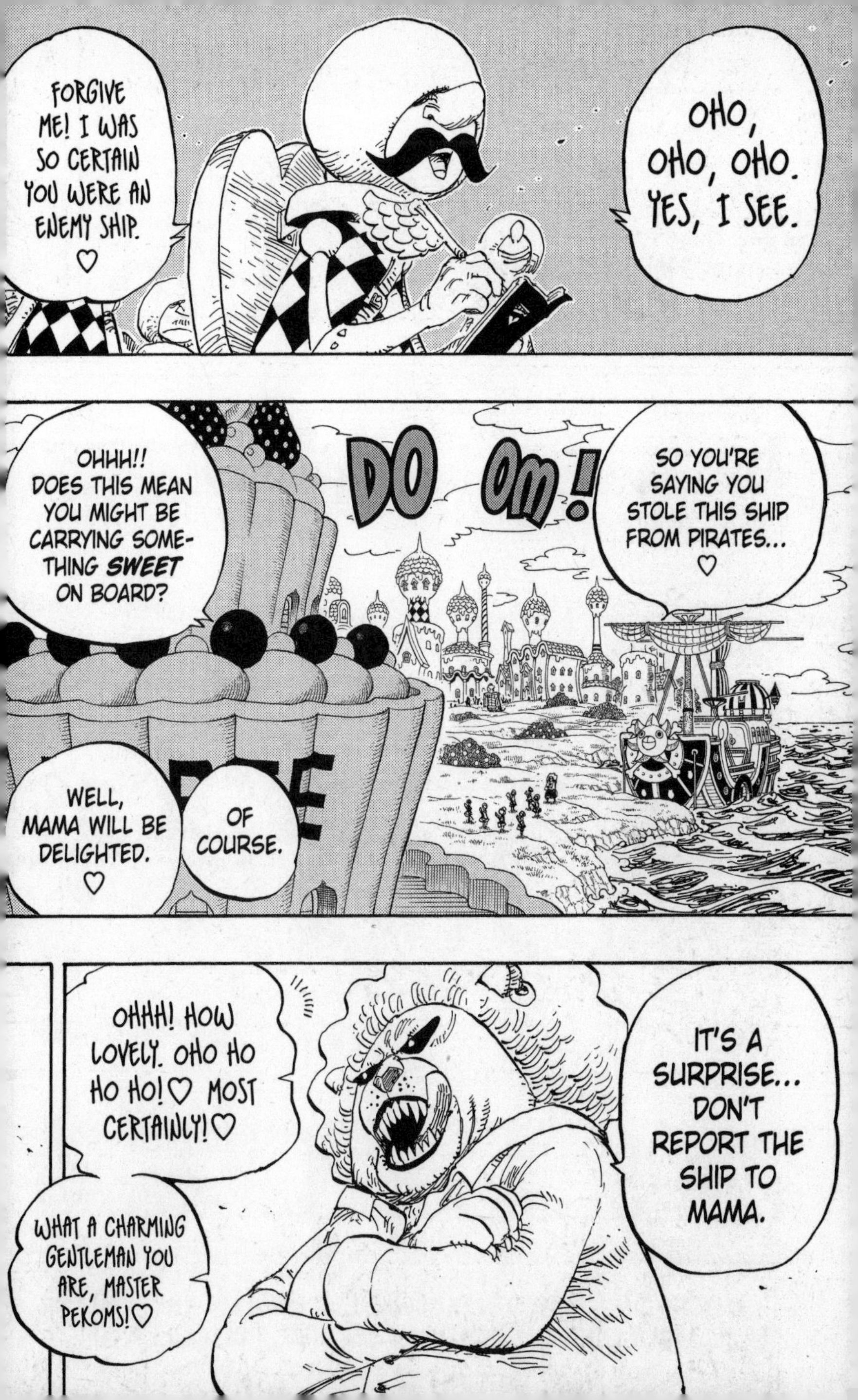
OHO, OHO, OHO. YES, I SEE.
FORGIVE ME! I WAS SO CERTAIN YOU WERE AN ENEMY SHIP. ♡
SO YOU'RE SAYING YOU STOLE THIS SHIP FROM PIRATES... ♡
DOOM!
OHHH!! DOES THIS MEAN YOU MIGHT BE CARRYING SOMETHING **SWEET** ON BOARD?
OF COURSE.
WELL, MAMA WILL BE DELIGHTED. ♡
IT'S A SURPRISE... DON'T REPORT THE SHIP TO MAMA.
OHHH! HOW LOVELY. OHO HO HO HO! ♡ MOST CERTAINLY! ♡
WHAT A CHARMING GENTLEMAN YOU ARE, MASTER PEKOMS! ♡

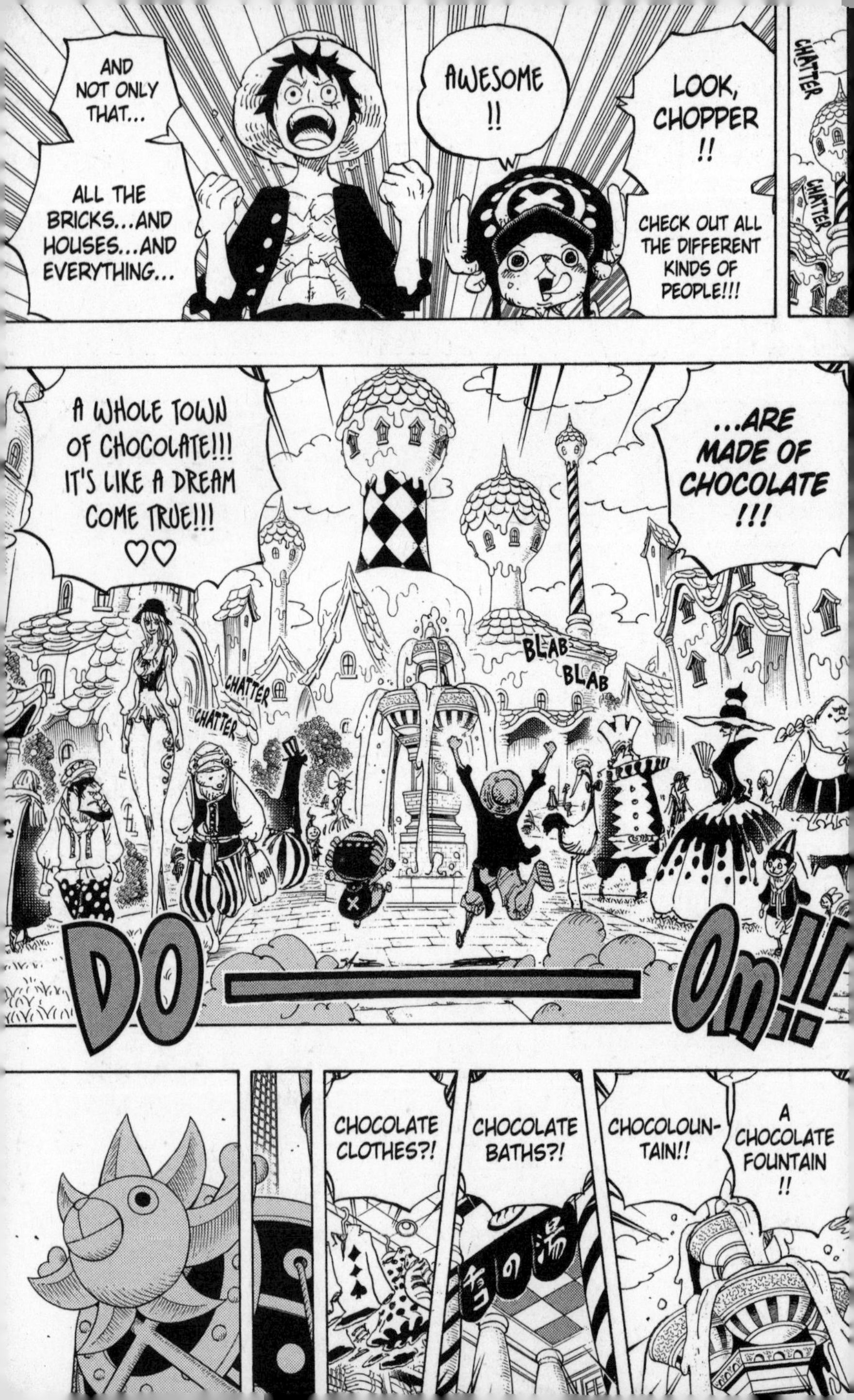
CHATTER
CHATTER
LOOK, CHOPPER !!
CHECK OUT ALL THE DIFFERENT KINDS OF PEOPLE!!!
AWESOME !!
AND NOT ONLY THAT...
ALL THE BRICKS...AND HOUSES...AND EVERYTHING...
...ARE MADE OF CHOCOLATE !!!
A WHOLE TOWN OF CHOCOLATE!!! IT'S LIKE A DREAM COME TRUE!!! ♡♡
BLAB BLAB
CHATTER CHATTER
DO——OM!!
A CHOCOLATE FOUNTAIN !!
CHOCOLOUN-TAIN!!
CHOCOLATE BATHS?!
CHOCOLATE CLOTHES?!

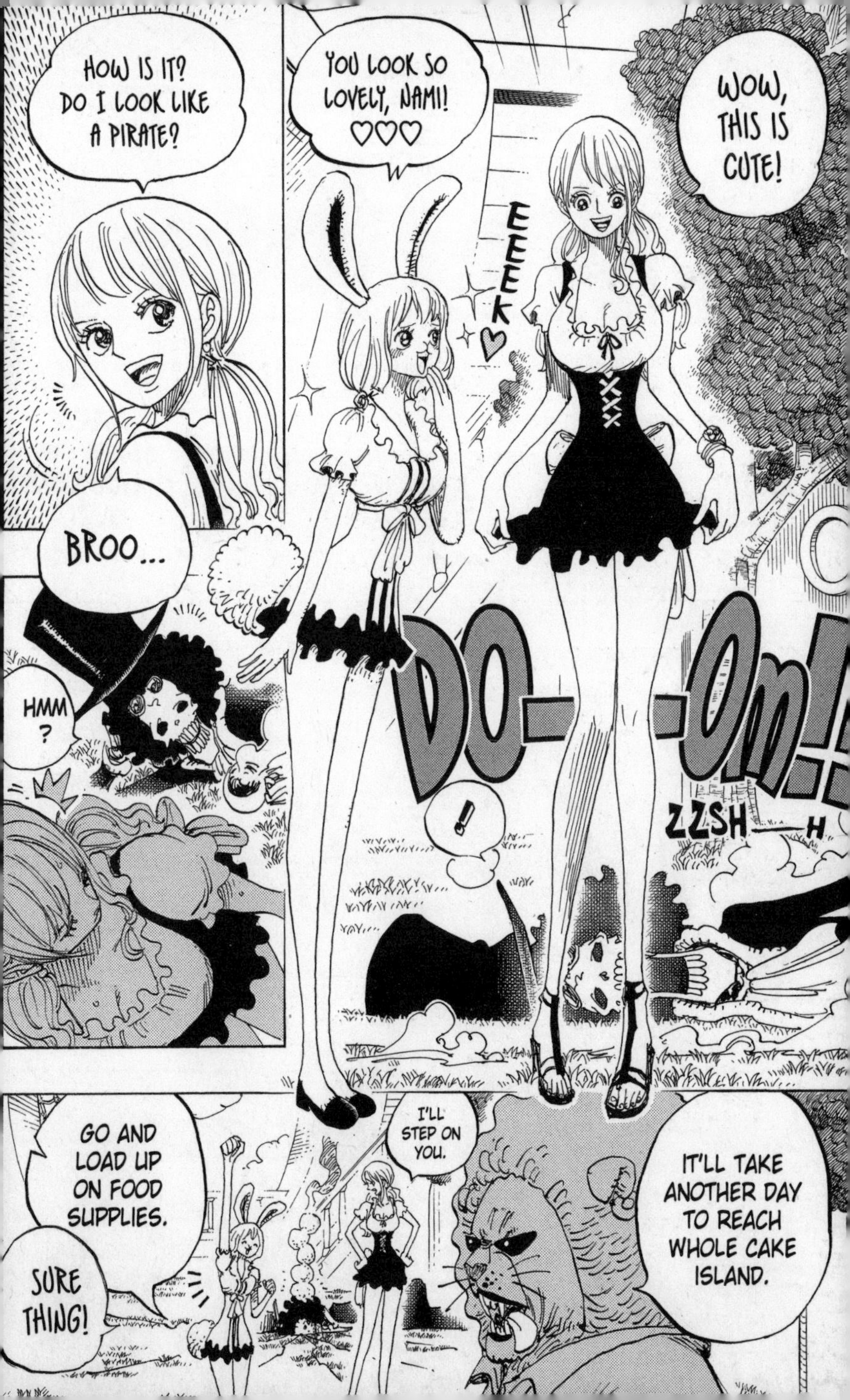
WOW, THIS IS CUTE!
YOU LOOK SO LOVELY, NAMI! ♡♡♡
EEEK ♡
DO--OM!!
ZZSH—H
!
HOW IS IT? DO I LOOK LIKE A PIRATE?
BROO...
HMM ?
IT'LL TAKE ANOTHER DAY TO REACH WHOLE CAKE ISLAND.
I'LL STEP ON YOU.
GO AND LOAD UP ON FOOD SUPPLIES.
SURE THING!

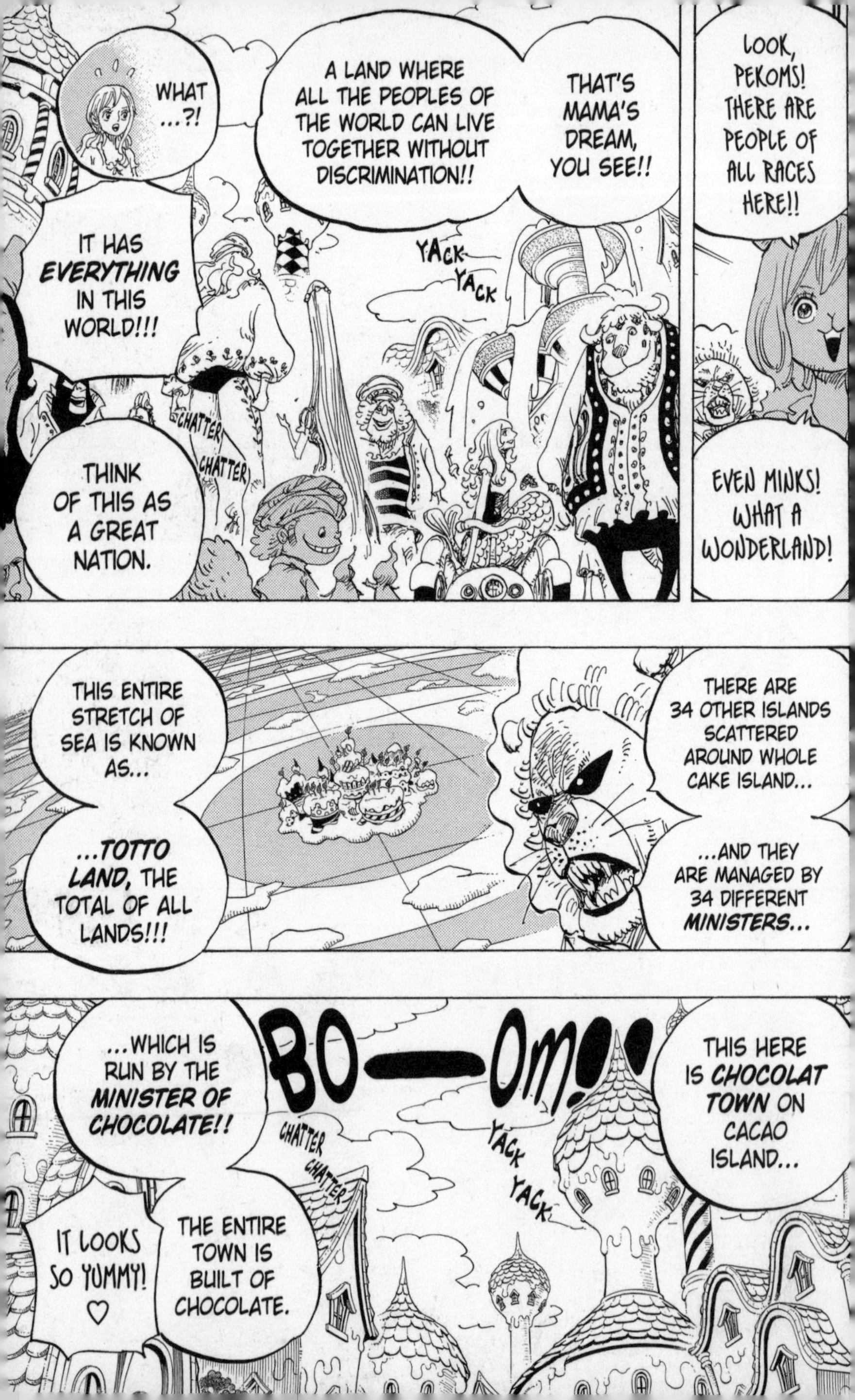
LOOK, PEKOMS! THERE ARE PEOPLE OF ALL RACES HERE!!
EVEN MINKS! WHAT A WONDERLAND!
THAT'S MAMA'S DREAM, YOU SEE!!
A LAND WHERE ALL THE PEOPLES OF THE WORLD CAN LIVE TOGETHER WITHOUT DISCRIMINATION!!
YACK YACK
WHAT ...?!
IT HAS EVERYTHING IN THIS WORLD!!!
CHATTER CHATTER
THINK OF THIS AS A GREAT NATION.
THERE ARE 34 OTHER ISLANDS SCATTERED AROUND WHOLE CAKE ISLAND...
...AND THEY ARE MANAGED BY 34 DIFFERENT MINISTERS...
THIS ENTIRE STRETCH OF SEA IS KNOWN AS...
...TOTTO LAND, THE TOTAL OF ALL LANDS!!!
THIS HERE IS CHOCOLAT TOWN ON CACAO ISLAND...
BO—OM!!
YACK YACK
...WHICH IS RUN BY THE MINISTER OF CHOCOLATE!!
CHATTER CHATTER
THE ENTIRE TOWN IS BUILT OF CHOCOLATE.
IT LOOKS SO YUMMY! ♡

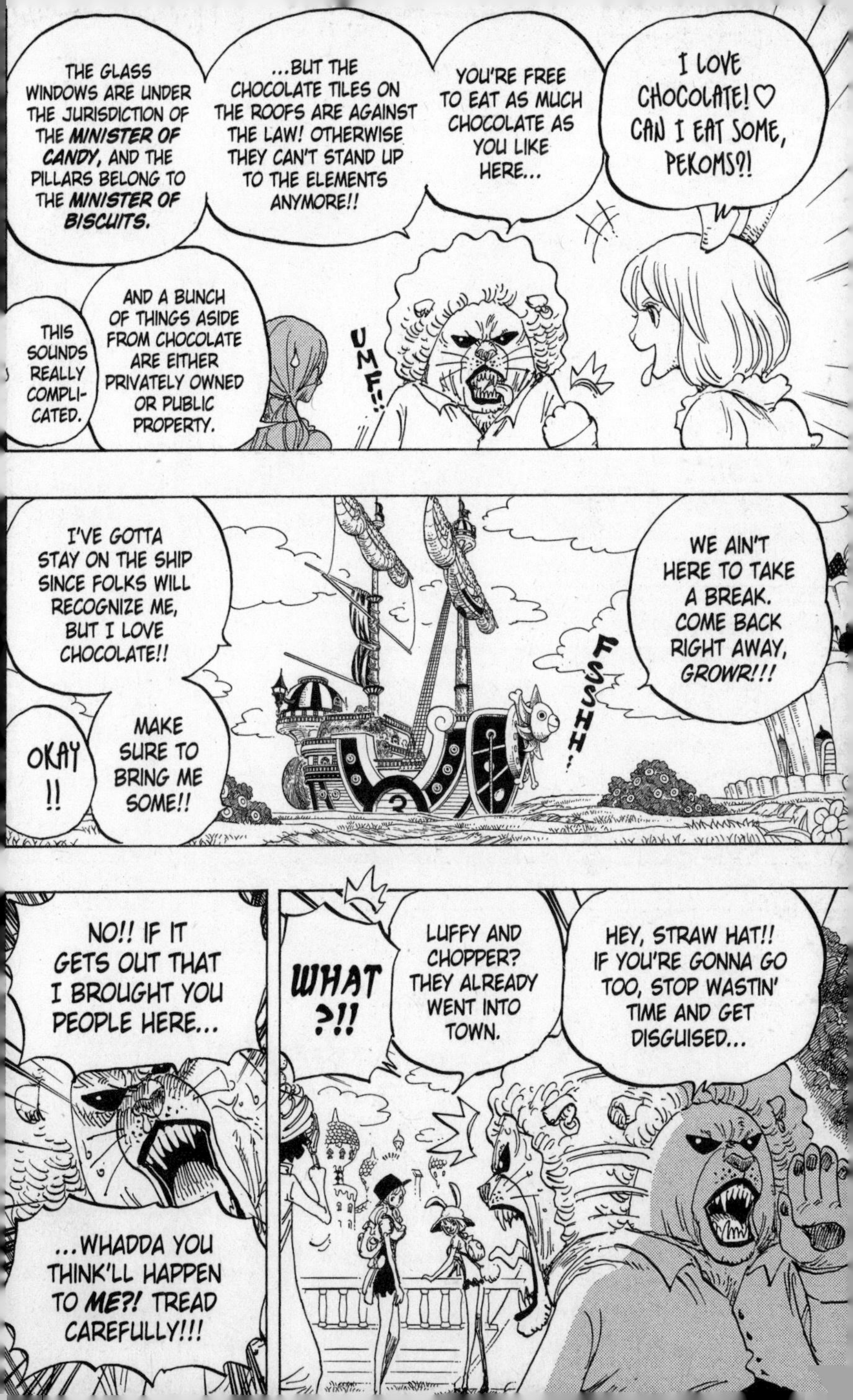
I LOVE CHOCOLATE! ♡ CAN I EAT SOME, PEKOMS?!
YOU'RE FREE TO EAT AS MUCH CHOCOLATE AS YOU LIKE HERE...
...BUT THE CHOCOLATE TILES ON THE ROOFS ARE AGAINST THE LAW! OTHERWISE THEY CAN'T STAND UP TO THE ELEMENTS ANYMORE!!
THE GLASS WINDOWS ARE UNDER THE JURISDICTION OF THE *MINISTER OF CANDY*, AND THE PILLARS BELONG TO THE *MINISTER OF BISCUITS*.
UMF!!
AND A BUNCH OF THINGS ASIDE FROM CHOCOLATE ARE EITHER PRIVATELY OWNED OR PUBLIC PROPERTY.
THIS SOUNDS REALLY COMPLI-CATED.
WE AIN'T HERE TO TAKE A BREAK. COME BACK RIGHT AWAY, *GROWR!!!*
FSSHH...
I'VE GOTTA STAY ON THE SHIP SINCE FOLKS WILL RECOGNIZE ME, BUT I LOVE CHOCOLATE!!
MAKE SURE TO BRING ME SOME!!
OKAY!!
HEY, STRAW HAT!! IF YOU'RE GONNA GO TOO, STOP WASTIN' TIME AND GET DISGUISED...
LUFFY AND CHOPPER? THEY ALREADY WENT INTO TOWN.
WHAT?!!
NO!! IF IT GETS OUT THAT I BROUGHT YOU PEOPLE HERE...
...WHADDA YOU THINK'LL HAPPEN TO *ME?!* TREAD CAREFULLY!!!

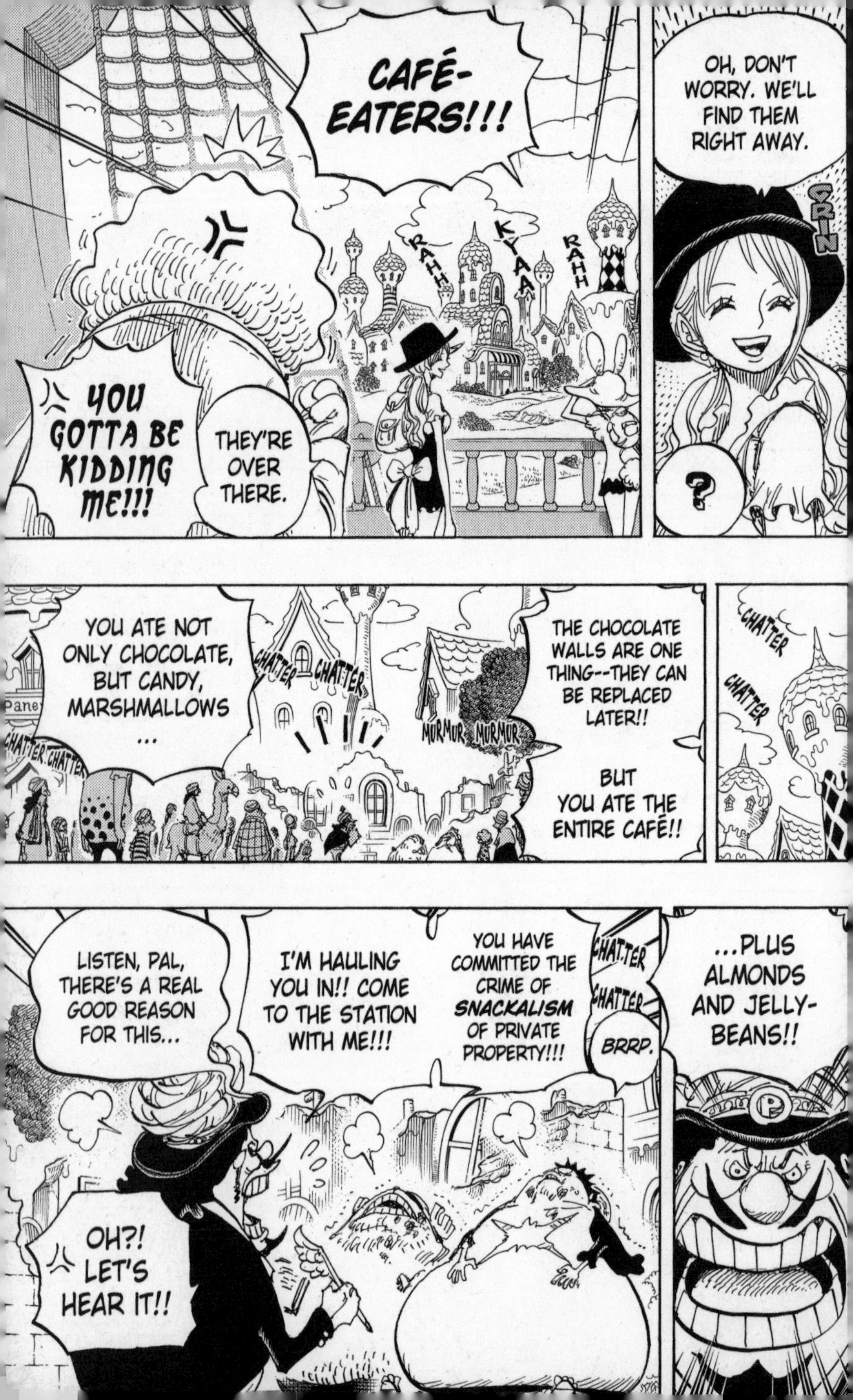
OH, DON'T WORRY. WE'LL FIND THEM RIGHT AWAY.
GRIN
?
CAFÉ-EATERS!!!
RAHH
KYAAA
RAHH
THEY'RE OVER THERE.
YOU GOTTA BE KIDDING ME!!!
CHATTER
CHATTER
THE CHOCOLATE WALLS ARE ONE THING--THEY CAN BE REPLACED LATER!!
BUT YOU ATE THE ENTIRE CAFÉ!!
MURMUR MURMUR
CHATTER CHATTER
YOU ATE NOT ONLY CHOCOLATE, BUT CANDY, MARSHMALLOWS ...
CHATTER CHATTER
...PLUS ALMONDS AND JELLY-BEANS!!
CHATTER
CHATTER
BRRP.
YOU HAVE COMMITTED THE CRIME OF SNACKALISM OF PRIVATE PROPERTY!!!
I'M HAULING YOU IN!! COME TO THE STATION WITH ME!!!
LISTEN, PAL, THERE'S A REAL GOOD REASON FOR THIS...
OH?! LET'S HEAR IT!!

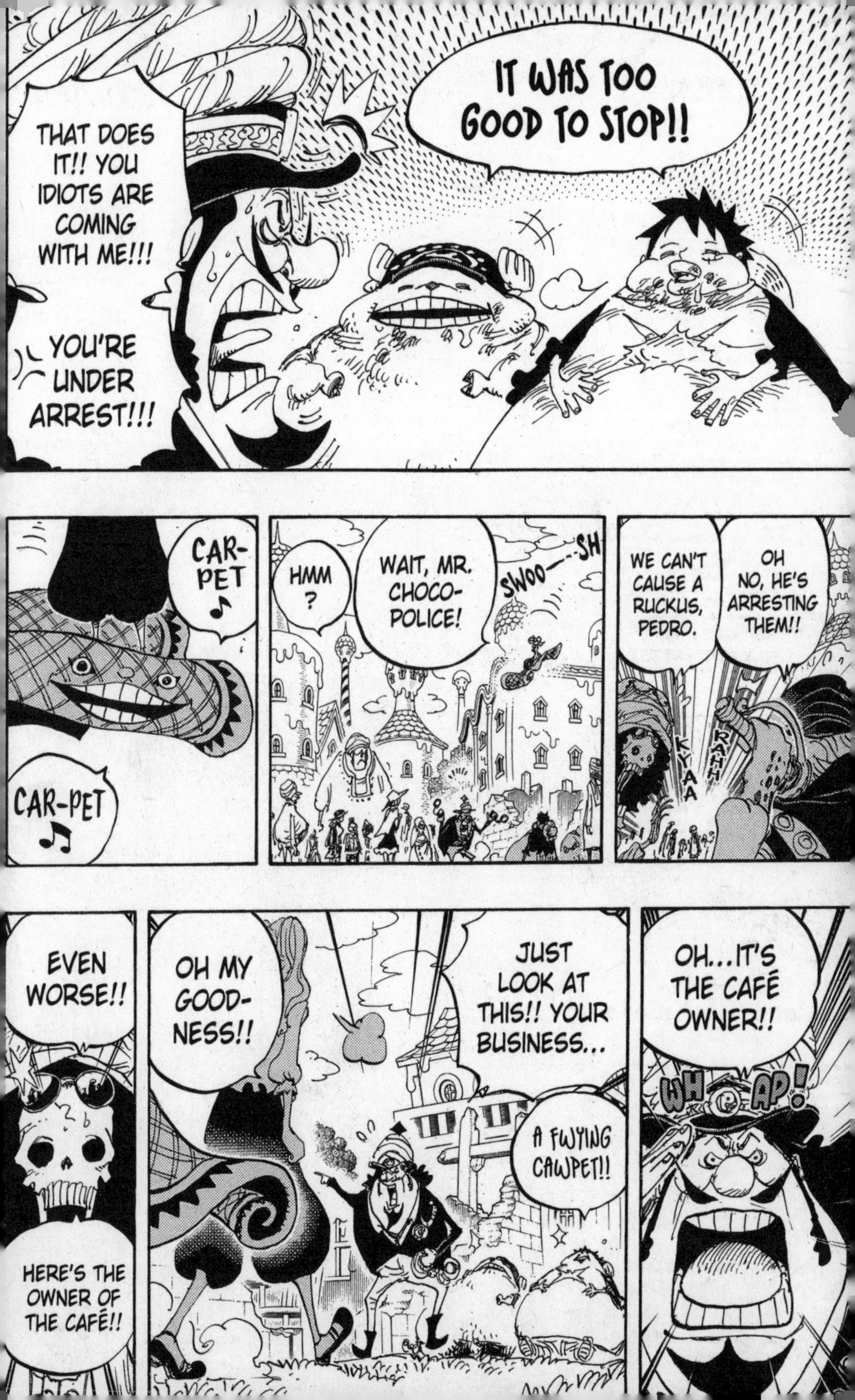
IT WAS TOO GOOD TO STOP!!
THAT DOES IT!! YOU IDIOTS ARE COMING WITH ME!!!
YOU'RE UNDER ARREST!!!
OH NO, HE'S ARRESTING THEM!!
WE CAN'T CAUSE A RUCKUS, PEDRO.
RAHH
KYAA
SWOO--SH
WAIT, MR. CHOCO-POLICE!
HMM?
CAR-PET ♪
CAR-PET ♪
OH...IT'S THE CAFÉ OWNER!!
WHAP!
JUST LOOK AT THIS!! YOUR BUSINESS...
OH MY GOODNESS!!
A FWYING CAWPET!!
EVEN WORSE!!
HERE'S THE OWNER OF THE CAFÉ!!

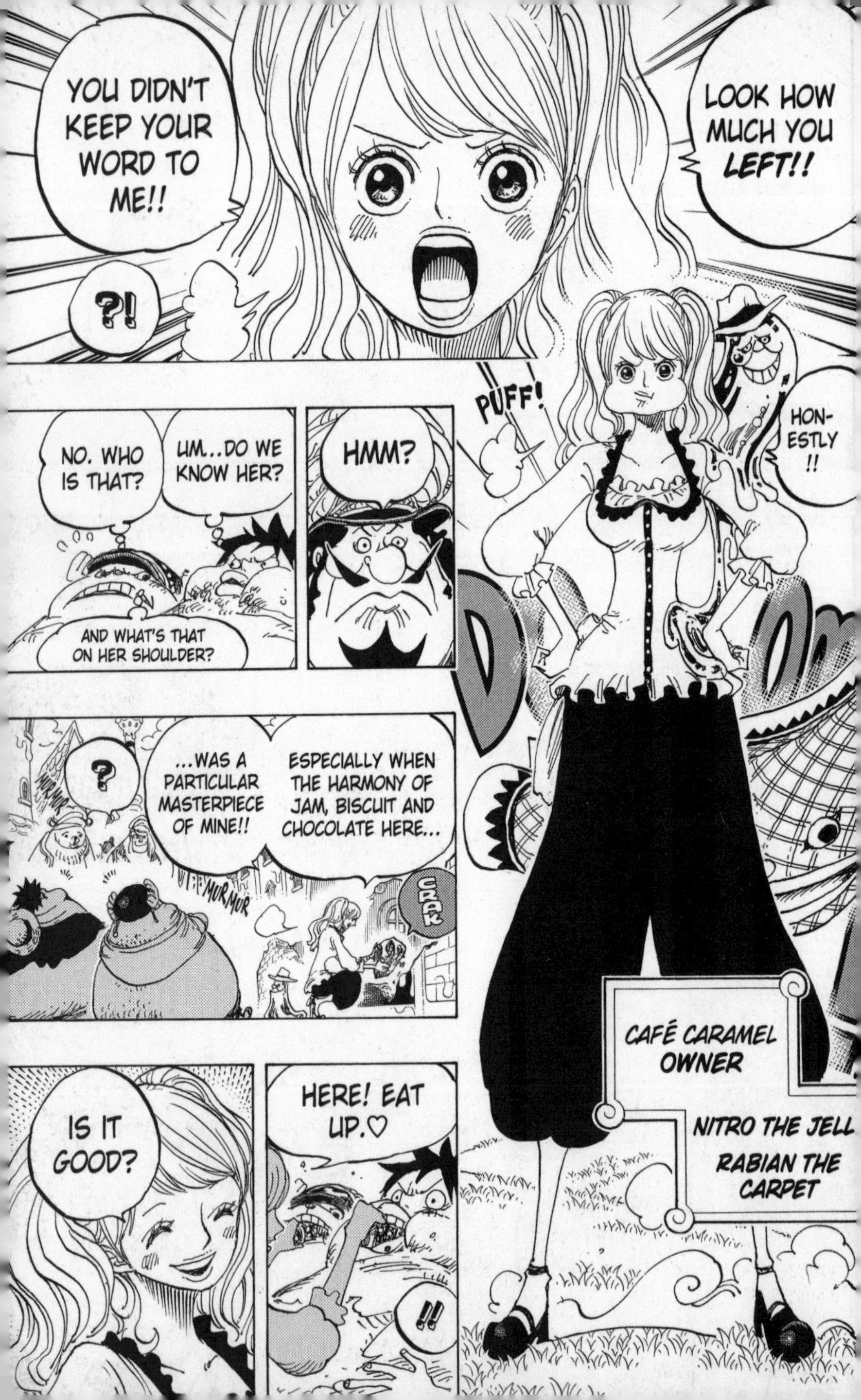
LOOK HOW MUCH YOU LEFT!!
YOU DIDN'T KEEP YOUR WORD TO ME!!
?!
HON-ESTLY!!
PUFF!
CAFÉ CARAMEL OWNER
NITRO THE JELL
RABIAN THE CARPET
HMM?
UM...DO WE KNOW HER?
NO. WHO IS THAT?
AND WHAT'S THAT ON HER SHOULDER?
ESPECIALLY WHEN THE HARMONY OF JAM, BISCUIT AND CHOCOLATE HERE...
...WAS A PARTICULAR MASTERPIECE OF MINE!!
CRAK
MURMUR
?
MURMUR
HERE! EAT UP.♡
!!
IS IT GOOD?

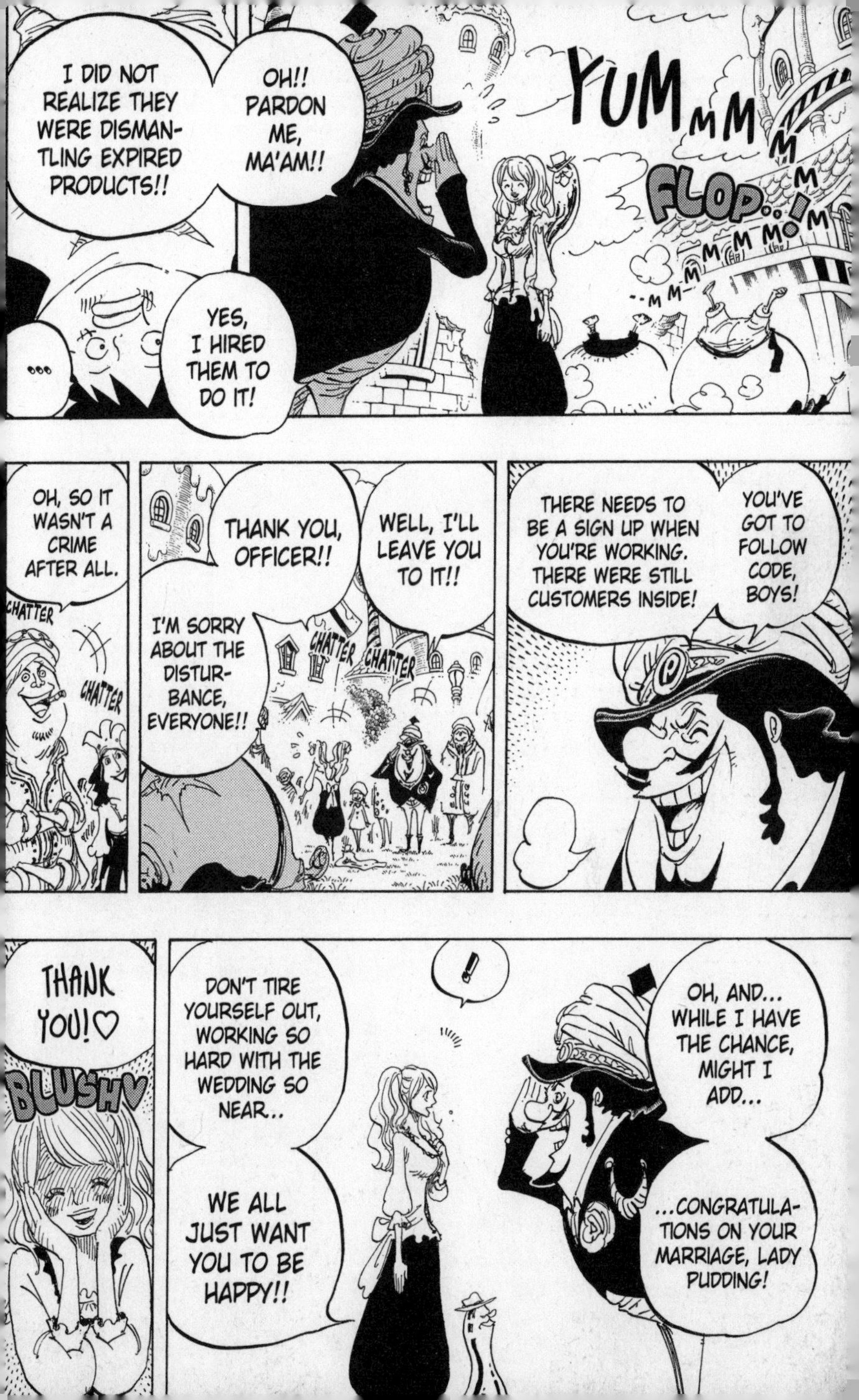
YUMMMMMM
FLOP..!
OH!! PARDON ME, MA'AM!!
I DID NOT REALIZE THEY WERE DISMANTLING EXPIRED PRODUCTS!!
YES, I HIRED THEM TO DO IT!
...
YOU'VE GOT TO FOLLOW CODE, BOYS!
THERE NEEDS TO BE A SIGN UP WHEN YOU'RE WORKING. THERE WERE STILL CUSTOMERS INSIDE!
WELL, I'LL LEAVE YOU TO IT!!
THANK YOU, OFFICER!!
CHATTER
CHATTER
I'M SORRY ABOUT THE DISTURBANCE, EVERYONE!!
OH, SO IT WASN'T A CRIME AFTER ALL.
CHATTER
CHATTER
!
OH, AND... WHILE I HAVE THE CHANCE, MIGHT I ADD...
...CONGRATULATIONS ON YOUR MARRIAGE, LADY PUDDING!
DON'T TIRE YOURSELF OUT, WORKING SO HARD WITH THE WEDDING SO NEAR...
WE ALL JUST WANT YOU TO BE HAPPY!!
THANK YOU!♡
BLUSH♥

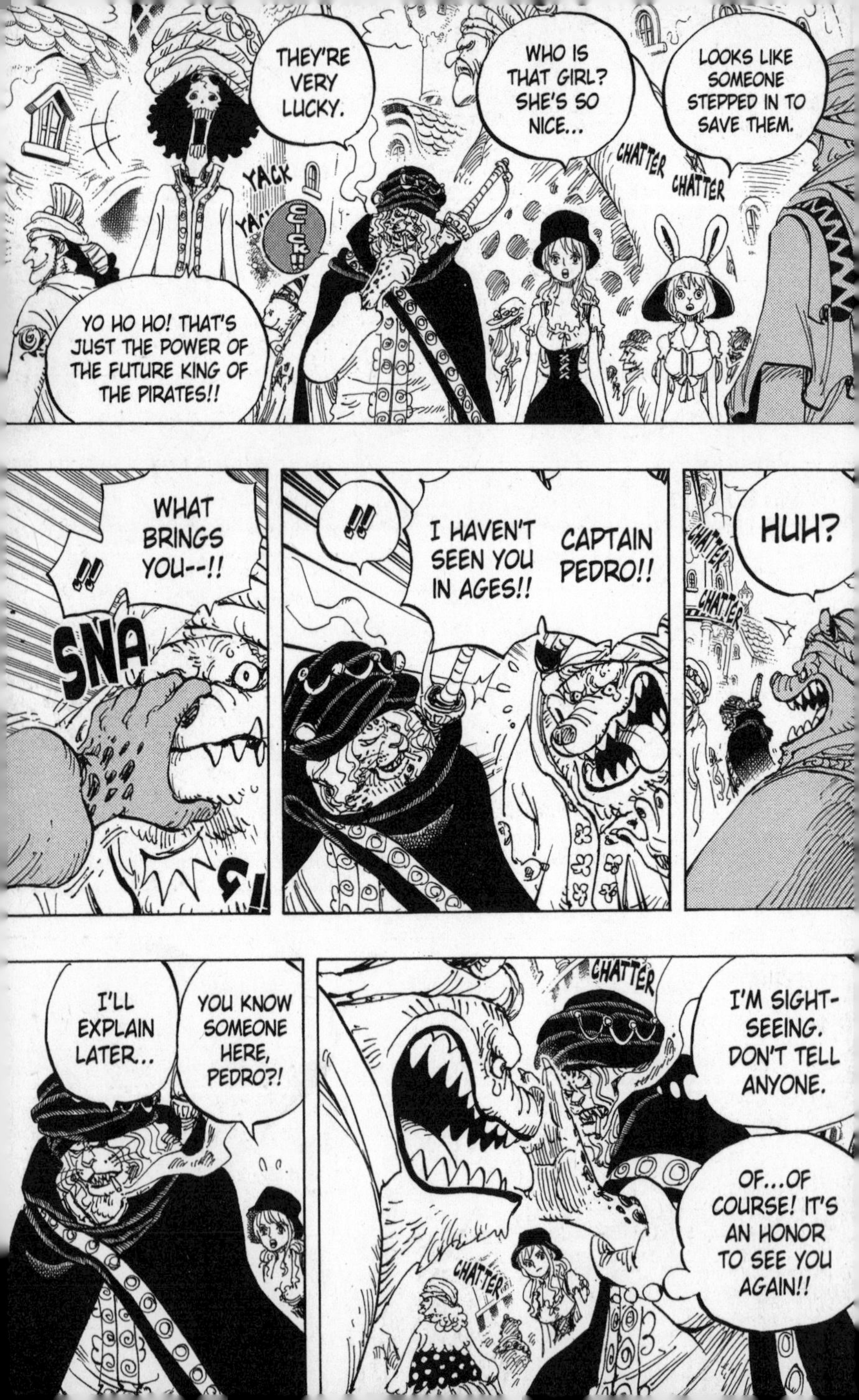

LOOKS LIKE SOMEONE STEPPED IN TO SAVE THEM.
CHATTER
CHATTER
WHO IS THAT GIRL? SHE'S SO NICE...
THEY'RE VERY LUCKY.
YACK
YACK
CLICK!!
YO HO HO! THAT'S JUST THE POWER OF THE FUTURE KING OF THE PIRATES!!
HUH?
CHATTER
CHATTER
CAPTAIN PEDRO!!
I HAVEN'T SEEN YOU IN AGES!!
!!
WHAT BRINGS YOU--!!
!!
SNA
G!
CHATTER
I'M SIGHT-SEEING. DON'T TELL ANYONE.
OF...OF COURSE! IT'S AN HONOR TO SEE YOU AGAIN!!
CHATTER
YOU KNOW SOMEONE HERE, PEDRO?!
I'LL EXPLAIN LATER..

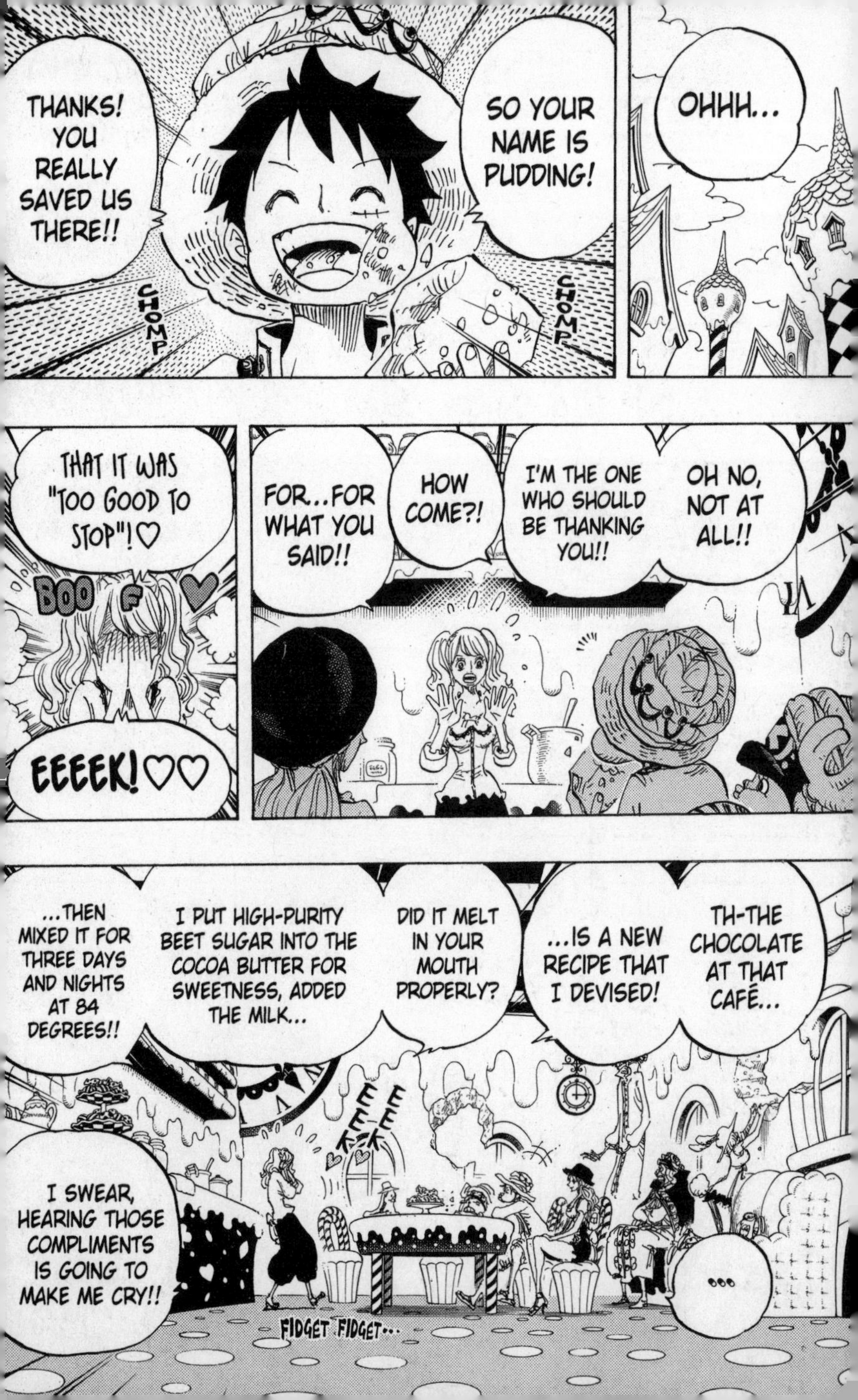
OHHH...
SO YOUR NAME IS PUDDING!
CHOMP
THANKS! YOU REALLY SAVED US THERE!!
CHOMP
OH NO, NOT AT ALL!!
I'M THE ONE WHO SHOULD BE THANKING YOU!!
HOW COME?!
FOR...FOR WHAT YOU SAID!!
THAT IT WAS "TOO GOOD TO STOP"!♡
BOOF
EEEEK!♡♡
TH-THE CHOCOLATE AT THAT CAFÉ...
...IS A NEW RECIPE THAT I DEVISED!
DID IT MELT IN YOUR MOUTH PROPERLY?
I PUT HIGH-PURITY BEET SUGAR INTO THE COCOA BUTTER FOR SWEETNESS, ADDED THE MILK...
...THEN MIXED IT FOR THREE DAYS AND NIGHTS AT 84 DEGREES!!
...
I SWEAR, HEARING THOSE COMPLIMENTS IS GOING TO MAKE ME CRY!!
FIDGET FIDGET...

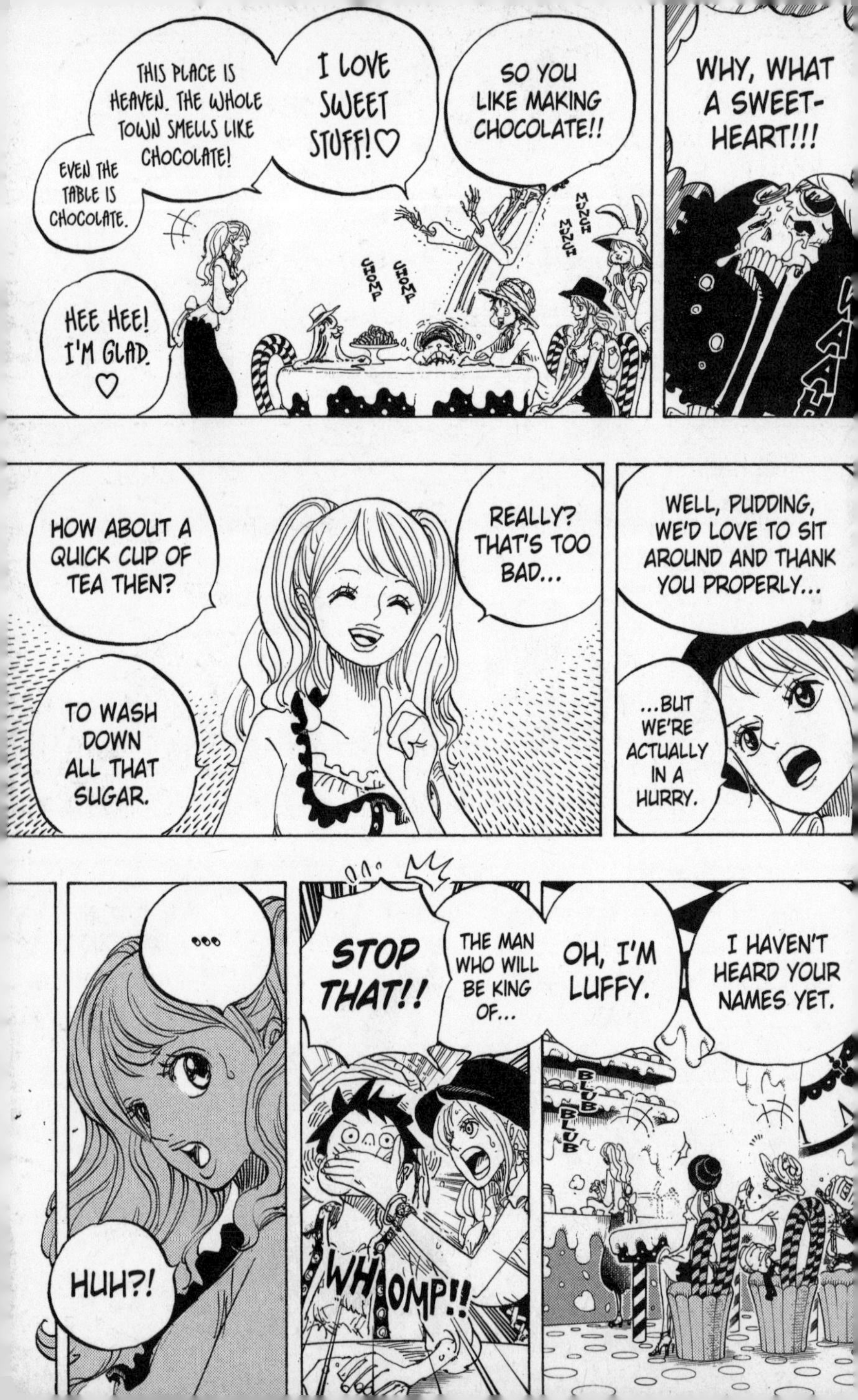
WHY, WHAT A SWEET-HEART!!!
SO YOU LIKE MAKING CHOCOLATE!!
MUNCH
MUNCH
I LOVE SWEET STUFF! ♡
THIS PLACE IS HEAVEN. THE WHOLE TOWN SMELLS LIKE CHOCOLATE!
CHOMP
CHOMP
EVEN THE TABLE IS CHOCOLATE.
HEE HEE! I'M GLAD. ♡
WELL, PUDDING, WE'D LOVE TO SIT AROUND AND THANK YOU PROPERLY...
...BUT WE'RE ACTUALLY IN A HURRY.
REALLY? THAT'S TOO BAD...
HOW ABOUT A QUICK CUP OF TEA THEN?
TO WASH DOWN ALL THAT SUGAR.
I HAVEN'T HEARD YOUR NAMES YET.
BLUB
BLUB
OH, I'M LUFFY.
THE MAN WHO WILL BE KING OF...
STOP THAT!!
WHOMP!!
...
HUH?!

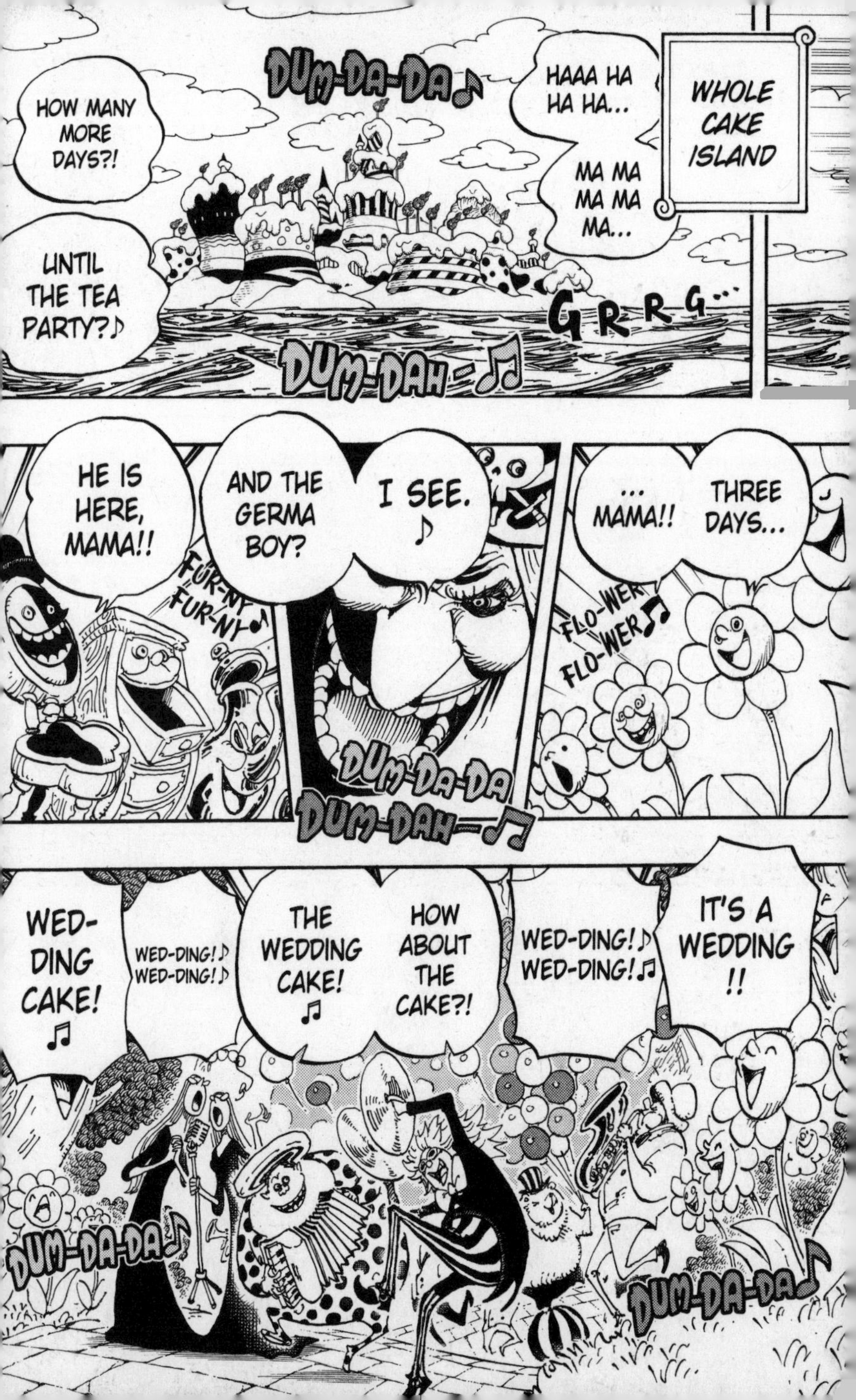
WHOLE CAKE ISLAND
HAAA HA HA HA...
MA MA MA MA MA...
DUM-DA-DA♪
HOW MANY MORE DAYS?!
UNTIL THE TEA PARTY?♪
GRRG...
DUM-DAH-♫
THREE DAYS...
...MAMA!!
FLO-WER FLO-WER♫
I SEE.♪
DUM-DA-DA DUM-DAH—♫
AND THE GERMA BOY?
HE IS HERE, MAMA!!
FUR-NY FUR-NY♪
IT'S A WEDDING!!
WED-DING!♪ WED-DING!♫
HOW ABOUT THE CAKE?!
THE WEDDING CAKE!♫
WED-DING!♪ WED-DING!♪
WED-DING CAKE!♫
DUM-DA-DA♪
DUM-DA-DA♪

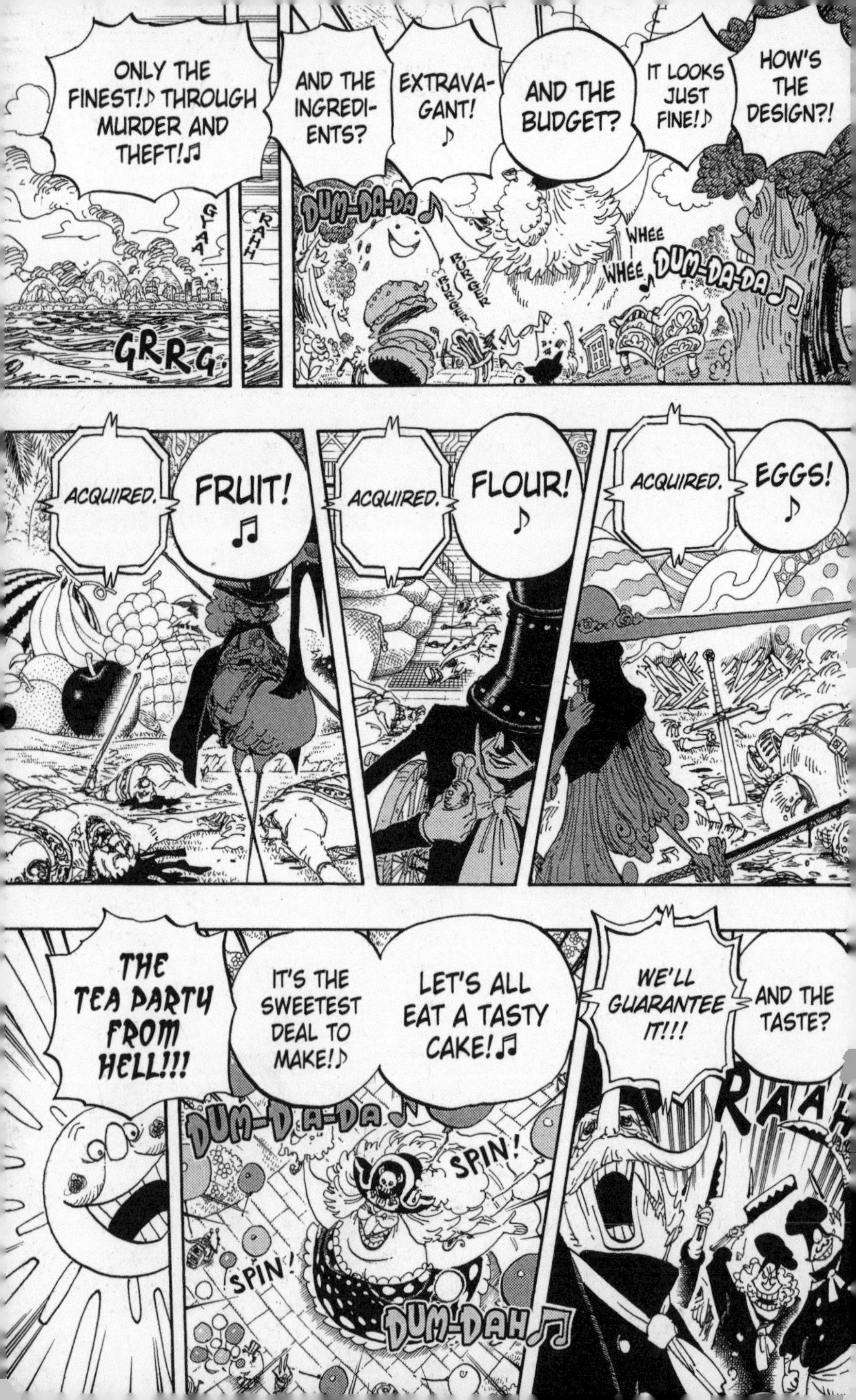
HOW'S THE DESIGN?!
IT LOOKS JUST FINE!♪
AND THE BUDGET?
EXTRAVAGANT! ♪
AND THE INGREDIENTS?
DUM-DA-DA♪
WHEE WHEE♪
DUM-DA-DA♫
BURGER BURGER
ONLY THE FINEST!♪ THROUGH MURDER AND THEFT!♫
RAHH
GYAA
GRRG
EGGS! ♪
ACQUIRED.
FLOUR! ♪
ACQUIRED.
FRUIT! ♫
ACQUIRED.
AND THE TASTE?
WE'LL GUARANTEE IT!!!
RAAH
LET'S ALL EAT A TASTY CAKE!♫
IT'S THE SWEETEST DEAL TO MAKE!♪
DUM-DA-DA♪
SPIN!
SPIN!
DUM-DAH♫
THE TEA PARTY FROM HELL!!!

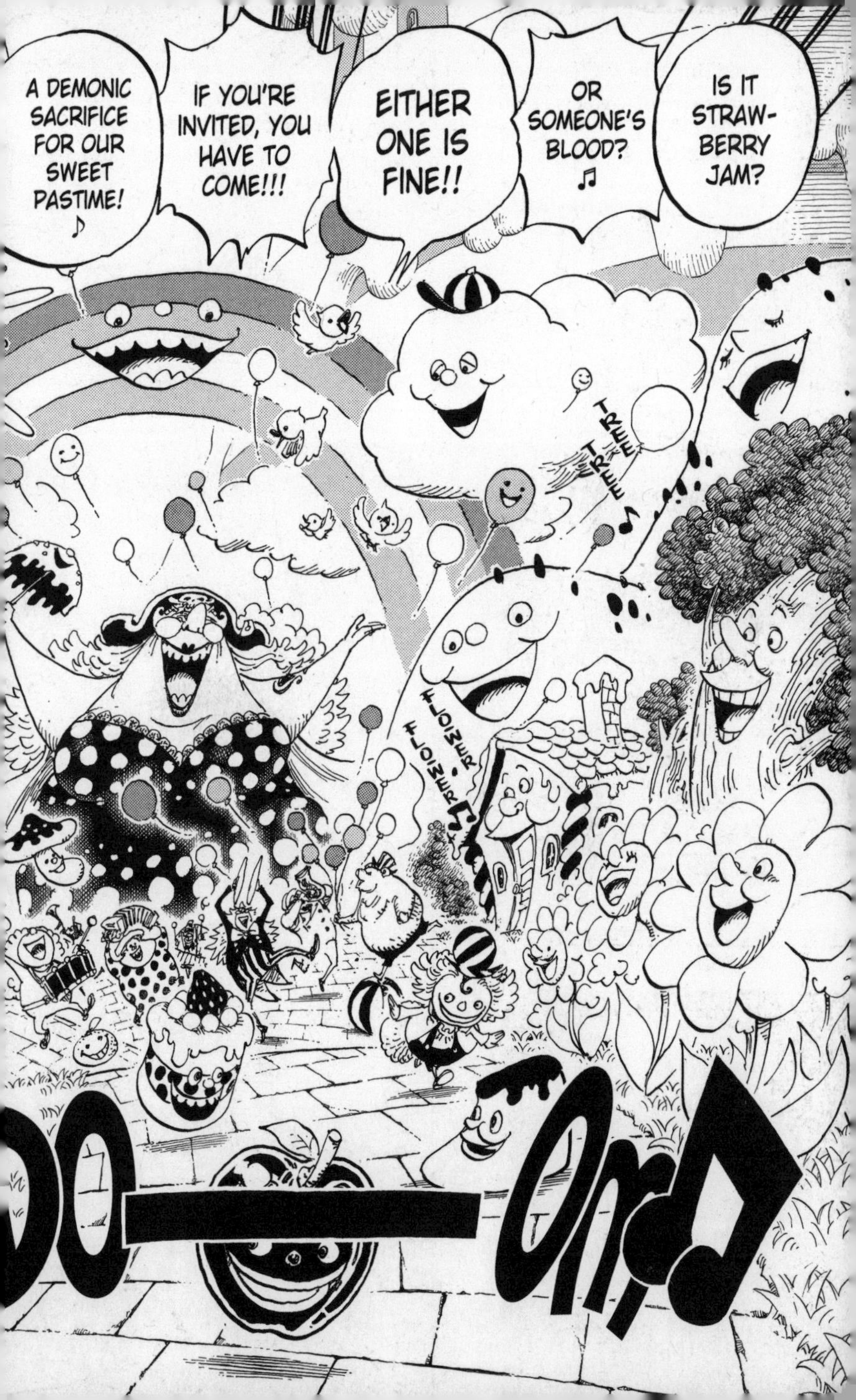
IS IT STRAWBERRY JAM?
OR SOMEONE'S BLOOD? ♫
EITHER ONE IS FINE!!
IF YOU'RE INVITED, YOU HAVE TO COME!!!
A DEMONIC SACRIFICE FOR OUR SWEET PASTIME! ♪
TREE TREE ♪
FLOWER, FLOWER ♫
DO—ON♪

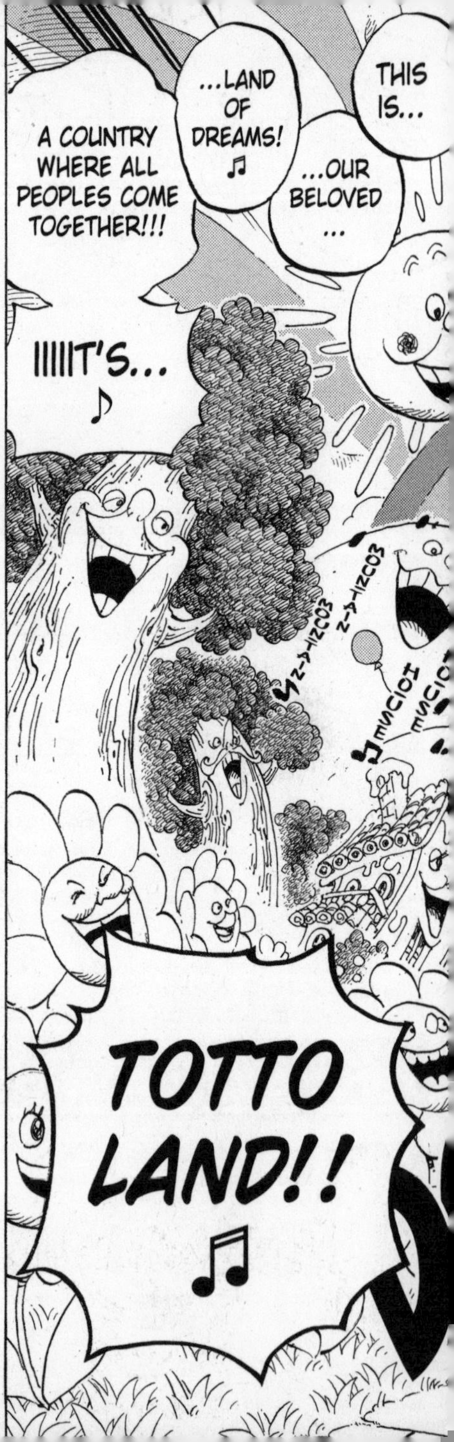
THIS IS...
...OUR BELOVED ...
...LAND OF DREAMS! ♫
A COUNTRY WHERE ALL PEOPLES COME TOGETHER!!!
IIIIIT'S... ♪
TOTTO LAND!! ♫

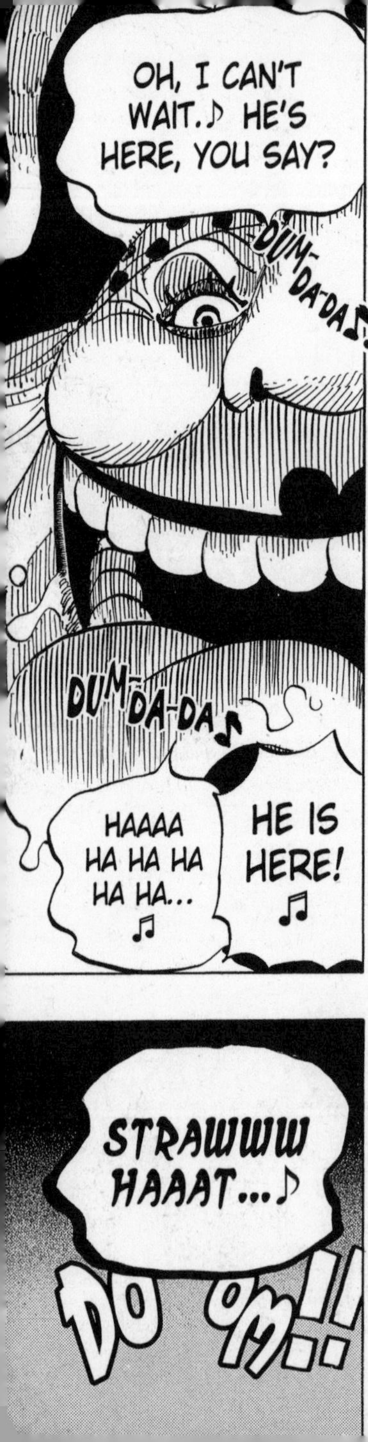
OH, I CAN'T WAIT.♪ HE'S HERE, YOU SAY?
DUM-DA-DA♫
DUM-DA-DA♪
HE IS HERE! ♫
HAAAA HA HA HA HA HA... ♫
STRAWWW HAAAT...♪
DOOM!!

KEY 7.23
WE'RE PUTTING OUT A MOVIE ON

★ Yes, it's movie time! One Piece Film Gold!! It comes out in Japan on Saturday, July 23, 2016. Is everybody ready for this one? At the time I'm writing this, they're running trailers in theaters and on the home page. Have you seen them yet? It's a two-part promotion. The first trailer features the music of the genius big band jazz singer I mentioned last volume, Mayumi Kojima! And the second trailer comes from these fine folks!!

Theme Song:
"Give Me Your Anger"
GLIM SPANKY

Did you listen to it? Talk about powerful! We're aiming for a real slick, cool and gorgeous movie this time around, and the music is a crucial part of the atmosphere. I suspect many readers might not be familiar with Glim Spanky yet, but you'll love that awesome singing voice! You'll get chills in the movie theater, I promise! Look forward to it!
Next up, allow me to introduce this fellow!! ⬇

Director: Pit Boss Hiroaki Miyamoto

★ He's the third series director for the One Piece TV anime!! A trustworthy man who helmed the ship for six years!! He was a huge help when it came to making the Paramount War as exciting as it should be, and clarifying some of the trickier details of Fish-man Island. He's an expert of the pause, and an entertainer who brings out tears and laughter alike! Let's see what he's got to offer us! Up next is an interview!!

A Comedy Routine from the Director and Executive Producer!

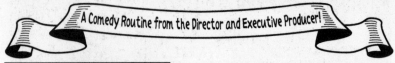

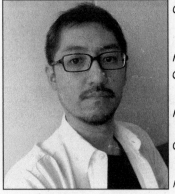

O (Oda): Here's the guy in charge of putting together Film Gold! It's our director, Pit Boss Hiroaki Miyamoto!!

M (Miyamoto): Yay! Why am I the pit boss?!

O: Oh, you just seem like you're really in sync with the staff. You're the guy who keeps the team together!

M: Well, if that's the way you meant it, I guess it's all right.

O: So first of all, why do we need to go to the theater to see this? What's wrong with a good old TV?!

M: Why are you mad about it?! Well, a movie and TV show are very different things.

O: Hey, that's just how I felt about it as a kid.

M: I see. Well, first of all, the budget for a movie is much, much different. When you put lots of money into crafting CG, music, big actors, and so on, not only does it enable more creative possibilities, it allows you to take expanded formats like 3-D, 4DX, and MX4D theaters into account while you're producing the movie. This is a film that reaches its greatest potential in the theater!

O: That's right. We're doing this movie in 3-D, 4DX, and MX4D. So it'll pop off the screen! I can't wait to see how we get to fully experience it in person!!

M: And with *Film Gold,* we're actually employing ten times the amount of CG as the previous movie! It's also got the highest number of musical tracks, so we want you to experience all the dynamic camera and sound work on a huge screen with 5.1 surround sound!

O: Gaah, I'm getting so pumped up!! The festival's gonna start!!

M: Yes, it is!! Get hyped with Luffy! Get angry with Luffy! Fight alongside Luffy!!

O: It's a movie you've got to feel for yourself! Come and see it, or I'll throw ya in the clink!!

M: Please don't threaten the audience!!

O: Oh, sorry...

M: Listen, everyone! Come and see this work of entertainment in the theater!!

O: Congrats on finishing up and gaining your freedom!

M: What am I guilty of? Oh…making a fun movie?

O: Check it out!!

★ Remember what the director just said about all that CG? Well, the people responsible for bringing the gorgeous Gran Tesoro to life are...

Kusanagi

The cutting-edge technicians of the anime world! They've returned after *Film Z* to bring the background of the story into stunning detail again!!

★ Next, we've got some supporting roles to announce. This misfit gang is bringing these kooky characters to the screen!!

Guest Voice Actors!!

Dice
Kobayashi Kendo

← Jimmy Meyers
Red-Eyed Owl →
Croquette

← Kent Beef Jr.
Pork →
Arata Furuta

Muscle Turtle
Ocarina

Mokin
Nadaru

Narrator
Masaharu Miyake

Mad Treasure
Shun Oguri

St. Kamael
Masakazu Mimura

← White Jack
Double Down →
Naoto Takenaka

Such a stunning lineup! All these people, just for these minor roles?! This is a feat only possible through the deep connections of friendship that *One Piece* has forged through its long run! Thank you all!!!

By the way, Hikari Mitsushima, who plays Carina, was once part of the group "Folder 5" that sang one of the *One Piece* anime theme songs! That's beautiful. Welcome back, Hikari!

COMING NEXT VOLUME:

The Straw Hats have faced their share of danger as they've navigated their way through the New World, but they've never met a foe like this! Can they outsmart Big Mom and rescue Sanji from his arranged marriage? Or is it time to start looking for a new cook…?

ON SALE AUGUST 2017!

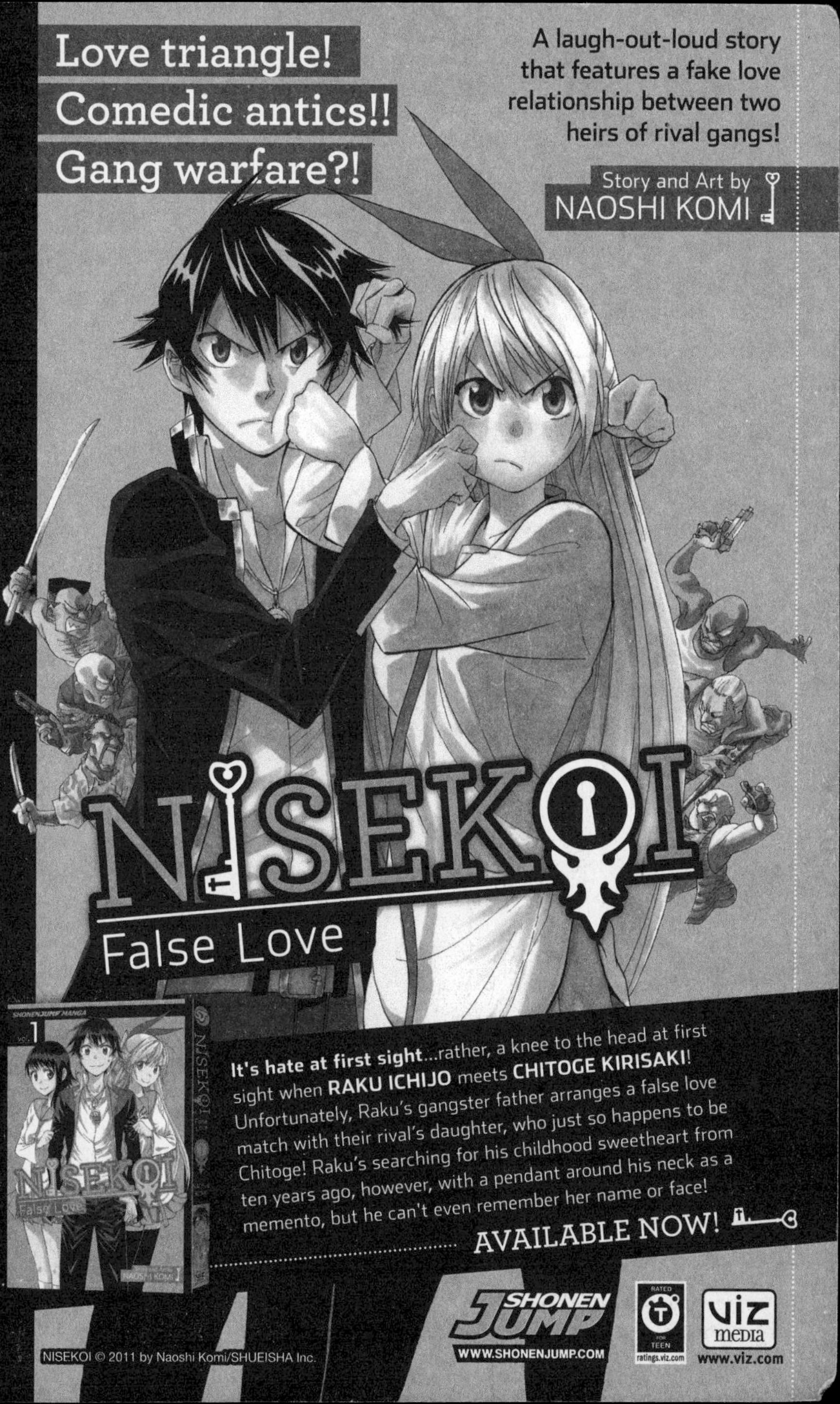

Love triangle!
Comedic antics!!
Gang warfare?!
A laugh-out-loud story that features a fake love relationship between two heirs of rival gangs!
Story and Art by
NAOSHI KOMI
NISEKOI
False Love
SHONEN JUMP MANGA
vol. 1
NISEKOI
False Love
NAOSHI KOMI
It's hate at first sight...rather, a knee to the head at first sight when RAKU ICHIJO meets CHITOGE KIRISAKI! Unfortunately, Raku's gangster father arranges a false love match with their rival's daughter, who just so happens to be Chitoge! Raku's searching for his childhood sweetheart from ten years ago, however, with a pendant around his neck as a memento, but he can't even remember her name or face!
AVAILABLE NOW!
SHONEN JUMP
WWW.SHONENJUMP.COM
RATED T FOR TEEN
ratings.viz.com
VIZ media
www.viz.com
NISEKOI © 2011 by Naoshi Komi/SHUEISHA Inc.

NARUTO

Story and Art by
Masashi Kishimoto

Naruto is determined to become the greatest ninja ever!

Twelve years ago the Village Hidden in the Leaves was attacked by a fearsome threat. A nine-tailed fox spirit claimed the life of the village leader, the Hokage, and many others. Today, the village is at peace and a troublemaking kid named Naruto is struggling to graduate from Ninja Academy. His goal may be to become the next Hokage, but his true destiny will be much more complicated. The adventure begins now!

WORLD'S BEST SELLING MANGA!

www.shonenjump.com www.viz.com

You're Reading in the Wrong Direction!!

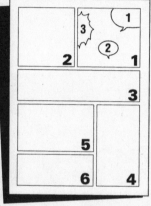

Whoops! Guess what? You're starting at the wrong end of the comic!

...It's true! In keeping with the original Japanese format, **One Piece** is meant to be read from right to left, starting in the upper-right corner.

Unlike English, which is read from left to right, Japanese is read from right to left, meaning that action, sound effects and word-balloon order are completely reversed...something which can make readers unfamiliar with Japanese feel pretty backwards themselves. For this reason, manga or Japanese comics published in the U.S. in English have sometimes been published "flopped"—that is, printed in exact reverse order, as though seen from the other side of a mirror.

By flopping pages, U.S. publishers can avoid confusing readers, but the compromise is not without its downside. For one thing, a character in a flopped manga series who once wore in the original Japanese version a T-shirt emblazoned with "M A Y" (as in "the merry month of") now wears one which reads "Y A M"! Additionally, many manga creators in Japan are themselves unhappy with the process, as some feel the mirror-imaging of their art skews their original intentions.

We are proud to bring you Eiichiro Oda's **One Piece** in the original unflopped format. For now, though, turn to the other side of the book and let the journey begin...!

—Editor